MUSIC

MU&SIC

Frank Granville Barker
Introduction by
Riccardo Muti

WINDWARD

For Agustin

Designed and produced by Breslich & Foss, London
House editor: Timothy Roberts
Picture Research: Vanessa Whinney and Imogen Graham
Design: Craig Dodd

WINDWARD

An imprint owned by
W. H. Smith & Son Limited
Registered No 237811 England
Trading as WHS Distributors,
St John's House, East Street, Leicester, LE1 6NE

ISBN 0 7112 0099 8

© text: Frank Granville Barker 1981
© introduction: Breslich & Foss

Illustrations originated in Great Britain
by Dot Gradations Limited, Essex
Filmset by Input Typesetting Limited, London
Printed in Great Britain
by Ebenezer Baylis & Son Ltd, Worcester
Bound by Leighton-Straker Bookbinding Company, Ltd, London

CONTENTS

Acknowledgments

The illustrations are reproduced by kind permission of the following: The Mansell Collection 1, 33, 40, 54, 65, 66, 76, 78, 87, 100, 122, 141, 157, 158, 164, 181, 232, 250, 258, 260, 261, 269, 276; Scala 2, 22, 23, 50–51, 154–5, 155 (right), 199, 266, 271; Zefa 13 (© Robin Smith), 35, 142, 283; Archiv für Kunst und Geschichte, Berlin 15, 16, 24, 29, 30, 32, 47, 55, 58, 268; Deutsches Theatermuseum, Munich 18; Bildarchiv Preussischer Kultur-besitz, Berlin (West) 25 (top), 45, 59, 148; Mozarteum, Salzburg 25 (bottom), 26, 27 (both); Nationalgalerie, Staatliche Museen Preussischer Kulturbesitz, Berlin (West) 30; Gesellschaft der Musikfreunde, Vienna 31; Beethoven-Haus, Bonn 34, 279; BBC Hulton Picture Library 19, 37, 43, 46, 84 (bottom left), 103, 120, 140, 188, 252, 253, 276, 277; Neue Pinakothek, Munich 38; Kunst-Dias Blauel 38, 138–9; Roger-Viollet 42; Mary Evans Picture Library 49, 50 (top); 52, 67, 58, 111 (© Mrs Barbara Edwards); Deutsche Fotothek, Dresden 56; Bildarchiv der Österreichische National-albibliothek, Vienna 60 (top), 62, 64, 134, 135, 167, 178, 265; Stadtbi-bliothek, Vienna 60 (bottom); Bulloz 70 (top), 217; Giraudon 70 (bottom), 151 (bottom), 206, 259, 262; E. T. Archive 14, 71, 145, 151 (top), 203; Royal College of Music 73, 80, 84 (bottom right), 102, 125; Victoria and Albert Museum 79, 81 (left), 87, 145, 151 (top), 227; Clive Barda 81 (right), 82, 131 (top), 143, 147, 170, 171, 173, 175, 177, 182–3, 186 (left & right), 190, 194, 195, 197, 202, 207, 213, 214, 219, 235, 238, 239, 242, 243, 244, 247, 251, 256, 273; Novosti Press Agency 84 (top left & right) 85, 88, 89, 94, 95 (right), 97, 223 (top & bottom), 224–5, 226, 229 (left & right); Sovfoto/Eastfoto, New York 90; Mike Davis Studios Ltd 91, 99, 119; Erich Auerbach 101, 127, 131 (bottom) 136, 237, 245, 274, 281; G. D. Hackett, New York 104, 106, 108; Nationalmuseum, Stockholm 110; Oslo Kommunes Kunstsamlin-ger Munch-Museet 112; Finnish Embassy 113, 115, 116; National Portrait Gallery, London 118, 123, 126, 162; The Bettmann Archive, Inc 128, 129, 130, 132 (all), 248; Schoenberg Institute Archives (Photo Florence Homolka) 133; Alte Pinakothek, Munich 138–9; Bibliothèque de l'opéra, Paris 146; Guy Gravett 150, 228; Donald Southern 152, 216, 218, 230; Art Institute of Chicago 156; MAS 159; The Metropolitan Museum of Art, New York 160; Royal Opera House Archives, London 161; English National Opera 163, 174, 189; Opera Magazine, London 165, 184, 236; National Gallery of Victoria, Melbourne 166; Artificial Eye Film Co Ltd 169; Andrew March 174; Spectrum Colour Library 179; Zoë Dominic 193, 211, 233, 241; Nancy Holmes 200; Erio Piccagliani 201; Bibliothèque Nationale, Paris 208, 209, 215; Metropolitan Opera, New York 220; Petersburg Press (© David Hockney 1980) 221; Reg Wilson 231; Carolyn Mason Jones 234; Nigel Luckhurst 246; Raymond Mander & Joe Mitchenson Theatre Collection 254; Cooper-Bridgeman Library 255; Internationale Bilderagentur, Zurich 267; EMI Records 272; Bayerische Staatsbibliothek, Munich 275; Museen der Stadt, Vienna 279

Author's Note

This book is addressed to the enthusiast who enjoys music in the concert hall and the opera house and would like to know more about it. The needs of the music student and the specialist are already well-catered for by a number of excellent histories which are both exhaustive and scholarly. Rather than attempt a similarly comprehensive and chronological account, I have concentrated on those composers whose works in orchestral, instrumental, vocal and operatic form are regularly performed today. For this reason the book is organized into four sections according to the most common types of performance: 'The Symphony Concert', 'The Opera', 'Recitals and Chamber Music' and 'Choral Music'. I have also chosen to discuss in non-technical language all the symphonic music of major composers such as Beethoven, Brahms and Mahler, rather than orchestral works by other composers which may be of interest to scholars, but which are rarely if ever heard. Similarly, I have given attention to the operas which have a place in the international repertoire, while only making passing mention of those which have fallen by the wayside as the result of changing tastes.

I have also outlined the lives of the leading composers. Music may be an abstract form of art, but its composers have inevitably been affected by their personal circumstances and the kind of society in which they worked. It is natural that we should want to know something of the men behind the music, not only because so many composers have been fascinating characters, but because it often explains why they composed in a particular style and manner that we recognize immediately. Anything which helps us to enjoy music more keenly is worthwhile, because music has always been composed first and foremost for our enjoyment.

A CONDUCTOR'S VIEW

Riccardo Muti

People who go to concerts and the opera often wonder how one becomes a conductor in the first place, and then what precise function the conductor performs. There are many different ways of becoming a conductor: some musicians have the ambition from the very beginning, others turn to it after a period as an orchestral player or a career as an instrumental soloist. In my own case I had no such ambition, and conducting came to me by a series of chance events or, as I like to think, through destiny. I did not even start out with any idea of making a musical career, because although my family all loved music they would have felt a musician's life far too precarious: my grandfather was a schoolmaster and my father is a doctor, both with a rather conservative outlook. They encouraged me, however, to take a good Italian's interest in music, and to play it as well as listen to it. When I was seven I was given a violin as a Christmas gift, which at the time was not at all the gift I had hoped for. At first it made me very unhappy, because in my childish way I wanted to play it straight away for my friends, with no thought of lessons, and the result was painfully unsuccessful. Then suddenly, for no reason I can explain, I began to love the violin and worked to master it. When I was nine I played a Vivaldi concerto in public, so that was my debut as a musician.

Five years later I started to play the piano in order to learn more about music. I believe that all string players should learn to play the piano a little, because it helps them to read and understand more complex music, polyphonic music. Then I found that I preferred the piano, because it enabled me to make music alone, without the need of an accompanist, so I abandoned the violin. After five years I went as an external student to be examined at the conservatoire at Bari, where Nino Rota was the director. He is mostly widely remembered as the composer of film scores, especially for Fellini's movies, but he was also a very fine composer of operas and chamber music. After he heard me play for my examination he gave me the maximum marks and told me that I should seriously think of becoming a professional musician. About this time my parents moved to Naples, where I began to study music more seriously. Chance again played a part, because the conservatoire in Naples is one of the oldest and best in the world, the conservatoire of Paisiello and Cimarosa. The Neapolitan piano school is very proud because it was founded by Sigismond Thalberg, one of the greatest virtuosos and teachers of the nineteenth century, and my teacher at the conservatoire was Vincenzo Vitale, who himself had been a pupil of a pupil at Thalberg. I studied with him at the conservatoire in the afternoons after my ordinary day at school, where I was preparing to go on to university.

Then in the year I gained my degree in piano, when I was twenty-one, chance played a part in my future once again. I was summoned one morning to see the director of the conservatoire in his office. I went along feeling afraid he was going to reprimand me for not having worked hard enough, but instead of that he asked me if I would like to conduct a concert with some of the students playing piano concertos with the student orchestra. He explained that there was no pupil in the school of conducting willing or able to conduct this concert, so he would like me to try. Although I was confused, feeling that something very strange was happening, I replied: 'Why not? Yes.' Later on I learned that when he had heard me play the piano for my degree examination he thought that I played with the orchestra in my mind rather than the piano. My programme had included Mussorgsky's *Pictures from an Exhibition*, but if I played this in an orchestral way it must have come naturally from within me, because at that time I did not even know the score of Ravel's orchestral version. There was only a week before the concert, so in that time I had to be taught how to give the orchestra the correct beat. Somehow I knew that this was to be the turning-point in my whole life, and when I finally stood in front of the orchestra for the first time my personality changed. It is not possible to explain my feelings at that moment, convinced that all the players must follow *my* ideas and *my* will, because nobody can understand it who is not himself a conductor. Yet until then I had never thought of becoming a conductor, only of playing the piano, but that one experience, even though it was just an experiment, was enough to convince me. It also convinced the teacher, because five minutes after I had begun the Bach double harpsichord concerto he telephoned the director of the conservatoire and said: 'We have a new conductor.'

From that day my mind was made up, though of course I had a great deal to learn. I was sure I had a conductor's sense of command, something one is born with, but I also realized that I had conducted my first experimental concert like a policeman on traffic duty. The conservatoire arranged another concert for me, but this time I prepared for a whole year, working two hours every week with the orchestra. Also I studied composition, which is very important for a conductor, who must have a thorough knowledge of harmony, counterpoint and orchestration. After this second concert in Naples, where the student orchestra was reinforced by players from the Teatro San Carlo and teachers of the conservatoire for a programme including Schubert's 'Unfinished' Symphony and works by Beethoven, Martucci and Pizzetti, I went on to Milan. There I was fortunate enough to study conducting with Antonino Votto, who had been the assistant of Toscanini and who passed on to me what he had learned from the maestro. He was very kind to me as well as being a very fine teacher, and I believe that the way in which I work with an orchestra still comes from my lessons with Votto. I finished my studies with him in 1966, and the following year I won the Guido Cantelli conductors' competition, which marked the real beginning of my career. My first important concert was in Florence with Sviatislav Richter, who played concertos by Mozart and Britten, and we enjoyed a great success. He was famous of course, while nobody really knew me as a conductor, so my success came as a surprise. I was invited by this orchestra, the Maggio Musicale, to give another concert with them a few months later, and on that occasion they asked me to become their principal conductor. This was to happen again when I first conducted the Philharmonia Orchestra in London and then the Philadelphia Orchestra. Just as conducting came to me by chance, without my seeking it, so the opportunities came to me to work with these fine orchestras.

The function of the conductor is to produce a unified interpretation — *his* interpretation — of a piece of music from all the players who make up the orchestra, and in order to do this he must have absorbed the music completely. He must be absolutely convinced about his interpretation before he stands in front of the orchestra, because only then can he convince the players, and through them the public. Orchestral players are very perceptive, and they know immediately whether or not the conductor has his ideas really clear: if he does, they respond, but if he has any doubts about his interpretation they will sense this insecurity at once, even though his technique may be perfectly secure. This whole matter of interpretation is solved in different ways by different conductors, so I can only describe my own way. When I decide to conduct a major work such as a symphony for the first time, I need to have the score on my piano for months before I start to study it. It may seem a strange idea, but for me it is a psychological approach to a psychological problem. I cannot pick up a score, open it and tell myself that I will begin working on it at once. I must first have the score on my piano where I can see it even though I am working on some other piece at the time. It becomes part of my room, waiting to be taken up. Eventually I will start to work on it, first by playing it at the piano, reading it in only a general way. The second stage for me is to study the music without using the piano, noting the form, the harmonies, all the details of its construction. Then I leave it aside again for one week or perhaps two before I make another study of the score, again without the piano. The fourth and last stage takes me back to the piano, playing the score until I feel I have absorbed it, and only then do I feel ready to go in front of the orchestra with it. This is a long process, so when I decide to add a new work to my repertoire I am planning two or three years in advance.

The actual sound of any performance is very important, because I believe that a good conductor has his own individual sound. Every orchestra, of course, has its own sound in some respects, but it can change this sound, as you hear at a conductors' competition for instance. There you may hear the same orchestra play the same work under three different young conductors, and the orchestra will produce three different sounds. The sound is the first reaction of the orchestra to a conductor's beat, reflecting his arm movement, which may be soft and long or hard and short. Then there is another sound, the sound that belongs to different music, so that Mozart must be played with a particular kind of sound that has nothing to do with Beethoven, and Beethoven with a sound that has nothing to do with Brahms. The conductor has in his arm, and inside himself, a natural sound that is part of his musical personality, which from his cultural experience he then applies so that he produces what he believes to be the right sound for each particular composer. This must happen even when the conductor moves from one orchestra to another. When, for instance, I conduct Mozart in Philadelphia, Berlin and London, I try to draw from these three very different orchestras the same sound — the sound that in my mind is the right sound for Mozart. It is terribly wrong to produce for Mozart a sound which is so big and robust that it belongs to the music of a much later period. This danger is always present, for we are so often playing the music of a composer with our minds affected by the experiences of music written since his time. The danger is even greater in the case of opera, where singers as well as conductors can easily make Rossini sound like Verdi, and Verdi sound like Puccini.

Sound is not interpretation, but is one aspect of it. If the sound is wrong, the interpretation will also be wrong though the right sound alone, with no formal command of the music, cannot produce a true interpretation.

I believe also that we are often mistaken today over the matter of interpretation, because so many musicians and scholars are certain they know the right style of playing the works of a particular composer. When we play Vivaldi, for instance, we try to be 'in style'; but this is just a dream which means nothing. Clearly we should be quite wrong to play Vivaldi's music as though it were by Brahms, but we cannot know the style of Vivaldi with any certainty. It was first played by different instruments than those which are played today, and in places with small acoustics. Neither the musicians nor the audiences of that period knew the sounds of cars and aeroplanes, the cinema and television, as we know them today. Their whole concept of sound was completely different from the concept we have now. Also I think that we concentrate too much today on finding a correct style, the only style, for a piece of music. We know that Brahms, on the other hand, would conduct his own symphonies in Vienna at different speeds from one night to the next. That was in the Romantic period when the performance of music was more free. Today we are inclined to think that a conductor is wrong if he changes tempi in this way, and we have lost the freedom that was enjoyed a century ago. Similarly we take too strict an attitude to the number of players involved in a performance of Mozart, for we can read in a letter which he wrote to his father from Milan that the orchestra playing one of his early operas there included twelve double basses, which he thought was fantastic and was delighted by. Of course, when I conduct Mozart I prefer to have an orchestra smaller than the one I would use for Brahms or Tchaikovsky, but it is pedantic to carry this too far. It is the spirit of Mozart that we should seek in both the sound and the interpretation.

When it comes to opera the function of the conductor is even more complex. In the first place he must have a natural feeling for the drama, because the music in an opera has a pulse which comes from the stage as well as the score. It is vital, therefore, that the conductor chooses the producer he will work with, or at least that he is able to say yes or no to the engagement of any producer the opera house might have in mind. Some opera houses engage a conductor and a producer who have never even met before, which is like a family arranging a marriage for their son or daughter, and this can be a disaster. The conductor is finally responsible for success or failure, because everything comes from the music: in the line of the production on stage you must see the equivalent of what you hear from the pit. The conductor may be mistaken in his choice of a producer, and in such a case he must accept responsibility for his mistake. I worked on one opera with a producer with whom I felt happy at the beginning, because when we discussed the interpretation I liked his dramatic concept and felt that the whole production would be fine. But his ideas did not work out in practice, because he did not understand what the music was saying, and so we failed. However, since I had accepted him as the producer, the responsibility for our failure was mine. In symphonic music there are fewer problems, but the conductor is always responsible for the outcome of a concert, whether it is a success or a failure. And this is fair, because if the conductor has the total command of the players for the performance, imposing his will and his interpretation on them, then his must be the final responsibility. It is the most exciting, challenging and rewarding of musical careers, and I would never want to change it for any other, even though I came to it in the first place through such a curious chain of circumstances.

THE SYMPHONY CONCERT

Haydn

The long and successful career of Haydn is the natural starting-point for our understanding and enjoyment of the symphony. Indeed, while it is not strictly accurate to refer to him as the 'father of the symphony', other composers having used the form before him, he is the earliest symphonist whose works have kept their place in the standard concert repertoire. He composed more than a hundred over a period of thirty-six years, continually experimenting until he established a pattern for them which has survived, with certain modifications, to the present day. It is largely due to him, in fact, that we still talk about the symphony orchestra and the symphony concert. He would be utterly astonished by the musical scene of today, with public concerts a natural way of life in countries as remote from his experience as Japan as well as in provincial cities throughout Europe, for he was a modest and thoroughly practical musical craftsman attempting no more than to satisfy the demands of the times in which he lived.

Most of his creative life, in fact, was spent in the service of princely patrons of a single family, catering to their tastes much as the television script-writer of today turns out episodes in drama serials for the entertainment of home viewers. However aristocratic his audiences may have been, he worked for most of his life strictly to commission, his aim being to please those who paid for his services. If he managed to express his own personality in the process, this was incidental. His career is also of remarkable interest in that it eventually moved from the private to the public domain, and that his social standing as a composer changed from being a rather high-class servant to becoming a celebrity who could turn down a royal invitation to Windsor in order to go back to his home in Vienna.

The son of a wheelwright, (Franz) Joseph Haydn was born at Rohrau, an Austrian village close to the border with Hungary, on 31 March 1732. His family had no connection of any kind with the world of music, which Joseph was introduced to almost by accident at the age of eight when he became a chorister at St Stephen's Cathedral in Vienna. With the inevitable breaking of his boy's voice, he had to leave the choir in 1749 and live, if not exactly by his wits, at least on very slender resources. Even though he spent the night after his dismissal sleeping in the open on a park bench, the teenage Haydn seemed to possess an overriding ambition not only to make music his life, but also to make his living by music. It was fortunate, as well as quite remarkable, that he should have the necessary determination to achieve

Haydn at the age of sixty, a composer of wide fame and artistic independence after years in the service of the Esterházy family

this goal. There was certainly little in his favour: he had no support from any influential quarter, nor had he any formal musical education other than that of a humble choirboy who had taught himself the rudiments of keyboard playing and struggled through a number of textbooks on composition with no teacher to guide him.

For the next twelve years Haydn led a life that was as varied as it was insecure, eking out a living by giving harpsichord lessons, performing in and later composing serenades, and accompanying singers at the keyboard. Two unusual aspects of Viennese life helped to improve his fortunes, and they deserve a mention in this context. First, the city's climate and a certain Latin vein in its culture had for centuries encouraged the activities of outdoor serenaders. A journalist of the time tells us that these serenades were quite elaborate, consisting of trios and quartets, usually taken from operas currently popular and accompanied by wind instruments or even by a whole orchestra. 'On summer nights', he specifies, 'the streets fairly swarm with serenading parties, and

Haydn's birthplace at the village of Rohrau, where his father, a wheelwright, encouraged the whole family to make music in the home

however late they make their appearance, even at an hour when most people are hurrying home to bed, heads soon appear at the windows and a crowd gathers round the players, clapping, applauding, demanding encores, and seldom dispersing until the serenade is over, when they will often troop after the players to another district.' These were public entertainments, entirely different from the private serenades in Spain, which a young man would pay a group of singers to perform with simple guitar accompaniment under the window of the girl he was courting.

Secondly, the large old houses of Vienna accommodated a remarkable cross-section of society under one roof, members of the aristocracy living on the ground and first floors, middle-class families occupying the couple of floors above, and poorer people like Haydn crammed into the attics. When chance led Haydn to rent a room up several flights of stairs in the Altes Michaelerhaus, he found himself under the same roof as the Dowager Princess Esterházy, whose two sons he was later to serve as court

musician for the thirty most formative years of his life, and, two floors higher, the Italian poet Pietro Metastasio, whose heroic and somewhat stilted verse dramas were used as the librettos of several hundred operas by composers such as Handel, Gluck, Arne and Mozart. (It is impossible to imagine three such distinguished personalities, drawn from such different social classes, living in one house in England at any period of time.) It was through Metastasio that Haydn met Nicola Porpora, the composer of some fifty operas and one of the outstanding singing teachers of all time. As a result of this meeting Haydn was engaged as accompanist for Porpora's singing lessons, thus supplementing his income and enjoying periods of good living at a critical time in his early career when he was on the verge of abandoning all hope of a musical future.

In a similarly unexpected fashion, his serenading activities had brought him, at the age of nineteen, his first commission as a composer. His group of musicians happened to serenade the pretty wife of Vienna's most popular variety comedian, who asked Haydn on the spot to write the music for a pantomime opera her husband was planning, the fee of twenty-five ducats making the budding composer, in his own words, 'regard himself as a very rich man'. 15

Prince Nicholas Esterházy, in whose palace Haydn was Kapellmeister with an orchestra and company of opera singers at his disposal

most elegant turns of phrase during the eighteenth century.

The door to a rosy musical future finally opened for Haydn in 1761, when he was appointed assistant Kapellmeister (director of music) at the country seat of Prince Paul Anton Esterházy. It was not long before Haydn was promoted to the senior post and the prince was succeeded by his brother Nicholas, who was to build a new palace, Esterház, reputed to rival Versailles in splendour. Prince Nicholas was to become one of the greatest benefactors of the arts in that famous age of patronage. The new palace, though remotely situated, was lavishly appointed, and not least for the requirements and ambitions of its director of music. There were two theatres, one for opera and the other for marionette plays, and also two concert halls. Haydn was required to compose whatever music the prince might fancy – operas, orchestral works and chamber pieces – and to conduct the performances and train the entire musical staff, which comprised about twenty-five players in the orchestra and a dozen singers for the opera. Prince Nicholas was undoubtedly demanding, but he had a real understanding of music and quickly developed a sincere friendship with his musical supremo.

Haydn made clear in his own words the advantages he enjoyed during the three decades he spent in the prince's service: 'My prince was pleased with all my work, and as conductor of an orchestra I could make experiments, observe what weakened and what strengthened and thereupon improve, substitute, omit and try new things. I was cut off from the world, there was nobody around to mislead and harass me, and so I was forced to become original.' The latter point was of the utmost importance, for unlike Mozart, who seems to have been born with his musical style already formed, Haydn was the kind of creative artist who needed to progress slowly and cautiously, reaching full maturity only through a lengthy process of trial and error. It was not strictly true, however, that he was cut off from the world: there was a regular stream of distinguished artists and musical *cognoscenti* making visits to Esterház, while he in turn was able to make occasional trips to Vienna and keep abreast of the new developments in the then musical centre of the world.

Haydn's considerable progress in the fields of opera, the string quartet and the keyboard sonata belong to other chapters: what concerns us here is his gradual extension and mastery of the symphony. The origin of the symphony is to be found in the Italian opera overture at the very beginning of the eighteenth century. Usually called the *sinfonia*, it was cast

All this, of course, represented only the first faltering steps in his progress, and it was not until 1759, at the age of twenty-seven, that he was appointed director of music and resident composer to the court of Count Morzin in Bohemia, for which he wrote his earliest symphonies. During this two-year appointment he also entered on what was to be a highly unsatisfactory marriage. He fell in love with the younger of two sisters who were his pupils for a time, and when she entered a convent he made the best of an unfortunate situation by taking the elder sister, Maria Anna, as his wife. Two remarks made by Haydn in later life summed up this sorry marriage. 'We grew fonder of each other, but I soon found that my wife was very irresponsible,' was the first. The second was even more damning: 'My wife was incapable of childbearing, and I was therefore less indifferent to the charms of other women.' People expressed the most distressing facts of life in the

16

in three movements and the pattern was always fast-slow-fast. This sequence of an Allegro movement followed by a shorter, more lyrical Andante, and then rounded off by another fast movement in dance rhythm (usually a Minuet) clearly anticipates the general form of the Classical symphony. Since their music bore no thematic or other connection with the actual operas which followed, these sinfonias were in fact frequently performed as independent orchestral works in concert programmes. There is a basic difference, however, between the opera sinfonia and the symphony proper. The symphony as we generally recognize it, a work for full orchestra in four separate yet related movements, was not born overnight but was the result of several changes which came about during the second quarter of the eighteenth century; it was Haydn who finally established its essential pattern and spirit.

The music of large-scale works in the late Baroque period had most often been contrapuntal, combining simultaneous parts (voices and/or instruments) each of which follows its own melodic path. In non-contrapuntal pieces – the concertos of Vivaldi, for instance – each movement was usually confined to the spinning out of a single idea or mood. In the symphony the importance of counterpoint is much diminished, while a greater profusion of ideas and extreme changes of key within each movement becomes the motive force, resulting in a greater sense of drama. The symphony is accordingly dramatic in essence, not as opera is dramatic because of its concern with human emotions, but in a purely musical sense, creating a constant flow of tensions by contrasting different keys as well as different themes one with another. The first steps towards transforming the sinfonia into the symphony took place almost simultaneously in several countries, with Giovanni Battista Sammartini (1700–1775) a leading figure in Italy; but it was German composers who seized on the new form with the greatest zeal, and from about 1740 onwards important 'symphonic' centres were established in Mannheim, Berlin and Vienna. The founder of the Mannheim School, Johann Stamitz (1717–57), formed an orchestra which became famous throughout Europe for its virtuosity, notably in respect of the dynamic range of its playing and its thrilling use of the crescendo. Stamitz was also responsible for introducing a contrasting, gentler theme into the opening Allegro movement, and for adding a fourth movement, another Allegro, after the Minuet to give the symphony a more balanced structure.

Perhaps the most important figure of all was Carl Philipp Emanuel Bach (1714–88), the second surviving son of Johann Sebastian, particularly for his development of sonata form. This form is fundamental to the symphony (as well as to overtures, chamber works and even vocal pieces). It is the pattern adopted for almost all Classical first movements, and though the term itself sounds a little dry and formidable, it can be described quite simply. It comprises a movement (usually in fast tempo) made up of three main sections, sometimes preceded by a slow Introduction. The first main part is the Exposition consisting of a first 'subject' (a theme or group of themes) in the principal key of the movement, a contrasting, usually quieter, second subject in the dominant of that key (if major) or its relative major (if minor), and a closing subject in the same key as the second. These different themes or groups of themes are connected by suitable bridge passages, and the exposition is usually repeated. Next comes the Development section, which might be regarded as a musical adventure in which themes from the exposition, or phrases from them, are presented in new aspects or combinations, with modulations into different keys. After this the Recapitulation section brings back the material from the exposition in its original order (this time all in the principal key). There may then be a short Coda to round off the movement with a flourish.

Sonata form could also be used in the second and fourth movements of symphonies, though it was not the usual practice with Haydn. The second, slow movement, an Adagio or an Andante, is generally more freely planned, often relaxed and song-like in character: it can be built from a single melody, though more than one may be employed. The third movement of the symphony gradually evolved from the gracious Minuet (as used in most of Haydn's symphonies) to the livelier, more humorous Scherzo, in both cases containing a middle section called the Trio which introduces a contrasting melody. The fourth movement, usually an Allegro like the first, might be in sonata form or designed as a rondo (a main theme repeated several times with different melodies, called 'episodes', between each of its reappearances).

It is a measure of Haydn's genius that he was able to produce more than a hundred symphonies without repeating himself or growing stale. Between 1760 and 1788 he sailed along from No 2 to No 92, composing most of them for the court of Esterház, the exceptions being the Paris series, Nos 82–87, and then Nos 88–92 for various private individuals. He crowned his achievement in the symphonic field between 1791 and 1795 with the series of twelve so-called London Symphonies, Nos 93–104, the most ambitious of all in scale and depth of expression. In view of such a large number it is hardly surprising 17

The orchestra of Haydn's day playing for an opera

that Haydn's symphonies vary in quality as well as style; yet even those which show evidence of haste in composition and lack subtlety of construction fall pleasantly on the ear, for Haydn was able to draw on an apparently inexhaustible fund of melody and was always a fine musical craftsman. His music is invariably fresh and bright in sound, its inspiration vigorous with a certain open-air quality. The remarkable thing is that so many of them, specifically designed two centuries ago to please Prince Esterházy

and his guests, still grip the attention and delight the senses of audiences today.

There are several reasons for the lasting appeal of Haydn's symphonies, stemming from the fact that, though conservative by nature, he introduced some quite revolutionary elements into the form. The music of the earlier, pre-Classical symphonists had suffered from the short-windedness of their themes:

18

Haydn overcame this by building up the short themes that are essential to symphonic development into spacious melodies. Then he used a distinctive style of counterpoint to add interest to the prevailing homophonic style (a melody in the main part supported by a simple, all-too-predictable accompaniment by the rest of the orchestra), thus creating a new richness of texture and instrumental colouring. Thirdly, he had strong roots in popular and folk music, so that gusts of country air frequently invigorate the elegant, *galant* atmosphere of the courtly milieu in which he worked, an innovation which frequently ruffled the powdered-wig sensibilities of the Establishment of his day. Finally, he was a man of natural vivacity with a boisterous sense of humour, which some contemporary commentators found 'playful' and 'alluring' but which others condemned as being altogether too frivolous. (This sense of humour, which Haydn shared with Beethoven, is quite distinct from the more sophisticated wit of Mozart.) His vivacity inspired him to invent a new kind of symphonic fourth movement, or Finale, in which he exploited a variety of whimsical effects, and two centuries later these high-spirited finales are universally regarded as being among his finest inspirations.

Any selection of individual Haydn symphonies for special mention is quite arbitrary, since so many of them are rewarding, yet a few can be cited as displaying different facets of his achievement. Two of the symphonies from his *Sturm und Drang* ('storm and stress') period are outstanding. The 'Trauersinfonie' ('Symphony of mourning'), No 44 in E minor, has a most beautiful Adagio for its second movement and an eerie Minuet offset by a Trio which both flows and glows; while No 49 in F minor, known as 'La Passione' because it was composed to celebrate the Easter of 1768, brings the expression of human grief into the abstract world of the symphony. In sharp contrast, the 'Farewell' Symphony of 1772, No 45 in F sharp minor, reveals the humorous side of the composer. The members of his orchestra had grown restive at their prince's protracted stay at the summer palace and were anxious to see their wives and families again, so Haydn dropped a heavy hint to their master by transforming the final Presto into an Adagio, in the course of which one group of instruments after another ends its contribution to the work, the players then leaving the platform until only two violins remain to whisper the closing bars. Nicknames were frequently given to Haydn's symphonies, reflecting the affection in which he was held, and we find one of the six he composed for Paris, No 83 in G minor, known as 'La Poule' ('The hen'). This name was given because of the 'clucking' descant to the

Johann Peter Salomon, the German violinist who settled in London to become an impresario and who commissioned Haydn's 'London' symphonies

second theme of the opening Allegro, which is a typical touch of his humour, though in its delicacy of orchestration and in the elegantly flowing first melody of its Andante this symphony clearly indicates the influence of Mozart upon the older composer.

Ironically, it was the death of his patron in 1790 that enabled Haydn to climb, or rather leap, to new heights as a symphonist. Prince Nicholas was succeeded by his son Anton who, though he added an annual salary to the generous pension his father bequeathed to the Kapellmeister of Esterház, had no great interest in music and disbanded the orchestra. At last Haydn was his own master, universally acclaimed, and free to accept whatever was offered him by professional impresarios, the new breed of men who were about to replace aristocratic amateurs as providers of the composer's livelihood with the passing of patronage from private into public hands. The enterprising Johann Peter Salomon, a German violinist who had established himself as the leading promoter of concerts in London, invited Haydn to 19

England, resulting in the two visits of 1791–2 and 1794–5 during which the twelve London symphonies were composed and performed with huge success. Spurred on by the availability of a larger orchestra than he had had at his disposal before, and put on his mettle by the knowledge that a highly cultivated audience expected nothing less than masterpieces from him, he surpassed everything he had done before. All are unusually impressive in scale, and all but one have slow introductions to the first movements which are either dramatic or mysterious in mood, filling the listener with a sense of suspense. He made free use of every device he had mastered over the years, the exploring and expanding of melodic development and harmonic range; the introduction of colour and folk-like elements into the Minuet and a continuing elaboration of the Finale.

Above all, Haydn gave each of these symphonies a personality of its own, once more looking forward to Beethoven, and in several cases this individual character has again resulted in appropriate titles being bestowed on them which the composer seemed positively to invite. It was inevitable, for example, that No 94 in G would be called the 'Surprise', the fortissimo chord which erupts after the statement of the delicate Andante theme by the strings having been deliberately inserted, in Haydn's own words, 'to make the ladies scream'. Similarly, the tick-tock accompaniment to the graceful melody of the Andante of No 101 in D ensured that the symphony would be nicknamed the 'Clock', while the timpani roll which begins No 103 in E flat in such original fashion led logically to the title of the 'Drum Roll'. These are not gimmicks but the composer's way of expressing his simple good nature; his effects are striking without endangering his basic regard for the form in which he was working. His command of this particular form was such that Mozart equalled it only in his three final symphonies, and Haydn was to remain the supreme symphonist until Beethoven broadened the musical horizon with his *Eroica* in 1804, five years before the older man's death in Vienna on 31 May 1809.

It is curious that Haydn, who was an accomplished keyboard player and whose late piano sonatas are highly impressive, should have done nothing outstanding in the field of the piano concerto; and of the various works he composed for other solo instruments with orchestra, only the Trumpet Concerto in E flat rises above the level of the agreeable to be counted a work of any consequence. It would seem that the idea of a solo instrument pitted against the orchestra did not fire his imagination as it did that of Mozart.

Mozart

Turning from the career of Haydn to that of Mozart is a saddening experience in human terms, for the man who was undoubtedly the most richly gifted genius the world of music has ever known was the most poorly rewarded. The miracle is that he should have achieved so much in his thirty-five years: a series of operas and piano concertos whose sheer perfection has never been equalled, and also a considerable number of enduring masterpieces in other forms. The word 'miracle' is not an extravagant claim; when Wolfgang Amadeus Mozart was born at Salzburg on 27 January 1756, Haydn was already twenty-three, and when he was buried in an unmarked pauper's grave in Vienna on 6 December 1791, the older composer was making his conquest of London and still had eighteen years of fame and fulfilment to enjoy. It is also miraculous that Mozart should win acclaim as a keyboard virtuoso at the age of six and then go on to compose his first sonatas at eight, his first oratorio at eleven and his first opera at twelve. There is, perhaps, an inevitable price to pay for being so precocious: if so, then he paid it in full. Fortunately for us all he happened to be a man whose personal and artistic lives were things apart, so that the suffering he endured in the one left no trace on the fruits of the other.

The system of aristocratic patronage under which Haydn had flourished never proved favourable to Mozart, and indeed was not geared to accommodate such a genius. The position of court musician provided security, and under a liberal patron such as Nicholas Esterházy could be pleasant enough, yet its holder was still a liveried servant. Mozart was by nature unsuited to such a position, not only because he was probably the first composer to realize that he was a superior being to his social masters, but because he also showed it in his behaviour. It was his misfortune to live before the French Revolution had changed the social face of Europe, for had he been born a few decades later he would probably have been able to assert himself as the mature Beethoven succeeded in doing. His childhood experiences as a touring prodigy must have played a considerable part in giving him a sense of superiority, even of arrogance, bringing him as they did into personal contact with Marie Antoinette of France and Maria Theresa of Austria. Royal praise of a child prodigy, however, was rarely more than a kindly gesture quickly forgotten. When Archduke Ferdinand of Lombardy, a son of that same Maria Theresa, asked her advice about engaging Mozart's services, she put in the imperial boot with a remark worthy of Wilde's Lady

Bracknell: 'It gives one's service a bad name when such people run about one like beggars.'

The constant influence behind the young Mozart's studies, concert tours and searching for patronage was his father, Leopold, a violinist, composer and Assistant Kapellmeister at the court of the Prince Archbishop of Salzburg. Leopold, quick to see the financial possibilities of his son's precocious musicianship, took him a few days before his sixth birthday to play the harpsichord at the Bavarian court in Munich, the first of many successful appearances by the boy wonder over a period of four years. This musical grand tour took in Vienna, Frankfurt (where the audience included the young Goethe), Brussels, Paris, London (where the first symphony was composed in their Ebury Street lodgings), The Hague, Geneva and many other cities. By the age of ten, Mozart was universally recognized as a star performer, on the violin as well as the harpsichord (soon replaced by the piano), while four years later, on 20 December 1770, he enjoyed his first triumph as a composer with the opera *Mitridate, rè di Ponto* in Milan, almost every aria being acclaimed with cries of 'Evviva il maestro!' After this he could scarcely be expected to find satisfaction serving the Archbishop in Salzburg, a city whose tastes he regarded as insufferably bourgeois and provincial.

Matters grew worse at the court with the appointment in 1772 of a new Archbishop, Hieronymus Colloredo, who was far less sympathetic to the Mozarts, father and son, than his predecessor had been. In fairness to him, he was not unreasonable in expecting them to work for the court which paid their salaries rather than travel through Europe for their own personal glory. On the other hand, while he retained the services of Leopold until the frustrated Assistant Kapellmeister's death in 1787, he heaped indignities upon the genius-son until he rebelled and tried all means of having himself dismissed. Events came to head in 1781 after the Munich success of *Idomeneo*, Mozart's first great masterpiece, when he was ordered to Vienna to join the entourage of the Archbishop, who was on a visit to the capital. A final argument ended in Mozart being literally kicked out of the official residence.

The twenty-five-year-old composer was now alone in the world, not only deprived of his official position but also of the advice and help of his prudent father. Having decided to gamble with a career in Vienna, he added to his problems fourteen months later by making an unsatisfactory marriage. A few years before, in Mannheim, he had fallen in love with Aloysia Weber, a girl of considerable beauty with a fine singing voice, who flirted with him for a time but then married another suitor. In the meantime, the Weber family had moved to Vienna, and it was with them that Mozart took lodgings. He was a vulnerable young man, and quickly fell in love with Aloysia's younger sister Constanze, and also being very unworldly he allowed the scheming Madame Weber to force him into marriage on 4 August 1782, by devious means which bordered on blackmail. (It is intriguing that Mozart, like Haydn before him, should marry a woman whose more attractive sister had turned him down.) The couple were genuinely fond of each other, yet they were far from being ideally matched, for Constanze's impracticality as a housekeeper only served to increase the debts which her husband incurred through his inability to manage his material affairs. The man who desperately needed a level-headed wife burdened himself instead with a flighty scatterbrain who lacked the intellect or culture to appreciate and encourage his genius.

Three weeks before his marriage Mozart had scored a triumph with *Die Entführung aus dem Serail* ('The escape from the seraglio'), resulting in a sudden upsurge of interest in his work by the Viennese. He gave many concerts, at which he played more than a dozen of the piano concertos he was then composing with such fluency and ever-increasing imagination. He moved easily among the nobility, but chose to spend his time with other musicians, writers, actors and even scientists, all men of ideas and some of them spokesmen of the new age that was about to dawn. When Leopold was persuaded to visit Vienna in 1785 he must have thought his son had finally made good, for he found a celebrated composer living in a stimulating *milieu*. Above all he must have treasured the declaration that Haydn made to him: 'I tell you before God and as a man of honour that your son is the greatest composer I know either personally or by reputation.' It was fortunate for the proud father, perhaps, that he died two years later and was spared all knowledge of the pitiful material state to which his son declined in the final years of 1788 to 1791.

The problem for Mozart was that he was virtually two beings in one. As a composer he was not only richly endowed but thoroughly practical, writing the kind of music that conditions demanded at a particular time. With the exception of his last three symphonies, he composed such works only when they were required of him, so that relatively long periods could go by without his writing in the form at all (the same consideration applied to his output of operas and piano concertos). He also designed his works to suit the abilities of specific performers and the taste of the audiences concerned. In personal matters, on 21

Above: *The boy Mozart playing the harpsichord at the Prince de Conti's tea-party in Paris during an early European tour with his father*

Opposite: *A highly romanticized painting of the young Mozart, already a prolific composer as well as a keyboard virtuoso*

the other hand, he was ingenuous as well as high-handed. He made friends with people whom he happened to like rather than those who in one official capacity or another might have helped him, thus minimizing his chances of securing any lucrative prestigious appointment. He also enjoyed living above his means, but when it came to dealing with his resultant petty debts he showed none of the flair of Wagner, who realized that in such matters nothing succeeds like excess.

It was his dual personality, on the other hand, which allowed him to continue to pour out elegant, sublime music as though he did not have a care in the world. Nowhere is this more evident than in his contribution to the symphony, which though less spectacular than his achievement in the field of the piano concerto, is none the less considerable. Throughout his early years he was strongly influenced by the Italian style in composition, which not only resulted in his frequent resort to the three-movement sinfonia, but also made him aim to entertain rather than to edify, to write flowing, song-like melodies in preference to the terse themes of the German school, and to lighten his faster symphonic movements with elements of *opera buffa*. Because he was so often on the move, however, his development did not follow any consistent course, so that a group of symphonies composed in 1772 for Salzburg have a more weighty nature, only to be followed by others in lighter, more Italianate vein. Then, during a later stay in Salzburg in 1773–4, he produced two sym-

Hieronymous Colloredo, the Archbishop of Salzburg who won a place in history by having Mozart literally kicked out of his service

phonies which suggested he was changing over to a course similar to that of Haydn. No 25 in G minor is unusually expressive, indeed almost stormy in mood, and it reveals a new subtlety in relating different themes so as to produce a unity of thought. Similar intensity of expression and more dramatic contrast of themes also characterize No 29 in A, which might be considered his first really serious symphony. Over the next twelve years Mozart returned only occasionally to the symphony, and not always with great distinction, though the period ended with the splendid 'Prague' Symphony (No 38 in D), a work both irresistible in melodic appeal and noble in expression.

And so we reach the three remarkable works with which Mozart crowned his career as a symphonist. They are remarkable in three respects: first, they were not composed to commission as all the others had been; secondly, they were dashed off in the course of about eight weeks when the composer's personal misery was at its most acute; and thirdly, their individuality and perfection come as a complete surprise after the inconsistent progress he had previously made in his symphonic writing. We shall never know why, in the absence of a commission, he wrote them in the first place, but we know from his letters and diaries exactly when and under what conditions the work was done. By 1788 the fickle Viennese public had turned its back on Mozart, failing even to appreciate *Don Giovanni*, which Prague had hailed with overwhelming enthusiasm the previous year. To add

to his troubles, Constanze was ill and in need of expensive medical attention. Begging letters written to his friend and fellow freemason, Michael Puchberg, reveal the desperate state of his finances. 'I still owe you eight ducats,' he wrote in June, 'but although at the moment I am not in a position to pay back this sum, I implore you to help me out with a hundred florins until next week.' A few days later he asked for a further loan – 'one or two thousand florins, at a suitable rate of interest . . . to enable me to work with a mind more free from care and a lighter heart, and thus earn more.' Puchberg sent him, not two thousand, but two hundred florins, and in July Mozart continued with even more pathetic letters. At the same time he made the following entries in his own record of works completed: '26th June – a symphony' (No 39); '25th July – a symphony' (No 40); '10th August – a symphony' (No 41, the 'Jupiter').

Although they were all composed under the same conditions, each of these symphonies has its own character and personality, the first tender and cheerful, the second meltingly sad, the last heroically triumphant. They provide, in fact, the final proof that the man and the artist in Mozart were beings apart. No 39 in E flat opens with a solemn Introduction, then the sonata elements are treated with great refinement in the song-like yet dramatically impressive themes of the Allegro. The Andante has a smiling, elegiac grace whose effect is heightened by brief passionate outbursts from time to time. The Minuet, by contrast, is ebullient, almost festive, while the final Allegro is virtually monothematic, 'learned' in its ingenious structure yet irrepressibly high-spirited. The symphony was aptly described as 'the swan song of Mozart's youth' by E T A Hoffmann, the novelist and amateur composer who changed his third name to Amadeus in homage to his idol. Wagner discerned a relationship between the symphony and Beethoven's Seventh, though he drew the distinction that 'in Mozart's music the language of the heart is shaped to graceful longing, whereas in Beethoven's conception this longing reaches out to the Infinite.'

As well as being one of the best known, No 40 in G minor is certainly one of his most advanced compositions, both melodically and harmonically. It is a symphony without trumpets and drums, which indeed would have no place in a work whose character is utterly fatalistic, almost a turning away from the world. (It is all the more surprising in view of its pessimistic nature that the first movement should once have hit the charts arranged as a pop number.) Yet there is nothing depressing about its music, each of its four movements overflowing with engaging melodies which speak more meaningfully to the

Facsimile of the 'Jupiter' Symphony, composed by Mozart in 1788 in a matter of two weeks when in desperate need of money for his sick wife

listener with every hearing.

The *galant* and 'learned' styles are drawn together with consummate skill in No 41 in C. The first theme of the opening Allegro is notable for its breadth and evolution, the Andante is a genuine expression of the soul in a manner foreshadowing the intensity of Beethoven's slow movements. The fourth movement is of revolutionary importance, an Allegro which makes the finale the weightiest point in the symphony. To bring off this feat, Mozart took a simple, easily recognizable theme and then manipulated it so that fugue and sonata elements are composed one against the background of the other. The listener can easily enjoy the music for its own majestic sake, without being aware of 'how it was done', though in historical terms it was of immense importance to the future of the symphony.

There are other orchestral works of Mozart which have won immortality, a variety of serenades composed for garden parties, like *Eine Kleine Nachtmusik* and the 'Haffner' Serenade, the popular Clarinet Concerto and five violin concertos, of which the three dating from the latter part of 1775 are quite masterly. All these have exquisite slow movements and infectious dance-like finales. Curiously, he never returned to the violin concerto though he gave us three notable examples whereas Beethoven, Brahms and Tchaikovsky were all content to write only one.

The concerto form was especially congenial to Mozart, for a solo instrument 'singing' against an orchestra has obviously much in common with his other favourite medium, the opera; and in the case of the piano concerto there was also the practical advantage that it allowed him to exploit his popularity as a leading virtuoso of his time. It should be stressed, however, that he was not a virtuoso in the flashy, athletic sense of later piano superstars, but in his brilliance of improvisation governed by impeccable good taste and in his production of singing keyboard tone. Appearances in concerts playing his own concertos were simply more lucrative than his other work, and if this sounds like expediency it should be remembered that such were the facts of life during the eighteenth century, which was not really the Golden Age that romantic idealists have subsequently imagined it to be. So far as composers were concerned there was only a thin veneer of gilt spread over a large mass of gingerbread.

The numbering of Mozart's piano concertos runs from 1 to 27, though the first four were in fact arrangements of music by other composers. Furthermore, 'No 7' is a concerto for three pianos and 'No 10' for two. Among the twenty-one original solo concertos there are several in the same key – four in C major, for example, and three in D major – so in order to identify them it is necessary to use their Köchel numbers. (Ludwig von Köchel was a scientist

Ludwig von Köchel, the scientist and music lover who carried out the task of cataloguing Mozart's six hundred works in chronological order

with an orderly mind who, as an admirer of Mozart's works, took upon himself the task of cataloguing them in what he considered to be a chronological sequence.) The first C major concerto is accordingly identified as K246, the last one as K503. Whereas a good number of the early symphonies, though pleasant enough to listen to, are almost routine minor works, all the piano concertos reveal the utmost fertility of imagination and continue to delight and stimulate: familiarity with them, far from breeding contempt, elicits ever-increasing admiration.

Concertos by earlier composers such as Johann Christian Bach (1735–82) had been relatively unsophisticated, designed in the *galant* style to do little more than charm the ear, and so written that the orchestra did little but accompany the soloist. Mozart elevated the piano concerto into a work in which soloist and orchestra enjoy an interplay of ideas on equal terms and are intimately related. In addition to creating this perfectly balanced relationship between the forces employed, he gave a unity to the three-movement form similar to that of the (usually) four-movement symphony, so that the piano concerto it-

Mozart and his sister Nannerl at the keyboard with their father in 1780–81. Their mother's portrait hangs on the wall

self became a genuinely symphonic form. His first movements follow the sonata principle, the orchestra providing the first exposition of the main themes, the soloist then joining in a fuller, more elaborate second exposition. Development and recapitulation sections follow, as in a symphony, but in the concerto the orchestra then falls silent for a cadenza, in which the soloist improvises on the thematic material, ending with a trill which cues in the other players for a brief coda. This is only a general guide to first movements, however, for Mozart frequently experimented within the pattern he had established. The second movement in most cases is like a lyrical aria, a clear reflection of operatic style. The finale is a rondo or sonata-rondo with lively melodies which the soloist treats in dazzling style and with scope for one or more cadenzas. In some cases a set of variations replaces the usual form for the second or third movement.

Mozart showed himself absolute master of the form with his fourth concerto ('No 9'), in E flat, K271, composed during the year in which he celebrated his twenty-first birthday. Here he opens the concerto in a way he was never to repeat: in the second bar the piano makes an utterly unexpected entry to answer the orchestra's opening phrase. There are other remarkable features too. The second movement is an unusually introspective Andantino, poignant in mood and elaborately extended, while the final Rondo, after presenting several perky tunes, suddenly digresses into a stately minuet with variations. Already, in 1777, he was experimenting with the piano concerto, raising it to new heights of expressiveness and making it very much his own; and he succeeded to such an extent that no composer since has surpassed his masterpieces in the form. Beethoven and Brahms may have produced bigger piano concertos, yet none of these works would be claimed even by the composers' staunchest admirers to be better than those of Mozart.

After K271 five years were to pass before Mozart embarked on his next group, written in Vienna during 1782 for performance at his concerts there and also for publication. Of these three concertos (K413–5) the one in A major, K414, most clearly demonstrates his aims as set down in a letter to his father: 'There are passages here and there from which connoisseurs alone can derive satisfaction; but these are written in such a way that the less learned cannot fail to be pleased, though without knowing why.'

After these relatively lightweight concertos he was occupied with other kinds of music for a time; then between 1784 and 1786 he produced no fewer than twelve great masterpieces, each of which explores some new expressive possibilities and therefore has its own individual character and special interest. All of them allow the soloist ample opportunities for displaying his virtuosity, yet none is shallow in the sense of the bravura concertos by Liszt and some later virtuoso-composers. Indeed, Mozart's concertos express some of his most profound musical thought below a surface which is immediately appealing and deceptively easy. A lengthy study would be necessary to do them full justice, though the receptive listener will readily enjoy them, in Mozart's own words, 'without knowing why': written from the heart of the composer, they go straight to the hearts of the audience. A few points, however, might be mentioned here, to draw attention to their variety of style and expression.

In the Concerto in B flat, K450, as in all the later concertos, the wind instruments play a vital role both as soloists and as a body. (They were optional in

Mozart and his wife Constanze, who was a devoted partner but who never understood his genius

some of the earlier concertos so that performances could be given by piano with string quartet.) This use of the wind gave a new wealth of colour to the concerto. The Concerto in G, K453, has been described as 'full of hidden laughter and hidden sadness', and it is certainly personal and even passionate, its first movement conveying emotional unrest despite the elegance of its unforgettable melodies. The tenderness of its Andante is also passionate, so that the joyousness of its Finale, a set of variations on a theme that might have been written for the bird-catcher Papageno in *The Magic Flute*, comes as a particularly delightful surprise. There is a similar contrast in the Concerto in C major, K467, march-like rhythms giving the first movement a military air, the wistful melody of the Andante sounding like an aria for the Countess in *The Marriage of Figaro*, and the Finale bustling with high spirits in the manner of an *opera buffa*. By contrast, the minor-key concertos, K466 in D minor and K491 in C minor, foreshadow Beethoven in their sombre colouring and sense of quite vehement drama. The A major Concerto, K488, deservedly one of the most popular of all, was composed at the same time as *The Marriage of Figaro*, and is an equally masterly work, mostly smiling but heart-searching too. The very last concerto, K595 in B flat, came in 1791 five years after his prolific period, and is filled with a sense of resignation, as though he knew he would not live out the year.

Beethoven

With the arrival – or one might even say eruption – of Beethoven upon the Classical scene, the music was changed at a stroke, never to return to its earlier sense of decorum. There are musical scholars who take the view that a composer's actual works are the only reality, divorced alike from the personality of the man himself and the social, political and cultural upheavals of the period in which he lived. 'If an artist's work,' writes Basil Lam in *The Symphony*, 'needs the commentary of biographical information to make it fully comprehensible, the work is to that extent a failure.' It is unlikely, however, that Beethoven would have composed the way he did if he had spent his creative life as a court musician prior to the French Revolution, an event which, significantly, Mozart did not mention once in his many letters of the time, and which Haydn also appeared scarcely to notice. It is equally unlikely that Beethoven's development, especially in his later works, was unaffected by his deafness, the most cruel affliction for any musician. The fact that his music was revolutionary and titanic surely indicates that he was influenced, indirectly at least, by the powerful forces the Revolution had released, just as the increasingly meditative, inward character of the works of his late period must be attributed to some extent to the fact that his deafness cut him off so much from the world. On the other hand, it can be dangerous and misleading to lay too much emphasis on such extra-musical considerations, for Beethoven remained essentially a Classicist: he may have strained the tradition he took over from Mozart and Haydn to its utmost limits, yet he never completely burst its bonds to become what one could truly call a Romantic composer.

Ludwig van Beethoven, who was born at Bonn on 16 December 1770, the son of a court musician, developed into the prototype of the unruly, independent man of genius, a fact of which he was clearly aware. So far as his personal behaviour was concerned, he once described himself as a man 'who did everything badly except compose music', while his conviction that he was destined for greatness found expression in a letter to his pupil, Archduke Rudolph: 'There is no loftier mission than to come nearer than other men to the Divinity, and to disseminate the divine rays among mankind'. He was the first composer to express such a sense of mission, and perhaps the first to realize that his music would not die with him, but would achieve immortality, appreciated more fully by future generations than it had been by the men of his own day. Though he never toppled over into megalomania, as Wagner was later to do, the knowledge that he had to fulfil a noble destiny made him become impatient even with his friends, and sometimes downright impossible to deal with. 'Living with Beethoven,' one of his friends is supposed to have said, 'would have been like living with a gorilla.' Others viewed him in a very different light. 'When I first saw him [in 1823] at Baden,' recalled Julius Benedict, 'his white hair flowing over his mighty shoulders, with that wonderful look . . . I was touched as if King Lear stood before me.'

However deficient in charm he might have been, Beethoven had a magnetic personality which attracted a variety of admiring, loyal friends, several of them from the Imperial family. It was these, no doubt, who saved him from investigation and prosecution for the inflammatory political ideas that he frequently expressed in public, and he was shrewd enough to realize their value in this respect. 'There is nothing smaller than our great folk,' he once said, 'but I make an exception of the archdukes'; and one can only admire the republican composer for using his privileged friends for his own ends. He was perfectly willing to accept them as patrons, but only so that he could follow his own path as a composer: he worked, not to commission, but in the light of his own personal inspiration. His insistence on creative independence entailed an ideal which was completely new and which was to have far-reaching effects on the future of all the arts. He was the first composer successfully to throw off the shackles of service to any paymaster and become his own man, and it is both a proof of his almost superhuman personal qualities and a sign of the times that he was encouraged to do so. Mozart had attempted to secure some measure of this freedom, though in a less radical way, but he had been born too soon to have any chance of achieving it. Beethoven, on the other hand, was the supreme example of the right man born at just the right point in history.

All the facets of the composer's personality and genius are to be found in the nine symphonies – nine, that is, if we ignore the so-called *Battle Symphony*, a well-paid indiscretion to celebrate Wellington's victory at the Battle of Vittoria in 1813. They span a period of twenty-four years and expand the form in every direction. The Symphony No 1 in C major, composed in 1799, has aptly been described as 'the instrumental swan-song of the eighteenth century', for while it lies within the tradition of Haydn and Mozart in many respects it introduces a few features which must have shocked its first audience in 1800 and which hint at what was to come later. The first movement starts on a discord, immediately arousing attention by tonal ambiguity; the Minuet discards the spirit of the graceful old dance for the more energetic abandon of the Scherzo; and the Finale allows the violins to have fun with false starts. These hints became more pronounced in the Symphony No 2 in D major, composed in 1802: the slow Introduction to the first movement is on a larger scale than any by Haydn, the Larghetto has an unusual wealth of themes in smoothly singing style, the Scherzo and Finale are nothing less than explosive.

Beethoven was by this time thirty-two and had been living in Vienna for ten years, so it is worth looking at the position he had established for himself. Having studied briefly under Haydn at the beginning of this period and later with other teachers he had quickly made his mark with a number of piano sonatas and chamber works, three piano concertos and the first two symphonies. It has so often been suggested that his work was misunderstood and undervalued in his lifetime that this myth should be scotched here and now. Most of his work was well received, even though a few of his innovations bewildered the critics, and he was widely recognized as the successor of Haydn and Mozart. He was also acknowledged to be the outstanding pianist of the day, a matter of considerable interest in view of his style of playing. He caused a sensation in 1792 when he first appeared on the Viennese concert scene, not because he was technically impeccable or a virtuoso with a superficially glittering style, but by virtue of the elemental power and fiery expressiveness of his performances. Indeed, no piano was safe with him. A friend who turned the pages for him when he played a Mozart concerto left this entertaining description of Beethoven the pianist: 'I was mostly occupied in wrenching the strings of the piano which snapped, while the hammers struck among the broken strings. Beethoven insisted on finishing the concerto, so back and forth I leapt, jerking out a string, disentangling a hammer, turning a page, so that I worked harder than he did.' Beethoven was often wildly inaccurate – and also wildly exciting. Perhaps the wisest critic of the time was the one who commented: 'He plays like a composer'. The general acceptance of this stormy, wilful genius makes clear the enormous change in public attitudes which had taken place in the space of a few momentous years of Europe's history.

1802, the year of the Second Symphony, was one of harrowing personal crisis as his deafness became ever more acute. On October 6 he wrote what is known as the 'Heiligenstadt Testament', a document intended to be read by his brothers after his death. 'I must live like an exile,' he railed, 'for if I approach near to people a hot terror seizes me, a fear that I

may be subjected to the danger of letting my condition be observed. Thus it has been during the last half year I have spent in the country: what a humiliation when someone stood beside me and heard a flute in the distance and *I heard nothing*, or the shepherd singing and again I heard nothing . . . Only art prevented my putting an end to my life. It seemed impossible to leave the world until I had produced all that I felt called upon to produce.' We have seen that in the case of Mozart personal problems did not seem to affect his work in any way at all; he was a totally Classical artist. Romantic composers, on the contrary, allowed their personal griefs to spill over into their work, Berlioz producing the *Symphonie fantastique* and Tchaikovsky his *Pathétique*. Beethoven, while he could not divorce his music completely from his life as Mozart did, was never-

Beethoven's workroom in Vienna, with one of the pianos which had been transported from one part of Vienna to another as he changed lodgings

Above: *Title page of Beethoven's* Eroica *Symphony. He scratched out the dedication to 'Bonaparte' on hearing he had declared himself emperor*

Opposite: *A portrait of Beethoven in 1819 showing him at work on the* Missa Solemnis *which took him five years to compose*

theless not the kind of man to indulge in Romantic excess of sentiment. The suffering that began with his affliction certainly affected his work, but far from driving him into any ill-disciplined expression of self-pity, it inspired him to compose music of which the theme and spirit suggest a determination to triumph over adversity, the *Eroica* Symphony and the opera *Fidelio* in particular.

The Symphony No 3 in E flat is indeed a heroic work, the most ambitious he had so far attempted and the most profound in expression. Significantly, too, it is the most carefully organized of his works up to that time, a miraculous structure in sound of which the first movement depends as much on tonal drama, the balancing of harmonies, as on thematic interplay. The huge span of this movement is always under perfect control, its heroic quality resulting from the treatment of the themes rather than from any particularly noble character of the themes themselves, the first subject in fact being identical with a melody from the overture to Mozart's juvenile opera *Bastien und Bastienne*, the second having an intimate, almost supplicatory appeal. Here is the pinnacle of sonata form, though that is a technical matter which need not concern the ordinary music lover, who has only to listen to the music to be bowled over by its expressive power. Similarly, a listener does not have to inquire why Beethoven chose to cast the Adagio as a funeral march of overwhelming intensity of feeling, universal rather than personal: it is enough simply to respond to its grandeur as what the poet Coleridge described as a 'procession in deep purple'. There is grandeur too in the Scherzo, for its bouncing main theme suggests triumph as well as exhilaration, qualities which are no less pronounced in the Trio section with its stirring introduction of the new melody by the horns. So much is new and daring about these three movements that the usual symphonic 31

Therese von Brunswick, in whom Beethoven found a loftiness of spirit to match his own, probably the 'Immortal Beloved' of his famous love letter

grows. The great glory of the work is the slow movement, an Adagio built upon one of sweetest and most tenderly flowing melodies the composer ever gave us. Berlioz declared that it produced an impression similar to that of reading the touching episode of Francesca da Rimini in Dante's *Divine Comedy*. This may be an over-fanciful comparison, yet it is not far off target. Is it also too fanciful to think that the symphony, which was first performed early in 1807, owes some of its happy character to the fact that it belongs to a period (1804–7) during which Beethoven enjoyed a romantic association with two aristocratic sisters, Therese von Brunswick and the widowed Josephine? There could be no question of marriage to either, for these were days when no aristocratic family would allow a daughter to marry a commoner, even one with the genius of Beethoven. It is just possible that the friendship of the two countesses, which certainly drew the usually solitary composer into a whirl of social activity, was partly responsible for the sunny nature of the Symphony No 4, the Violin Concerto and the Piano Concerto No 4 in G major produced during these years. It could also be an indirect reason for his laying aside work on the Symphony No 5 in C minor, which he had begun early in 1804, until the end of 1807.

The Fifth, probably the best-known of all symphonies, no doubt owes some of its celebrity to the story that he described its opening as 'Fate knocking at the door', an apt description of the four-note motive which recurs in one guise or another in the three subsequent movements. Its use as an introduction to Allied broadcasts in World War II indicates how universally this idea has survived in the popular imagination. This terse theme, with the rhythm it establishes, dominates and unifies the whole symphony. The Andante, a theme with variations, has been likened to 'a song of mankind marching towards freedom', an interpretation which suggests it was the result of sudden inspiration whereas in fact, like most of his major works, it involved Beethoven in a lengthy process of chiselling into its final form. The Scherzo, a movement of uncanny power, has also been subject to romantic interpretations, among them the famous description in E M Forster's *Howards End* – 'first of all the goblins, and then a trio of elephants dancing'. Of more direct musical interest is the bridge passage between the end of this movement and the final Allegro, a passage of unparalleled suspense which suddenly broadens out by a hair-raising crescendo into the blaze of the triumphant Finale, in which trombones are used for the first time in a symphony. The effect of the work is perhaps best summed up by Goethe's comment to the young Men-

finale could not have made a worthy summing up, and it is typical of Beethoven that he should have come up with a totally unexpected solution. The idea of combining elements of variation form and fugue is not so startling in itself (Haydn had occasionally done so); the real surprise is that he should return to a theme he had used several times before, a gracious melody presented in its simplest form in a dance for small orchestra, then in the ballet music for *Prometheus* (1800), and again in the theme of the Piano Variations of 1802. The melody is put forward in a number of guises, graceful, jubilant and always colourfully scored, culminating in a grandiose coda. Not only is this a triumphant finale; it is also the inevitable outcome of what has gone before.

It could easily seem that with the *Eroica* Beethoven had carried the expressive possibilities of the symphony as far as they could go; yet six more followed, each entirely different from the others, each valid on its own terms, and all but the last kept, if only by a whisker, within the Classical boundaries. With No 4 in B flat, there is a reversion to a more intimate style, even though the symphony opens with a shadowy, brooding Introduction, out of which the first subject

delssohn: 'How big it is,' he growled, 'quite wild! Enough to bring the house about one's ears!'

His contemporaries never knew what Beethoven would get up to next, and they must have been amazed by his next symphony, No 6 in F major, the *Pastoral*. Here he moves from the inner world of the spirit to the outer scene of nature, resorting to five movements instead of the customary four and giving each a descriptive title. It should be mentioned at this point that unlike Mozart, who apparently did not even notice the beauties of nature and to whom even Venice was just another city in which to make music, Beethoven responded strongly to the world around him. He developed the habit of composing out of doors, often on long, solitary walks. Asked on one occasion where he found ideas for his music he replied: 'They come unsummoned, directly; but indirectly I could take them with my hands out of the open air, in the woods, incited by moods which are translated by the poet into words, by me into tones'. The *Pastoral* Symphony is his most direct expression of this response to the natural world, though he took pains to emphasize that the titles of the movements, such as 'Scene by the Brook', should not be taken too literally but only as 'expressions of feelings rather than depiction'. In spite of the bird calls of his second movement, and the rustic band which strikes up in the third, this symphony is not realistic 'programme music' such as Richard Strauss was to create in his tone poems. There are many other touches for the listener to appreciate as pictures of the countryside, but structurally this is still a Classical symphony, and however much it may differ from the others it holds a rightful place in the logical series of symphonic works which reveal Beethoven's total musical personality.

The Symphony No 7 in A major makes a return to the energy of the *Eroica* and the Fifth, even surpassing that energy in the Finale, which has been called 'a triumph of Bacchic fury'. After the slow Introduction, in fact, the symphony lives up to Wagner's declaration that it represents 'the apotheosis of the dance'. The second movement is not the expected Andante or Adagio but an Allegretto, contrasting with the other movements because of its gentler colouring rather than by means of a slower tempo. After this outburst of daemonic force, which excited the public but puzzled the critics, one of whom thought the composer must have been drunk when he wrote it, the Symphony No 8 in F major is a little gem in more relaxed mood. Its delicacy, wit and easy manner, however, should not tempt us to dismiss it as in any way a minor work, for its relative shortness is the result of Beethoven's skilfully making his ideas

Sketches of Beethoven, showing the short legs which made him 'leap and run rather than walk' and his unusually high forehead

superbly compact. Its central movements are not the usual Andante and Scherzo, but an Allegretto Scherzando followed by Tempo di Minuetto, and the whole symphony, though delightfully easy to listen to, is planned with uncommon care and precision.

More than a decade passed before the completion and first performance (7 May 1824) of the Symphony No 9 in D minor, the 'Choral', on which Beethoven worked intermittently for about six years. This was not only due to the scale and revolutionary nature of the symphony itself, but was symptomatic of his work during the final period of his life. To add to the tragedy of his deafness he suffered generally poor health, resulting in his withdrawal from other people more and more into himself, developed unnecessary fears about his financial affairs, which were in fact quite sound, and in 1816 unwisely took upon himself the guardianship of his nephew Karl, a pathetically deceitful and hostile creature on whom the composer lavished possessive affection to morbid excess. Faced by all these practical problems he can scarcely be blamed for feeling that the world had little or nothing to offer him, and it is no exaggeration to say that he found happiness only in the music which formed 33

Life-mask of Beethoven made in 1812, the weight of the wet plaster having emphasized the bone structure at the expense of the softer features

suggestive of the most barren loneliness, but after only a few bars the titanic first subject thunders in. This theme is contrasted with a second subject that includes a varied group of attractive melodies. The second movement is a powerful and intensely rhythmic Scherzo with stunning drum passages, the whole creating the effect of superhuman energy being released. The third movement, marked Adagio molto e cantabile, is indeed song-like, using the theme-and-variations form but with two different sublimely beautiful themes. After much deliberation the composer finally hit on a wonderful plan for leading into his choral finale: each of the preceding movements is briefly reviewed and rejected in turn, rejection being made by glimpses of the great tune of the movement proper, which first reveals itself in cellos and basses, then jubilantly with full orchestra. The initial clamour returns momentarily, this time to be calmed by the bass soloist in recitative. For his text Beethoven chose verses from Schiller's *Ode to Joy*, which he had first thought of setting to music some thirty years previously, verses expressing ideas of universal brotherhood, joy in nature and love of the world's creator. Even though sketches exist for a tenth symphony, it is difficult to imagine anything surpassing the glory of the 'Choral', in which he seems to have condensed his whole personal and artistic credo. This greatness, both of personality and artistry, was duly recognized on his death three years later: the schools in Vienna were closed for the day of his funeral, which was attended by twenty thousand people including all the leading musicians, writers and performing artists of the city. One cannot help wondering whether some of the older mourners on this occasion thought back to the lonely, almost furtive burial of Mozart thirty-six years earlier.

Although the symphonies, like the string quartets, embody all the finest qualities of Beethoven's work, his concertos are scarcely less noteworthy. The Piano Concertos Nos 1 and 2 are both first-rate works which fully deserve their continued popularity even though they do not advance on the form as Mozart left it. With No 3 in C minor, however, the individual voice of Beethoven can be heard, in the majestic stride of the first movement, for example, and the passionate undercurrent of the central Largo. No 4 in G major has always been a universal favourite on account of the ethereal beauty of its melodies and the sheer poetry of the keyboard writing. Even with familiarity, the sound of the soloist before the orchestra's exposition of the first movement themes is spell-binding, while the question-and-answer form of the Andante is perhaps the most remarkable dialogue between piano and orchestra ever conceived. The heroic,

itself in his own mind. That music accordingly became ever more concentrated and in some cases too 'difficult' for his contemporaries to grasp. The Choral Symphony, however, won the favour of many critics at its first performance, at the end of which the now totally deaf Beethoven was unaware of the tumultuous applause until a friend motioned to him to turn round to acknowledge it. Today we have no problem in responding to its music, and the introduction of vocal soloists and chorus into the last movement is no longer a disturbing element as several subsequent composers have followed this practice.

34   The first movement opens with a brief prelude

A concert in the Beethovenhalle at Bonn

triumphant themes of the opening movement of the Concerto No 5 in E flat merit its title of 'The Emperor', though Beethoven himself did not supply any such name for it. Once heard, the melody of the Adagio is never forgotten, while the final Rondo is Beethoven in his most unbuttoned, exhilarating mood. The Violin Concerto in D major is an absolute masterpiece, the most satisfying in the violinist's entire repertoire, created for the instrument's very soul. Here again one finds Beethoven scrupulously observing Classical form yet filling it out with music of the most delicate poetry and feeling.

A final word might be said about the overtures, *Prometheus*, *Egmont* and the three with the title *Leonora* intended at different times for the opera later known as *Fidelio*. Characteristically, Beethoven adheres to sonata form, but stretches it to the limits because of the intensity of the musical ideas he wanted to express. As in the symphony, he expanded and perfected Classical form to a point from which there could be no return, and beyond which

it could scarcely proceed any further. It is not exaggerating to claim that he left virtually nothing for later composers to achieve within the tradition he had inherited; so though he was not himself a Romantic composer, and might even have disapproved of the various courses which Romantic music was to run, he virtually drove his successors to abandon most of the Classical principles he had followed and throw themselves into the new movement for good or ill. Only Brahms, perhaps, was consciously aware of this predicament, for although he wanted desperately to turn the tide, he waited until 1876, when he was forty-three and more than fifty years had passed since the first performance of the 'Choral', before presenting his own first symphony to the world. Other composers embarked on the new voyages of discovery made possible by the Romantic movement, all with positive intentions, yet never admitting even to themselves that there was really no alternative open to them. Tacitly, however, they were admitting that Beethoven had already done all that could be done within the framework of the pure Classical style.

ROMANTICISM

The dividing lines between different creative styles such as Classical and Romantic are never so easy to draw as tidy-minded music historians would like them to be. Simple definitions just will not do, because they are always oversimplifications which leave too many important considerations out of account. To declare, for instance, that Classical music is objective whereas Romantic music is subjective suggests that Haydn, Mozart and Beethoven were somehow computer-like, composing music which avoided any expression of their personal feelings, which is obviously absurd. Similarly, to declare that the Romantic composers 'freed' themselves from the disciplines of traditional forms overlooks the fact that they continued to use them even in the most unlikely contexts – such as Verdi's choosing a fugue to round off his comic opera *Falstaff*. It should also be remembered that the two styles co-existed for a time: Weber, the arch-Romantic opera composer and German idealist, died a year before Beethoven, whom Schubert survived only for a year.

There are, nonetheless, a number of differences between the two schools which we can readily grasp, and they stem for the most part from causes of a non-musical nature. The composer's place in society was radically transformed, for he had ceased to be the employee of a city, a court or the church. Only Beethoven had won any measure of real independence, though even he had relied for much of his livelihood on aristocratic patrons, however generously they had allowed him to go his own way. Now in theory entirely his own man, the composer was in fact the servant of the public, whose needs were met by a rapidly growing network of concert societies and music festivals. If, like Mendelssohn, he was able to provide the kind of music this vast, predominantly middle-class public liked, then he became a success. If, on the other hand, he chose to ignore the taste of the time and composed for himself and an ideal posterity, then he was driven to become the 'difficult', unsociable artist of popular imagination. Composers in this latter category often tended to think of themselves as belonging to an élitist breed of men apart, priest-prophets of the art of the future.

The use of the word 'artist' is not without significance, because the composers of the nineteenth century thought of themselves in that light. They did so with good reason, moreover, because once they had been freed from the shelter of private patronage and let loose into the world they began to make contact with writers and other kindred creative spirits. Indeed, Weber, Schumann and Berlioz all wrote about music as well as composing, while Wagner not only wrote his own librettos but poured out so many books and essays on music, drama and philosophy that it is remarkable he found the time to compose so much. This new breed of composers took a keen interest in all the new ideas floating in the air, scientific and nationalistic as well as artistic, above all they were fascinated to the point of obsession by literature, and whereas their predecessors had been content in instrumental music to express purely musical ideas, the Romantics set out to rival the breadth of ideas which could be expressed in words. It had always been common practice, of course, for composers to set words to music, in songs, masses and opera, but the new vogue was to make instrumental music suggest or describe specific scenes, even tell stories. This process started with Weber, Beethoven's contemporary, and in time developed into the graphic symphonic poems of Liszt and Richard Strauss.

Romantic literature moved during the first half of the nineteenth century from the natural and urbane to the fantastic and larger-than-life, as exemplified by Jane Austen's *Pride and Prejudice* (1813) and Emily Brontë's *Wuthering Heights* (1847). There is a world of difference between these two English novels, the difference being aptly summed up by Walter Pater's definition of Romanticism as 'the addition of strangeness to beauty'. It is not surprising, then, that Romantic music should also concern itself largely with the marvellous and the supernatural, as Berlioz did spectacularly in his *Symphonie fantastique* of 1830. Composers quickly developed a new interest in the natural world about them, not the simple nature celebrated by Beethoven in the *Pastoral* Symphony, but Nature with the all-important capital 'N', a force with which they felt they had a special relationship by virtue of their being set somewhat apart from other men. Yet another aspect of Romanticism, in music as well as in literature, was the emphasis it placed on man as an individual, not just as a member of a society which confined people within carefully defined classes from which there was little or no means of escape. Setting corresponding store by his own individuality, the composer deliberately sought originality, sometimes to the point of egotism, thus separating himself even further from the Classical composer who had repressed some of his creative instincts in the process of working to order.

Any brief attempt to outline the characteristics of Romantic music can easily mislead the reader into thinking that its composers were something of a wild bunch, and it is true that some of them had their eccentric moments. On the whole, however, they exercised sufficient self-control not to go over the top in their use of their new freedom. Most of them still continued to use the traditional forms of the symphony, sonata and string quartet, though taking certain liberties within these forms which would not have occurred to Mozart, and which would have offended his sense of good taste. (Ideas of what is or is not good taste, it should be remembered, are constantly changing, so that behaviour which is considered *de trop* in one generation becomes the norm in a later one, and yesterday's *enfant terrible* gradually becomes the respectable Grand Old Man of today.) Within the Romantic movement there were always two distinct groups, the radicals like Berlioz, Liszt and Wagner on the one hand, and conservatives like Mendelssohn, Brahms and Bruckner on the other. An appraisal of the early Romantics will show how this split in the ranks arose, and it will also separate those composers whose chief interest to us lies within

the scope of orchestral music (Mendelssohn and Berlioz) and those whose importance lay in other musical areas (Schubert in the world of song, Schumann in song and piano works, Weber in the opera).

Weber

Although his major significance, and therefore his life, lies in the section of this book dealing with opera, the music which Carl Maria von Weber (1786–1826) composed for orchestra is historically important – and also immediately enjoyable. It is so likeable, in fact, that its recent neglect is difficult to explain. His opera overtures such as *Der Freischütz* and *Oberon* are frequently used to open symphony concerts, but while there are several different recordings of all his concertos, indicating that the public like them, these works are now rarely if ever played in the concert hall. The second half of the twentieth century has seen a huge gulf develop between the music-lovers who go to concerts and the managements who put them on. The latter, encouraged by the critics, carry their policy of trying to 'educate' the public some-

A fanciful painting entitled 'Last Thoughts of Weber' which epitomises the popular idea of the Romantic composer

38

times to the point of denying the audience the kind of music it really wants to hear in favour of less popular works. Those composers who are both popular *and* respected by the establishment get a fair hearing, but many works by less fortunate composers are no longer featured in the concert hall even though public affection for them is proved by the number of times they are played on the radio in listeners' request programmes.

Weber's two piano concertos and his *Konzertstück* for piano and orchestra have suffered this form of neglect. The composer was himself a brilliant pianist, and the exceptional size of his hands, which enabled him to play tenths as easily as octaves on the keyboard, encouraged him to write virtuoso passages which are strikingly effective and almost need to be seen as well as heard. He designed his concertos to please and exhilarate his audience as bravura works rather than as exercises in symphonic construction and style, making the utmost expressive use of the colour and richness of the piano's sound, and he was an absolute master of the difficult art of balancing the solo instrument against the greater weight of the orchestra. The first movement of his Piano Concerto No 1 in C major intriguingly combines an almost military dash with gentler elements of almost salon charm, the Adagio has haunting passages in which the delicacy of the piano's voice is contrasted with the more sombre colours of horns, violas and two solo cellos, while the final Allegro dances along its course in irresistible high spirits. His Piano Concerto No 2 in E flat is bolder and more serious in style, with a first movement which pays more attention to the principles of sonata form. Its slow movement is a landmark in Romantic style, at once highly ornamental and vocal: his ability to make the piano 'sing' a decorative melody clearly influenced Chopin.

We have Weber's own account of the reasons for giving the name *Konzertstück* to the work he originally intended as a third piano concerto. 'I have an F minor piano concerto planned,' he wrote to his friend Johann Rochlitz. 'But as concertos in the minor without definite, evocative ideas seldom work with the public, I have instinctively inserted into the whole thing a kind of story whose thread will connect and define its character – moreover, one so detailed and at the same time dramatic that I found myself obliged to give it the following headings: Allegro, Parting; Adagio, Lament; Finale, Profoundest misery [followed by] consolation, reunion, jubilation.' Julius Benedict

has left an even more intriguing account of hearing Weber play the piece at home with a running commentary on the story it was intended to suggest, a piece of nonsense about a lady in a tower dreaming about her knight who is fighting in the Holy Land, and who finally returns in triumph after she has experienced a fearful vision of his death. In fact Weber never referred to this 'programme' again and did not have it published, for he disliked the idea of labels being attached to music. So although he was almost certainly the first composer to envisage what we call programme music, he drew back from it himself, because his aim was not to illustrate a detailed story but to prompt the listener to exercise his own imagination. His own simple headings for the movements of the *Konzertstück*, while evoking pictures in the listener's mind, do not prevent the music from following its own natural course. It is brilliantly constructed, not on lines such as Beethoven would have adopted, but on Weber's own, the result being a genuine Romantic concerto exploring new possibilities in keyboard expression and presenting wonderful melodies with a distinctive flavour which is the composer's own.

Response to the colour of an instrument's tone was highly characteristic of Weber. He was especially attracted by that of the clarinet, which could sound both melancholy and jubilant, and he wrote a concertino and two concertos for it. The Concerto No 1 in F minor opens with an Allegro that is by turns dramatic and elegiac, its darkly brooding mood anticipating the atmosphere of the Wolf's Glen scene in *Der Freischütz*, while the central Adagio includes a dialogue between the solo clarinet and a trio of horns which conjures up a German woodland scene. The finale of the Concerto No 2 in E flat employs the Polonaise rhythm whose extrovert brilliance Weber loved so much. Other concertos for the bassoon and the horn testify to his ready response to individual instrumental timbres, which interested him more than purely formal matters. The fact that he was never really at home with strict sonata form accounts for his lack of success with the symphony, for though he composed two early examples they lack the imaginative power and appeal of his concertos. As an opera composer he naturally sought to make any solo instrument, whether piano or clarinet, play in what can only be described as a singing style, which is essentially Romantic. That he avoided Romantic excesses was due to his upbringing, with its strong Classical links – he was, after all, the cousin of Mozart's wife, *née* Constanze Weber, and had studied with Michael Haydn, the younger brother of Joseph. It is the dual nature of Weber's music which makes

Opposite: 'The Symphony' by Moritz von Schwind, a friend of Schubert and an admirer of Beethoven (whose bust appears in the bottom panel)

39

it so fascinating, and its neglect in the concert hall is to be regretted.

Schubert

The name of Franz Schubert (1797–1828) is associated first and foremost with song, then with piano and chamber works; yet two of his symphonies are among the best-known all over the world, the so-called 'Unfinished' and the 'Great' C major. He composed nine altogether, if we include the one in E major which was sketched out but left incomplete (No 7). They have defied all attempts to place them into any general category other than Romantic. The first five all date from his teens, No 1 in D major from 1813 when he was a sixteen-year-old schoolboy, and while they are modelled on Haydn, Mozart and early Beethoven there is a flavour to their music which can immediately be recognized as Schubertian. They are full of beguiling melodies, occasionally plaintive yet mostly reflecting the gaiety of the composer's own Viennese nature, and they convey the impression of being composed with remarkable fluency and ease. What makes them Romantic is not anything particularly novel about their form, but the song-like flow of their melodies, their harmonic freedom and a glowing warmth of instrumental colouring which is somewhat like that of Weber. These qualities even break through in the Symphony No 5 in B flat which uses the modest orchestra of Haydn and has a Mozartian grace.

The Symphony No 8 in B minor, the 'Unfinished', raises an interesting question: did Schubert ever intend to add further movements? He did certainly sketch out a third movement, a Scherzo which makes a complete contrast to the radiant lyricism of the slow movement, and some scholars believe that the tragic march which forms the first *entr'acte* of the music for *Rosamunde* was originally intended as the finale of the symphony. On the other hand, the 'Unfinished' has been thought by others (including Brahms) to be complete as we know it, Schubert having said so much in its two magnificent movements that there is nothing more that he could have said. The argument will no doubt continue for ever in academic circles, but for those who simply enjoy music there is cause to be eternally grateful for this symphony in which melody is of supreme importance. The word 'tune' is appropriate here, because instead of the short themes which Classical composers had found most suitable for symphonic treatment, Schubert uses long, self-sufficient melodies. The first movement is dramatic, in the symphonic sense, yet it does not achieve this effect by changes of tempo, the speed in

Portrait of Schubert, the most unassuming and genial of the great Viennese composers, in an uncharacteristically serious mood

fact being a leisurely pace never encountered before in an opening Allegro. The second movement, an Andante, consists of three main themes which really make up one idea, and it exerts its unique magic by the unfolding of these sublime melodies with considerable repetition rather than by working them out in traditional symphonic style. What makes this the first truly Romantic symphony has little to do with its form, still less with any literary associations or programme; its novelty lies more in Schubert's harmonic sensitivity and in his feeling for warm instrumental colouring.

The Symphony No 9 in C major, the 'Great', was admired by Schumann for its 'heavenly length', though it should be pointed out straight away that the sheer beauty of the melodies makes the listener unaware of its length. Schumann also praised the music's interchange of vivid emotions and its singing qualities, the instruments of the orchestra 'conversing with one another like human voices'. There can be no denying that Schumann was apt to slip into over-poetic language when writing about pieces of music which he admired, but there is no other way of describing the announcement of the opening theme by unison horns, and there are similar magical moments throughout the work. Wealth of melody alone does not account for the universal esteem with which the symphony is regarded. It represents the culmination of Schubert's instrumental thinking throughout his brief lifetime and his final mastery of the symphonic form with which he had wrestled. It is one of the most cruel ironies of musical life that he never heard any of his symphonies performed, even though he had worked on them so hard and so successfully. He died in 1828, yet No 9 was not performed until 1839, in Leipzig, and No 8 had to wait until 1865 for its first performance, in Vienna.

So far as orchestral music was concerned, Schubert's only success came with the incidental music for *Rosamunde*, a play by Helmina von Chézy, a lady of infinitely more ambition and persistence than taste or talent. (She also wrote the disastrous libretto for Weber's *Euryanthe*.) Her play died a well-deserved death on its second night, but Schubert's music won high praise, and has remained popular ever since. Nevertheless, during his lifetime he was known mostly as a song-writer and even in that capacity only to a circle of friends and to the small audiences at his occasional public recitals.

Early Romantic Concertos: Hummel, Field, Chopin

Though he was a pianist and violinist of some stature, Schubert curiously never turned his attention to the concerto, a form which would have been well suited to his warm lyrical gift. Fortunately there were other composers who were quick to seize on the Romantic possibilities of the piano concerto, as Weber did. Among the first was Johann Hummel, whose life began in the full bloom of the Classical era and extended well into the Romantic: he was born of Hungarian and German descent at Pressburg (now Bratislava) on 14 November 1778, and died at Weimar on 17 October 1837. He went at the age of seven to Vienna, where his father conducted an orchestra, and he not only studied with Mozart but lived for a time in the composer's home. His many successful tours took him everywhere from Scotland to Russia, and he was considered the equal of Beethoven as a composer during his lifetime. Subsequent generations found his amiable, highly polished music lacking in substance, but thanks to the gramophone several of his best concertos and chamber works have come to enjoy a new lease of life.

His Piano Concerto in A minor is a particularly attractive work, which shows the influence of Mozart in the clarity of its orchestration and in its formal balance, yet which has long-spanning melodies and delicate ornamentation anticipating something of Chopin's style. (It can be fascinating to play a recording of this concerto to friends unacquainted with Hummel and ask them to spot the composer: guesses will range from Weber, Mendelssohn and Chopin to even later composers.) Hummel tends to decorate his themes, even the subjects of his sonata-form first movement, rather than develop them as Mozart and Beethoven would have done, while the rondo theme of the final Allegro is engagingly soft in feeling, marking a definite move into the world of Romanticism.

Thanks no doubt to his studies with Mozart, Hummel composed, and seems to have played, with delicacy and refinement – qualities which are also found in the work of John Field, an Irish virtuoso-composer who deserves a place in musical history as the man who invented the piano nocturne. Like Hummel, he was to be eclipsed in the Romantic concerto form by Chopin, but he exerted a strong influence on the Polish composer and his own concertos have been restored to considerable favour after a long period of neglect. His father taught the violin, his grandfather the piano, and it was the latter instrument for which he showed an early aptitude. Born in Dublin in July 1782, he made his professional debut ten years later, moved to England the following year and produced his first concerto in 1799. He went to Paris for his first trip abroad, quickly moving on to St Petersburg, where he rapidly established himself as a social as well as a musical celebrity. Apart from a three-year return to London and Paris, he passed the rest of a happily dissolute life in Russia, dying in Moscow on 23 January 1837. More is known of his music than of his life, for what autobiographical material he left is largely fiction, which he invented with a delightful Irish disregard for accuracy.

His early concertos glitter with ornamental passages and have perky rondo tunes, but his more important contribution is the poetic singing style of his piano writing, especially in the last of his seven concertos. He was no master of form, and his orchestration sounds naive to ears accustomed to the concertos of more distinguished composers. He did not, after all, have the solid musical training of Hummel, whose concertos have a strong structural sense even when their chief aim is to show off the pianist's virtuosity. Field was nevertheless one of the most original of a whole generation of pianist-composers who designed concertos and solo piano pieces to parade their mastery of the instrument which had replaced the harpsicord and which was constantly developing in expressive and dynamic potential. Such concertos, in which the orchestra is reduced to

41

an accompanying role, do not afford such deep musical experiences as those of Mozart and Beethoven, yet music which gives lasting pleasure to performers and audiences alike is never to be dismissed.

Chopin (1810–49) takes the place of honour among the composers of this school, his two concertos being the only ones to have kept a permanent and regular place in the repertoire. (Consideration of his life and his music for solo piano belongs to a later chapter.) Both concertos date from his early years, and the fact that he never returned to the concerto in his maturity suggests quite clearly that he realized his limitations in large forms involving the orchestra. He was only nineteen when he wrote the poetic yet carefree work which we know as the Piano Concerto No 2. He originally played it in March 1830 at his home in Warsaw with a small orchestra and an invited audience crowded into the family drawing-room. So enthusiastic was the reaction that on 17 March he was able confidently to introduce his most ambitious work to date to a public seething with curiosity after a good deal of publicity about the local genius.

It is interesting to glance at the peculiar nature of this concert, given at the Warsaw National Theatre, because it shows how muscial tastes and manners have changed. The programme opened with the cus-

tomary overture, then Chopin played the first movement of the concerto. This was considered sufficient for the audience to think about for the moment, and it was followed by a horn *divertissement*, only then did the composer return to the platform to play the remaining two movements of his concerto. Although he had to play on a piano of his own, which was too soft-toned for a large auditorium, enthusiasm knew no bounds and the critics were lavish with their praise the next day. 'His music', wrote one, 'is full of expressive feeling and song, putting the listener into a state of subtle rapture, bringing back to his memory all the happy moments he has known.' At a second performance given five days later, Chopin had the use of a superior Viennese piano borrowed for the occasion, and his more exciting performance drew from one critic the comment that 'Fate has given Chopin to the Poles as it has given Mozart to the Germans'. Was nationalist enthusiasm going too far? Not if we are to believe Schumann when he subsequently wrote: 'We may be sure that a genius like Mozart, were he born today, would write concertos like Chopin and not like Mozart.'

Before commenting on the music itself, it should perhaps be explained why this concerto is listed as No 2. Its success prompted Chopin to compose a new Concerto in E minor (now known as No 1), and in the course of a journey across the Continent he lost the orchestral parts of the F minor, which so delayed printing that the E minor was published first.

The first movements of both concertos follow sonata form, beginning with the double exposition of the main themes, but it is the piano part which catches one's interest, the orchestral writing being relatively undistinguished – though not nearly as weak as the composer's detractors have tried to make out. The slow movements have a unique poetry which is Chopin's own, a tenderness that never palls, and there is engaging bravura in the finales with their Polish dance melodies. The composer was to go on to greater things in his music for solo piano, but it is a measure of his youthful genius that the two concertos, written when he was nineteen and twenty, could never be mistaken for the work of anyone else. The melodies have an individuality which a master craftsman such as Hummel could never stamp on any of his work, and the decoration of the melodic line for the piano is never like icing on a cake but an integral and importantly expressive part of the music as a whole. Both concertos stand head and shoulders above those of Weber, Field and Hummel in the Romantic repertoire, and they remain as popular as the even more satisfying masterpiece by Schumann of a decade later.

Portrait of Chopin by Eugène Delacroix, who described the composer as 'the truest artist I have ever met, whom one can admire and value'

Paganini

No outline of the rise of the Romantic movement would be complete without a mention of Niccolò Paganini, for although his music does not contribute significantly to the newly emerging style he was probably the greatest violinist the world has ever known; and as a personality he sums up all that was most sensational in the liberation of the artist which took place during this period. The story of his life was even charted before he was born at Genoa on 27 October 1782, his mother having had a dream in which an angel told her that her future son would be a famous violinist. Niccolò's father, whose was an accomplished amateur performer on the mandolin, took this portent so seriously that he made the poor boy practise on the violin as soon as he could hold one. Niccolò emerged as a virtuoso in public at the age of eleven, sending audiences into raptures of amazement, and after two years of more advanced studies in Parma he set off in 1797 on the first of his concert tours. Unfortunately his success turned him into a teenage gambler and heavy drinker to such an extent that his whole future was seriously endangered. The way in which he was rescued from his addictions was typical of his extraordinary career: an aristocratic lady carried off the nineteen-year-old prodigy to her country estate in Tuscany where she taught him love-making while he taught himself new techniques on the violin. No researcher has ever discovered the noble lady's identity, a mystery which gave rise to rumours that he had been in prison during this period for having murdered one of his mistresses – rumours whose publicity value he appreciated too much to attempt to refute. He similarly encouraged the widely believed story that he had sold his soul to the devil in exchange for his apparently superhuman skill.

Emerging from his secluded love-nest in 1804, Paganini was appointed organizer of music at the court of the Princess of Lucca, the sister of Napoleon. The salary was meagre, but he had the compensation of living in luxury with a bevy of court beauties at his disposal. It took him eight years to drag himself away from these delights to embark on his conquest of Europe, earning a princely living from his concert fees. Unlike poor Mozart, who was usually rewarded with snuff-boxes and other decorative gifts, Paganini demanded cash. During his year's visit to England he made a profit of £17,000, a veritable fortune in the 1830s. Some idea of his effect upon audiences can be gathered from an account of his London debut, when he played the first of his six violin concertos: 'With the tip of his bow he started the orchestra in a grand

Paganini, who was believed to have sold his soul to the devil in return for his almost superhuman skill as a violinist

military movement, with a force and vivacity as surprising as it was new. At the end of this introduction he commenced with a soft, dreamy note of celestial quality, and with three or four whips of his bow elicited sounds that mounted to the third heaven. A scream of astonishment and delight burst from the audience at the novelty of the effect'. The members of the orchestra, for whom he had only played his entry and exit cues at rehearsal, were just as intoxicated by his playing, so that none of them noticed a candle had set fire to the music at one of the desks until someone in the audience had sufficiently recovered his wits to draw their attention to the flames. He retained his magnetic personality to the end, improvising on a violin even on his deathbed in Nice on 27 May 1840. The legend of his diabolism continued after his death, the church authorities refusing to allow him to be buried in consecrated ground, so that his body was moved around from one grave to another until 1926.

The most popular and substantial of his works is 43

the Violin Concerto No 1 in D major, which is delightful listening even if it is not a masterwork in the sense of the concertos by Beethoven, Mendelssohn and Brahms. The military opening of the first movement is followed by a memorably lyrical contrasting melody which far greater composers would have been proud to write. The soloist's part naturally exploits every virtuosic trick of the trade. The short Adagio is expressive in the manner of an operatic aria, while the piquant final Rondo has all the sparkle one would expect of such a master of the instrument. The other concertos all have fine moments, though the technical fireworks soon begin to sound flashy and empty. The solo Caprices combine a good deal of charm and lyrical appeal with dazzling bravura passages. One of them has become immortal as the inspiration for lavish sets of variations by other composers, most notably Brahms and Rachmaninov, but extending even to a rock setting by Andrew Lloyd Webber in 1978. As a composer Paganini may be a second-rater, but he holds a unique place in musical history as the first instrumental superstar, a virtuoso whose influence on violin playing is incalculable.

GERMANY AND AUSTRIA

Mendelssohn

A man of highly cultivated taste and a background which inclined him towards a basically Classical style, Felix Mendelssohn cannot be considered a thorough-going Romantic, yet he travelled some way along the new stylistic path particularly in his musical landscapes. His two most famous symphonies, the 'Italian' and the 'Scottish', reflect his impressions of these countries which he found so fascinating on his travels, while *The Hebrides* is surely the most vivid seascape prior to Wagner's overture to *The Flying Dutchman*. His music is less turbulent than that of Schumann or Berlioz: indeed, in its ease and good nature it seems to mirror the nature of the man himself, one of the most fortunate as well as prodigiously talented of all composers.

From the day he was born, 3 February 1809, Mendelssohn led a charmed life. His family were wealthy Jewish bankers in Hamburg, so he grew up in comfort and with the knowledge that he would never suffer any of the privations which have beset so many other composers. He was nevertheless trained to work hard from the beginning: his parents took the education of their children so seriously that the young Felix was made to get up every morning at five o'clock to start his studies in good time. By the age of eleven he had made several appearances on

the concert platform as a pianist and also had a number of compositions to his credit. His *Midsummer Night's Dream* Overture, a masterpiece by any standards, was written at the age of seventeen. A year later he took up the cause of Bach's then forgotten *St Matthew Passion* and in 1829, in spite of a good deal of jealous opposition, conducted its first performance since the composer's death some eighty years previously. He was a tireless champion of neglected music by others, which he either played or conducted in his concerts throughout Europe. He conducted Schubert's symphonies, for instance, and as a favourite virtuoso he popularized Beethoven's Piano Concerto No 4 in England. In addition to his composing and his concert tours he held the post of conductor of the Gewandhaus Orchestra in Leipzig, where he was also teacher of piano and composition at the Conservatoire.

The Mendelssohns moved to Berlin three years after the birth of Felix, so he had the advantage of growing up in a centre of musical activity. At the age of twelve he met Weber and was highly enthusiastic about his music, which left its mark on much of his own work. In the same year he also visited Goethe in Weimar with his teacher Carl Zelter. The German poet, who by that time was a living legend throughout Europe, had heard the young Mozart improvise at the keyboard almost fifty years previously, yet he considered Mendelssohn even more precocious. Just how precocious he was became clear in 1826 with the composition of his *A Midsummer Night's Dream* Overture, which while skilfully constructed in sonata form managed to suggest all the magic of Shakespeare's play. The prolonged woodwind chords at the opening breathe out the sylvan setting to perfection, the fairy-like first main theme remains unequalled for its delicate poetry, the more ceremonial second theme vividly suggests Theseus's court; these are followed by no less inspired music for the lovers and then the rustics, complete with the descriptive braying of the donkey to indicate the 'translation' of Bottom. Both in its control of form and its superb orchestration, especially the evocative woodwind writing, this is a masterpiece any great composer could have been proud of writing in his full maturity. Sixteen years later, Frederick William IV of Prussia commissioned incidental music for a production of the play in Potsdam, and Mendelssohn was miraculously able to recapture this first fine youthful rapture in several numbers which have become as famous as the Overture. The Scherzo, the most extended he ever composed, captures the very spirit of fairyland, also creating an unforgettable portrayal of Puck, while the Nocturne is one of the most melodiously

Mendelssohn, a composer of wide culture who championed music by neglected masters and won further fame as a conductor

sublime pieces of night music of all time. It would no doubt have astonished Mendelssohn to learn that the Wedding March was to accompany real-life brides to the altar not only up to the present day but also for the forseeable future. For millions of people it has become synonymous with either the greatest day or the greatest mistake of their lives.

If it is remarkable that Mendelssohn in his teens should have responded so sensitively to Shakespeare, it is scarcely less surprising that he should have fallen under the spell of Scotland some years later, in 1829. He was the most cosmopolitan of men, aristocratic in his refinement, accustomed to the society of the rich and famous in elegant surroundings, yet the romantic wildness of Scotland struck a rich chord in his imagination. His friend Karl Klingemann, who accompanied him on the tour, was less enthusiastic, writing in a letter home: 'The Highlands and the sea together brew nothing but whiskey, fog and foul weather'. He also wrote of the composer

that 'as an artist he gets along better with the sea than does his stomach'. Seasickness apart, however, Mendelssohn was fascinated by his visit to Fingal's Cave, sketching down on the spot the first eight bars of what was to become a landmark in the development of 'nature music', even though it took him three years to complete the piece to his satisfaction. He did not attempt any programme in *The Hebrides*, setting out simply to convey the mood of the seascape and the effect it had on his own imagination, and it is a measure of his genius that he was able to do this in traditional sonata form. The first two themes suggest a calm sea with only a gentle swell, then the third brings with it loud calls from horns and trumpets, together with cries representing gulls and other sea birds. Calm and storm alternate, and the coda finally dies out quietly and mysteriously, as though the composer wants to let the sea keep its secrets to itself.

There is no programme either in the 'Scottish' Symphony (No 3 in A minor), though again he was immediately inspired by a specific scene, 'the half-ruined grey castle on the meadow, where Mary Stuart lived in splendour and saw Rizzio murdered'. It was in the Queen's ruined chapel that he conceived the idea of the brief, melancholy Introduction to the symphony, which took him twelve years to complete. He conducted its first performance in Leipzig in March 1842, then in London a few months later, when he obtained Queen Victoria's permission to dedicate it to her. How Scottish, the reader might ask, is this symphony? The second movement, marked Vivace and really a Scherzo, has a Scottish-type dance tune introduced by the clarinet, while there is a tartan tang to the brisk first theme of the Finale. Perhaps it would be most accurate to describe the symphony as not having any strong Scottish connection, rather a sombre atmosphere reflecting a general sense of history which Mendelssohn experienced as he stood in the old chapel of Mary Stuart, an ill-fated woman who fired the imaginations of so many Romantic writers and composers.

The 'Italian' Symphony (No 4 in A major) is a different matter, its music positively drenched in Southern sunshine. The composer visited Italy in 1830, and like all tourists fell completely under the spell of Rome, Florence and Naples. He completed the symphony in 1833, favouring London with its first performance. Its music sounds so fresh and spontaneous that one wonders why he was dissatisfied with it and always intended to revise it, resulting in its not being published until after his death. The first movement has irresistible athletic grace, the Andante has often been called a Pilgrim's March inspired by a religious procession seen in Naples – 45

Opposite: *A scene from* A Midsummer Night's Dream *for which Mendelssohn composed his famous overture at the age of seventeen*

Above: *Fingal's Cave, which Mendelssohn visited on his tour of Scotland and immortalized in his descriptive overture* The Hebrides

though it owes just as much, if not more, to the equally solemn slow movement of Beethoven's Symphony No 7 – and the Finale presents two dance tunes in the rhythm of the Roman saltarello and a third in that of a Neapolitan tarantella.

As felicitous a work as the 'Italian' Symphony is the popular Violin Concerto in E minor, which shares a place of honour in the repertoire with the more ambitious yet not more perfect concertos by Beethoven and Brahms. It is highly original in construction, its three movements thematically related to one another and also joined together by means of linking notes or passages. The beautifully lyrical first movement also breaks with tradition by placing the cadenza between the development and recapitulation sections – an idea taken up by Sibelius many years later. The Andante is a fine example of Mendelssohn's gift for serenity of melodic utterance, while the Finale sparkles with the youthful exuberance of the *A Midsummer Night's Dream* music. His Piano Concerto No 1 in G minor is unashamedly virtuosic in the Romantic manner of Hummel and Field, with soloist and orchestra plunging together into the impetuous opening. An unexpected feature of the concerto is the passage for horns and trumpets which links the first movement to the second, and the sec-

ond to the third. The scoring, whether of the tender Adagio or the scintillating Presto finale, is as wonderfully polished as that of the 'Italian' Symphony, an example of exquisite craftsmanship.

The poise and grace of Mendelssohn's easy melodies reflect the happy side of his nature, the sparkle of his scherzo movements is indicative of his considerable wit in conversation and correspondence, while the sometimes feverish activity of some allegro movements are clear reminders of his restless nature. It was this last, an inability to relax, which constantly undermined his generally delicate health, though his death in Leipzig on 4 November 1847, was undoubtedly hastened by the shock of the death of his sister Fanny, to whom he had always been devoted and with whom he had shared his musical thoughts, during the previous year. The side of his character which was less attractive is a certain moralizing tone, which led him, with many other Germans of his time, to look down his nose at 'frivolous' Italian music, and which gives his oratorios and other sacred music an undeniable stuffiness. His other music, however – chamber works, piano pieces and songs as well as the orchestral works discussed here – are free of that pompous element and merit respect as well as affection.

47

Schumann and Liszt

Although they may initially seem strange bed-fellows, Schumann and Liszt belong to the same chapter of musical history because as well as being born only a year apart they responded with equal enthusiasm to the invigorating new climate in which they grew up. Both of them radically enriched the solo piano repertoire, Schumann also bringing fresh ideas to the world of German song, exerting their most important influence in the field of intimate, small-scale works, yet neither could resist the lure of the more ambitious forms of orchestral music. Schumann, an introvert by nature, cautiously held on to certain traditional principles, whereas the extrovert Liszt was quick to grasp and develop every new possibility that the Romantic movement opened up. As composers they represent the two sides of the Romantic coin, Schumann the more conservative side which was to continue with Brahms, Liszt the radical side looking forward to the most revolutionary figure of all, Wagner. In the latter half of the century Brahms and Wagner would confront one another directly as champions of entirely different schools of music, but in the case of Schumann and Liszt the dividing line is teasingly difficult to define.

Born at Zwickau in Saxony on 8 June 1810, Robert (Alexander) Schumann inherited an almost obsessive love of literature from his father, who was a bookseller and publisher, and a streak of unhealthy morbidity from his mother, a combination which made him too poetic and introspective to be able to cope with the ruthless everyday world. (His mind, in fact, became deranged in 1854 and he spent the last two and a half years of his life in an asylum.) As a young man he fell in love all too easily and frequently, and would write with straight-faced sincerity such flowery phrases about his girlfriends as: 'Were I but a smile, how would I flit about her eyes'. He was saved from priggishness thanks to his taste for champagne, cigars and other healthy addictions. His family made him study law, but happily – for one dreads to think what his antics in court might have been like – he threw this up at the age of twenty to devote his life to music.

In spite of his impulsive nature this particular act was no mere whim, for he had displayed outstanding musical ability as a child: he had begun to study the piano seriously from the age of seven, making his first fumbling attempts at composition two years later. His dream of becoming a celebrated concert pianist was shattered in 1832 when he permanently injured his right hand in the course of a crackpot

experiment to strengthen the fingers, but this may have been a blessing in disguise since it made him devote the rest of his time to composing rather than touring as a virtuoso. During the next few years he wrote some of his finest music for the piano, and he might well have confined himself to keyboard composition and songs all his life had it not been for his marriage to Clara Wieck in 1839 after several years' courtship. (This was bitterly opposed by her father, who feared it might interfere with her career as a concert pianist, and who refused to give the couple his blessing.) It was Clara who persuaded Schumann to turn his attention to the symphony, and from 1841 onwards he applied himself to this form of composition for which he was not by nature ideally suited. This is not to say that his symphonies are undistinguished; but he could not write them with the command and vivid imagination that he brought to the keyboard.

Once his mind had been made up, Schumann was a quick worker, so the Symphony No 1 in B flat was sketched out in four days and nights in January, the orchestration completed in February and the first performance given at the Leipzig Gewandhaus on 31 March 1841, with Mendelssohn conducting. Its warm reception encouraged Schumann to produce his next symphony as a birthday surprise for Clara six months later. This was less successful, so Schumann withdrew the score, which he revised twelve years later to be published as No 4 (in D minor). These two are unanimously considered his finest symphonies, in which his inspiration runs most freshly.

Schumann admitted that No 1 was influenced by a spring poem he had read. 'At the very beginning,' he wrote, 'I should like the trumpets to sound as if from on high, like a call to awaken. In what follows of the Introduction there might be a suggestion of the growing green of everything, even of a butterfly flying up, and in the following Allegro of the gradual assembling of all that belongs to spring.' He even thought of titles for the four movements – 'Spring's Awakening', 'Evening', 'Merry Playmates' and 'Spring's Farewell' – but he abandoned these fanciful ideas before the symphony was published. The symphony, however, has continued to be given the nickname of the 'Spring', and in a general sense it is appropriate, for the music is emotional in an almost youthfully exuberant way. The slow Introduction of the first movement gives way to a boisterous main Allegro theme, with a gentler second subject, and a surprise comes with the introduction of a new, tender melody for strings in the coda. The slow movement is a sensuous meditation on a melody which reminds us that Schumann was a natural songwriter, its calm mood unbroken by any contrast until just before the end, when a new theme on hushed trombones hints at the subject of the Scherzo, which follows without a break. There is a novelty here, Schumann writing two entirely different Trio sections. The melodies of the final Allegro have a rather fussy yet propulsive vivacity which is a special Schumann hallmark.

The Symphony No 4 is his most original, for he consistently follows through his favourite device of developing all his thematic material from a few basic ideas presented at the beginning. The slow Introduction to the first movement contains three concise melodic germs which recur in all the subsequent ones, a practice quite new to symphonic construction. Berlioz had reintroduced the *idée fixe* of the first movement of the *Symphonie fantastique* into the other four, but here Schumann goes much further, initiating a method which later composers would extend in their own different ways, Liszt's thematic transformations, Wagner's leitmotif and Tchaikovsky's motto themes. In this symphony Schumann also eliminates the customary breaks between movements, thus keeping up a steady train of musical thought all the way through the music. Yet another break with tradition is found in the first movement, where there is no recapitulation section, the coda following hot on the heels of the development. Apart from all these structural novelties the symphony has always claimed public affection for its rich vein of melody, notably the haunting tune shared by oboe and cellos in the Romance, the bouncing theme of the Scherzo, and the exhilarating march-like main subject of the Finale which appears like a burst of sunshine after a mysterious introductory section.

The Symphony No 2 in C major composed in 1845–6 is the most traditionally formal of the four, giving the least freedom to Schumann to exploit the poetic side of his nature. The Symphony No 3 in E flat, the 'Rhenish', is a very different matter, directly inspired by the sights of the Rhineland which he came to know so well after his appointment as director of music at Düsseldorf in 1850. It owed its inception, he candidly admitted, to the impression made on him by the sight of Cologne Cathedral in bright sunshine, by the magnificent ceremony surrounding the installation of Archbishop von Geissel as a cardinal and by the outdoor revelry of the Rhinelanders. The work must accordingly be considered his nearest approach to pictorial symphonic music, though it illustrates his own emotional reactions to what he saw rather than making any attempt to describe the scenes and events themselves. Surprisingly in these circumstances, the first movement is strictly Classical in form, the most regularly and tautly constructed of all his first move-

Central aisle of Cologne Cathedral, whose exterior was one of the inspirations for the last symphony to be composed by Schumann, the 'Rhenish'

ments. The Scherzo is really a slow rustic Ländler (an early form the waltz) with a main theme in a naive folksong style which is developed with considerable ingenuity. There follow two slow movements, the first a disarming song-without-words, the second a majestic, exalted piece of contrapuntal writing eminently suited to the ecclesiastical occasion it depicts. The Finale makes a striking return from Gothic grandeur to the bustle of everyday life, its sprightly music creating a holiday spirit. Although there are traditional elements in the symphony, its pictorial qualities and the subjective warmth of Schumann's style take it a long way from the path established by Haydn and closely followed by Beethoven and Schubert even when they spread their imaginative wings most freely.

Undoubtedly the most popular of all Schumann's large-scale works, the Piano Concerto in A minor is 49

Above: *Schumann with his wife Clara, who encouraged him to turn to the symphony and who first played his piano concerto*

Opposite: *Frescoes at Pisa on the 'Triumph of Death' which inspired Liszt's* Totentanz *('Dance of Death') for piano and orchestra*

Below: *Liszt at the piano, being admired by (l to r) Alexandre Dumas, Berlioz, George Sand (seated), Paganini and Rossini*

Engraving by Doré for Dante's Inferno, *which also inspired the* Dante Symphony, *one of Liszt's most ambitious programmatic works*

also his most original and consistently inspired. It developed from an independent *Phantasie* for piano and orchestra composed in 1841 which intuition told him should be held in reserve for the first movement of a future concerto. He duly added the Intermezzo and Finale four years later, and the work was given its first performance at Dresden on 4 December 1845, followed by another at Leipzig a few weeks later, both with Clara as soloist. It is a work which stands on its own, quintessentially Romantic and therefore unlike any concerto by Mozart or Beethoven, and equally far removed from those by Schumann's con-

temporaries. It is not a bravura piece like those of Weber and Mendelssohn, or the later concertos by Liszt, as Schumann made clear when he wrote to Clara: 'I can't write a concerto for virtuosos; I must think of something quite different'.

The thematic material of the first movement has a similar quality to that of Mendelssohn, whose example he also followed by dispensing with the customary opening orchestral exposition, but the general style is intimate as soloist and orchestra weave a wealth of variations on the rapturous melody which dominates throughout. The movement is not strictly monothematic, yet secondary subjects are derived from this one theme or the peremptory piano flourish of the opening. It is fascinating to listen to this melody running the whole gamut of emotions – wistful, joyous, martial, majestic and jocular in turn. Alto-

words between those who regarded Wagner as the Messiah of new music and those who believed just as fervently that Brahms represented the only hope of saving all that was of value in musical tradition from the onslaught of revolutionary ideas. Today this seems absurd, since Wagner's work was confined to the opera house and that of Brahms to the concert hall, but during the latter half of the nineteenth century reason went out of the window as the two sides engaged in battle. Poor Brahms, who played no part himself in this war of ideas, found himself dragged into it against his will, set up by the one side as a saviour and by the other as a stuffy reactionary. And as so often happens in such circumstances, those who championed his music did so largely for the wrong reasons, entirely failing to see what actually lay behind its Classical form and structural techniques.

Brahms, who was born in Hamburg on 7 May 1833, was provided with a brief musical education by his father, a professional horn and double-bass player, but though he quickly proved to be an excellent pianist it was some time before he made any impression in a serious way. For five years he played mainly in dock-side taverns, then in 1853 he set off with a refugee Hungarian violinist on a modest concert tour during which he met Joseph Joachim, for whom he would subsequently write his powerful violin concerto. Later in that same year he called on Robert and Clara Schumann, both of whom enthused over the youthful piano sonatas he had composed. He must have been astonished as well as delighted a few weeks later when an article by Schumann was published in a leading journal declaring that he had been waiting for a new composer to 'spring, like Athene, fully armed from the head of Zeus. And such a one *has* appeared; a young man over whose cradle Graces and Heroes have stood watch. His name is Johannes Brahms, and he comes from Hamburg where he has been working in quiet obscurity.' An unknown twenty-year-old could hardly ask for more. More important, however, are Schumann's specific comments on the music that Brahms played for him, which was 'turbulent in spirit' and which drew him into 'ever more enchanting spheres'. A Romantic himself, Schumann would not have written in such terms about music which was academically Classical: what he was so quick to recognize was the warmth and colour illuminating Brahms's music from within.

The difference between Brahms and most of the other composers of his time was that he imposed a strict discipline on his musical language whereas they were inclined to allow expressiveness to degenerate from time to time into sentimentality on the one hand or cheap rhetoric on the other. He was also a perfectionist, so that however immediate the original inspiration for a composition might have been, he would never allow it to be performed or published until he was absolutely satisfied that it was as right in every detail as he could make it. It was because of the scrupulous care he took with his work that he was quite unjustifiably accused of being dry and over-academic, this misconception being reinforced by his outwardly uneventful life. There are those portraits, too, with the magnificent philosopher's head giving the impression of an unapproachable intellectual. It is necessary, whenever we try to understand his music, to remember that his personality was in fact very different from the legend created by Wolf and other Wagnerite partisans. His bachelor life should not mislead us into believing he was incapable of romantic affection. It was his misfortune to fall in love with Clara Schumann, who relied upon his affectionate support during the two terrible final years that her husband spent in an asylum. When Robert Schumann died on 29 July 1856, Clara and Brahms decided for reasons we shall never know to go their own separate ways, but their friendship re-

Silhouette of Brahms accompanied by a hedgehog—a reference to the fact that his favourite Viennese restaurant was called 'The Red Hedgehog'

Drawing of Clara Schumann—one of Brahms's closest friends—accompanying Joseph Joachim, for whom Brahms wrote the Violin Concerto

mained the strongest emotional element in the latter's life. He experienced several other emotional involvements as well, being highly susceptible to the charms of young women, yet he was afraid of what he once described as the 'fetters of matrimony'. The lighter side of Brahms is clearly revealed in his own Hungarian Dances and also in his admiration for the waltzes of his friend Johann Strauss. And as soon as he was able to settle in Vienna thanks to the offer of a musical appointment there, he quickly found the gaiety of the Austrian capital more to his taste than the bourgeois sobriety of Hamburg.

The first major work of Brahms, the Piano Concerto No 1 in D minor, is Romantic in the fullest sense of the word. In the first place, it was his means of working the personal crises he experienced with the Schumanns out of his system, and it took him three years of intense anguish to do so. He originally began to compose the music in 1854 in the form of a sonata for two pianos, perhaps as a piece to be played by Clara and himself, then for a period he re-sketched it as a symphony, and only by 1857 did he complete it as a massive concerto of some fifty minutes' duration. The whole work is infused with an intense personal passion which is never to be found in any of the concertos of Mozart or even Beethoven. Its music does not paint a picture or tell a story, as that of Berlioz or Liszt often sets out to do, but it does

express a personal drama, Brahms's own. There is no programme, a device which Brahms rejected throughout his creative career, but it is impossible to listen to the destiny-laden first theme of the opening Maestoso without sensing the composer's deep emotional involvement. In this, and also in the grandeur of its symphonic structuring, Brahms added a new dimension to concerto form. Another surprising feature is that the composer, who was a formidable virtuoso, deliberately refrained from allowing the piano to dominate: on the contrary, the soloist has to fight for his life *against* the orchestra. The concerto proved too hard a nut for the audiences of the time to crack, and it was loudly hissed when Brahms played it in Leipzig in 1859. His Piano Concerto No 2 in B flat, composed a quarter of a century later, won public and critical approval more easily, for although it is also unusually long and elaborate, cast like a symphony in four movements, its reflective lyricism and tranquillity give it immediate appeal. It is also an essentially Romantic work, not because it is personal and dramatic, but by virtue of the glowing warmth of its melodies and the tonal colouring of the piano part. Again this is a 'symphonic' concerto far removed from the brilliant, rather superficial display-pieces of other Romantic composers, but its seriousness of purpose does not prevent its being immensely rewarding to the soloist and readily accessible to the listener.

Although his first piano concerto had revealed his ability to think in symphonic terms and his early chamber music had made clear his command of sonata form, Brahms was so wary of the symphony itself that he did not present the Symphony No 1 in C minor until he was forty-three and widely acclaimed as a leading composer in the grand manner. The reason why some sixteen years passed between its first sketches and its completion in 1876 was that Brahms was such a fervent admirer of Beethoven's symphonies, he doubted anyone could add anything of value to what they had already said. He also knew that when he did eventually make his bow with a symphony everyone would judge it by the standards of Beethoven, and this sense of responsibility daunted him. It is, in fact, precisely what happened, though fortunately the long-awaited work was not only warmly received but actually paid the compliment of being hailed as the 'Tenth' – that is, the logical successor to Beethoven's Ninth. This nickname came all the more readily because the big theme in the Finale of this symphony bears a certain resemblance to the broad melody in the last movement of the Beethoven Ninth. Brahms was hardly enraptured when this was pointed out to him: 'Any fool can hear that,' was his tart rejoinder. There is no doubt, however, that he had worked most diligently to produce a first symphony which could stand comparison in scope and profundity with those of his idol.

Brahms was fortunate to find in Eduard Hanslick a critic who not only championed his debut as a symphonist but who understood exactly what he had set out to do. 'This new symphony,' Hanslick wrote of the Vienna premiere on 17 December 1876, 'is so earnest and complex, so utterly unconcerned with common effects, that it hardly lends itself to quick understanding.' He went on to assert, however, that once it had been heard a few times 'even the layman will recognize it as one of the most individual and magnificent works of the symphonic literature'. His only fear was that Brahms seemed to favour 'too one-sidedly the great and the serious, the difficult and the complex, at the expense of sensual beauty'. Few critics have ever written so perceptively about a major new work and been proved absolutely correct by history: Hanslick responded immediately to the Faustian conflicts of the first movement, the influence of the world of German song in the Andante, and the majestic progress from darkness to light in the lengthy and complex Finale. It is curious that he did not seem to spot a certain similarity of expressive design to Beethoven's No 5, which also follows a path from C minor tension to C major triumph. Brahms disappointed his followers only with the third movement: they were no doubt expecting an energetic scherzo in the manner of Beethoven, whereas Brahms, who never provided any of his symphonies with a true scherzo movement, offers here an elegant interlude which alternates between pastoral calm and a mood of slight agitation.

As though from relief at having made his serious mark with his first symphony, Brahms took only a year to compose his Symphony No 2 in D major, in an altogether more genial and sunny vein. His friends and the Viennese public in general were at once delighted by the new work, which was described as being 'so merry and tender, as though it had been especially written for a newly married couple'. Although it is as impeccably constructed as the other Brahms symphonies, its easy flow of warm melody gives it something of the quality of a serenade. There is a touch of solemnity about the short Adagio, with its broad opening cello theme, but the three other movements find Brahms at his most Romantically beguiling. After this the Symphony No 3 in F major strikes a comparatively heroic note which is emphasized by the use, for the only time in his symphonies, of a brief motto, the three notes F – A(flat) – F. We know that the composer adopted this

motto in his youth, *frei aber froh* ('free but happy'), but in no way does its appearance here suggest a programme for the symphony. Its combination with the more feminine main theme of the first movement simply helps to make the music more dramatically condensed, and its reappearance in the final Allegro binds the work together. As with the Symphony No 2, the third movement is a gentle Intermezzo.

When it came to his Symphony No 4 in E minor, of which he conducted the first performance himself in 1885, the composer was surprisingly cautious about the reception it would be given – surprisingly because his second and third symphonies had met with immediate acclaim and he was by this time revered. Indeed, for a genius who relentlessly pursued his own chosen path, paying no heed to changing fashion and refusing ever to court popular favour, he had enjoyed remarkable success with the public. Early in the 1860s he had established himself as a distinguished conductor as well as pianist, and with the success of his middle symphonies he found himself deluged with invitations to appear all over Europe. (He received many invitations to visit England, but declined them because he feared sea travel.) These demands on his time became so great that he was forced to take long summer breaks in the country to be able to compose undisturbed. He would go to Baden-Baden, where Clara Schumann had a holiday house, to Ischl where Johann Strauss had a villa, and to lakeside villages where he would not be pestered by budding composers seeking the Master's advice on their work.

The new symphony, which was to be his last, was, in the words of Hans von Bülow, one of the few musicians of the time who admired both Brahms *and* Wagner, 'gigantic, utterly original, brazenly individual'. It did seem, in fact, that Brahms had deliberately set out to test his mastery of formal construction, sacrificing in the process some of his gift for melody. It showed, as Hanslick was quick to appreciate, his 'sovereign mastery of all the secrets of counterpoint, harmony and instrumentation . . . the logic of development combined with the most beautiful freedom of fantasy'. It is this 'freedom of fantasy' which is so important, for it is the quality which makes nonsense of the vicious attack on Brahms by Hugo Wolf quoted earlier. The tensions of the first movement, the dark profundity of the slow movement, the playful yet masterful tone of the movement nearest the composer ever came to a scherzo, the final Passacaglia with its thirty variations and coda on an eight-bar bass theme – all these elements make up a magnificent and unique contribution to symphonic literature. It is also a symphony

57

Brahms, the composer of the Romantic period who imposed a strict Classical discipline on all his symphonic writing

which the ordinary concert-goer can enjoy simply for the sake of its exhilarating music, for its appeal does not depend in any way on a knowledge of the technical feats achieved in its composition. The last word belongs to Hanslick, who summed up in a sentence every music critic would give up his right arm to have written: 'It is like a dark well; the longer we look into it, the more brightly the stars shine back!'

In addition to the symphonies and piano concertos Brahms wrote two fine concert overtures, the *Tragic* and the *Academic Festival,* and the 'St Anthony' Variations. He also gave the violinist the only concerto to equal Beethoven's in both grandeur and popularity. (Mendelssohn's stands with them in its formal perfection, yet it does not share their depth of expression.) This Violin Concerto in D major was written

expressly for Joachim, who was frequently consulted on technical matters throughout its composition, and as a compliment to whom the Finale was given its Hungarian flavour and abandon. The first movement abounds with haunting melodies and is equally notable for the imagination with which they are developed; the second, with a sublimely simple theme which represents the essence of Brahms the Romantic, gives unusual prominence to a solo oboe as well as to the violinist; the Finale is positively cheeky, yet it taxes the soloist to the utmost. The concerto was considered so difficult to play that at first violinists other than Joachim fought shy of it. Eventually, however, it established itself as a favourite work with players and public alike, winning for its composer affection as well as respect. It is the final paradox of Brahms that he should have been accorded such affection by the Viennese, for he never, as man or artist, consciously strove to win the approval of anyone, dedicated only to the service of music itself.

Hans von Bülow, the conductor and pianist who was one of the few musicians of his time to appreciate the music of both Brahms and Wagner

When he died on 3 April 1897, Vienna gave him a funeral of great splendour which may not have been in keeping with the simple life he had chosen to lead, but which proved that the city which had failed to honour Mozart a little over a century before had finally learned to appreciate the men who had made it great.

Bruckner

Few of the great composers of the nineteenth century had to struggle so hard as Anton Bruckner, who did not win recognition at home until late in life and who made little impression abroad until many years after his death. This was due not to the nature of his music, which is not difficult to come to terms with, but to a combination of external circumstances. In the first place, he was a late starter in composition, which caused his whole career to be overshadowed by that of Brahms, nine year his junior. He was also a man of naive character with a clumsy manner which made it difficult for him to make friends either socially or professionally. Finally, because he openly declared his admiration for Wagner, he was drawn into the battle fought out between the champions of Wagner on the one hand and Brahms on the other. He never played any active part in these squabbles, devoting his energies to his massive symphonies; but he became a hapless victim of the cross-fire. He lacked, alas, the fighting spirit that might have brought him the fame and material rewards his music merited.

Born in the Austrian village of Ansfelden on 4 September 1824, he belonged to one of the lowliest groups of European society, the Catholic peasantry, which had an unquestioning faith in God and a strong love of nature, but no sophistication or even awareness of social change. When he became a composer it was to serve and glorify his Maker rather than to gain anything for himself. If he became an innovator in the process this was because he could only write music in accordance with his genius. Like his father and grandfather before him, Bruckner started out as a schoolmaster with the additional duties of village organist and choirmaster. It was not until he was thirty-two that he secured the appointment of organist at Linz, where he was able to become more familiar with the works of Beethoven and first encountered the music of Wagner. He lived in Linz for thirteen years, but for half that period he turned his back on the few sacred works he had already composed and devoted himself to study with a teacher in Vienna, where he spent several weeks each year. Only when he had mastered a thorough theoretical groundwork did he begin to write music again, revealing his genius for the first time in the Mass in D minor of 1864. It is significant that this mass should precede his Symphony No 1 in C minor, because there is a strong affinity between Bruckner's symphonies and his masses. He tended to treat the central sections of the latter as sonata movements with dramatic episodes interspersed, while all the finales of his symphonies – and some their first movements too – rise to chorale-like climaxes. His masses and symphonies also share a similar monumental character, and his symphonic writing was so influenced by the proportions of his masses that he was forced to break away from the Classical form of Beethoven, whose music he revered. Curiously perhaps, he was helped in his search for a suitable symphonic formula by his encountering the music of Wagner, not by adopting the dramatic master's style but by combining certain elements of his Romanticism with the strict techniques he had mastered in Vienna.

It has been said that Bruckner did not so much compose nine symphonies as write one symphony

Bruckner, the composer who was overshadowed by Brahms throughout his life and whose symphonies did not win wide recognition for many decades

material is treated spaciously in slow-moving blocks of sound often dominated by the brass. His slow movements do not have the characteristics of the song-without-words favoured by so many other composers, but are painstakingly developed Adagios – or an Andante in the case of the Fourth Symphony – in two alternating sections of deeply-felt melody. The Bruckner Scherzo is usually weighty, though driven along with strong rhythmic impetus, while his Finales, which frequently open like his first movements, involve a number of themes subjected to elaborate development and eventually combined in a chorale-like apotheosis. While they all adhere to this same basic form, each affords the listener an individual musical experience. They have been conveniently grouped into three periods – the first three in minor keys, Nos 4, 5 and 6 more Romantic works in major keys, and the last three thematically linked to his sacred music – but this does not take into account the variety achieved within each group.

The most popular is the Symphony No 4 in E flat, which while conforming fairly closely to his usual pattern has a particularly happy melodic inspiration derived from the composer's Austrian background. Its music speaks with the voice of nature, through the suggestion of awakening dawn and the murmuring of a forest in its first movement, the almost Schubertian elegiac charm of its Andante, the hunting calls of its Scherzo and the exultant marches and

Page from Bruckner's exercises for Simon Sechter, the pedantic theorist with whom he studied every aspect of compositional technique for seven years

nine times over. Like all epigrams, this is only partly true. Unlike the nine symphonies of Beethoven, which reveal a steady development and a general tendency towards greater length and complexity, Bruckner's follow a consistent formal pattern. All are in four movements, and despite the descriptive labels he once suggested for the Fourth ('Romantic') Symphony they are all non-programmatic. The first movements usually emerge from a mysterious, indefinite harmonic muttering, following the example of Beethoven's Ninth, a work which had a profound and lasting impression on Bruckner; and the melodic fanfares of its Finale. The optimistic tone of the symphony helps to dispel the notion that Bruckner was an over-stolid figure, despondent over his failure to win immediate recognition. He resolutely followed the creative course he had set himself and never lost his inner artistic confidence. He remains enigmatic as a man, for he combined but was never able to resolve his sturdy peasant character with the delicate sensibility that made him a composer of such originality. He was subject to mental instability, a condition aggravated by his sexual repression and the narrowness of his intellectual outlook. He was susceptible all his life to the attractions of teenage girls, none of whom responded to the clumsy older man whose idea of a love-token was inevitably the gift of a prayer book. Obsessed by music and religion, he took no interest whatsoever in literature or the theatre even after he moved permanently to Vienna in 1868. Ignoring the stimulating life of the Austrian capital, he led a monotonous round of composition and teaching relieved only by his occasional visits to Paris, London and other cities in the role of organ virtuoso. (It was his lifelong interest in the organ which largely dictated the style of his orchestration.) In spite of his friendship with the much younger Mahler, who as conductor championed his works, he remained very much an outsider in musical Vienna up to his death on 11 October 1896.

Mahler

Throughout the nineteenth century German composers had been famous above all else for their allegiance to the symphony, but after the death of Brahms only Mahler was to follow this tradition, and even he could not work within its formal bounds. The natural heir to the Romantic movement, he carried it to its ultimate point. Unwittingly perhaps, he prepared the ground for Schoenberg to make a complete break with the symphony by discarding the tonal principle upon which it had been founded. Gustav Mahler, who was born in the Bohemian village of Kalischt on 7 July 1860, seems to have been destined for a tragic life. He was the second of twelve children, of whom five died at an early age from diphtheria, while his favourite brother died at thirteen and another brother committed suicide. He grew up with death an ever-present reality. His childhood was also made unhappy by the frequent quarrels he witnessed between his father and mother, so it is hardly surprising that he withdrew into himself and the dream world he created as a refuge from the suffering around him. Happier influences on his childhood development

were his love of nature and the music that he heard, military music from the nearby barracks and folk-tunes sung by local Slav servant girls. All these influences were to come together in his music, which expresses a sensuous love of nature together with a very real consciousness of the imminence of death, and which features strident marches and gentle, folk-like songs. He poured his feelings, hopes and fears into all his work, so that the symphonies are all to some extent spiritual portraits of their composer.

Mahler had taught himself to play the piano so well by the age of eight that he was able to give lessons to a younger boy. His father, quick to spot his talent, arranged for him to study music in addition to his standard education, and he was admitted in 1875 to the Vienna Conservatoire, where he carried off prizes for piano playing and composition before leaving with his diploma in 1878. He knew that he was in no position to earn a living as a composer, and after a couple of years struggling as a tutor he decided to become an opera conductor at the age of twenty. It is almost certain that he took this step for purely financial reasons, quite unaware that in fact he had quite remarkable talents in that direction. After three years of unrewarding work in minor opera houses he was appointed second conductor at Cassel, where he first became aware of his own potential, and after that he moved by way of Leipzig and Prague to Budapest. It was in the Hungarian capital that he showed the first signs that he was to become one of the world's greatest conductors. He was superb in Mozart, for instance, prompting Brahms to declare: 'To hear the true *Don Giovanni*, you must go to Budapest'. Subsequently he made an international career, notably in Vienna and at the Metropolitan Opera and the Philharmonic Society in New York, where he was greatly admired. He drove his players to despair with his demand for perfection and his autocratic methods. This work reduced the time available for composition, but it certainly helped him to become a master of orchestral writing.

He completed his Symphony No 1 in D major in 1883 and conducted its first performance a year later, when it was unfavourably received. Today it is a popular repertory work. Originally he presented it as a symphonic poem in two parts and five movements, to each of which he gave a descriptive title, but he later dropped programmatic titles and one movement altogether, and indeed it should be regarded as a pure symphony composed on fairly traditional lines. Its slow first movement is alluringly melodic, suggesting the awakening of spring in music of the utmost freshness. The second movement is a dancing Scherzo in the form of the simple Ländler so popular

Mahler as a young man in 1881 at the beginning of the career as a conductor which poverty forced him to take up at the expense of composition

with Schubert and Bruckner, after which there comes a grotesque march movement inspired by a painting of a huntsman's funeral procession accompanied by the creatures of the forest whose lives he had threatened. The Finale progresses from ferment at the opening to a joyous conclusion, drawing on themes from earlier movements.

The next three symphonies all involve voices as well as orchestra, Mahler choosing poems from *Des Knaben Wunderhorn* ('The boy's magic horn'), a collection of German folk poetry that inspired much of his music. Voices had been brought into the sym-

phony before, beginning with Beethoven's Ninth, but Mahler carried the idea much further than any other composer, so that the line between the symphony and the song-cycle becomes difficult to draw. (The song-cycle *Das Lied von der Erde* – The song of the earth – is largely symphonic, at least in Mahlerian terms.) Whereas Beethoven had resorted only once to the inclusion of song in a symphony, and then only for the final movement, Mahler brought songs into four of his symphonies, and regarded them as an integral part of his symphonic writing. The Symphony No 2 in C minor includes a contralto soloist in the fourth movement who is joined by solo soprano and chorus for the fifth, and the unusually large orchestra is augmented by bells, harps and organ. It has been called a symphony of destiny, starting with an Allegro maestoso suggesting the death of a hero in his struggle for his ideals, ending with a jubilant assurance of the Resurrection. As a contrast to this symphony inspired by thoughts of death and the life beyond, the Symphony No 3 in D minor is a celebration of nature. It is scored for large orchestra, with solo contralto, a women's chorus and a boys' chorus, and it has a most unusual structure, an immensely long first movement followed by five short ones. The first movement opens with what has been labelled as the 'awakening call' for eight horns in unison, a theme which is later subjected to many transformations, as is the contrasting march. The music has a complexity that has divided scholars as to whether or not the movement is in sonata form at all. The tone becomes more gracious in the Minuet and Scherzo movements which follow, the fourth movement brings the sombre feeling of a 'Midnight Song', the fifth a chiming gaiety, and the purely instrumental final Adagio an intense lyricism. The Symphony No 4 in G major, which has a soprano soloist in the last movement, is much shorter and its first three movements adhere more closely to the Classical symphonic pattern than anything Mahler had composed before. All three of these works are more accessible than their structural complexities might suggest, for Mahler was a superb songwriter who filled his scores with long, lithe melodies rather than the more terse themes used by many symphonists.

Just as the symphonies Nos 2, 3 and 4 constitute a trilogy reflecting Mahler's struggle for an enduring religious belief – he renounced his Jewish faith in 1897 to become a Roman Catholic – the next three symphonies, all purely instrumental, form an interrelated group. They show the composer reverting to a more Classical style, partly because there are no vocal texts to provide an obvious programme; yet

'How the animals buried the hunter', from a drawing which inspired the grotesque march of the third movement of Mahler's First Symphony

they still reveal certain extra-musical ideas. The Symphony No 5 in C sharp minor, for instance, opens with a stern funeral march, interrupted by two episodes of passionate lamentation, and its second movement may be considered a stormy continuation of the first. The central Scherzo, which features a horn solo in its main theme and has two contrasting Trios in Ländler style, is designed on a colossal scale. The fourth movement, a gentle Adagietto scored for strings and harp alone (often played on its own in the concert hall), is followed by a highly contrapuntal final movement. The Symphony No 6 in A minor is more unified in thematic material and formal layout as well as more consistent in mood, its tragic tone heightened by the prominence of brass and percussion. It is in four movements, of which the last is itself as long as any complete Mozart symphony. Except in the song-like Andante, march-like themes and fateful rhythms give the music a pessimistic character which reflects Mahler's obsession with thoughts of death. Even the Scherzo, though vigorous, has a sinister quality on account of its lurid orchestration. After this the Symphony No 7 in E minor brings a sense of emotional relief, for its five movements progress from a mood of urgency to one of joy, taking in two Nocturnes on the way, enchanting pieces lightened by touches of guitar and mandolin.

Never a man to worry about the economics of performance, Mahler went so far over the top in his Symphony No 8 in E flat, calling for eight vocal soloists, a boys' choir and two mixed choirs as well as mammoth orchestra, that the work has been dubbed the 'Symphony of a Thousand'. It falls into two parts, the first a setting of the medieval hymn *Veni, creator spiritus*, the second of the closing scene from Part II of Goethe's *Faust*. Whether the work should be called a symphony at all is debatable, though the first part is in sonata form of an unorthodox kind. It was a correspondingly huge success when the composer conducted its first performance in 1910 in a hall built especially for the occasion, but today it is only rarely given, despite its considerable melodic appeal, brilliant orchestral writing and the sense of sheer excitement it generates. After this optimistic hymn to life, the Symphony No 9 in D major represents his most poignant encounter with the thought of death. (He did in fact die less than a year after its completion.) Purely instrumental, it is in the customary four movements though none of them follows traditional sonata form. Although the first movement has two main themes, Mahler elaborates them in an improvisatory way rather than developing them symphonically. The Scherzo, a Ländler with two Trios, is sardonic as though to suggest a dance of death, and the third movement also, entitled Rondo–Burleske, has a cruelly mocking character. To complete this picture of despair, the last movement is a sustained Adagio of solemn beauty. Although the music expresses its composer's personal grief over the futility of life as he saw it, listening to it is in no way a depressing experience.

It was his superstitious nature that prevented Mahler calling *Das Lied von der Erde* a symphony, not the fact that it employs two soloists throughout. Had he included it among his symphonies it would have been his ninth; and he believed that he would die after completing nine. It consists of settings of seven Chinese poems in German translation celebrating the joys of youth, beauty, the intoxication of wine and spring, in between songs of sorrow and farewell. They are among the loveliest songs ever written, and the orchestral contribution is imaginative and inspired. The unfinished Symphony No 10 in F sharp minor, which is occasionally performed in the completed version prepared by Deryck Cooke, makes it clear that Mahler was still continuing to explore new possibilities within the form, however radically he had changed it in so many respects. This was inevitable in the case of a composer who had declared: 'The symphony is the world! The symphony must embrace everything.'

Significantly, it was not until the 1950s that Mahler's symphonies became widely popular. His music at once looks back with nostalgia to the optimistic Romantic period and forward to a future bereft of hope. In this he seemed to express the feelings of the post-war years, in which people all over the civilized world found themselves facing a breakdown of established moral and religious beliefs, a dangerous confrontation between opposing political ideologies and even the possibility of a nuclear holocaust. The pessimism, even the self-pity that characterize so much of Mahler's music found a ready response, especially among a younger generation which otherwise had little interest in orchestral music.

A final point that should be made is that Visconti's film *Death in Venice*, based on the novel by Thomas Mann, tends to identify the character of Gustav von Aschenbach with Mahler. This is utterly misleading, for there is no connection at all between the fictional character and the composer, who died in Vienna on 18 May 1911 from a congenital heart condition exacerbated by over-work.

Mahler in 1911, the year of his death, when he had finally achieved fame as a composer as well as a world-wide reputation as a conductor

Richard Strauss

Although even more important in opera than orchestral music, Richard Strauss (1864–1949) has won a place of honour in the concert hall for the tone-poems he composed before the turn of the century. These popular and original works fall into two main categories, the descriptive and the 'philosophical', though these frequently overlap. *Don Juan*, composed when Strauss was only twenty-five, and his first completely mature work, is a striking example of his descriptive genius, for it gives a vivid portrait of the amorous hero in pursuit of his ideal, carries him through several encounters and ends with death in a duel. Strauss preferred his programme to be accepted in general terms as his 'poetic idea' rather than in any precisely detailed sense. The music is breathtaking in its impetuous surge, melodic freshness and scintillating orchestral writing. This was followed a year later by *Tod und Verklärung* ('Death and transfiguration'), a 'philosophical' tone-poem with a few descriptive details. The music falls into four continuous sections and might be seen as an Allegro in free sonata form, with slow introduction and epilogue. It is not at all stark, as its title might suggest, but warmly emotional and alive with dramatic contrasts. The Death motif is a syncopated figure, reflective rather than tragic, while the Transfiguration motif when it arrives in its complete form is broad and impassioned, indeed almost erotic. In the course of its progress the music features startling dissonances and novel harmonies that have been so widely copied that it is difficult to appreciate how much they puzzled audiences at the time.

The later tone-poems grew more elaborate and even more assured. *Till Eulenspiegel* (1895) is in rondo form, the two themes associated with Till recurring in a variety of guises. Till is an altogether engaging rascal, whose pranks are vividly described in the course of the piece: he rides his horse through a busy market, overturning the stalls, makes fun of priests and philistines, and tries to be a Don Juan. At the end he is brought to judgment, and we hear him pleading his innocence of the charges thundered against him. After the graphic episode of his execution Strauss cannot bear to leave him, so a brief, hectic coda presents him as a legend after his death, a man who, like Falstaff, brought fun and laughter to the world. In contrast to this musical jest stands *Also sprach Zarathustra* (1896), a work in which the composer paid his homage to the philosopher Nietzsche. Strauss made his purpose quite clear: 'I did not intend to write philosophical music or to portray in music Nietzsche's great work. I meant to convey by means of music an idea of the development of the human race from its origin, through the various phases of religious and scientific progress, up to Nietzsche's idea of the Superman.' As with all the tone-poems of Strauss, *Also sprach Zarathustra* can be appreciated and enjoyed on a purely musical level without paying any attention to its programme.

The last two tone-poems, *Don Quixote* and *Ein Heldenleben* ('A hero's life'), were written as companion works. Having sketched the tragicomic figure of the Spanish knight whose vain search for heroism leads to insanity, Strauss tried to present in *Ein Heldenleben* a more general and free ideal of true heroism, that which reveals the inward battle of life and leads towards the elevation of the soul. *Don Quixote* (1897) is described as a set of 'fantastic variations on a knightly theme' and features a solo cello and a solo viola representing Don Quixote and Sancho Panza respectively. Episodes from Cervantes' novel are graphically described. *Ein Heldenleben* (1898) is autobiographical, the composer's defiant reply to his critics, whom he caricatures while extolling his own achievement with thematic material quoted from his earlier works. It is fortunate that he composed this before writing his *Sinfonia domestica* (1903), an inferior piece with movements headed with such mawkish tags as 'Parents' happiness' and 'Childish play'. This four-movement symphony was followed twelve years later by the one-movement *Alpine Symphony*, which also falls below the level of his other programmatic works. Strauss also wrote several concertos and the neo-Classical *Metamorphosen* for twenty-three stringed instruments, all works of interest. Even more successful, however, are the *Four Last Songs* (1948), the last music he composed, which deserve mention here since they have orchestral accompani-

Richard Strauss and his wife Pauline, with whom he enjoyed a stormy marriage which he made the subject of his opera Intermezzo

ment and are therefore always performed in the concert hall as opposed to the recital room. Strauss had passed through a period in which his inspiration had flagged, but there he seems to have recaptured the spontaneity of his early years, notably in the radiant melodies. The songs express tranquillity, tenderness, confidence and resignation, the last ending with the question 'Is this perhaps death?' The voice part soars with blissful ease, yet it is completely integrated with the orchestral accompaniment.

65

FRANCE

Berlioz

It is ironical that the first out-and-out Romantic symphony, the *Symphonie fantastique* by Berlioz composed in 1830, should have been the work of a Frenchman. In general the French have always shown leanings towards reason rather than sentiment, and this habit of letting the head rule the heart has constantly influenced their attitudes towards the arts as well as social and political matters. This can most easily be seen in the drama when we compare the formal, rather cold perfection of Racine's tragedies with the less neatly constructed yet imaginatively far richer *Hamlet* and *King Lear*. Hector Berlioz, who was born in the small town of La Côte Saint-André on 11 December 1803, happened to move to Paris, officially to study medicine, at exactly the right time for a man of his particular temperament and genius. From the beginning he was extravagantly affected by poetry: anyone who, in his own words, was 'seized with nervous shuddering' on reading Virgil was destined for something more exciting than becoming a country doctor. He was in fact to formulate and fulfil the ideals of Romanticism in music, and achieve enduring fame – except in his own country, where, standing apart from the mainstream of French music, he has remained a neglected figure to this day.

Berlioz has left us a racy account of his early life in his *Memoirs*, lambasting the musical establishment of Paris in the process even though it was unexpectedly sympathetic to him in his student days. Armed only with the ability to play the guitar and the flute plus a few youthful compositions, he managed to enter the Paris Conservatoire, where in 1830 he finally (at the third attempt) won the Prix de Rome which allowed him to study for three further years at the Villa Medici in Rome. Between 1827 and 1830, besides falling under the spell of Beethoven's symphonies and of Shakespeare's plays, he became involved in the Romantic literary movement spearheaded by Victor Hugo. It was in his revolutionary published Preface to *Cromwell*, a play which was unfortunately ill-suited to the stage, that Hugo proclaimed that art was by its nature evolutionary and dynamic and that the old Classical formulas spelt only rigidity and decay. His equally bombastic *Hernani*, later to become internationally famous as Verdi's opera *Ernani*, was a literally riotous success, leading to fights between the pro- and anti-Romantic factions, Berlioz active among the former. The *Symphonie fantastique* was conceived in this heady atmosphere, and because it enshrines the whole spirit of the Romantic movement,

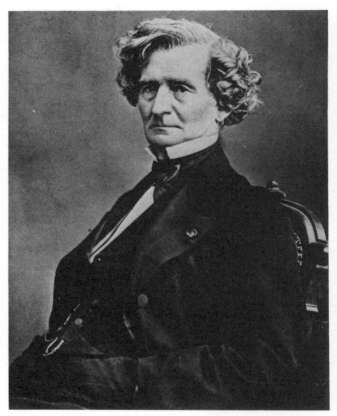

Berlioz, the unruly genius who disconcerted the French musical taste of his time by the heady, Romantic nature of his music

its excesses and also its contradictions, it deserves close attention. It still has the power to astonish the twentieth-century music lover hearing it for the first time, so one can easily imagine the shock-waves it sent through the first Paris audience and the affront it gave to the composer's more conservative colleagues. 'Indifferent drivel' was the comment of the usually charitable Mendelssohn in one of his rare lapses of judgment. Whether you happen to like the *Symphonie fantastique* or not, it is anything but indifferent: the whole point is that it was completely *different* from any other symphony previously composed.

The story behind the work concerns the beautiful Irish actress Harriet Smithson, whom Berlioz had seen in 1827 as Ophelia and Juliet with an English theatre company playing in Paris. Highly susceptible to feminine charms, he promptly fell in love with her. Actresses, however, are renowned for giving the cold shoulder to their stage-door admirers, which is precisely what Miss Smithson did to the then undistinguished Berlioz. She not only left his letters unanswered, but departed from Paris two years later without once having condescended to meet him. The indignant composer worked out his frustration and bitterness in the *Symphonie fantastique*, so we have the delightful irony of a vain, empty-headed actress, by breaking a composer's heart, inspiring one of the most original of musical masterpieces. The couple eventually met a few years later, were married (with Liszt as one of the witnesses), and lived unhappily for seven years until they wisely decided to separate. Meanwhile, Miss Smithson was featured in the symphony as the ardent theme of the first movement, a theme which also returns in the four subsequent movements to represent what Berlioz himself called his *idée fixe*.

There are many musicologists who urge us to ignore the personal story behind the symphony and simply listen to the music and study it as we do in the case of Mozart or Beethoven. This is not a very valid proposal, however, in view of the fact that Berlioz not only had printed the 'programme' of the symphony and issued it to the first audience, but went so far as to subtitle the work 'Episode in the Life of an Artist'. It is true that he subsequently asked concert-goers to forget both programme and subtitle, but as he had so strongly stressed their importance at the time of composition and first performance they cannot be swept aside so easily. Also, the music does illustrate the programme so vividly that there is no reason why listeners today should not share in the experiences depicted in the five movements. The first, 'Reveries and Passions', deals with feelings of rejection and jealousy; the second, 'At a Ball', finds the hero in a ballroom where his beloved presumably spent the evening dancing with other men; and the third, 'In the Country', depicts the serenity of nature rather in the manner of Beethoven's *Pastoral* until the appearance of the *idée fixe* suggests impending doom. The last two movements represent the nightmares which the hero suffers after taking opium to try to forget his unfulfilled love: the 'March to the Scaffold' in which he witnesses his own execution after murdering his beloved, then the 'Dream of a Witches' Sabbath' in which he sees her taking part in diabolic revelry. In these last movements Berlioz seems to have anticipated the grisly event of 1864, when the cemetery in which Harriet Smithson had been buried was demolished. He felt it his duty to attend the exhumation and reburial of the body of his first wife. As the gravediggers removed the coffin its lid came away to reveal the head already parted from the rest of the corpse – in the composer's own words, 'the ungarlanded, withered, hairless head of my poor Ophelia'.

CONCERT A LA VAPEUR.

'Concert à la Vapeur', a caricature reflecting the general bewilderment caused by Berlioz's unconventional concerts

So much for the sensational aspect of Berlioz's Romanticism: now for its contradictory side. The *Symphonie fantastique* not only had a detailed programme, but much of its thematic material was taken by Berlioz from his earlier works, a song he wrote as a boy, a cantata he composed while a student, and the unfinished opera *Les Francs Juges*. All this suggests that the *Symphonie fantastique* is a hotchpotch of musical ideas thrown together in a fit of self-pity. In fact, nothing could be further from the truth, for Berlioz constructed the work so that it expressed his inner drama in purely musical terms, thus standing as a legitimate symphony without its programme. Above

'Witches flying to Sabbath', a print depicting the kind of scene which Berlioz conjures up in the last movement of his Symphonie fantastique

all, it has remarkable unity, not only because its main subject, the *idée fixe*, appears in a variety of guises in all five movements, but because this theme, which is unusually long (forty bars) and irregularly phrased, influences the whole melodic character of the symphony. The first movement does not follow sonata form, but has a closely argued form of its own: after a spacious slow Introduction comes the exposition of the *idée fixe* subject, then the rest of the movement consists of a subtle development section which finally comes to rest on solemn chords without recourse to the customary recapitulation and coda sections. The second movement is a waltz, at once glittering and graceful. The pastoral third movement is quite novel, opening with a solo call on the cor anglais which receives a distant answer from a solo oboe, giving the effect of idyllic peace. At the close, however, Berlioz creates disturbing tension when the cor anglais is answered, not by the former soloist, but by rumbles of thunder from four timpani tuned to form a chord. The heavily orchestrated 'March to the Scaffold' evokes a grotesque atmosphere, culminating in a guillotine stroke which cuts short the soft playing

of the *idée fixe* by a solo clarinet. A parody of the *Dies Irae* plainsong helps to turn the dramatic screw in the witches' dance of the finale. Apart from the addition of an extra movement (which Beethoven had already done in the *Pastoral*), Berlioz follows the general formal pattern of the symphony, showing how even the most revolutionary Romantic ideas could be incorporated into the Classical mould without breaking it altogether.

Two later symphonies make more radical breaks with tradition, *Harold in Italy* featuring a viola soloist and *Romeo and Juliet* introducing voices into four of its seven movements. The first of these 'not quite symphonies' was commissioned in 1834 by Paganini, and for its inspiration Berlioz turned to *Childe Harold's Pilgrimage* by Lord Byron, whose extravagant verses and even more extravagant life fired the imagination of so many composers of the Romantic period. His choice of subject was no doubt also influenced by the time he had spent in Italy as winner of the Prix de Rome, enjoying the scenes of its picturesque country life as much as the artistic treasures of its cities. *Harold in Italy* is largely built around a single theme, following the example of the *Symphonie fantastique*, this time a haunting, rather melancholy melody given to the solo viola which represents Harold himself. The hero does not take much part in the four 'scenes' of the work: he observes them and reflects upon them. The music is much more varied than this programme suggests, with a Pilgrims' March as the second movement, a Mountaineer's Serenade for the third, and an Orgy of Brigands for the finale. In spite of the prominent part played by the viola this is not a concerto in any sense, and indeed Paganini refused to perform it when he saw the score, deciding it would not give him the amount of limelight his vanity demanded.

Although the form of *Romeo and Juliet* is generally symphonic, Berlioz makes the drama more explicit here than in the two earlier works, and while he was later to compose the impressive operas *Benvenuto Cellini* and *The Trojans*, he may be said to have expressed himself more successfully in this Shakespearean dramatic symphony, free from the practical limitations which stage performances imposed on his imagination. The purely orchestral sections, the 'Love Scene', 'Queen Mab Scherzo' and 'Death Scene', are among the composer's most brilliant and successful achievements, with the Queen Mab music a triumph of descriptive writing. It translates the tripping words of Mercutio's speech into a shimmering web of orchestral sound that can only be described as musical gossamer. Here, as indeed throughout all these radically conceived symphonies, Berlioz proved himself a trail-blazer in orchestration, enriching music with fresh resources of harmony, instrumental colour far more exotic than that of his Romantic predecessors or contemporaries, and a variety of structural novelties. His influence extended in all directions, to later symphonies in cyclic form – that is, with the use of a recurrent theme in different movements – to the symphonic poems of Liszt, and even to the music dramas of Wagner. He had a uniquely sensitive ear, many of the colourful effects he produced in the 'Queen Mab Scherzo' and the *Roman Carnival* Overture remaining unsurpassed to the present day; while his treatise on orchestration, published in 1844, is itself a classic.

Berlioz was thirty-six when he composed *Romeo and Juliet* and had another thirty years to live, but he did not compose so much in that period as might have been expected. There are, it is true, two masterpieces in the oratorio *The Childhood of Christ* and the epic opera *The Trojans*, but the creative pulse of the 1830s slackened considerably. This was no doubt due largely to the indifference or positive hostility shown towards his music in his own country, though his disappointment must have been offset by its more ready acceptance abroad and its championship by Liszt and other leading composers. He was also active in other fields, having published his first writings on music as early as 1823 and become a music critic ten years later for the *Rénovateur*, from which he moved on to the more influential *Journal des débats* and *Gazette musicale*. He also began a career as a conductor, in which capacity he undertook extensive tours of Germany, Austria, Hungary, England and Russia. These activities were not taken up from choice but because they provided an income which was not forthcoming from his composing, and the fact that he was forced into such work must have caused him much bitterness. His personal life had its tragedies too. After the death of Harriet in 1854 he married again, this time an indifferent singer, Marie Recio, who made a good wife until she died eight years later. Tragedy struck again in 1867 when the son of his first marriage, Louis, died at the age of thirty-three.

There is a wonderful description of Berlioz by Théophile Gautier which refers to his having 'a splendid head, like an exasperated eagle'. Berlioz had plenty of cause to feel exasperation, and from the pinnacle of his genius gazing down on the mediocrity of French musical life he was indeed as solitary as an eagle. He never gave up the struggle as an artist, however, nor did he lose his sense of humour, even of the absurd, when pouring out a full measure of his bitterness in his *Memoirs*. This book makes fascinating reading, for Berlioz comes across as an extraordinary man, yet one with whom the twentieth-century reader can readily identify. He is, in fact, a perfect example of modern man as well as a tremendous genius born before his time. Extravagantly imaginative and highly strung, he was saved from despair and self-pity by the hard-headed survival instinct of the provincial Frenchman. What made him unique was his combination of this sense of the practical with an idealism he never relinquished. It is movingly expressed in a letter he wrote to a friend upon hearing from a Russian girl with whom he had enjoyed an affair: 'I suffer keenly, yet I am grateful to her for reviving the pain I was trying to forget. There are so many kinds of love; the kind I feel is the true full-blown poetic love. I have known it since the first time, and nothing is more beautiful. It alone, and the love of art, can raise men's souls to the divine. With it, the world grows radiant, the whole of nature glows . . . one loves, that's all, one loves!' Those words give a good indication of the Romantic spirit which Berlioz expressed so radically in his music.

Apart from Berlioz, whose work was misunderstood and largely ignored by his countrymen, French composers produced little outstanding orchestral music

Gounod, primarily an opera composer, whose symphonies and other orchestral works are still played in France though neglected elsewhere

movements which is full of attractive melodies and is most imaginatively scored with deft touches of Spanish colouring as implied by its title. But the orchestral output of both these composers is small, even insignificant, compared to that of Saint-Saëns, a man of outstanding intellect and prodigious talent who was a very fine composer though not among the greatest.

Saint-Saëns

In the archives of the Paris Conservatoire can be found the manuscript of a short piano piece by Saint-Saëns bearing the date 22 March 1839. It is no masterpiece, but the date shows that its composer was less than four years old. This is more significant than might at first appear, because Camille Saint-Saëns (born in Paris on 9 October 1835) was so completely obsessed with making music during his early childhood that he had no time to develop most of the ordinary human emotions. (Mozart, of course, was

Opposite: Anna Pavlova as the Dying Swan, in a solo dance set to music by Saint-Saëns

Below: *Saint-Saëns*

during most of the nineteenth century, though Paris was the undisputed capital of the operatic world. The public flocked to the opera and to the piano recitals of Chopin and Liszt, but had neither the opportunity nor the inclination to take an interest in orchestral concerts, so it is not surprising that French composers turned their attention elsewhere. Opera and song, for example, were the chief concerns of Charles Gounod (1818–93) and Edouard Lalo (1823–92), though both men occasionally tried their hands at symphonic music. Gounod's two symphonies were favourably received and are still performed occasionally in France, but it is not difficult to understand their neglect elsewhere. Although they temper the all-too-obvious influence of Schumann with a certain Gallic delicacy, they have insufficient personality to hold their own against composers whose genius was more naturally suited to the symphony. Lalo has at least enjoyed more enduring success with one work,

70 the *Symphonie espagnole*, a violin concerto in five

similarly precocious – but also all too human.) His natural mastery of the keyboard was such that he was delighting invited guests at salon recitals by the age of seven, and at ten made his phenomenal public debut with an orchestra. His programme consisted of two concertos, by Mozart and Beethoven, with solo works by Bach, Handel and Hummel sandwiched in between. He played everything from memory, a rare practice at that time, and when an encore was demanded he offered to play any of the thirty-two Beethoven sonatas. He was spared the fate of the travelling child prodigy by being put to compositional studies instead, though he continued to play publicly right up to his death at the age of eighty-six. His first two symphonies came in 1853 and 1857, both showing an effortless mastery of traditional writing in the manner of Mozart and early Beethoven. In the latter year he also became organist at the Madeleine, the most coveted post in France. In 1858, still only twenty-three, he began his series of concertos, five for piano, three for violin and two for cello. All are works of lyrical charm and impeccable craftsmanship, and have endured along with his tone-poems *Danse macabre*, and *Le Rouet d'Omphale*.

The Piano Concerto No 2 in G minor is a splendid work combining Romantic lyricism with a truly Classical poise. It is perhaps because it defies convenient labelling that it has become somewhat neglected outside France. This is a great loss to both pianists and concert-goers; its superb pianism is as rewarding to the sensitive virtuoso as its melodic grace and imaginative structure are satisfying to the listener. The brilliant variations of the first movement are followed by a Scherzo of Mendelssohnian sparkle and a final Presto in exhilarating tarantella rhythm. The Piano Concerto No 4 in C minor, which prompted Gounod to hail Saint-Saëns as 'the French Beethoven', is even more original and ambitious. It is cast in two movements, each divided into two parts, and is based on two recurring themes. There is great variety of mood – solemn, tender and almost frisky – but the composer's mastery of form holds these elements together in an integrated design.

It looks forward, in fact, to the most ambitious of his orchestral works, the Symphony No 3 in C minor, commissioned by the Royal Philharmonic Society and first performed in London in 1886. This work is dedicated to Liszt, not only from friendship, but also because it employs the Lisztian idea of theme-transformation – whereby a basic theme or motto recurs throughout a work, changing its character according to context. There are four movements, joined together to form two pairs. The work calls for a large orchestra, with additional parts for two pianos and organ, resulting in its nickname, the 'Organ' Symphony. The music is mightily impressive (though marred by some bombast in the Finale) and merits the occasional performances it is still given today.

Although a purist in style, Saint-Saëns is perhaps most widely known for two works which do not follow any standard form. The *Danse macabre* began life as a song but was soon turned into the orchestral piece we know today, a triumph of atmospheric music. After a harp has sounded the strokes of midnight, Death's fiddle plays a slithering waltz to chromatic woodwind accompaniment and the rattle of bones provided by the xylophone, a parody of the *Dies Irae* stealing in before the oboe sounds the cock-crow of dawn. Its novelty outraged the first audience in 1875, provoking such a barrage of shouts and boos that the composer's aged mother fainted in her seat. A more extended piece, *The Carnival of the Animals* for two pianos and orchestra, is unique in that it expresses wit in music without descending into mere buffoonery. It represents the streak of Parisian urchin humour in Saint-Saëns which he usually kept hidden behind his academic public image; indeed, this 'grand zoological fantasy' was intended only for private performance. When eventually published it caught the public's fancy and has never diminished in popularity. The suite includes movements of superb parody, the elephants portrayed by double basses playing Berlioz's feather-light Dance of the Sylphs and the tortoise by the playing of an Offenbach can-can at an agonizingly slow pace. There are many beautiful movements too, notably 'The swan', which not only became the most popular solo cello piece but also provided Anna Pavlova with the dance that immortalized her, 'The Dying Swan'. Two smaller works, both for violin and orchestra, have won similar popularity: the Introduction and Rondo Capriccioso and the *Havanaise*, dazzling showpieces with immediate tuneful appeal and stylistic elegance.

Posterity's judgment on the music of Saint-Saëns has been as fickle as the changes in fortune he experienced during his lifetime. For all his talent he was never awarded the Prix de Rome, given to so many lesser French composers; and his operatic masterpiece *Samson et Dalila* was premiered by Liszt at Weimar in 1877, fourteen years before the Paris Opéra grudgingly decided to stage it. (The somewhat cynical composer must have derived satisfaction from the fact that it quickly became one of the Opéra's biggest successes.) He enjoyed little family life, for after the tragic deaths of his two children in 1878 he remained with his wife for only three years before deserting her for ever without a word of explanation. He was devoted to his mother, and after her death transferred his affection to the dogs which were his table companions when he dined at home. A conservative in his musical outlook, he fell out of fashion after 1886 when a new school of composers emerged with César Franck as their figurehead.

Ten years later, however, his fortunes changed and he became a living legend, extravagantly fêted abroad as well as at home. Aristocratic society courted him, he was invited into the artistic circle of Marcel Proust, and on his visits to London he was received as warmly by Queen Alexandra as by Victoria before her. In 1902 he was asked to write a march for the coronation of Edward VII, which he attended, and in 1915 he was sent by the French government as an official representative at the San Francisco Exhibition, for which he provided a noisy choral work entitled *Hail! California*. It was fortunate that he enjoyed travel, for he spent his last years moving from one country to another to receive yet more honours. He retained his waspish wit as well as his stamina, and must be one of the few men who ever deflated Sir Thomas Beecham. When the ebullient English maestro asked him what he thought of his conducting, Saint-Saëns blandly replied: 'My dear young friend, I have lived a long time and I have known all the *chefs d'orchestre*. There are two kinds; one takes the music too fast, and the other too slow. There is no third kind.' The composer's last journey was to be to Algiers, where on 16 December 1921, at the end of a day spent in piano practice, letter-writing and his usual game of dominoes, he died shortly after retiring to bed.

Franck

There was little, if any, sense of adventure in French musical life during the mid-nineteenth century, its general tone being bland and conventional. The composer who eventually brought about a change in the seventies was neither a Frenchman by birth nor a likely standard-bearer for a new movement. Although he made Paris his home in his early teens, César Franck was born at Liège in Belgium on 10 December 1822. His musical career began in spectacular fashion, for his father realized the boy had a rare talent as a pianist and planned recital tours for his young prodigy. The family then moved to Paris so that César could have further private study before entering the Paris Conservatoire in 1837. Five years later, instead of being allowed to complete his composition studies and compete for the Prix de Rome, he was whisked back on to the concert circuit by his father. He could doubtless have made a career as a concert artist, for he was a virtuoso on both the piano

and the organ; but that would not have satisfied his ambition as a composer. He at last broke free of his father's influence by marrying an actress's daughter, to the horror of his bourgeois family. The ceremony itself, which took place in Paris at the height of the 1848 Revolution, was given a romantic touch when bride and groom had to be lifted by the insurgents over street barricades. It did not remain a romantic union, however, for Franck's wife became as great a tyrant as his father had been, and the only understanding and affection he ever enjoyed were given to him by his students in later years.

He spent the next twenty-four years teaching untalented private pupils, a chore relieved only by his work as organist at a succession of Paris churches, and by his new-found opportunities for composition. Of all composers he took the longest time to develop a mature and distinctive style, and it was not until 1872, when he was appointed professor of organ at the Conservatoire, that he reached his full powers. His official organ classes quickly developed into discussions of the new musical ideas of the day, notably

Franck, the organ virtuoso whose fame as a composer was not established until the latter part of his life thanks to his students

those of Wagner and his followers, which the other professors rigidly ignored. Among his pupils were the future composers Ernest Chausson and Vincent d'Indy, whose enthusiasm for his music proved the final spur to his creative imagination. All his major chamber and orchestral works belong to the last decade of his life. Of his Liszt-inspired symphonic poems, *Le Chasseur maudit* ('The accursed huntsman') has become the best known. It tells in graphic musical terms the story of a huntsman who refuses to halt the chase when church bells call him to prayer and is punished by himself being hunted to the death by the devil. Scored for a very large orchestra, it is an exciting piece of programme music which still conforms to the composer's Classical roots. He did not write a concerto, a surprising omission for a virtuoso, but the Symphonic Variations for piano and orchestra soon established itself in concert pianists' favour. Unlike most sets of variations, which treat a single theme, this work is constructed on two themes. Its characteristic melodic style and strange harmonic twists make it a rewarding pendant to the standard concerto repertoire.

The Symphony in D minor is undoubtedly Franck's outstanding orchestral achievement, and also the only French symphony other than Berlioz's *Symphonie fantastique* to win worldwide admiration. It is curious that he should have waited until he was sixty-six before completing a symphony, for he had begun as a composer with four piano trios and had always admired Classical forms. However, he spent his middle years writing music either specifically for the church or of an ecclesiastical nature, none of it very distinguished. When he came to the symphony he had at last developed a powerful individual style, and the work is startlingly original in several respects. It has only three movements, though the second combines the functions of slow movement and Scherzo, and cyclic form, always favoured by Franck, is featured when the Finale recalls themes from the preceding movements. After a brooding slow Introduction, the first movement builds up in its main Allegro section to an unforgettable singing theme often referred to as the 'faith motif'. The second movement has an equally memorable melody, of a gentle, melancholy character, which by a stroke of inspiration the composer gives to the plaintive voice of the cor anglais. The Finale brings the most joyous music that Franck ever composed to round off what has become one of the most popular symphonies. It was not appreciated at first; the more academic French composers and critics disliked its chromaticism and, above all, its use of the cor anglais. No Classical composer, they fulminated, would ever

have introduced the instrument into a symphony (overlooking the fact that Haydn had done so in his 'Philosopher' Symphony more than a century earlier). However, within a very few years, thanks to its continued championship by Franck's devoted followers, it had taken its rightful place in the repertoire.

The symphony was Franck's last purely orchestral work. Two years later he was knocked down by a bus, suffering injuries which were not properly treated and which led to his death on 8 November 1890. His style lived on in the works of those who had studied with him, though they were minor composers whose music is not regularly heard outside France. Vincent d'Indy (1851–1931) is known only by an occasional performance of his *Symphony on a French Mountaineer's Song*, which is not really a symphony nor, though it includes a piano which enters as a solo instrument from time to time, a concerto. It is built on a pastoral theme which appears in all there movements, with a few subsidiary melodies giving contrast. It is best described as an orchestral fantasia, inspired by the landscape of the Cévennes, a mountain range in southern France, and most readily enjoyed for its fresh, almost open-air tunefulness and the charm of its exquisite orchestral colouring. Ernest Chausson (1855–99), who was even more strongly influenced by Wagner than was d'Indy, is also remembered chiefly for one symphonic work, the *Poème* for violin and orchestra. It is a lush, Romantic piece, but despite its title has no programme or literary association. It owed its publication and initial success to the generosity of the Spanish composer Albéniz, who provided the money for publication and Chausson's advance royalties without ever letting his friend know. Apart from the equally Romantic *Poème de l'amour et de la mer*, Chausson's other works, which include a symphony and an opera both strongly influenced by Wagner, have failed to stay the course. It must be remembered, however, that he reached artistic maturity only a couple of years before his death in a bicycle accident.

It would be wrong to think that France was short of distinguished composers before Debussy's arrival on the scene towards the end of the century. Berlioz, Saint-Saëns and Franck may have been the only important orchestral composers, but Gabriel Fauré contributed a great deal to the song, chamber music and solo piano repertoires, while Jules Massenet and Georges Bizet enriched the opera. Bizet (1838–75)

Opposite: *Nijinsky as the Faun in the ballet he choreographed to Debussy's evocative music of* Prélude à l'Après-midi d'un faune

"L'APRÈS MIDI D'UN FAUNE"
(NIJINSKY)

7me Saison
des

BAKST

Ballets
Russes

NIJINSKI, dans l'"Après-Midi d'un Faune"

deserves an honourable mention here for his Symphony in C, composed when he was seventeen but never performed during his lifetime. It lay in manuscript in the archives of the Paris Conservatoire, completely overlooked, until 1935 when it was discovered by chance and performed in Basle under Felix Weingartner. Its elegance and freshness delighted its first audience, and the work reveals that Bizet had a precocious talent like that of Mendelssohn, for its melodic fluency is accompanied by an astonishing grasp of symphonic structure. It is strictly Classical in design and in the treatment of its themes, but several of the melodies themselves look forward to the music of his maturity: in particular, the Finale introduces a light-hearted march which anticipates the parading street urchins of *Carmen*. The symphony leaves many music-lovers regretting that Bizet did not compose more for the concert hall.

Debussy

A revolutionary change in French music came with Debussy, a man whose creative genius was as startlingly original as that of Wagner, though the two composers represent opposite poles of artistic ideals and style. Claude Debussy, who was born at Saint-Germain-en-Laye on 22 August 1862, reacted against the excesses of Romanticism, its over-emotionalism and lapses into stridency. Everything he composed is fastidious, miraculously achieving the most impressive results by means of under- rather than over-statement. Even when his music calls for an unusually large orchestra, it is never loud.

He studied at the Paris Conservatoire, where he was considered a gentle and charming boy; but beneath this outward personality he was already developing a musical style of his own which ran contrary to everything that the institution's conservative academics tried to teach him. From the age of fourteen he began writing songs, piano pieces and occasional chamber works, and was able to earn a little money as a pianist. In 1880 he secured a place as pianist in the household of the wealthy Mme von Meck, the discreet patroness of Tchaikovsky, and four years later he won the Prix de Rome for his cantata *L'Enfant prodigue*, but though this brought him four years' further study in Italy he was never influenced by musical trends there, remaining completely his own man. He continued his self-education after returning to Paris, and although he fell for a time under the spell of Wagner's operas he soon largely rejected their influence, apart from a lifelong fascination with the delicate orchestral colouring of *Parsifal*. His chief inspiration was to come from an entirely different source, resulting in 1894 in a masterpiece unlike anything composed before, the *Prélude à l'Après-midi d'un faune* ('Prelude to the afternoon of a faun').

Debussy's interest in the arts generally was focused particularly on the painters of the Impressionist school headed by Claude Monet, and he translated the style of this movement into the world of music. His own Impressionism was a form of composition designed to evoke particular moods through rich, varied and often elusive, harmonies and instrumental timbres. His orchestral works in this style differ from Romantic programme music in that they do not tell stories or 'describe' detailed scenes: their aim is to conjure up a mood or atmosphere in very general terms, employing such means as a suggestive title, the occasional suggestion of natural sounds and evocative dance rhythms. His pieces are less strenuous and emphatic than a symphonic poem of Liszt or Franck, relying on 'themes' which might be only brief motifs combined into a musical mosaic. Colour thus becomes an all-important feature of his music, a feature which his imaginative command of the or-

Debussy, the most delicate and fastidious of stylists, who introduced Impressionism into music and effected a 'quiet revolution'

chestra allowed him to treat in a unique way. Because his rhythms are often as ambiguous as his melodies the structure of his music is fluid. It would be wrong, however, to think that because his music conveys often vague and dream-like impressions he was hazy in his craftsmanship: on the contrary, every note is set in its context with the utmost precision, as carefully as a brush-stroke in a Monet painting. No scores have ever been constructed with greater discipline and sense of order than the five superb orchestral pieces by Debussy. Five may seem a small number, but each one is an absolute masterpiece.

The *Prélude à l'Après-midi d'un faune*, inspired by a pastoral poem by Mallarmé, perfectly creates an amorous daydream in a score of unsurpassed voluptuousness and the utmost delicacy. Within the span of only nine minutes the music conjures up the faun drowsing in the afternoon sun, never certain whether the seductive nymphs who satisfy his desires are real creatures or dreamed. The magical spell begins with a meditative solo flute, then a woodwind chord, a rippling of harp colours and soft horn calls prepare for the most subtle example of musical scene-painting. Gradually the orchestra grows more animated, an ecstatic theme suggesting the vision of the nymphs, and with the same gentle inevitability it dies down again, through a passage for flutes, two solo violins, tremolo strings and hushed cymbals, to the drowsiness of the opening. Mallarmé, when he first heard the music, is reported to have said: 'I never expected anything like it. The music prolongs the emotion of my poem and paints its scenery more passionately than colours could.' Because Debussy made the scene almost visual, dancers have been unable to resist the piece. Nijinsky first choreographed it and danced in it for the Ballets Russes in 1912, and among the many subsequent versions have been Serge Lifar's, in the form of a solo dance, and the notable one by Jerome Robbins for New York City Ballet.

Nocturnes, which followed five years later, is a set of three movements giving impressions of the play of light in the evening. The first, 'Nuages' ('Clouds'), uses gently moving chords to suggest the lazy march of clouds across the sky, a wistful song for the cor anglais expressing the loneliness of the scene. The second, 'Fêtes', is altogether livelier, depicting a scene of constant revelry. It builds up into a march, bright with brass, which then dies away into the silence of the night. 'Sirènes' adds to the orchestra a choir of women's voices which sing wordlessly to suggest the alluring laughter of the Sirens teasing the crews of passing ships.

The sea was the subject of Debussy's next orchestral work, *La Mer*, a set of three symphonic sketches. Here again it would be unprofitable to look for any definite pictures or episodes, for the music does not present a sea-picture in the sense of Mendelssohn's *Hebrides* Overture. It has perhaps most fittingly been described as 'a seascape without figures', for it presents emotional responses to the sea itself, open water without men or ships upon it. Debussy did not compose this music, as might be imagined, on a Mediterranean beach but more prosaically at Eastbourne.

England also supplied a certain inspiration for 'Gigues', the first of the three orchestral *Images*, for it includes the tune 'The keel row'. The second of them, 'Iberia', has proved the most popular, and is often played on its own in the concert hall. It is more brightly coloured and extrovert than his other music, the composer responding warmly to the spirit of Spain even though he knew it only at second hand, having crossed the border just once for a brief visit to San Sebastian. The French 'panel' of the three *Images* is 'Rondes de printemps', an evocation of springtime dance festivities which makes use of two popular folksongs. Debussy's last orchestral work, *Jeux* ('Games'), was composed for the Ballets Russes and first performed in 1913 with choreography by Nijinsky of which the composer strongly disapproved. It has kept the stage, though the highly original music is heard much more frequently in the concert hall than in the theatre.

For a man who had such a considerable effect on music, Debussy led an uneventful life – apart from his two marriages and many love affairs. On his first wedding morning, in 1899, he had to give a piano lesson to pay for the reception, but his second wife was a woman of some wealth, and by 1908 he was himself achieving financial security. A year later his health began to deteriorate, preventing his reaping the full rewards of his success, and on 25 March 1918 he died before the end of the war which had added despair to the pain he suffered in his last year.

Ravel

It is inevitable that the names of Debussy and Ravel should so often be coupled, for these outstanding French composers of the early twentieth century were equally fastidious stylists, of wide culture and interested in all the arts. It would be quite wrong, however, to look too hard for similarities in their music. Ravel was less revolutionary than Debussy, drawing much of his inspiration from the past and combining an almost neo-Classical concern for clear-cut melodies and forms with a Romantic fondness for pictorial descriptiveness. In contrast to his extrovert music, Maurice Ravel was a man of considerable reserve whose personal inhibitions distanced him even from his friends of longest standing. He was born at Ciboure of mixed Swiss and Basque descent on 7 March 1875, but grew up in Paris and studied at the Conservatoire there, remaining within the academic circle until he was thirty. Although clearly a musician of outstanding promise he was unsuccessful in his repeated attempts to win the Prix de Rome, and in 1905 he was eliminated by the jury in the early stages of the competition in spite of his list of compositions including the brilliant *Jeux d'eau* for piano and the three songs with orchestra, *Shéhérazade*, which have become classics.

Considering that Ravel is such a master of orchestral writing, comparable to Rimsky-Korsakov and Richard Strauss, it is surprising that so many of the works we hear in the concert hall were originally written for the piano. One of the most charming of these is the Suite *Ma Mère l'Oye* ('Mother Goose'), which he wrote in the form of piano duets in 1908

Ravel, whose glittering orchestral works include Daphnis and Chloe, La Valse *and other ballet scores equally popular in the concert hall*

for the children of some close friends. Two years later he orchestrated the five movements, and in 1912 the music was used for a ballet. The style conjures up a world of fairytale guaranteed to delight any child's imagination. The lucid scoring bears out Debussy's claim that Ravel possessed 'the finest ear that ever existed', for its colours are superbly blended and contrasted. Another piano work, a habanera, was drawn upon for the third movement of the *Rapsodie espagnole* (1907), an elaborate four-movement evocation of Spain scored for a large orchestra with a whole battery of percussion which is used to sparkling effect. *Le Tombeau de Couperin* (1917) was first written as a piano suite of six movements, each dedicated to the memory of friends killed in action during the war, but it is most familiar in the arrangement the composer subsequently made for small orchestra, in which two of the movements are omitted. As its title suggests, it represents Ravel's leanings towards a classical style, yet its piquant flavour is unmistakably modern. Another piano work familiar in its orchestral guise is the *Valses nobles et sentimentales*.

Ravel's music is always strong in rhythm, so it was only natural that he should have been asked to compose for the Ballets Russes in 1909 when Serge Diaghilev began to commission new scores for his company rather than use existing ones. He began work on *Daphnis and Chloe* without much enthusiasm, soon laying it aside in order to write the opera *L'Heure espagnole*. When he took up the ballet score again he did so with ever-increasing interest and lavished so much care on it that it was not completed until 1912. It is significant that Ravel designated *Daphnis and Chloe* as a *symphonie chorégraphique* because its score is constructed symphonically, with leitmotifs for Daphnis, Chloe and the other characters. A large orchestra is involved, and also a chorus of mixed voices who sing wordlessly. As it follows the story of the ballet, the music ranges through many moods, all of them clearly expressed in Ravel's exotic harmonies and magically evocative melodies. One of the greatest of all ballet scores, on a par with those of Tchaikovsky and Stravinsky, it stands on its purely musical merits as strongly as any symphony.

Ravel's rhythmic mastery is revealed in two definitive large-scale dance movements for orchestra, the *Boléro* (1927) and *La Valse* (1920). *Boléro* was written in response to a challenge to write an extensive piece based on pure repetition of musical material without variation. Ravel succeeded brilliantly, thanks to his skilful orchestration, building his exotic, hypnotic tune to a great climax and giving the piece its final twist in a surprise modulation (change of key) – the first in the piece. *La Valse* is a brilliant evocation

Set design by Bakst for the 1912 Fokine ballet of Ravel's Daphnis and Chloe, *in which the principal roles were danced by Karsavina and Nijinsky*

of the Viennese ballroom in which the waltz rhythm builds in great washes of sound to ever greater heights of delirium, exaggerated to the point of grotesque parody.

In contrast to these unique works, Ravel returned in 1931 to the Classical form of the piano concerto, composing two fine examples. The Piano Concerto in G major is an immediately appealing work, in keeping with the composer's own declaration that the music of a concerto should be 'light-hearted and brilliant, and not aim at profundity or dramatic effects'. Its flavour reminds us that jazz was very much in the air at the time; it was once said that it gives out a whiff of jazz every now and then 'just to show that father can still keep pace with the boys on their night out'. Ravel's Piano Concerto for the Left Hand was written for the Austrian pianist Paul Wittgenstein, who lost his right arm in the 1914–18 war. It is more dramatic in tone than the other concerto, compressed into one movement, and more heavily orchestrated, making it a formidable challenge to the player. Both concertos reveal Ravel's rare ability to combine Classical perfection of form with a modern tone of voice.

During the last few years of his life Ravel was prevented by illness from composing anything of consequence. His powers of speech and movement had been seriously affected by head injuries incurred in a car accident, though he remained perfectly clear in his mind. Apart from his concert tours, which had taken him to the United States as well as to most European countries, he had always led a fairly quiet domestic life, first with his parents and then with his brother; but now he was reduced to spending his time looking over the fields from the balcony of his villa. He hated this inactivity, frequently complaining, 'I've still so much music in my head.' He was never able to write it down, however, and it was a merciful release when he finally died on 28 December 1937.

SPAIN

For the greater part of three centuries Spanish music developed apart from the rest of Europe. The brilliant tradition of church and keyboard music dating from the Renaissance continued through the eighteenth century, and local forms of opera developed; but conditions were not propitious to the growth of orchestral music. The distinctively 'Spanish' style of music grew up in the *zarzuela* (a form of comic opera) and in folk music; but it was composers from elsewhere who first transplanted the style into orchestral music: Glinka (*Spanish Overture* and *Summer Night in Madrid*), Rimsky-Korsakov (*Spanish Capriccio*), Lalo (*Symphonie espagnole*) and Chabrier (*España*); while the nearest thing to a Spanish opera that we see regularly is Bizet's *Carmen*. These composers all found the Spanish idiom irresistible by virtue of its alluring melodies and vital yet elusive rhythms. Sometimes the flavour of their music is only of the travel poster variety, but in the case of *España* it is so authentic that Manuel de Falla once wrote: 'I venture to say that no Spaniard has succeeded better than Chabrier in giving us the version of a *jota* as it is "shouted" by the peasants of Aragón.'

Even when Spain finally entered the international music scene it was with two Catalan composers, Isaac Albéniz (1860–1909) and Enrique Granados (1867–1916), who devoted themselves almost exclusively to works for solo piano. Albéniz produced a youthful piano concerto in the rhetorical style of Liszt, with whom he studied in Rome and Weimar, but he was quick to realize that he would never master the medium of the orchestra. Granados tried his hand at a symphonic poem, *Dante*, and he also expanded his masterly piano suite *Goyescas* into an opera, from which the Intermezzo has become a popular concert piece; but like Albéniz he was at home only when writing for the keyboard.

By good fortune the greatest of all Spanish composers was a man so completely characteristic of his country that his music was able to express its very soul. Manuel de Falla was born at Cádiz on 23 November 1876 into a well-to-do musical family, receiving his first piano lessons from his mother. From his earliest days he exerted the strictest artistic self-discipline. He studied first at Cádiz, then in Madrid with Felipe Pedrell, a champion of Spanish folk music. Falla learnt from him to identify with the native music of Spain, and under this influence he composed his masterly two-act opera *La vida breve* ('Life is short'). This gave him the confidence to embark seriously on a career as a composer, so at thirty-one

he set off to Paris, where he remained for seven years, moving in the circle of Debussy, Ravel and Stravinsky. French composers were at that time keenly interested in the Spanish idiom, and Falla found in their Impressionism a technique which might have been made to measure for the musical style he was developing. He began work on his *Nights in the Gardens of Spain*, which he described as 'symphonic impressions for piano and orchestra', in 1909, though he did not complete it until seven years later after he had returned to Spain. Its music evokes scenes and memories, but is not programmatic: the three nocturnes simply express poetic moods of sensuous charm with undercurrents of characteristic Spanish melancholy and a tragic sense of life. The whole work is alive with colours subjected to the play

Falla, the most distinguished of modern Spanish composers, all of whose music is characterized by his colourful native idiom

of different lights and shadows, a wonderful evocation of Spain.

Falla's two most familiar concert works are suites drawn from ballets, their music appropriately embodying all the characteristic features of the Andalusian style. *El amor brujo* ('Love the magician') was written in the white heat of inspiration in 1915 for Pastora Imperio, the most celebrated of all flamenco dancers. The scenario deals with a loving couple whose courtship is menaced by the ghost of a former lover of the girl, and their successful outwitting of this vengeful spirit. Falla's music is overpoweringly effective, most of all in the 'Ritual Fire Dance', of which he later made a brilliant piano arrangement and which has become one of those tunes played by every conceivable instrument or ensemble. In con-

trast to the barbaric force of this and the 'Dance of Terror' are enchantingly delicate sections such as the 'Pantomime' with its poignantly beautiful melody in the tempo of a Cádiz tango. The whole score is the very essence of Andalusian music, though it does not draw on a single folktune, and its orchestration places Falla on a par with Rimsky-Korsakov and Ravel.

For *El sombrero de tres picos* ('The three-cornered hat'), Falla turned to a peasant folk-tale about the humiliating of a pompous *corregidor* (village magistrate) who tries to seduce the wife of a miller. It was first staged as a mime-play in Madrid in 1917, then revised in 1919 for Diaghilev's Ballets Russes with choreography by Léonide Massine and designs by Picasso. An elaborate work, its music creates the per-

Picasso costume design for The Three-cornered Hat, *Falla's best-known score for Diaghilev's Ballets Russes and a popular concert work*

John Williams (left) and Julian Bream, two great virtuosos who have continued the long tradition of guitar and lute playing

fect atmosphere for the different scenes, a sultry working afternoon and a starlit, mysterious night of revelry, as well as providing dances appropriate to the individual characters. Actual folktunes are included, though the main dances – the miller's *farruca* and the hectic *jota* of the final scene – have original melodies. The composer's orchestral mastery is superb. It is surprising that he completed no other work for full instrumental forces. His Harpsichord Concerto, written in 1926 for Wanda Landowska, has only five accompanying instruments, marking a new austerity of style.

The horrors of the Civil War made Falla withdraw into himself, his health becoming so undermined that he did not leave his house for a period of four years. He was invited in 1939 to give a concert tour in Argentina, and once there he decided to make the country his home. In these last years he grew reclusive, living up to Stravinsky's description of him as 'withdrawn as an oyster' and 'unpityingly religious', devoting his creative energies to a project which had occupied his mind ever since the 1920s, the setting of an epic Catalan poem combining the legend of lost Atlantis with a pageant of Spanish history. The score of *La Atlántida*, which he left incomplete on his death on 14 November 1946, was finished by his friend and pupil Ernest Halffter. Sadly, none of the Spanish composers who followed Falla has matched his genius.

Some attractive orchestral music was composed by Joaquín Turina (1882–1949) and Jesús Guridi (1886–1961), the former's *Sinfonia sevillana* and the latter's symphonic poems *Una aventura de Don Quixote* and *Leyenda Vasca* both drawing strongly on the Spanish idiom. Their music has been little performed outside Spain. Widely popular, on the other hand, is some of the music of Joaquín Rodrigo, born at Sagunto on 22 November 1902, who has pursued a remarkably active career in spite of the blindness that overtook him at the age of three. His leaning has always been towards Classical forms, in particular that of the concerto, writing such works for piano, violin, cello, harp and, commissioned by James Galway, flute. Naturally for a Spaniard, his two finest concertos feature the guitar, the *Concierto de Aranjuez* and the *Fantasia para un gentilhombre*, the former having become the most celebrated of all works for guitar and orchestra. It succeeds miraculously in pitting the intimate sound of the solo instrument against the weight of the orchestra. The central Adagio is the most expressive and subtle of the three movements, a set of variations, while the Finale subjects a single theme to continual exploration of sparkling contrapuntal vivacity.

Rodrigo, the blind composer whose Concierto de Aranjuez *has become the most popular of all guitar concertos*

A major problem for Spanish music since 1939 has been that many composers left their homeland after its Civil War and have lived in exile, sometimes becoming absorbed into the cultural styles of the countries they adopted. One who chose England, Roberto Gerhard (1896–1970), had previously worked in Germany under Schoenberg and developed a keen interest in twelve-note and serial techniques; his music has little Spanish character. He came eventually to regard himself as an English composer, but his style is best described as cosmopolitan. His Concerto for Orchestra, Violin Concerto and several symphonies certainly prove him a most accomplished and original composer, and he exerted a considerable influence on the musical scene in England even though his works remain outside the general repertoire.

RUSSIA

For centuries Russian music existed solely in two forms, folk music on the one hand, the chants of the Russian Orthodox Church on the other. All types of art music were imported from the West, usually from Italy. There were a few native Russian composers, among whom Dmitri Bortniansky (1751–1825) made genuine efforts to implant some kind of Russian idiom into the choral and instrumental music he wrote after being sent by Catherine the Great to study in Italy. Establishing a national style, however, was an uphill battle, because there was no conservatoire in Russia, so that composers were obliged to seek their training in Germany or Italy. Furthermore, audiences in the concert hall or opera house looked down on anything which drew its inspiration from folk art. Even Mikhail Glinka (1804–57), who came to be regarded as the 'father of Russian music', was obliged to study abroad and had some of his operatic music dismissed as 'the kind of stuff coachmen whistle in the streets'. Like his successors Alexander Dargomijsky (1813–69) and Modest Mussorgsky (1839–81), Glinka was almost exclusively concerned with opera, leaving no orchestral works of note; but the lead he gave in seriously attempting to establish a Russian school of music was important for all types of music. Largely due to him a group of mainly amateur composers known as the 'Five' came into existence, and though they soon went their own ways, their shared ideals finally brought to birth the kind of music we recognize as Russian.

They were a curious group, consisting of Mily Balakirev, its leader and a highly capable conductor; Mussorgsky, a government clerk; César Cui, a military officer; Borodin, a research chemist; and Rimsky-Korsakov, a naval officer. Balakirev, born at Nizhny-Novgorod on 2 January 1837, failed to organize his remarkable talents and his career followed an erratic course as he took up one teaching or conducting post after another in the effort to establish the nationalist cause. He composed slowly, completing very few works, yet his influence was considerable. The Piano Concerto No 1 in F sharp minor, written when he was only eighteen, has an individual Russian flavour in spite of showing the influence of Chopin. The Symphony No 1 in C major is his most extended work, so full of originality and charm that it deserves to be heard more often, though it is less immediately striking than the masterly symphonic poem *Thamar*, overwhelming in its opulence of sound. *Thamar* had a direct influence on Rimsky-Korsakov's *Scheherazade* and also on Debussy's *L'Après-midi d'un faune*. Balakirev's fanaticism alienated the younger composers who had joined his cause, and who consequently deserted him to go their separate ways. He died at St Petersburg on 29 May 1910 a disappointed man, though he had lived to see Russian music truly established.

Cui (1835–1918) fared even more unhappily, for his many works are virtually forgotten. With Mussorgsky's genius directed towards opera, it was left to Borodin and Rimsky-Korsakov to compete with the more cosmopolitan Tchaikovsky in the concert hall.

Borodin

The illegitimate son of a prince, Alexander Borodin was born in St Petersburg on 12 November 1833 and given the name of one of his father's servants. Although he showed early musical talent, composing several chamber works in his teens, he was encouraged to study for a medical career and developed a passionate, lifelong interest in chemistry. On the musical front he began with a keen admiration for Mendelssohn, which after meetings with Mussorgsky widened to embrace similar sympathies for Schumann and Glinka, and then after coming into contact with Balakirev in 1862 he took up the nationalist cause. Although he always regarded composition as secondary to his scientific work, he took it seriously enough to produce a small number of major works which make up in quality what they lack in quantity. His opera *Prince Igor*, for instance, was begun about 1870, but remained incomplete on his death seventeen years later. It is mentioned here because the Polovtsian Dances from its second act are popular in the concert hall. Furthermore, their style is clearly discernible in all three of his symphonies.

Of the three symphonies, only the first two were completed by his death. No 1 in E flat appeared in 1867, but had to wait two years for its first public performance. It showed immediately that for all his amateur status he was quite capable of sustaining the complex form of the symphony. A persuasive case has been put forward, in fact, that his symphonies are more thoughtfully developed as well as more truly Russian in spirit than those of Tchaikovsky, though they have never attained the same degree of popularity. They all express, moreover, his strong individual qualities, a sure command of both the epic and the intimate, and a melodic style which combines Western and Oriental elements, the result no doubt of his mixed Russian and Caucasian ancestry.

With the Symphony No 2 in B minor, completed in 1876 after many interruptions, Borodin fully revealed his originality. There are suggestions in the

The Russian Five, the composers who set out to create a truly national style. Above: *Borodin;* Opposite, clockwise from upper left: *Cui, Balakirev, Mussorgsky and Rimsky-Korsakov*

music of a medieval Russian pageant, complete with warriors, troubadours and legendary heroes, yet there is no loss of formal control. The power and brilliance of the orchestration helps to make the work one of the most impressive of all Russian symphonies, and one which has retained its popularity with audiences everywhere.

One of Borodin's shorter pieces, the orchestral sketch *In the Steppes of Central Asia* (1880), is still a concert hall favourite and the obvious inspiration of Rimsky-Korsakov's even more celebrated *Scheherazade.* Though too short to be considered a major work, it epitomises the blend of the Oriental and the Russian in his music. Composed as incidental music for one of a series of *tableaux vivants* of episodes from Russian history, devised to celebrate the twenty-fifth anniversary of the reign of Alexander II, it depicts an Eastern caravan crossing the steppes with an escort of Russian soldiers. As a tone poem it is brilliantly descriptive, revealing the remarkable command of orchestration that this self-taught amateur composer had developed over the years. His professional colleagues might have regarded Borodin's death in St Petersburg on 27 February 1887 as a loss to science, but later generations would agree that it was a far greater loss to music.

Rimsky-Korsakov

The most gifted and most fortunate of the Russian nationalist composers was Nikolai Rimsky-Korsakov. He was born at Tikhvin on 6 March 1844 into a wealthy, music-loving family, but although he showed considerable aptitude for the piano as a child his chief ambition was to follow his elder brother into a naval career. At the age of twelve he accordingly entered the Naval College in St Petersburg, where the richness of the city's musical life seems to have given him second thoughts about his future. The opera made a lasting impression on him, though his earliest compositions were to be in the instrumental and orchestral fields. His music teacher introduced him to Balakirev, who suggested that the fledgling composer, then eighteen, should try writing a symphony. Rimsky-Korsakov took the advice seriously and began the Symphony No 1 in E flat, but any immediate hopes of making a musical career were dashed when his naval duties took him to sea for a period of three years. He continued work on the symphony nonetheless, actually completing it on board his ship while it lay at anchor in Gravesend Harbour on a visit to England. The work was given its first performance on his return to St Petersburg at the age of twenty-one. It is not particularly individ-

85

Set design for the Polovtsian Dances from Borodin's Prince Igor. *The ballet has been revived many times, and the music is often played as a concert suite*

ual, partly because of its composer's inexperience, but mainly because his talent was not suited to conventional forms.

Fortunately he was quick to realize the true nature of his creative gift, which was the ability to conjure up worlds of fantasy allied to a remarkable, indeed unique command of orchestral colour. Just as his best operas were fairy tales peopled by dream-like characters, so his orchestral music took the form of freely constructed symphonic suites with exotic or magical programmes. Three years after the nondescript symphony came *Antar*, based on an Oriental fairytale, and already the characteristics of his mature works become evident, sinuous melodies and brilliant colouring anticipating the more celebrated *Scheherazade*. The success of *Antar* (sometimes called the Symphony No 2) led to his being offered the post of professor of composition at the St Petersburg Con-

servatoire in 1871, when he was only twenty-seven. He was allowed to accept by the naval authorities, who conveniently appointed him Inspector of Military Bands two years later, enabling him to devote his full attention to the study of orchestration. He turned more and more to the opera about his time, though in his operas the orchestra rather than the voice plays the more memorable part.

Half of Rimsky's best-known orchestral works are in fact suites drawn from the operas, suites which include such popular pieces as 'The flight of the bumble bee' (from *Tsar Sultan*) and 'The dance of the tumblers' (from *The Snow Maiden*). Among the true orchestral works, the colourful virtuosity of the *Capriccio espagnol* may have been equalled in orchestral showpieces by Stravinsky and Ravel, but it has never been surpassed; while *Scheherazade* exerts a magic of its own. The stories of the *Arabian Nights' Entertainments* made an immediate appeal to Rimsky-Korsakov, and he must have delighted in the idea behind them. They are supposedly related by the quick-witted Scheherazade to her husband the Sultan, who

Nijinsky as the Golden Slave in the Fokine ballet Scheherazade *created to the exotic symphonic suite by Rimsky-Korsakov*

Princess, the Baghdad festival and the ship that is dashed against the rock bearing the statue of the bronze warrior. He warned the listener, however, not to pay too much literal attention to his motto themes. 'These are no more,' he wrote, 'than purely musical material or themes for symphonic development . . . Appearing as they do each time under different moods, the self-same themes correspond each time to different images, actions and pictures.' By allowing himself complete musical freedom, rather than tying himself down to literal story-telling in musical terms, the composer gives the listener the corresponding freedom in his imaginative response. It is this unique aspect of *Scheherazade*, a bonus to its wealth of melody and its dazzling orchestration, which makes it so fascinating.

It is not too fanciful to suppose that the composer's liking of magical adventures was a compensation for his uneventful personal life, which was exclusively devoted to composition and teaching. (Among his pupils was the young Igor Stravinsky.) He worked so hard, in fact, that he suffered a period of nervous exhaustion for two years, fortunately recovering to enjoy a further seventeen years of intense creativity, becoming the most popular and most powerful figure in Russian music. When he died in St Petersburg on 21 June 1908 he was regarded as the country's greatest composer, and it was some time before changing tastes relegated him below Tchaikovsky in the field of orchestral music and Mussorgsky in the opera.

Tchaikovsky

If Tchaikovsky had not existed, Hollywood would surely have invented him. He lives up to the popular image of the neurotic composer by virtue of his hyper-sensitive nature, by a marriage that was brief and ludicrous even by Hollywood standards, and by his astonishing friendship with a wealthy patron, Mme von Meck, whom he glimpsed only once when the carriages in which they were travelling happened to pass in the street. Finally he died of cholera, brought on by drinking a glass of unfiltered water in a restaurant, just nine days after conducting the first performance of the *Pathétique* Symphony whose final movement has been described as carrying composer and listener 'to the very brink of the grave'. This generally accepted portrait of Peter Ilyich Tchaikovsky should be treated with some caution, however, for it is a little too good to be true. Almost all composers have been sensitive souls, most suffered the disappointment of having their works initially received with some critical coolness, and many have displayed a certain degree of eccentricity in one form

has vowed to put to death each of his successive wives after the first night of marriage. In order to stay alive she thinks up such irresistible stories for a thousand and one nights that the Sultan continues to put off her execution until he finally decides he cannot live without her. (Her stories are certainly more entertaining than the television serials apparently inspired by her success.) It was the exotic setting and sense of utter fantasy of the stories, rather than the actual adventures they recounted, which attracted the composer, so the symphonic suite is not in any way like such Richard Strauss tone poems as *Don Juan* and *Till Eulenspiegel*, in which the listener can follow the programme detail by detail. Rimsky-Korsakov explained in his autobiography that he had four separate episodes from *The Arabian Nights* in mind when he composed *Scheherazade*: the narrative of Prince Kalandar, the story of the Prince and the

or another. Tchaikovsky was in fact more fortunate than many other composers: the generosity of Mme von Meck gave him financial security for many years, his marriage was a cloud which passed over in a matter of weeks, he enjoyed happy travels abroad to meet other famous personalities of the time, and a good deal of his work quickly became popular with the public. Also, it should be stressed that much of his music is sunnily melodic and much is high-spirited.

Although he showed considerable aptitude for the piano as a child, Tchaikovsky could not expect much encouragement in the unmusical town of Votinsk, where he was born on 7 May 1840. When the family moved to St Petersburg eight years later he was sent to a boarding school, where he spent a year of considerable misery, then after his parents left the city he was allowed to live with various family friends during his early period as a student at the School of Jurisprudence. Although he went on to complete his law studies his mind must have been more concerned with music, for about this time he began to compose as well as play the piano. The death of his mother from cholera in 1854 affected him deeply, almost certainly implanting in him the streak of morbid pessimism which was to overshadow the rest of his life, as though he knew he would himself die from the same terrible disease. Four years later he graduated as a lawyer and secured a minor post at the Ministry of Justice, where he does not seem to have taken his work too seriously. An amusing anecdote related by his brother Modest describes how he once absent-mindedly chewed to pieces an important official document he was delivering from one department to another. In 1862, at the age of twenty-two, he made the bold decision to take up a musical career and enrolled in the new St Petersburg Conservatoire founded by the pianist-composer Anton Rubinstein.

At this time Tchaikovsky had only an amateur's knowledge of music, appearing to have no inkling at all about Schumann's work or even to be certain as to the number of Beethoven symphonies. It should be remembered that St Petersburg, though an important and beautiful city, had no great musical life: concerts were mostly given by amateur orchestras, and the repertoire was chosen by those composers who had been imported from France, Germany and Italy and so reflected their own particular tastes. There was a body of church and folk music, but in other respects Russian music had only begun with Glinka (1804–57), whose opera *A Life for the Tsar* was first performed in 1836. With his entry as a student at the Conservatoire Tchaikovsky's horizons were widened, because Rubinstein, though conservative

Tchaikovsky in academic guise on 13 June 1893, five months before his death, when Cambridge University conferred a doctorate of music on him

in his teaching, was forward-looking in the concerts which he directed for the Imperial Music Society, introducing works by Liszt, Berlioz and Wagner. Tchaikovsky's compositions of this period did not show any outstanding promise, but he must have made a good impression as a student, because when Nicholas Rubinstein, Anton's brother, decided to open a conservatoire in Moscow he invited the young man to join him in 1866 as a teacher of theory. The salary was small, but at least Tchaikovsky had finally become a professional musician. He found Moscow a more congenial place than St Petersburg, but he was slow to make any headway creatively. His Symphony No 1 in G minor, rich in invention if rather weak in formal construction, was poorly received in 1866, when only two of its four movements were played. He was not consoled until two years later when Mily Balakirev, who had succeeded Anton Rubinstein as director of the Imperial Music Society, arranged for a complete performance which proved an extraordinary success. Tchaikovsky, scarcely able to believe this turn for the better, appeared on the platform to acknowledge the applause holding his

Nadezhda von Meck, the wealthy patroness who gave Tchaikovsky financial independence but never met him

hat in his hand and looking as scared as the proverbial rabbit.

Balakirev was his good angel once again in 1869, when he suggested that Tchaikovsky should compose a work on the theme of *Romeo and Juliet*. Although Balakirev was only four years his senior, and was destined to be completely overshadowed by the younger man, Tchaikovsky regarded him with veneration at that time and was immensely flattered by his suggestion to take on such an ambitious project as this fantasy overture. All through the period of its composition he sent draft after draft of the music to Balakirev for his approval and made numerous alterations to the score in deference to his advice and criticisms. *Romeo and Juliet* was completed in November of that year and played with considerable success the following March. Tchaikovsky was still not satisfied, however, revising it a few months later into the form we know it today. Its composition gave him a good deal of trouble, but its lasting popularity proves that it was worth all the care he lavished on it. His first undoubted masterpiece, this so-called Fantasy Overture is really a symphonic poem, a more

successful one, incidentally, than any by Liszt. It does not attempt to tell literally the story of the star-crossed lovers of Verona, but in its portrayal of Friar Laurence on solemn bassoons and horns and its haunting love themes, of which the principal one is among the most beautiful melodies ever composed, it is a triumph of musical characterization. A sense of drama is created by the contrast between the love music and the powerful, strongly rhythmic allegro theme depicting the warring families of Montagues and Capulets. The work combines the passionate melodic spontaneity of a composer who has just discovered himself with a remarkable mastery of form.

If Tchaikovsky appears to have been moving very slowly in the field of orchestral compositions this was largely because he was much concerned at that time with opera, a form in which it took him several years to find his feet. It certainly strikes us today as a pity that he allowed three years to elapse between *Romeo and Juliet* and his Symphony No 2 in C minor, known as the 'Little Russian' on account of its use of Ukrainian (or 'Little Russian') folk tunes. It was given with great success in 1873, but again the self-critical composer decided on drastic revision. Representing a considerable step forward in close symphonic thinking on his first symphony, it is a work of warm melodic appeal which also springs a variety of harmonic and rhythmical surprises. Although Tchaikovsky never belonged to the Russian nationalist school he was the first composer to show that folk material could profitably be incorporated into the symphony (a practice which Shostakovich was later to follow with equal success). The work has remained the most popular of his early symphonies because it is formally satisfying as well as providing the wealth of fine tunes and glowing orchestral colours that make Tchaikovsky such a favourite with the large public audience. The Symphony No 3 in D major, which followed in 1875, is a curious step backwards, more of a suite than a true symphony in its five movements, though its music is highly enjoyable on its own terms. In historical terms it is important for the new expressive intensity of its slow movement, an Andante elegiaco, and because Tchaikovsky, following the example of Berlioz in the *Symphonie fantastique*, introduces a waltz into the symphony. The finale is a Polonaise, which prompted the title 'Polish' being given to the symphony when it was played in London in 1899. One English musicologist has claimed that Tchaikovsky did not object to this name being attached to it, which was hardly surprising as he had then been dead for six years! The composer, in fact, never considered any such title.

That same year of 1875 saw the first performance 89

The country home of Tchaikovsky near Klin, now a museum, where he spent most of his last years in comfortable seclusion close to nature

of the famous (some critics would say notorious) Piano Concerto No 1 in B flat minor, which was the cause of a bitter breach between Tchaikovsky and Nicholas Rubinstein, to whom he had intended dedicating the work. The composer, then thirty-four and just beginning to feel confident in his abilities, played the concerto privately on Christmas Eve, 1874, to Rubinstein and a few other friends. At the end, his respected colleague denounced it as 'worthless and unplayable', adding that many of its passages were 'manufactured and clumsy beyond possible correction' and its whole conception was 'trivial and commonplace'. Though utterly mortified by this criticism, Tchaikovsky fortunately had the courage of his convictions and went ahead with the orchestration, which he completed within a couple of months. He then dedicated the concerto to Hans von Bülow, who gave the first performance in Boston on 25 October 1875, during a tour of the United States. Six weeks later its Russian premiere was an immediate success with the public. It is pleasant to record that Tchaikovsky and Rubinstein were reconciled several years later, and that the latter eventually became one of the concerto's most enthusiastic exponents. We should not be too hard on Rubinstein, for the piano part is tremendously difficult to play and some of its more spectacular passages are undeniably vulgar in their obvious attempt to raise the roof. On the other hand, the concerto is full of memorable tunes and brilliant touches of orchestral colour, and the fact that it has attracted the world's leading pianists and conductors for more than a century indicates that it is neither unplayable nor trivial. Its popularity, which extends to a vast number of people who rarely, if ever, go to symphony concerts, has caused some academics to look down their noses at it, but such snobbery does not alter the fact that it is a very fine concerto by any standards. Two other piano concertos are less impressive, No 2 in G major being so repetitive that its melodies outstay their welcome,

and the meandering No 3 in E flat, of which only one
movement was completed, having a principal melody
which to Anglo-Saxon ears is embarrassingly reminiscent of the song 'What shall we do with the drunken sailor'. The Violin Concerto in D major, however,
is deservedly a favourite repertoire work, ably constructed, rewarding to the soloist in spite of its technical hazards, and both exciting and melodically
attractive to the listener. An unusual work for solo
cello and orchestra, the *Variations on a Rococo Theme*
finds Tchaikovsky writing with almost Classical elegance. With the Dvořák and Elgar concertos it tops
the list of concert cello works.

Tchaikovsky's life reached crisis point in 1877
when, with several major works to his credit, he was
beginning to find his professional duties at the Moscow Conservatoire not only irksome but a hindrance
to the more important call of composition. He was
also finding it increasingly difficult to live with the
knowledge that he was homosexual, so in a desperate
attempt to 'go straight' he decided on marriage. It is
unlikely that this step could have had a happy outcome even with a sympathetic, understanding
woman, and it was downright impossible with the
one he chose, Antonina Milyukova, one of his students, who happened to have an insatiable sexual
appetite. Within a few weeks the desperate composer
had twice deserted his wife and attempted suicide,
and he was saved only by being packed off to Switzerland. There, out of the blue, came the offer by Mme
von Meck to make him a generous annual allowance
to enable him to give up teaching and devote all his
attention to composition. It also meant that he was
free to travel, so he moved on to Venice to complete
the symphony he had begun earlier in the year but
which he had laid aside to work on his opera *Eugene
Onegin*. He had to send home for the draft of the
score, which was then lost for a time by the Venice
post office (Italian postal services being as inefficient
then as they are today); but at last he was able to
produce his finest symphony, No 4 in F minor.

This symphony deserves special attention because
it is the only one to which Tchaikovsky provided a
definite programme and therefore gives us an insight
into his personality. He revealed the ideas behind
each of its movements in a series of letters to Mme
von Meck, declaring also that 'never before have I
felt such affection to any of my compositions'. He
described the ominous theme which horns and bassoons thunder out at the beginning of the Introduction as representing 'Fate, the inevitable power that
hangs over our heads like some Damoclean sword'.
The second movement, an Andantino, 'shows suffering in another stage. It is a feeling of melancholy

Benois design for the Rat Soldier in The Nutcracker,
Tchaikovsky's happiest and most easy-going ballet score

such as fills one when sitting at home exhausted by
work; the book has slipped from one's hand; a swarm
of memories fills the mind . . . We regret the past,
yet we have neither the courage nor the desire to
begin life anew'. Concerning the Scherzo he recorded
that 'no definite feelings find expression here. We
think of nothing, but give free rein to the fancy,
which humours itself by evolving the most singular
patterns. Suddenly there arises the memory of a
drunken peasant and a ribald song . . . Military music passes in the distance'. The note regarding the
last movement reveals that Tchaikovsky was not the
negative pessimist he has sometimes been thought:
'If you can find no pleasure in yourself, look about
you. Mix with the people . . . A popular festival is
depicted . . . How merry they all are! And do you
still say that the world is steeped in grief? No, there
is such a thing as joy . . . Rejoice in the happiness of
others, and it will still be possible for you to live.' If 91

there is some contradiction in this programme for the symphony, there is an even greater contradiction when we analyze the symphony itself, for it is so skilfully organized on purely musical lines that it makes compulsive listening without recourse to any programme. The work is full of contrasts, yet these are brilliantly integrated, the music being constructed according to a pattern as subtle and logical as that of any Classical symphony, though very different in kind.

The two later numbered symphonies, No 5 in E minor and No 6 in B minor, the *Pathétique*, are similarly large-scale and have achieved the same degree of popularity as No 4. Both have come in for some critical disapproval, probably because they *are* so popular with the concert-goer all over the world. It is significant too that the musical experts who disapprove of Tchaikovsky tend to be negative in their approach, complaining about qualities which are absent from his symphonies rather than drawing attention to the many impressive and highly individual qualities they actually do possess. The very originality which the general public accepts with pleasure often baffles the experts. On the strength of the symphonies Nos 4, 5 and 6, with their wealth of memorable melody, their richness of orchestration and the masterly organization of their material, Tchaikovsky earns a place among the greatest symphonists. His last word on the subject, the concluding Adagio of the *Pathétique*, forged an entirely new path which later composers such as Mahler found ideal for their own symphonic journeyings.

In addition to symphonies, concertos and dramatic overtures, suites from the ballets *Swan Lake*, *The Sleeping Beauty* and *The Nutcracker* feature regularly in concert programmes, for Tchaikovsky was the first composer to provide music for the ballet which can justly be said to stand on its own feet and not simply serve those of the dancers. His was a case of the right man appearing at the right time, because while the ballet in Western Europe suffered a severe decline in the second half of the nineteenth century, it entered a period of glory in St Petersburg under the directorship of Marius Petipa (1818–1910), a French dancer, choreographer and ballet master who first went to Russia in 1847. Classical ballet became ever more refined yet also more dramatic in the hands of Petipa, who naturally welcomed the rich and powerful music of Tchaikovsky after the scores so limply put together by tea-shop tunesmiths like Ludwig Minkus (1827–1907) with whom he had previously worked.

At first the Russian audiences complained that Tchaikovsky's ballet music was 'too symphonic', a reproach the composer most probably accepted as a compliment, for in his skilful use of key structure and his imaginative balance of symphonic passages with lighter dance music for the virtuoso *divertissements* he had deliberately set out to create what might be called symphonic ballets. He must have taken delight in writing this music, for whereas his later symphonies express the unhappy, introvert side of his nature, the ballet scores seem to recall the joy of his happy childhood, especially in *The Sleeping Beauty* and *Nutcracker* with their fairytale atmosphere. They also gave him the perfect opportunity to indulge his love of pretty tunes with an exotic flavour. The composer whose symphonies Nos 4 and 6 are filled with thoughts of suffering and death escaped into the witty, carefree dance music for Puss in Boots and the White Cat, Florine and the Blue Bird, the love music for Aurora and Désiré in *The Sleeping Beauty*, the charm of the Arabian and Chinese Dance and Waltz of the Flowers in *Nutcracker*. His ballet music has remained unsurpassed, though it has been equalled by Stravinsky in a very different style. Like the gentle Serenade for Strings and the noisy 1812 Overture, it reminds us that Tchaikovsky was not always the gloomy soul-baring composer that legend would have us believe.

Rachmaninov

The style of Tchaikovsky, which combined nationalism with a late Romantic idiom, was so popular with Russian audiences that it is hardly surprising many young composers followed the same path. The most successful was Sergei Rachmaninov, born on 1 April 1873 into an aristocratic, land-owning family at Oneg in a province lying between Moscow and St Petersburg. His father was so extravagant and impractical that the family fortune declined until he was forced to sell off his estate. When the parents later separated, Sergei went with his mother to St Petersburg, where he entered the Conservatoire at the age of ten and became the star student. He went on to Moscow, where he played his First Piano Concerto at a public concert two weeks before his nineteenth birthday and saw his first opera, *Aleko*, produced in the following year. These youthful successes brought little financial reward, and on completing his studies he was obliged to take up teaching and routine work as an accompanist, much to his distaste. It was not until 1897 that he made a really ambitious bid to establish himself as a composer, but his First Symphony was so poorly conducted by Glazunov in St Petersburg in 1897 that Rachmaninov actually left the hall for a time. He later recalled the performance as 'indescribable torture'. He never published the symphony, and even destroyed the manuscript score. It was not performed again during his lifetime, but in 1945 was reconstructed from the orchestral parts and was immediately recognized as being superior to the two later symphonies.

For two years Rachmaninov was inconsolable, the humiliation of his failure convincing him that his career as a composer was over, and he withdrew into seclusion to lick his wounds. His friends, worried by his ever-increasing despair and depression, finally persuaded him to consult Dr Nikolai Dahl, a distinguished psychoanalyst who was also an enthusiastic amateur musician and could therefore be relied upon to take a special interest in his patient. The good Dr Dahl deserves the world's gratitude for successfully ridding Rachmaninov from his burden of anxiety and frustration. His help was certainly appreciated by the composer, who dedicated to him the Piano Concerto (No 2) that he completed after his recovery, one of the most popular ever written. With this triumph in 1901 he found himself in constant demand as pianist and conductor. Five years later he left Moscow to live in Dresden, where he found the peace and quiet to compose another symphony and the tone poem *The Isle of the Dead*. In 1908 he was lured back to Moscow, but only for a brief visit, for he was about to embark on the restless life of the international concert pianist. He became one of the most celebrated pianists of all time, bringing a prodigious technique and outstanding interpretative sensitivity to the works of Schumann, Liszt and Chopin as well as giving definitive performances of his own piano compositions. After the Russian Revolution he made his home in the United States, which he left only for his European concert tours. As time went by he lost the inspiration to compose, but he continued to dazzle the public with his playing to the end, his last concert taking place only a few weeks before his death in Beverly Hills on 28 March 1943.

In form and style Rachmaninov's music belongs to the nineteenth century, for it is tonal and follows traditional symphonic lines. It is nevertheless highly personal, so that none of his symphonies and concertos, or the brilliant *Rhapsody on a Theme of Paganini* for piano and orchestra could be mistaken for the work of any other Russian composer. It is the mark of the great composer that his music should be immediately recognizable from even a few bars, and Rachmaninov is assured of his place in musical history. Critics have complained that he is prone to fall back on alluring melodies with an undeniably sentimental appeal. These can be justified, however, because they sincerely express his musical personality. They should be judged on their own merits; they can

only be admired in the piano concertos even if they are less successful in the symphonies.

The early Piano Concerto No 1 in F sharp minor was revised by Rachmaninov in 1917, but while he made the treatment of the thematic material rather more sophisticated he wisely retained its youthful impetuosity. Though more boisterous than the later concertos, it features the kind of haunting slow melodies which distinguish his more mature style and the writing for the piano makes it clear that he had a natural grasp of its expressive potential similar to that of Liszt and Chopin. Its weakness lies in the last movement; its fast sections are simply brash and noisy, while its main feature is yet another reflective slow melody. The Piano Concerto No 2 in C minor suffers from no such defect, for it provides the thematic contrasts which are needed to sustain interest and create a sense of symphonic tensions. Again it is the slower, long-breathed melodies which dominate, but both main subjects in the first movement have an urgency that saves them from cloying, and the music is spiced with writing of such sparkle for the soloist that the total effect is one of exhilaration. The Finale also has a second theme of a languorous character, but the main theme is so ebullient that this lyrical relief has a completely logical place in the scheme of the movement. The Piano Concerto No 3 in D minor is altogether more ambitious and elaborate, and with the Brahms concertos the most difficult in the repertoire. The premiere in New York in 1909 was not the success Rachmaninov had hoped for, but when he played it there a few months later with Gustav Mahler conducting, its full grandeur was revealed. It is recognized as one of the most original works in the form. In addition to the Rachmaninov's characteristic melodic appeal, it reveals more intensity of expression and greater assurance and imagination in the orchestral writing.

After a disappointing Fourth Piano Concerto, which is rarely performed, Rachmaninov produced a final masterpiece for piano and orchestra in the *Rhapsody on a Theme of Paganini* (1934) which is more accurately described as a set of variations. The theme, taken from a set of Caprices for unaccompanied violin had previously been adopted by Brahms and Liszt and has attracted other composers after Rachmaninov. Rachmaninov's treatment of the theme is perhaps the most successful of all, the twenty-four variations ranging so wide that they exploit every aspect of pianism with such subtlety that it is sometimes difficult to spot the theme itself under its different disguises. This need not worry the ordinary listener, however, for the whole work affords a feast of melody and virtuosity as well as revealing the composer as a master of variation form comparable to Brahms and Elgar.

The symphonies lapsed from critical favour during the anti-Romantic trend of the middle of the century, but they were rehabilitated with the virtual re-discovery of Symphony No 1 in D minor. It was seen to be a natural successor to the symphonies of Borodin and Tchaikovsky, yet a work of considerable power with a voice of its own. Its tone is more heroic than that of the two later symphonies, and its somewhat sterner themes are treated with discipline. Had it not been so disastrously performed at its premiere in

Rachmaninov, who spent half of his life abroad, the last twenty-five years in the United States, yet whose music is wholly Russian

1897 Rachmaninov might have developed as a symphonist along the lines it set down; but when he returned to the form some ten years later he was understandably nervous and turned instead to the riper, more succulent melodic style of the Second Piano Concerto. The Symphony No 2 in E minor is enjoyable, thanks to its wealth of memorable tunes, though they do not present any compelling symphonic argument. Its Scherzo, for instance, starts out with a theme whose healthy pulse suggests it could have been profitably developed, but this gives way to a highly emotional melody for the violins which seems oddly out of place. The Scherzo of the earlier symphony is more consistent. The Symphony No 3 in A minor (1936), whose three movements are related by a motto theme, is more refined and economical than No 2, but the creative pulse is slack. Its first movement shows the composer still faithful to sonata form, and although it has only three movements the presence of a Scherzo central section in the Adagio places the symphony within the traditional mould. In the West Rachmaninov is regarded as a symphonist who did not fulfil his early promise. In the Soviet Union he was considered a bourgeois decadent for some time after the Revolution, but his symphonies are now regarded as the link between the generations of Tchaikovsky and Prokofiev.

Scriabin

Among the large number of relatively minor Russian composers, Alexander Scriabin (1872–1915) stands out for an originality bordering on the eccentric. He spent his late twenties mostly as a concert pianist and as Piano Professor at the Moscow Conservatoire, then in 1903 gave up this work to concentrate on composition. His works include ten sonatas and other works for solo piano, a piano concerto and several symphonies, but he remains best known for three orchestral works inspired by his obsession with theosophic mysticism. His aim was to produce an experience of ecstasy through the senses and then to achieve truth through that ecstasy. Such theories rarely lead to anything very substantial in music or the other creative arts, but Scriabin at least enjoyed a measure of success with *The Poem of Ecstasy*, a huge, opulent and almost intoxicating score full of lush melody and even more lush harmonies. The earlier *Divine Poem* calls for only slightly less ambitious orchestral forces, and *Prometheus: the Poem of Fire*, besides including a demanding obbligato piano part, was intended to be complemented in performance by a continuous light display of ever-changing colours. An occasional hearing of these works is a fascinating

Cover design of the first edition of Scriabin's Prometheus, *an orchestral 'poem' intended to be performed with an elaborate lighting display*

Prokofiev, a versatile composer who was as much at home with film and ballet scores as with his many symphonic works

experience thanks to the harmonic richness of the music which Scriabin evolved from the chromaticism of Liszt and Wagner. He achieved a unique and sometimes magnificent blend of colourful sound in his music.

Prokofiev

Unlike Rachmaninov, who never returned to his homeland after 1917, Sergei Prokofiev left it in 1918 for a period of sixteen years and then went back to spend the rest of his life there. He was born at Sontzovka in the Ukraine on 23 April 1891, and by his tenth birthday he had composed several piano pieces and an opera as well as manifesting outstanding talent as a pianist. His early compositions, including the two piano concerts written in 1912 and 1913,

showed a well-developed and highly original musical personality, one which struck Russian audiences as enjoyably outrageous on account of its violent rhythms and audaciously comic melodic material. The Piano Concerto No 1 in D flat is a fine example of this early style, a work cast in a single movement. Its opening is poundingly rhythmic, the brilliant scale passages for the soloist leading into a skittish tune. There is a central slow section of nostalgic lyricism, so utterly Romantic that it strikes a note of near-parody in its context, and the concerto ends with a return to the brash, carefree music of the opening. The piano writing is so brilliant that few virtuosos have been able to resist it.

Composition always came easily to Prokofiev, and he was able to work to every kind of commission, including ballet scores and film music. His early in-

95

terest in ballet resulted in the *Scythian Suite* and *Chout*, staged by the Ballets Russes. Other works of the wartime period included the popular *Classical Symphony*, a most affectionate essay in traditional style. His reason for writing it in 1916–17 was purely practical. Usually he composed at the piano, but in order to test his 'musical ear' he wrote this piece without the aid of any instrument, limiting himself to conventional patterns and chords. The result is a symphony constructed within the eighteenth-century framework, yet with almost impudent melodies and a twentieth-century tone of voice. It must have surprised him that this became one of his two most widely known works (the other being *Peter and the Wolf*). When he went to the United States in 1918 on a concert tour he enjoyed huge success as a pianist but created some hostility by his music, which was mistakenly regarded as 'Bolshevist'. His opera *The Love for Three Oranges* was unfavourably received in Chicago in 1921, and indeed is a rather silly piece, though the orchestral suite he made from it is attractive and deserves its popularity. He met with more understanding when he returned to Europe, but he was encouraged by the cultural climate in Paris to enter on an avant-garde phase which now seems rather self-conscious. On his return home in 1934 he turned back to the more direct style which was more natural to him.

The cinema inspired three of his finest scores, the witty *Lieutenant Kijé* (1934), the colourful *Alexander Nevsky* (1939) which was later adapted as a cantata, and the powerful *Ivan the Terrible* (1945). Two classical ballet scores, *Romeo and Juliet* (1936) and *Cinderella* (1944), rank among the greatest in the repertoire, so filled with melody that the music is highly rewarding to listen to in the concert hall – though it is even more satisfying when played for the ballets. For fourteen years he enjoyed success in the Soviet Union, but then he was criticized by the authorities for committing 'formalistic deviations and anti-democratic musical tendencies'. The whole subject of state interference in the arts is beyond the scope of this book, but it cannot be ignored completely as it has affected the course of Soviet music over the past fifty years. Censorship has always existed in one form or another: Donizetti and Verdi were obliged to submit all their librettos to the Austrian authorities in Italy, British dramatists were subject to the whims of official censorship for more than two hundred years after John Gay upset the establishment with *The Beggar's Opera* in 1728, and writers were severely persecuted in Hitler's Germany and Franco's Spain. Tsarist Russia had always kept a tight control over even such respected writers as Tolstoy, Turgenev and Dostoev-

sky. Censorship of pure music – music not associated with any text – was a new problem the Soviet composer had to face, and it led to crises in the lives of Prokofiev and Shostakovich among others.

Prokofiev was fortunate for most of his career. His film music and the opera *War and Peace* had patriotic subjects, and his symphonic works are characterized by bold rhythms and jaunty tunes which are 'democratic' in that they have direct appeal. His Symphony No 6 in E flat minor, which was first heard in 1947, showed a more stark melodic style and was both introvert and tragic in its mood. When he was subjected to official criticism he at first defended his work, but after a time his self-confidence deserted him and he wrote an abject letter admitting his 'artistic errors', as a result of which he was restored to favour and even awarded a Stalin Prize in 1951. His creative will, however, was undermined by this experience, and he composed nothing more of any real distinction before his death in Moscow on 7 March 1953. The episode was particularly saddening as he had previously enjoyed a pleasant enough relationship with the authorities and had made a sizeable and valuable contribution to twentieth-century music as one of the few composers of his time to express himself in a modern idiom and still appeal to a wide audience.

In addition to the works already mentioned, he composed two fine violin concertos in a seductively lyrical style, strong yet tender and spiced with a sense of fantasy. Both are truly symphonic in style, and written with great understanding of the expressive qualities of the violin. After the *Classical*, he did not enjoy any comparable success with a symphony until No 5 in B flat, which is traditional in its construction but daringly novel in its detail. Its successor, which caused the composer so much trouble, is an equally impressive symphony though not so immediately appealing. Prokofiev is one of the rare composers who brought wit to his symphonic writing, so it is not surprising that he also provided a uniquely amusing work for the concert hall in the shape of an 'orchestral fairy tale for children', *Peter and the Wolf*. This involves a narrator who tells how a young boy captures a wolf which has terrorized his animal friends, the orchestra commenting on each stage of his adventure. Such a piece could have easily become trivial, but the composer's light touch and the employment of different solo instruments to represent each character, with a string quartet for Peter himself, give it true musical interest. In its unpretentious way it is characteristic of a composer of originality whose music, even at its most serious, rarely fails to entertain.

Shostakovich

Dmitri Shostakovich, who was born in St Petersburg on 25 September 1906, became the first major Russian composer to embark on his career after the Revolution and pass his whole life as a Soviet citizen. It is impossible to tell, therefore, to what extent his music was a purely personal expression and how much it was tailored to suit the demands of state control. Official disapproval of his opera *Katerina Ismailova* in 1936, on the grounds that it adopted 'the worst of decadent Western manners, producing an art that was offensive and harmful to Soviet citizens', certainly caused him to withdraw his Fourth Symphony which was already in rehearsal. It was generally believed, on the other hand, that he accepted the official line, and he headed the score of his next symphony with the words 'A Soviet artist's response to just criticism'. The sincerity of this recantation is

Shostakovich, the Soviet composer who dominated the symphony throughout the middle years of the twentieth century

uncertain, however, since a book published in 1979 and purporting to contain his private views dictated to a friend, reveals a sense of violent bitterness towards his ideological masters. The truth is still not clear, and may never be known, because doubts have been cast on the authenticity of these posthumous revelations. So one must ask the simple question: if he really resented artistic conditions in the Soviet Union, why did he stay there? It was his own disinclination to travel which kept him at home: there was no restriction on his going abroad, and had he wished he could have settled in the West, where the royalties from the publication and performance of his music would have made him a wealthy man. Also, in spite of the two occasions on which he was subjected to official criticism, he was honoured as few composers have been honoured elsewhere, and he was able to become, in the words of *The Times* newspaper's obituary, beyond doubt 'the last great symphonist'.

Although the young Shostakovich had to choose between becoming a composer or a concert pianist, the decision was made for him at the age of nineteen

when his Symphony No 1 in F major proved to be not only remarkably successful but also astonishingly original. Other composers have impressed with their first symphony, but usually within an established framework and familiar idiom. Shostakovich, on the other hand, communicates a vital personal experience in his music which reveals what might best be described as instant maturity. Its slow movement, above all, expresses a range of deep feeling that is not found in the comparable youthful works of Mendelssohn and Bizet, and which makes one think back to Mozart. Shostakovich, unfortunately, did not sustain this level of inspiration as Mozart did, and his works include a good deal of music of disappointing quality.

His second and third symphonies, both one-movement works involving a chorus, have little of interest in the matter of thematic development, and there is far too much empty gesturing in the music. The fault in both cases is probably due to the composer's determination to express a sense of patriotism – and patriotism has invariably led to bombast and banality in music. (Beethoven's *Battle Symphony*, for example, is a sheer embarrassment.) The Symphony No 4 in C minor, which Shostakovich cautiously withheld from performance for more than twenty years, is an altogether more important work, deeply intense in its personal vision, rich in detail and securely constructed. Even so, it does not reveal the mastery of form that one would have expected from a composer who had begun his symphonic career so brilliantly. This mastery finally came with the Symphony No 5 in D minor, the composer's most popular and arguably his finest work. It is ironic that it should be his 'response to just criticism', for even though he may have written this inscription with his tongue in his cheek the work has greater cohesion than anything he had produced before. The first movement is gentle and spacious, though a section of martial grotesquerie supplies a delightful touch of irony. There is another whiff of irony in the Trio section of the Scherzo, a movement which represents the skittish side of the composer at his best. This is followed by an intense and rhapsodic Largo, a movement of unalloyed expressive beauty. The final Allegro non troppo opens with the brass, which have been silent in the Largo, in a stirring theme in march rhythm, a theme which eventually finds its contrast in a quieter section introduced by solo horn. A final apotheosis of the march theme rounds off the work with a sweeping grandeur not heard since the Second Symphony of Sibelius or the symphonies of the grander nineteenth-century composers.

Shostakovich was to compose ten more symphonies, only two of which sustained this level of inspiration, before his death in Moscow on 9 August 1975. Three wartime symphonies, beginning with No 7 in C major, the 'Leningrad', have not fared very happily since the events which inspired them have receded into history. The 'Leningrad' (1941) has all the boldness of a recruiting poster – and also all its empty rhetoric; No 8 in C minor, which has the character of anti-war protest, wins a more sympathetic response, though again the material is not controlled in a truly symphonic way; and No 9 in E flat strikes a totally unexpected note of comedy and self-parody which makes it an entertaining work but ultimately an insubstantial one. The last five symphonies are not very satisfying either, Nos 11 and 12 having programmes related to Russian history, No 13 involving a solo baritone and chorus in settings of poems by Yevtushenko, No 14 being more of a song cycle with orchestra, and No 15 being most noteworthy for its ingenious treatment of musical quotations from Wagner and Rossini. The Symphony No 6 in B minor, however, is a work of dark eloquence with a strong sense of unity, which has failed to equal the popularity of its immediate predecessor mainly because of its pessimistic tone. With the Symphony No 10 in E minor Shostakovich combined all his best qualities into the most logically constructed of all his scores.

Other works by Shostakovich which are encountered from time to time include two unpretentious piano concertos, the first with an additional solo part for trumpet, which please by virtue of their attractive melodies and frisky rhythms. Two violin concertos are rather less appealing; the two cello concertos, made famous by Mstislav Rostropovich, are more substantial. Shostakovich composed music for a ballet, *The Age of Gold*, whose scenario is an example of the most naive political propaganda. Although the ballet is now mercifully forgotten, the best of the music was made into a five-movement orchestral suite which makes a riotous impact in the concert hall. Even in such light-hearted pieces as this, Shostakovich stands head and shoulders above other Soviet composers.

Aram Khachaturian (1903–78) is widely known for the exciting 'Sabre Dance' from the ballet *Gayaneh*, produced by the Kirov Ballet in 1942, but his once-popular Piano Concerto in D flat has lost ground. The noisy exuberance of his music is captivating on first hearing, but with repeated listening its superficiality becomes all too apparent. No composer can survive simply by rattling the same old sabre over and over again. Few other Soviet composers have made any impact abroad.

Stravinsky

Although he was born at Oranienbaum on 17 June 1882, and though he studied with Rimsky-Korsakov for six years, Igor Stravinsky spent the greater part of his life abroad and gradually developed from a Russian composer into a cosmopolitan one. He thus contrasted with Rachmaninov, whose style remained fundamentally nationalistic throughout his long residence in the United States. Stravinsky also had a very different musical personality from Prokofiev and Shostakovich, his juniors by nine and twenty-six years respectively, because he belongs so completely to the twentieth century while their music is rooted to a great extent in the nineteenth. He began to dominate the musical scene with his earliest works, and he kept his place in the forefront by responding positively and successfully to every change in musical outlook which occurred during his long career. An artistic chameleon, he adopted one style after another with bewildering speed and dexterity, mastering every one of them. While there is one immediately recognizable Beethoven and one Wagner, there are at least three different Stravinskys, the extrovert master-colourist of the early ballet scores, the delicate etcher of the neo-Classical opera *The Rake's Progress* (1951), then the serialist of *Threni* (1958).

A scene with the evil Kastchei from the Royal Ballet version of Firebird, *the first of Stravinsky's great ballet scores*

For many people, however, Stravinsky has remained the composer of the three magnificent early works written for the Ballets Russes. They have become classics even though they were branded as difficult and, in the case of *The Rite of Spring*, downright scandalous when first performed. It was by a stroke of incredible luck that Stravinsky was invited by Sergei Diaghilev to compose the music for *The Firebird* in 1909, for he had at that time produced nothing of any substance. Diaghilev's artistic intuition was phenomenal, for on the strength of two orchestral works, *Scherzo fantastique* and *Fireworks*, neither of which lasts for more than five minutes, he entrusted his protégé with a most important commission for his new company. Stravinsky's music was strongly influenced by Rimsky-Korsakov, and was considered over-complicated. The celebrated Anna Pavlova declared 'I shall never dance to that nonsense' and withdrew from her role as the Firebird to be replaced by Tamara Karsavina at the Paris premiere in 1910. This was a tremendous success and established the composer overnight. The music is distinguished by its rhythmic force and colourful orchestration, contrasted by a good deal of sinuous, oriental melody. Stravinsky later adapted music from its nineteen numbers into a suite of six movements for a reduced orchestra, and it is this version, rather than the complete ballet score, which is popular in the concert hall. With *Petrushka* (1911) the composer developed even more alert rhythms and employed orchestral colours that were deliberately more raw, adding

touches of *verismo* in the music for the circus characters. The score is more complex and compact than that of *The Firebird*, but it scarcely prepared the public for the revolutionary step forward he was to take with his next ballet score, *The Rite of Spring*.

The basic dramatic idea for *The Rite of Spring* came to Stravinsky two years before he began to think about the music for it. 'I had dreamed a scene of pagan ritual,' he recounted later, 'in which a chosen sacrificial virgin dances herself to death, but this vision was not accompanied by any concrete musical ideas.' When they eventually came to him these ideas were perfectly suited to his vision: music expressing such primitive mystery and violence had never been heard before, and Jean Cocteau described it with brilliant aptness as 'a pastorale of the pre-historic world', a pastorale whose landscape is far removed from that of Beethoven's nature symphony. The premiere of the ballet at the Théâtre des Champs-Elysées on 29 May 1913 caused riotous scenes of a ferocity rare even for the volatile Parisian audience. It was more favourably received in concert performances,

Karsavina as the original Firebird in Stravinsky's celebrated ballet which was first presented by Diaghilev in Paris, 1910

and the composer came to the conclusion that the music belonged to the concert hall rather than the theatre. It is not, however, a really symphonic composition, for it consists of a string of more than a dozen episodes, each of which is complete in itself. The melodic ideas are brief and simple, limited to very few notes; it is the complex rhythmic and metric treatment of them that makes the score so endlessly fascinating. A huge orchestra is involved, making *The Rite of Spring* the composer's most massive score in terms of sheer sound. It seems he felt he had gone as far as possible in this direction, for in later works he reduced his instrumental forces in search of ever-increasing spareness and clarity.

The ballet *Pulcinella* (1920), based on themes by Pergolesi, calls for three singers and a small orchestra excluding percussion. Though made up of elegant eighteenth-century tunes, *Pulcinella* is entirely characteristic in its tangy harmonies and briskness. A year earlier, the ballet with narration *The Soldier's Tale* had cut the orchestral players down to seven, while *Les Noces* ('The wedding'), produced in 1923, had the singers and dancers accompanied only by four pianos and percussion.

Stravinsky's personal fortunes, as well as his musical style, had also changed during this period. He and his family had gone to live in Switzerland in 1914 for health reasons, intending to return to Russia, but with the Revolution in 1917 came the realization that his properties would be confiscated and he therefore opted for exile in Western Europe. He left Switzerland in 1920 to settle in Paris, where he became a French citizen in 1934, and after *Les Noces* he ceased to compose any music that could truly be described as Russian. Having given up all his roots, he followed his innermost personal convictions wherever they led him. In addition to the lightly scored ballets which followed the massive *Rite of Spring*, he wrote a variety of chamber music, short piano pieces and songs, culminating in the Octet for Wind Instruments in 1923 which marked a new change of style. No longer was he just conceiving music for small forces: he now adopted a style which is conveniently described as neo-Classical. His compositions from the time of the Octet until *The Rake's Progress* in 1951 reveal a return to the Classical principles of balance, purity and objectivity, as opposed to the Romantic mannerisms of emotionalism and programme music. Like other neo-Classical composers, Stravinsky was looking for a way out of Romantic subjectivity other than the somewhat rigid twelve-tone system evolved by Arnold Schoenberg; and he found his answer in the orderliness of the Classical style. The Classical tradition was, in his own words, 'a living force which

Stravinsky, a composer who adopted every new musical style during his long career including primitivism, neo-Classicism and serialism

animates and informs the present', and the works he composed between 1923 and 1951 showed that his acceptance of traditional values in no way lessened his originality or his modernity of expression. Even his Symphony in C (1940) and Symphony in Three Movements (1945) are in no reversion to the past but belong wholly to their time. The Concerto for Piano and Wind Instruments (1924) is novel in several respects. The soloist is accompanied by an orchestra consisting of nineteen wind instruments, four timpani and double bass – thus omitting the singing strings that traditionally played so important a part in the concerto. Even more unusual is that, although it is cast in three movements, Stravinsky described it as 'a sort of passacaglia or toccata, in the style of the seventeenth century seen from the point of view of today'. The Capriccio for Piano and Orchestra (1929) is a further example of his experimenting with old forms, for he explained that he had in mind the capriccio in terms of a fantasia allowing for the juxtaposition of different episodes. He also confessed to being influenced in this work by 'that prince of mu-

sic, Carl Maria von Weber'; he was prepared to turn to an arch-Romantic in his own pursuit of neo-Classical aims.

In 1939, with war imminent, Stravinsky left Europe to start a new life in the United States, where a year later he settled in Hollywood – a curious choice for a neo-Classicist, one might think – and became an American citizen at the end of the war. In 1953 he began to experiment with serialism, which can be found in parts of the ballet suite *Agon*, which was produced by New York City Ballet in 1957, and composed his first completely serial work a year later in *Threni*. He continued to compose until a few years before his death, his works becoming ever more condensed. In 1962, his eightieth year, he paid a visit to Moscow and Leningrad, where he was received with all due honour, though no doubt more in memory of his early works than those he was then composing. He had, after all, turned his back on the conservative styles of the Russian composers who had remained at home. Declining health caused him in 1969 to move from Hollywood to New York, where he died on 6 April 1971. Unpredictable to the last, he had chosen to be buried, not in his native country or in either of his adopted countries, but on the island of San Michele in Venice.

101

CZECHOSLOVAKIA

There had long been a strong musical tradition in the lands of Bohemia, Moravia and Slovakia which were combined in 1918 as the independent nation of Czechoslovakia, but because they were ruled by the Habsburgs as part of the Austrian Empire for several centuries before then their composers had had no national identity. During the eighteenth and nineteenth centuries they contributed a great deal to European music, chiefly in various German centres. The Bohemian Johann Stamitz (1717–57), for instance, was one of the earliest composers to establish the form and style of the symphony at Mannheim, where he also instigated new standards of performance and conducting; while the Benda family was associated with the courts of Frederick the Great and other German rulers. When the music historian Dr Burney visited Bohemia in the 1770s he called it the 'conservatoire of Europe' and was amazed by the musical activities flourishing even in remote country villages. Mozart had a special affection for Prague, which appreciated his work more warmly than any other capital, and which commissioned his *Don Giovanni* and *La clemenza di Tito*. With the rise of nineteenth-century nationalism a distinctively Czech style of music developed, finding its first great leader in Smetana, whose chief claim to international status rests on his operas but who also wrote some outstanding instrumental music.

Smetana

The early career of Bedřich Smetana followed a haphazard course. Born at Litomyšl on 2 March 1824, he was at first encouraged by his father, a brewer and amateur musician, to learn both violin and piano. He responded so keenly that he made his first public appearance as a pianist at the age of six. After this promising beginning, however, he had little formal education in music, though he did not lack ambition. When he was seventeen, and spending a good deal of time playing the piano in the homes of the wealthier citizens of Pilsen, he wrote rather grandly in his diary: 'I wish to become a Mozart in composition and a Liszt in technique.' He never reached either of these heights, but he did become a highly accomplished composer with a worldwide reputation that has not dimmed. There are two other interesting points about this diary entry. Firstly, it was written in German, for this was the language spoken in his home and he did not learn Czech until he was over thirty. Secondly, Liszt was to prove a kind and helpful friend to him. Having failed in his attempt to establish him-

Smetana, the 'father' of Czech music who first expressed his country's national spirit in his operas and orchestral works

self as a piano virtuoso, Smetana decided in 1847 to open his own music school, writing to Liszt for advice and a loan and enclosing his Six Characteristic Pieces for piano suitably dedicated to his idol. Liszt provided him with advice but ignored the plea for money. Ten years later, however, he at least paid him a rare compliment. Smetana, visiting Weimar specifically to meet Liszt, was taunted at a musical soirée by an arrogant Viennese conductor for belonging to a race which had not produced a single composer capable of writing worthwhile Czech music. Liszt at once sat down at the piano, played the Six Characteristic Pieces to the admiring assembly, and then declared, 'Here is a composer with a genuine Czech heart, an artist by the grace of God'.

Smetana chose the symphonic poems of Liszt as his models for the six orchestral pieces which make up his most substantial orchestral work, *Má vlast* ('My country'), composed at intervals between 1875 and 1880. By that time he had already been overtaken by deafness, so that though present at their first performances he could not hear a note of the music. No less than his operas, *Má vlast* served to establish him as the 'father' of Czech music, for the melodies and especially the rhythms have a distinctive national quality about them. The symphonic poems were all directly inspired by the Czech countryside, its rivers and valleys, or by legends about the country's past heroes. Fortunately the listener need not know the programmes of the six pieces in order to enjoy them: each stands on musical merit alone. Each is also self-contained, though there are themes which recur during the cycle, so that it is more fully appreciated in its entirety. A knowledge of the programmes behind the individual symphonic poems also adds to the listener's enjoyment of the music, for it is uncommonly graphic.

The cycle opens appropriately with *Vyšehrad*, the name of a rock above the Vltava river which, according to legend, was the seat of the princes of Bohemia. Smetana wrote of this poem: 'The harps of the minstrels introduce the songs about the events at Vyšehrad, its glories, tournaments and battles, up to its final decline and ruin. The work ends on an elegiac note.' There is a wealth of warm melody typical of the composer, a solemn tune suggestive of past glories, with the brass adding glints of pomp and ceremony, a march section followed by music of battle, then the reflective close. *Vltava*, the most popular piece of all, and frequently played on its own in concerts, is a picture in sound of a journey along the river which rises in the southern tip of Bohemia and crosses the country to reach Prague in a majestic sweep. Central to the poem is a memorable spacious theme representing the river itself, while subsidiary melodies suggest scenes glimpsed on the way: a hunting party, a rustic wedding featuring the national dance, the polka, and later a more delicate dance for the legendary water nymphs. *Šárka* forms a complete contrast, an uninhibited example of musical blood and thunder which tells the story of the leader of a group of Amazonian women who has sworn to be revenged on all men because of her own lover's infidelity. She tricks a band of soldiers, whose leader falls in love with her, and then her followers kill them all. This savagely graphic piece is followed by the pastoral poem *From Bohemia's Woods and Fields*, the music of which suggests the variety of the Czech countryside, and which has become almost as familiar as that of *Vltava* in the concert hall. The two final poems, *Tábor* and *Blaník*, return to Bohemia's legendary past, and both make impressive use of the Hussite chorale of the fifteenth century which the revolutionary movement of the nineteenth century revived as its anthem. *Má vlast* as a whole appeals to music-lovers everywhere by virtue of its memorable melodies and richly imaginative orchestration, while for Czechs it is also a musical vision of their country and its history. Smetana, alas, never heard the complete work, for he was already deaf by the time of its first performance in 1882, and he died in Prague on 12 May 1884.

Dvořák

The most prominent Czech composer in the world's concert halls is Antonín Dvořák, whose last three symphonies are among the most frequently played in the whole repertoire and whose Cello Concerto towers above all others. He was one of those composers who succeeded against almost impossible odds, for he was born in the humblest circumstances in the village of Nelahozeves on 8 September 1841, son of a butcher and innkeeper. As a boy he scraped a fiddle outside his father's inn for the entertainment of tourists, and learnt at the village school how to sing and play music at an amateur level. At the age of twelve he was sent to live with an uncle in a small town where a schoolmaster gave him more formal instruction in piano, organ and theoretical studies. Schooldays over, he returned to his father to help in the business, but eventually won his consent to go off to Prague for more advanced musical training.

Dvořák, the village innkeeper's son who always retained his love of the Czech people and countryside in spite of his world-wide travels

Drawing of the first performance at Carnegie Hall, New York, of Dvořák's Symphony No 9, 'From the New World', on 15 December 1893

There he managed to eke out a livelihood by playing the viola in a private orchestra and by supplying the music in a tavern. From 1862 until 1873, during which period he added to his financial difficulties by marrying, he played in the orchestra of the National Opera and later as a church organist, composing only when he had enough money to buy music paper. His composition of a patriotic hymn brought him some local recognition, but it was not until 1875 that he won the unexpected championship of Brahms and the Prague-born critic Eduard Hanslick in Vienna, which led to the award of an annual stipend from the Austrian Ministry of Culture. Only then was he able to devote himself to a full-time career as a composer. Three years later, his Slavonic Dances and several chamber works established his reputation first in Germany and then in England, where his music was later to enjoy a considerable vogue. He was far from satisfied with his early compositions, many of which he destroyed in manuscript, and some of which he held back from publication for a considerable time. Not until many years after his death did his four early symphonies become known, and the numbering of the five mature ones revised. Now that they have all been published in the right order, and recorded, we can see that they show a gradual and logical development.

The four symphonies of 1865–74 are somewhat uneven in quality, but they deserve to be heard more often in the concert hall. While there are strong traces of Beethoven in their ambitious slow movements and of Wagner in their harmonic writing they are mostly highly individual in style and rich in melody. The first of the symphonies, which may well have been his first orchestral work, shows that Dvořák had mastered the technique of orchestration very early. With the Symphony No 5 in F major he finally asserted his nationalism, bringing the spirit of the Bohemian woodlands into the first movement and the racy rhythms of Czech dances to a Scherzo otherwise Classical in form. It was a transitional work leading to the four mature masterpieces.

By the time he came to compose the Symphony No 6 in D major, Dvořák was familiar with the first and second symphonies of Brahms, so a comparison was inevitable between his new work and the latter's symphony in the same key. Brahms's influence is discernible in the gentle opening of the first movement, one of those apparently innocent melodies which are capable of subtle treatment and development. In this Dvořák reveals a mastery of form not found in the earlier symphonies, and in this respect, as well as in the orchestration, he is clearly indebted to Brahms, but there is enough of his own impetuous temperament to give the music a strong Czech accent. This is clearest in the Scherzo, a lively furiant, the kind of Bohemian dance that he had played outside his father's inn. Dvořák never used actual folktunes: his melodies are original, though nationalistic in flavour.

From this symphony onwards he developed along lines that were entirely his own. Like Schubert, Dvořák had a natural gift for melody, and was able to organize melodies into symphonic form. He was the most unsophisticated of men, delighting in such simple pleasures as train-spotting, breeding pigeons, and playing skittles (though one wonders whether he did not play up, with an impish sense of fun, to the image which had been thrust upon him). 'I shall remain,' he once wrote, 'what I have always been – a simple Czech musician'; but we should not take too seriously this probably tongue-in-cheek remark; for his music reveals considerable sophistication underneath its engagingly tuneful surface.

The most impressive of all his symphonies, No 7 in D minor, was composed for the London Philharmonic Society, a direct result of the success in England of its predecessor. Dvořák's awareness of his new responsibility was testified by his statement in a letter that it 'must be such again as to make a stir in the world'. It is the most intense of his symphonies, and has a keen sense of inner conflict and closely-knit structure that forms a perfect arch from the brooding opening to the energetic and majestic close. The themes of the first movement are bold and urgent, leading to a particularly dramatic development section, more thoughtful than anything in the earlier, more genial symphonies. There is a hint of tragedy even in the warm melodies of the long slow movement, which expresses a variety of deep emotions before dying away in a mood of serenity, almost resignation. The Scherzo is vigorous, serious rather than capricious, and has a contrasting pastoral Trio. It paves the way with inevitable logic to a final Allegro whose themes seem to fight for supremacy up to the exultant coda in the traditional grand manner. The symphony is Dvořák's tribute to the Classical spirit of Beethoven and Schubert, composed as though to prove that he could hold his own with the greatest of symphonists, a fact that the enthusiastic audience at the London premiere in 1885 was quick to appreciate.

The composer subsequently seems to have felt free to indulge in a style of more easy-going charm, and the Symphony No 8 in G major, completed four years later, treats a wealth of appealing melodies in an almost rhapsodic manner; it is simpler in harmony and in instrumental technique. With a touch of irony he offered this least academic of all his symphonies to Cambridge University on the occasion of his receiving an honorary Doctorate of Music. Though its structure is satisfying, it does not observe the 'rules' of sonata form: the themes of the first movement, for instance, are contrasted one with another rather than developed. There is some sorrowful expression in the Adagio, which shows up the high spirits of the other movements to full advantage. The third movement forms a delightful contrast, its main tune having the smiling lilt of a slow waltz. Towards the end a national flavour is introduced in an amusing dialogue between oboe and bassoon, in the spirit of the composer's Slavonic Dances. Dvořák's sense of fun breaks into the last movement too, for after a trumpet fanfare which seems to be preparing for a free-for-all Bohemian folkdance the music suddenly switches to a stately processional theme and only after some delightful variations on that theme takes on the expected fairground gaiety and bustle. The symphony was not such an immediate success as No 7, but eventually became one of the most popular all over the world.

However, it is above all the Symphony no 9 in E minor, subtitled 'From the New World', that won Dvořák the affection of the public. Its curious history shows how chance can play an important part in shaping a composer's style and fortunes. If a wealthy wholesale grocer in New York had not married a lady with a keen love of music the composer would not have given us the symphony at all. It was this lady, Mrs Jeannette Thurber, who, seeking a celebrated composer to direct her National Conservatory of Music in New York, hit on the bright idea of inviting Dvořák. America made a deep impression on him when he arrived in 1892; he was particularly struck by the plight of the blacks and Indians. As a Bohemian patriot whose own country suffered under the despotic rule of the Habsburgs, he felt compassion for these ill-treated people of the New World. At the same time, despite his success with American music-lovers, he began to long to be back in his homeland. These sentiments combined to give his new symphony its special character. It is more loosely constructed than the other symphonies, but the richness and inspiration of its melodies are irresistible. Its subtitle, incorrectly translated, misled commentators for a time, for they believed the work to be a 'New World' symphony expressing Dvořák's response to the American environment. His subtitle, on the contrary, meant exactly what it said: the symphony was a greeting to his fellow-countrymen *from* the New World. Far from being in any way Americanized, its is more positively Czech than any other of his symphonies.

Dvořák is concerned here not so much with form as with a variety of rich and memorable melodies, which he dresses up in different guises and re-introduces into subsequent movements. There is a slow Introduction to the first movement, but its rather solemn tone quickly gives way to the boisterous first main theme of the Allegro, based on the pentatonic (five-note) scale which has characterized much of the world's folk music from earliest times. The second main tune of the movement bears a certain similarity to 'Swing low, sweet chariot', though it would be unwise to stress this as evidence of American influence. In the famous Largo a cor anglais plays a plaintive melody now widely known as the spiritual 'Goin' home'; the melody is in fact Dvořák's own, an expression of his longing to return to his homeland, and the words now sung to it were added many years later. For the third movement the composer turns to the hectic Czech furiant, with reminiscences of the opening movement before and after the Trio. The latter was once happily described as depicting 'a Bohemian inn where Schubert happens to be the guest'. The last movement recalls themes from all three earlier movements (as had Beethoven's Ninth Symphony), but not until it has presented two of its own, the first for horns and trumpets against short chords for the rest of the orchestra, and the second for clarinet. Dvořák always chose the right instrument or instruments to give the most striking flavour to his melodies. He plays his final ace in the coda, combining the main theme of the first movement with that of the last movement to produce a majestic climax. He has been criticized in some quarters for having kept an eye on the box-office; but few people could fail to respond to the symphony's abundant lyrical charm and sheer human warmth. When it was first performed by the New York Philharmonic Orchestra on 15 December 1893, the audience called for Dvořák to take a bow after the second movement, and at the end he was obliged, in his own words, 'to thank them from my box, like a king!'

This was to be his last symphony, but before he left New York he composed another major work, the Cello Concerto in B minor. It has enjoyed a similar enduring success, and might be considered his most impressive masterpiece. Melodically it is almost as rich as the Ninth Symphony. The problem of balancing the cello against the full orchestra is solved more successfully than in any other cello concerto and, while the music is splendidly rewarding for the soloist, the work is also truly symphonic in character. Dvořák was adamant that it should not be a mere showpiece for the virtuoso, vigorously rejecting the request of Hanuš Wihan, for whom it was written, to add a concluding cadenza. 'The Finale,' he wrote to his publisher, 'closes with a gradual diminuendo like a sigh – with reminiscences of the first and second movements, the solo dying away to a pianissimo. Then the sound begins to swell again, and the last bars are taken over by the orchestra, which provides a tempestuous ending. That was my idea, and I cannot change it.' There is nevertheless plenty of scope for the soloist to prove his technical and expressive skill, so that the concerto has been eagerly adopted by every great cellist. As with the Ninth Symphony, the composer's mind and heart were with his homeland when writing it.

After his return to Prague in 1895 Dvořák produced a number of symphonic poems but devoted most of his energies to the opera, composing *The Devil and Kate* and *Russalka* for the Prague National Theatre in whose orchestra he had once played. His dramatic works, however, have made little impression outside Czechoslovakia, his worldwide reputation resting on the symphonies, the concertos for cello and (though to a much lesser extent) violin. There are many shorter orchestral works including the very fine, unjustly neglected Symphonic Variations and the *Carnival* Overture and the Slavonic Dances which fully deserve their popularity. The Czech idiom of Dvořák's music has never impaired its instant appeal to audiences in all countries, and his death in Prague on 1 May 1904 was mourned the world over.

Janáček

The natural heir to Smetana was not so much Dvořák as Leoš Janáček (1854–1928), who was born at Hukvaldy, a village in the mountainous district of Moravia. He was primarily an opera composer, but deserves a mention at this stage by virtue of one highly original orchestral work, the Sinfonietta of 1926. He described the piece himself as 'a very nice Sinfonietta with fanfares', which is the most modest of understatements. It was dedicated to the Czech Armed Forces, which the patriotic composer regarded as the defender of his country's newly-won independence. It was at a military band concert in a park that Janáček heard the fanfares which inspired so much of the music. There are five contrasting movements, without symphonic treatment in the customary sense; rhythms and intervals are gradually transformed and developed in a highly individual

Janáček, who had to wait until he was more than sixty before recognition came to him, pictured in the garden of his home at Brno

but clear and logical manner. The first movement (for brass alone) typifies this; it opens solemnly with a phrase for tubas, bass trumpets and timpani, and gradually becomes brighter and livelier as all nine (!) trumpets join in. Several ideas are introduced in the second movement, notably a vigorous folk-dance for the oboes and a more lyrical melody for oboe and flute, which do not seem to be related at first but which are eventually shown to have an affinity to one another. Its final flourish reintroduces the full brass of the opening movement. With the central Moderato the mood changes: strings and woodwind sing out a serene, nostalgic melody, after which brass chords introduce an unexpected touch of the sinister. The fourth movement consists of a single striking tune repeated with a number of changes of rhythm and instrumental textures. There is interesting development of the main theme of the last movement, which is introduced in rather innocent form by the flutes, then given added emotional character by clarinet and oboe, next turned into a Scherzando and finally reaching a huge climax, with the full complement of brass bringing back the whole of the first movement, now accompanied by the rest of the orchestra. The work perhaps seems complex on first hearing, but soon exerts such a spell that one regrets that Janáček did not compose more orchestral music in the last, most fruitful period of his life. The only comparable work is the Rhapsody *Taras Bulba*, composed in 1915–18 and hardly less impressive than the Sinfonietta.

HUNGARY

Bartók

The international reputation of Hungarian art-music virtually began with Bartók. There had been a native school of music in Hungary in the nineteenth century, but the only first-rate composer it produced, Franz Liszt, became a cosmopolitan figure who worked mainly abroad. His Hungarian rhapsodies are ostensibly national in spirit, but like the Hungarian dances of Brahms are in fact based on gypsy music rather than the true Hungarian folk music that inspired so much of Bartók's work.

Béla Bartók, who was born at the village of Nagyszentmiklós on 25 March 1881, was to take his musical birthright far more seriously. He studied at the Budapest Academy of Music and first made his mark as a concert pianist, like his slightly older compatriot, Ernst von Dohnányi (1877–1960), whose fame as a composer rests on the one work for piano and orchestra, *Variations on a Nursery Song*. At first Bartók

fell under the influences of Brahms and Liszt, then of Richard Strauss, but he found the most important and lasting stylistic inspiration in 1905 when he began to make a systematic survey of Hungarian folk music with his friend and fellow composer Zoltán Kodály (1882–1967). His editing of this material, as well as folk music from neighbouring countries, remains a major contribution to the study of ethnic music. Its influence can be heard in all his mature works, including those which he composed after leaving Hungary for the United States in 1940.

After a spate of works which have remained unpublished, mostly indebted to Strauss, he composed the large-scale *Kossuth* Symphony, a rousingly patriotic piece. It is really a symphonic poem in ten descriptive sections employing thematic transformation in the manner of Liszt. This established his name abroad, being performed in Manchester only a few months after its Budapest premiere in January 1904. There followed two orchestral suites, but for a number of years, having accepted a teaching post at the Budapest Academy, he composed mainly piano and chamber works. This period also saw the production of the opera *Bluebeard's Castle* and music for two ballets, *The Wooden Prince* and *The Miraculous Mandarin*, familiar in the concert hall even though not often staged. It was not until 1926 that he composed the first of his three piano concertos for the practical purpose of having something new to offer in his concert repertoire. His other major orchestral music was written to commission, the Music for Strings, Percussion and Celesta (1937) for the Basle Chamber Orchestra and the Concerto for Orchestra (1944) for the Boston Symphony. These works represent the more extrovert side of his character, whereas the equally imaginative chamber music he composed throughout his life reveals more of the inner man. He had suffered from poor health since his childhood, and as he grew older he withdrew more and more into himself, his mental distress aggravated by the fate of his country, which was ruled by the Habsburgs in his early years and then, after a brief period of independence, by the Nazis. Even though he was able to escape to New York, he never settled there as contentedly as other composers had done, but remained a homesick, displaced Hungarian until his death on 26 September 1945.

There is great variety in the style and expressive character of the concertos. An unusual aspect of the Piano Concerto No 1 is its emphasis on the percussive quality of the instrument, which allows it to hold its own against the orchestra as it hammers out fragmentary themes devoid of ornamentation. The slow movement is even more unusual in that the soloist 107

Bartók (fourth from left), photographed by his colleague Zoltán Kodály on a field trip to collect folk songs at the village of Darázs

is partnered by a battery of percussion including timpani, side drum, bass drum, triangle and cymbals. In the second Concerto Bartók keeps the pianist busy in music of contrapuntal complexity reminiscent of Bach – though with a pronounced twentieth-century accent. Its second movement combines Adagio and Scherzo elements, while the Finale treats themes from the first movement in new rhythmic guises. After these aggressively virtuosic works with their often harsh brilliance, the Concerto No 3, written in the last year of his life, is unexpectedly serene in mood. The opening theme is song-like and highly ornamented, and the first movement continues in this tender vein. The Adagio is reflective, marked *religioso*, with a delicately scored Trio based on bird-calls which the composer had heard and written down in North Carolina. There is a good deal of intricate fugal writing in the final Rondo, but it is gayer in spirit than anything in the earlier concertos. The Violin Concerto in B minor is different again, a virtuoso piece with warm, full-bodied melodies and effective harmonic contrasts.

Of Bartók's symphonic-style works without a soloist, the Concerto for Orchestra has always been by far the most popular. Cast in five movements, it was originally designed to exploit the virtuosity of the players of the Boston Symphony Orchestra, and its title is explained by its tendency to treat single instruments or instrumental groups in a *concertante* or solo manner. The first and last movements are composed in sonata form, respectively highlighting the brass and the strings, while the second, a Scherzo, features pairs of wind instruments which follow one another like couples dancing at a ball – bassoons, oboes, clarinets, flutes and muted trumpets in turn. The composer explained that 'the general mood of the work represents, apart from the jesting second movement, a gradual transition from the sternness of the first movement and the lugubrious death-song of the third to the life-assertion of the last one.' In its richness of thematic material, its clean textures and subtlety of varying rhythms, this is a work of powerful originality and imagination, no mere pretext for virtuoso display. Because it is also strongly tonal, melodic and relatively straightforward in formal structure, the Concerto for Orchestra constitutes the ideal introduction to contemporary music.

The same might be said of the Music for Strings, Percussion and Celesta, which is complex in its organization yet so spontaneous in its communicative qualities that it is readily enjoyable. Bartók probed into the possibilities of music freed from tonality, and much of his writing involves interweaving lines of counterpoint which are not always easy for the ear to follow, but he adopted these procedures because they seemed to him the logical way to express his musical ideas: he was never, like Schoenberg, a theoretician deliberately planning a new method of composition. There is also a violent, 'barbaric' impulse in much of his music, stemming from his interest in primitive dance rhythms. He himself said: 'I do not care to subscribe to any of the accepted contemporary musical standards. My ideal is a measured *balance* of these elements.' By achieving this balance he became one of the most progressive composers of the time without alienating himself from the musical public.

SCANDINAVIA

For a long period German composers dominated orchestral music as completely as Italians did the opera, giving the impression that most other countries were virtually inactive in that field during the latter part of the eighteenth century and the early part of the nineteenth. This is true to a considerable extent, because even where the more sophisticated musical forms were to be found at all they were little more than imitations of the styles inaugurated and developed by the two trend-setters of Europe. Music in England suffered a decline from the death of Purcell until the advent of Elgar (notwithstanding such composers of the second rank as Boyce, Arne, Sterndale Bennett, Parry and Stanford); while in the Scandinavian countries, distanced from the main centres of activity, the only truly native music was based on their folk culture. Johan Helmich Roman, for instance, was honoured with the name of 'father of Swedish music', though his sinfonias simply reflected the Italian and German styles of the early eighteenth century. The Scandinavian countries were so backward that their musical public recognized only imported music and refused to believe that they could possibly produce any art-music of their own. This attitude was so prevalent in Sweden that the country's one great symphonist, Franz Berwald, (1796–1855) was shamefully cold-shouldered throughout his long life. Only a century after his death did his countrymen begin to recognize his worth, and his music still remains virtually unknown in the rest of the world.

Grieg

Unlike Berwald, Edvard Hagerup Grieg enjoyed a comfortable and successful life, receiving early recognition in his native Norway. He was born at Bergen on 15 June 1843, of Scottish descent on his paternal side, his great-grandfather having settled in Bergen in 1746 after the Battle of Culloden. Links with Britain were maintained, for Edvard's father was the British Consul in Bergen. The boy's musical talent was inherited from his mother: an accomplished pianist, and a regular performer at local concerts, she gave him his first piano lessons at the age of six. He must have been a responsive pupil, for he composed his first piece, a set of variations, only three years later, and at fifteen he was considered so talented that he was sent to the Leipzig Conservatoire for more serious studies. There he came under the influence of Schumann, whose piano concerto, which Grieg heard Clara Schumann play in Leipzig, was to be the inspiration behind his own concerto, the best-known of all his works. It is fortunate that he did not return straight home when his studies in Germany were finished, for had he done so he would probably have become just another Scandinavian composer working in the style of the Leipzig school and might never have found his national identity.

He wisely spent most of the year 1863 in Copenhagen, which was at that time the chief centre of Norwegian as well as Danish cultural activity, and where he quickly became aware of the Scandinavian heritage previously unknown to him. 'For the first time,' he wrote in an autobiographical sketch, 'I learned to know the northern folktunes and my own nature.' For the next three years he divided his time between Denmark and Norway, gradually coming to grips with the latter's folk music upon which he subsequently drew so consistently for his compositions. Ironically, however, it was on a visit to Rome in 1865 that he first met his great compatriot, Henrik Ibsen, for whose drama *Peer Gynt* he was later to write incidental music. These were principally years of continued study in an attempt to find his creative personality, becoming the first real Norwegian composer in the process. At the same time he was establishing his name with groups of songs and piano pieces, so that when he finally settled in Norway in 1866 he was widely respected as the country's musical leader. He was therefore in a favourable position to promote concerts and, within a year, founded the Norwegian Academy of Music. At the same time he married his cousin Nina Hagerup.

From the age of twenty-three, Grieg was able to lead what might well be considered a settled life for

Above: *Grieg with his wife Nina, a distinguished soprano who played a great part in making his songs widely popular*

Opposite: *A Rackham drawing of Peer Gynt with the King of the Trolls, a scene for which Grieg composed a suitably grotesque dance*

a composer: his work both as creative and performing artist, augmented by state bursaries, ensured him freedom from financial worries. He suffered all his life from frequent bouts of ill-health as the result of a severe attack of pleurisy in his teens, yet he was sufficiently determined to overcome this handicap and make annual concert tours to promote Norwegian music throughout Europe. Although he championed the works of several of his compatriots, it was his own music which always attracted the most attention, so that he became accepted everywhere as *the* Norwegian composer. His reputation in the concert hall rests on a handful of works, above all the Piano Concerto in A minor, which he composed at twenty-five, a surprising fact when we consider that he lived to be sixty-four. Basically, however, he was a miniaturist, most at ease when writing songs or short piano pieces. It is significant that he quickly abandoned his youthful attempt at a symphony, and that he also laid aside the sketches he made for a second piano concerto. Aware of his limitations, he knew that his musical ideas were potent enough in

themselves but generally unsuitable for lengthy extension and development, and he also realized that his fondness for folk-style music similarly precluded him from large-scale compositions.

The Piano Concerto must be regarded as the exception which proves the rule – so well, in fact, that it fully deserves its place among the handful of crowd-pulling concertos. It makes a warm appeal on a first hearing which does not lessen with familiarity, and in this respect it is very like Schumann's concerto in the same key, which it strongly resembles in form even though its melodies carry an authentic flavour of Norwegian folk music. (It is surely not without significance that a dozen recordings couple the two concertos.) The whole work is full of melodic invention to delight the listener, with brilliant yet never merely superficial keyboard writing to appeal to the virtuoso pianist. Grieg the nationalist is much in evidence in the first movement, for both the jaunty first theme and the impassioned second subject have an immediately recognizable Northern character. The languorous melody of the slow movement is one of

Edvard Munch lithograph for a performance of Peer Gynt, *with incidental music by Grieg*

the composer's finest inspirations, reflective at first, then rising to a dramatic central climax before it dies down to its original mood ready for the sudden contrast of the piano's launching into the Finale. This has two main themes, the first suggestive of the Norwegian dance known as the *halling* and the second a pastoral subject introduced by the flute.

It was inevitable that Norway's two most famous sons should come together, even though they were geniuses of very different orders. Ibsen remains a towering figure in world drama, whereas Grieg is a minor figure compared to such international musical giants as Bach, Mozart or Wagner. When he was asked to compose incidental music for *Peer Gynt*, however, Grieg rose splendidly to the occasion, providing twenty-two numbers for this verse drama which caught its satirical character to perfection. He subsequently chose the best and most substantial of these pieces for two orchestral suites, of which the first has always been the more popular. The music of its four movements shows that although he was by nature a writer for the piano he also had a flair for effective orchestration. 'Morning' is a pastoral Allegretto with an undulating melody delicately coloured by the woodwind; 'The death of Aase', scored for muted strings, is made poignantly expressive by skilfully shifting harmonies; 'Anitra's dance' has a piquantly scored tune which conjures up exactly the right exotic atmosphere for the Bedouin girl setting out to seduce the hero with her dancing; and 'In the hall of the mountain king' features a grotesque dance for dwarfs, building up to a frenzied finale. By contrast, the *Holberg Suite*, while clearly bearing Grieg's

own fingerprint, is a deliberate pastiche of Baroque dances.

It would be pointless to search for any great profundity of thought or expression of dark personal feeling in the music of Grieg because it so faithfully reflected the even course of his life and the good-natured ease of his personality. Success came to him early, and he was fortunate too in his marriage to a singer who understood his work and was able actively to promote and popularize his many songs. Far from resting on his easily won laurels, however, he was highly conscientious in all his work, revising his piano concerto, for example, throughout his life until it reached the form in which we know it today. He became a witty after-dinner speaker, and was known to fly into a temper only when he felt that a fellow-composer had been unfairly attacked by the critics. A republican in politics, he was not greatly impressed by the honours heaped on him by the royal families of countries he toured either as pianist or conductor, though he found they could be turned to practical advantage. 'Orders and medals,' he once confessed, 'are most useful to me in the top layers of my trunks, for customs officials are always kind to me at the sight of them.' He was mourned as a national hero on his death on 4 September 1907.

Sibelius

There has always been something enigmatic about both the personality and the music of Jean Sibelius, the severe-looking Finn who put his country on the musical map. Born at Hämeenlinna on 8 December 1865, he came from a family with no musical tradition, though like his sister and younger brother he learnt to play an instrument, the violin, as a child. He nursed the ambition to become a concert artist for many years, even auditioning as a violinist for the Vienna Philharmonic Orchestra as late as 1891 after he had already composed a number of chamber works. In spite of his obvious musical inclinations, however, he was pushed by his family into studying law when he went to university. Like so many other composers, he resisted parental pressures to become a respectable barrister and insisted on changing over to a course of musical studies, and he was fortunate in having Ferruccio Busoni, with whom he was to form a lifelong friendship, among his teachers. When he went on to Berlin for further training in 1889 he learnt more from the music which he heard in the concert halls, where the repertoire was infinitely wider than anything Helsinki had provided, than from his formal lessons there. He was most impressed of all by a Finnish work, the *Aino* Symphony of Robert Kajanus, conducted by its composer, thus developing nationalist leanings early in his career.

After returning to Finland for several months, where he became engaged to a daughter of the prominent aristocratic Järnefelt family, appropriately called Aino, he went on to Vienna. Busoni had given him a letter of introduction to Brahms, but the German master characteristically refused to see him, so Sibelius found a teacher for himself, Karl Goldmark, the prolific composer now remembered only for his opera *Die Königin von Saba* ('The Queen of Sheba') and his symphony subtitled *Rustic Wedding*. Whatever he learnt in matters of technique, however, Sibelius was in no way influenced by German music: all his mature works are completely Finnish in character, recognized as such even by listeners who know the country only from books and travel posters. This achievement is all the more remarkable when we remember that the Finland in which he grew up was still a grand duchy of Tsarist Russia, largely governed by a Swedish minority. Although he entered the first Finnish-speaking grammar school as a boy, his family always spoke Swedish at home, so he did not become fully proficient in his national language until he was a young man.

He found nationalist inspiration by immersing himself in the *Kalevala*, the great Finnish epic which meant to his countrymen what the *Iliad* and *Odyssey* meant to the Greeks, and which he first drew upon for his *Kullervo* Symphony. Its first performance in 1892, when he was twenty-six, brought him immediate success and parental permission for his marriage to Aino Järnefelt. The work was ambitious in scope, calling for two soloists and chorus as well as orchestra, and lasting eighty minutes, but Sibelius soon withdrew it. The occasional performances it has been given since his death have only confirmed the wisdom of his decision, for in spite of some interesting passages it falls far below the standards of his seven later symphonies. During the next three years he produced *En saga* and the *Four Legends*, all of which were considerably revised after their first performances. It was during this period that he fell briefly under the spell of Wagner following a visit to Bayreuth, but he quickly reacted against Wagnerism and turned instead to the symphonic poems of Liszt as a more suitable model for his music. The *Legends* follow this format, as do half a dozen other works spread over the years and culminating in *Tapiola* (1925), his last major composition. (They are now usually referred to as 'tone-poems', a term which has replaced the original one used by Liszt.) Three of the four *Legends* are programmatic, describing various adventures of Lemminkäinen, a typically tough and

fearless Nordic hero, a Siegfried with a touch of Don Juan, while the other, *The Swan of Tuonela*, is more of a mood-piece. Solo cor anglais and muted strings dominate this brooding evocation of the swan floating majestically on the river which surrounds the land of death. All these early works reveal a remarkable mastery of the orchestra, with the most resourceful use of the strings reminding us that the composer was a formidable violinist, and in their taut construction they often look forward to the symphonies.

National recognition took a material form in 1897 when the Finnish government awarded him an annual pension, so that like Grieg before him, Sibelius was relieved from the economic pressures which most composers have had to endure. This was necessary in his case as he was not the most astute of businessmen, selling the rights of his *Valse triste* outright for the equivalent of £5 and thus losing a fortune in royalties when the piece became a worldwide hit played by every kind of orchestra from the New York Philharmonic to the Palm Court. He also

Sibelius as a young man about the time he began composing his first major orchestral works, the Kullervo Symphony *and* En Saga

113

won recognition abroad, especially in Anglo-Saxon countries, so that until the war of 1914 he was regularly invited to Germany, England and the United States. He enjoyed these trips, which allowed him to indulge in high living, with good food and drink at the top of his list. He realized, however, that social distractions could adversely affect his career, so in 1904 he decided to leave Helsinki and live in the country. 'Give me,' he said, 'the loneliness either of the Finnish forests or of a big city.' (Paris and London, he had found, were large enough to afford him solitude, whereas Helsinki was not.) He finally chose the village of Järvenpää, some twenty-five miles outside the Finnish capital, where he named his villa Ainola after his wife; and there he lived for the remaining fifty-three years of his life.

Financial security probably helped him to decide to embark on his series of symphonies in 1899 rather than to fulfil commissions, (though he composed the patriotic *Finlandia* that year), and it is on the foundations of those works that his reputation has endured. The Symphony No 1 in E minor shows him already a master of form as well as orchestration, and still at thirty-three strongly influenced by Tchaikovsky, whose *Pathétique* had been composed only six years previously. It makes a strong impact, the lush opening theme of the slow movement and the extrovert big tune of the finale having a Tchaikovskian appeal, the Scherzo generating almost physical excitement, and the whole work abounding in sudden, vivid contrasts. The Symphony No 2 in D major, which followed two years later, is similar in character though less even. The music of its first movement unfolds with such ease that its strength and originality tend to be overlooked: many of its individual themes and ideas appear to stem from a common source, a procedure which has led some commentators to imagine Sibelius was breaking with sonata form – whereas he was rather developing it with a new subtlety. The slow movement is rhapsodic in style, first sombre and then restless, and there is a more playful restlessness in the Scherzo. The final movement is rather a let-down, for what is offered as the expected big tune turns out to be rather lame, its frequent reappearances eventually leading to near-banality.

After this second symphony Sibelius shed all Russian influences and developed a symphonic voice and style entirely his own, exploring entirely new ground with each of the subsequent five symphonies. This change came appropriately enough with the turn of the century, for the first two symphonies belong to the nineteenth century and the others to the twentieth in conception as well as time. With the

Symphony No 3 in C major, completed in 1907, it is clear from the beginning that Sibelius knows exactly where he is going. In its restraint the first movement is more classical than anything in the earlier works, as clear in outline as a symphony by Haydn, but at the same time its musical ideas grow so naturally and inevitably one from another that there are no breaks in the musical argument. If ever the word 'athletic' can be applied to the movement of a symphony it is here, for the music is all muscle and no fat. The second movement is altogether more relaxed, a series of musings rather than variations on a gently elusive melody. Even more original in construction is the finale, which falls into two separate sections of equal length, this giving the impression that the symphony is in four movements when there are in fact only three.

The next two symphonies are in the strongest possible contrast to one another, representing Sibelius at his most introspective and then at his most extrovert. With the Symphony No 4 in A minor he seems to be reacting against the self-indulgence and opulence of so much music of the time, the first decade of the century in which Mahler was composing symphonies of enormous length and Richard Strauss was using the orchestra to produce orgies of colourful sound. Sibelius gave his answer in a work which is condensed to the point of terseness, with hesitant rhythms and a general mood of despair, as though he were prophesying in 1911 the destruction that would come to Europe three years later with the First World War. Curiously though, the Symphony No 5 in E flat, composed in 1915 and revised for the first time a year later, sounds a heroic, optimistic note. It caused its composer a great deal of trouble, for it was not until 1919 that he reworked it to his final satisfaction into the form in which we know it today. The first movement opens in an atmosphere of foreboding, and there is a good deal of tense drama and restlessness in the course of the music, but gradually it increases in energetic drive to reach a triumphant climax in a brilliant coda. The slow movement is one of the most delicate in all the Sibelius symphonies, a theme with variations in pastoral, quite sunny mood, though with hints of dark clouds in the sky. There are hints also of thematic material to come in the third and last movement, which is carried relentlessly forward on two main themes, the first mysteriously bustling and the other with a bold outline that earned the description of Thor swinging his mighty hammer. The tingling physical excitement of this finale has helped to make the Fifth the most popular of the later symphonies.

Sibelius had gradually moved away from conven-

Sibelius with his wife Aino at their villa, named Ainola after her, in the village of Järvenpää some twenty miles from Helsinki

tional sonata form, and with the contemplative Symphony No 6 in D minor it becomes difficult to designate first and second themes or trace thematic development in traditional terms. No doubt largely for this reason it was received with some puzzlement in 1923, and it has never gained wide favour, though today its musical argument seems logical enough, and easy to follow when compared with more recent experiments with symphonic form. The one-movement Symphony No 7 in C major departs even further from tradition, but in its own way integrates his musical ideas in a way for which there is no description other than symphonic. Within this single movement the character of the material experiences many changes of character and tempo, so that certain sections suggest scherzo qualities while others give the impression of the usual slow movement. For years after this there were rumours that Sibelius was composing another symphony, but no such work ever materialized, even though he had assured several interested conductors that it was either close to completion or actually finished. His last major work was

Tapiola, a virtually monothematic tone-poem expressing the very soul of the Scandinavian forests in all their lonely majesty, and it makes a fitting summing up of the composer's mastery of resourceful orchestration and vivid musical imagination. It was completed in 1925, when Sibelius was sixty, and followed only by incidental music for *The Tempest* and finally three short pieces for violin and piano in 1929. Then came twenty-eight years of silence before his death in Järvenpää on 29 September 1957, at the age of ninety-one.

It has been suggested that his retirement, like his failure to deliver the promised eighth symphony, was due to a sudden drying-up of his creative inspiration, and this may well have been the case. It is also possible that he felt he could not surpass the achievements of the Symphony No 7 and *Tapiola* and therefore chose to retire gracefully rather than produce works of lesser stature. He had, after all, generously repaid his country for the moral and material support it had given him: the symphonies and tone-poems place him in the top international league. Curiously, however, these works which have always been loved and admired in the Scandinavian countries, Britain, Germany and the United States have never met with great success in the Latin countries. 115

Sibelius at Ainola, chosen because he preferred to live 'in the loneliness of the Finnish forest or of a big city'

The masterpiece which has broken all national barriers is the Violin Concerto in D minor, which has won itself a place among the half-dozen most popular works in the form. Dating from 1903, and revised two years later, it has the romantic flavour of his early compositions, with a rhetorical first movement, a lush slow movement and an irresistible dancing finale which Donald Tovey happily described as 'a polonaise for polar bears'. Naturally, in view of the composer's own virtuoso abilities, it has all the qualities which appeal to the violinist.

Throughout his retirement Sibelius remained a respected figure in world music, often beset by tourists in the retreat where he already had to cope with visits from a family of five daughters, fifteen grandchildren and twenty-one great-grandchildren. Streets

and parks were named after him, a Sibelius Prize was instituted which benefited Stravinsky and Shostakovich among many others. On his eighty-fifth birthday the President of Finland drove out to the Villa Ainola to pay the nation's respects, while his ninetieth was celebrated with more than a thousand telegrams, gifts from all the Scandinavian kings, cigars from Winston Churchill and a broadcast from London of a birthday concert conducted by Beecham. No composer could ask for more.

Nielsen

The Danish composer Carl Nielsen, who was born on the island of Fyn of humble parents on 9 June 1865, played as a military bandsman before taking up any serious musical studies. He led a comparatively uneventful life, holding various conducting and academic posts and devoting all his free time to composition. By dint of sheer perseverance he became so celebrated in Denmark that his sixtieth birthday was treated as a national event. Recognition abroad came more slowly, and it was not until some years after his death in Copenhagen on 2 October 1931 that his contribution to the symphony began to be appreciated, and even then in a haphazard fashion. His six symphonies are only rarely encountered in the concert halls of Britain or the United States, yet all have been recorded, the best of them being available in half a dozen different versions by leading orchestras with conductors of international stature. Scholars and music historians have proved uncertain where to place him: in some quarters he is regarded as one of the most important modern symphonists, while *The Concise Oxford History of Music* (1979), a volume which runs to almost a thousand pages, dismisses him in a footnote as the composer of incidental music for an obscure Danish play.

His music in the symphonies is broad and powerful, with melodies that are clear in outline and strong in their dramatic and emotional impact on the listener. Most have titles – *The Four Temperaments* (No 1), *Espansiva* (No 3), *Inextinguishable* (No 4) – which are indicative not of any programmatic element but of their general spirit. Their neglect is difficult to explain, because Nielsen's music is quite as accessible and rewarding as that of the later Sibelius symphonies. An original aspect of Nielsen's style is his concluding a symphony in a different key from that in which it began, a concept known as 'progressive tonality' – though this is a technical matter which need not concern a listener wishing only to enjoy symphonies which have a lyrical and dramatic character all of their own.

BRITAIN

After the death of Purcell in 1695 the fortunes of native British music fell into such a sorry decline that it might be said to have died altogether in any real creative sense. The collection of overtures by William Boyce (1711–79) under the title *Eight Symphonies*, published in 1760, makes pleasant listening but can scarcely be considered of major importance in a period which saw such a wealth of glorious music being produced elsewhere in Europe. Attempts have been made to claim Handel as an English composer because he spent his mature working life in London and became a naturalized British subject, but this is blatant cheating born of desperation. One must simply accept the fact that, while it developed a flourishing tradition in poetry, drama and the novel, England failed to produce a composer of international stature for two centuries, until Elgar appeared on the scene. This may bruise her national pride; but it is perhaps not so surprising if we realize that, whereas Italy and Germany were made up of a variety of states whose rulers supported court orchestras and operas, England was a unified country with a single court in London. After the Tudors and Stuarts it saw German monarchs who were rarely interested in music at all and never concerned with specifically English music. The aristocracy too, settled in country homes convenient for the practice of field sports, had little taste for music beyond the call of the hunting horn. Had Gluck, the son of a huntsman, been born in England, he would probably have become no more than a gamekeeper on some desolate Yorkshire moor.

During the eighteenth century there was plenty of music-making in London and elsewhere, but no first-rank English composer emerged. Thomas Arne (1710–78) was, with Boyce, the leading English contemporary of Handel, and wrote some charming theatre music, of which 'Rule, Britannia' remains a famous example. During the Classical and early Romantic periods the most promising composers seem to have died young and thus failed to fulfil the expectations raised by their early works. Thomas Linley junior (1756–78) died in a boating accident. Stephen Storace (1762–96) was a pupil and close friend of Mozart – his sister Nancy sang Susanna in the Vienna premiere of *Figaro* – but he died too young fully to develop his brilliant talent for comic opera in the Mozartian style. George Frederick Pinto (1785–1806) wrote several remarkable chamber pieces that seem to anticipate Schubert, before his untimely death at the age of twenty-one.

In the nineteenth century the concerts which took place in London and the larger cities were attended by growing audiences from the upper and middle classes, but it was not to hear English music or native performers. Similarly, the founding of the Three Choirs Festival in 1724, the Royal Philharmonic Society in 1813 and Manchester's Hallé Orchestra in 1857 did little or nothing to help English music. Audiences gathered to pay homage to Chopin, Liszt and Mendelssohn in the concert hall just as they flocked to hear Italian singers in Italian operas, and even when Covent Garden decided to have an opera in English, the management commissioned the German Weber to compose *Oberon*. Well-to-do families encouraged their daughters to play the piano agreeably and to sing drawing-room songs, but brought up their sons to regard any participation in musical activities as unmanly, fit only for decadent foreigners. Even the intelligentsia, so sensitively responsive to literature, paid scant regard to music. The gibe that Britain was a 'land without music' may have been cruel, but it was not undeserved.

There was a continuing tradition of folk music, of course, but this was associated with the 'lower orders' and was not considered by musicians to be of any importance until Cecil Sharp (1859–1924) collected and published a large body of songs and dances early in the twentieth century. Only through him did the British become aware at last of the valuable store of native music they had so long ignored.

In the middle of the nineteenth century Britain produced three composers of considerable gifts and serious intentions, Arthur Sullivan (1842–1900), the Welshman Hubert Parry (1848–1918) and the Irishman Charles Villiers Stanford (1852–1924). They pursued different courses, though they shared the distinction of being knighted. (The bestowal of honours on musicians was a feature of the reign of Victoria, who though less musically discerning than Prince Albert, took a deep interest in music. She even made entries in her diaries after her visits to the opera which reveal a certain critical flair, frequently penetrating and sometimes quite vitriolic.) Sullivan reached his peak in operetta, Parry in church music and Stanford in opera and song; yet all three sought to make a name in orchestral music. That none of them succeeded in composing enduring music was not due to any lack of craftsmanship or integrity: their work simply had insufficient imagination or personality to compete with the best European music; and such fame as they enjoyed at home waned with the advent of Elgar. Their symphonies have vanished from the repertoire though a few of their shorter works are occasionally to be heard – Sullivan's Overture *Di ballo*, a fine concert piece; Parry's *Symphonic Variations*; and Stanford's Irish rhapsodies.

Arne, a prominent English composer at a time when the German-born Handel dominated the musical scene

Elgar

Although he received no formal musical education to equip him for composition, Edward Elgar grew up in an environment in which music was of paramount practical importance. He was born near Worcester on 2 June 1857, and his family moved into that city two years later so that his father could more conveniently manage his music shop there. In addition to this business, his father served as church organist and piano-tuner, also joining in the active musical life of the city which was one of the centres of the Three Choirs Festival. The young Edward learned to play both piano and organ, but quickly proved his preference for string instruments by teaching himself to play the violin. He showed early signs of his ultimate ambition too, teaching himself composition. 'I am

self-taught,' he declared in later life, 'in the matter of harmony, counterpoint, form and, in short, the whole of the "mystery" of music . . . When I resolved to become a musician and found that the exigencies of life would prevent me from getting any tuition, the only thing to do was to teach myself. I read everything, played everything, and heard everything I possibly could.' After a year in a lawyer's office, he worked from the age of sixteen until he was past thirty as a local musician, taking pupils, playing in concerts and occasionally conducting. His main conducting post for five years was that of the staff band at a lunatic asylum, which surely makes him unique in one respect among the great composers.

For all his own forceful ambition, Elgar needed encouragement from outside himself, and he was fortunate enough to find this in his marriage to Caroline Alice Roberts in 1889. The daughter of a major-general who had retired to a country house in Worcestershire, she not only satisfied his social ambition to marry into a county family but was sufficiently musical to stimulate and sustain his creative imagination. (It is significant that he composed no major work after her death in 1920, though he lived until 1934.) The couple met when Alice decided to take lessons from him. She was too tactful ever to recall what he was like as a teacher, though another of his female pupils recorded that he showed quite plainly that 'teaching was the most loathsome thing in his life' and that he spent most of the time during lessons eyeing his golf clubs in a corner of the room. His social ambition and his keenness for outdoor activities are not irrelevant; they were significant elements in Elgar's complex personality. He developed into a typical Edwardian country gentleman with a bombastic sense of patriotism that is expressed in the *Pomp and Circumstance* Marches, aspects which have unfortunately and mistakenly been given far too much attention. Elgar should not be judged on the strength of his occasional 'public' pieces alone any more than Tchaikovsky should be assessed by his *1812* Overture, Sibelius by *Finlandia* or Beethoven by his *Battle Symphony*. His true creative stature is revealed in his major works – *The Dream of Gerontius*, the 'Enigma' Variations, *Falstaff*, the symphonies and concertos – all of which put him among the front-rank European composers, transcending time and place.

Although choral compositions occupied much of his time between 1889 and 1906, several orchestral works of this period indicate his ultimate goal – the symphony. The early Serenade for Strings, for example, completed in 1892 after he had made a new

The Photographer taking a picture of all the characters in Frederick Ashton's ballet version of the Enigma Variations

home in Malvern, shows not only his remarkable understanding of the expressive potential of the string orchestra, but also a masterly handling of the thematic material. The music, reflective in character, has a mellowness that is surprising in a composer at the beginning of his career, and Elgar gives the work unity by recalling in the Finale two snatches of melody from the opening movement. Symphonic skill becomes more apparent with the *Cockaigne* Overture, subtitled 'In London Town', which though a vivid sound-picture of the bustling metropolis is cast in a form which can be analyzed in terms of exposition of themes, development, recapitulation and coda. The orchestration is nothing less than brilliant, showing that Elgar had much of the flair of Richard Strauss for creating varied sound textures and colours. Strauss, incidentally, was among the first musicians on the Continent to recognize the genius of Elgar.

The most original and inspired of his early works came with the 'Enigma' Variations, for which he is perhaps celebrated above all else; and it came almost by accident. He was improvising at the piano one day, showing his wife the different ways in which certain of their friends might play the same melody, when she cleverly suggested that he should turn the idea into a 'proper' composition. Its nickname arose later when Elgar hinted that a larger theme, never actually stated, could be played simultaneously with his own original one. Many suggestions regarding this other melody have been put forward, but it is difficult to fight down the suspicion that no such tune ever existed and that Elgar, who had a keen sense of humour, was simply leg-pulling, revelling in the thought of sending out generations of musicologists on a wild goose chase. There is certainly a touch of mock-modesty in a letter he wrote at the time: 'Just completed a set of variations, thirteen in number, but I call the finale the fourteenth because of the ill-luck attaching to that number. I think that in each variation I have looked at the theme through the personality of another Johnny. I don't know if it's too intimate an idea for print, but it's distinctly amusing.' The variations certainly have their amusing moments, but far from being 'too intimate for print' proved to be his most popular work. Each variation bears the initials of the friend it represents, and each is a very clear character portrait: 'C.A.E.' is an appropriately tender tribute to his wife; 'R.B.T.' switches from grumpy bassoons to flutes to describe a friend whose voice would suddenly jump an octave in pitch; 'W.N.' makes gentle fun of a neighbour who was a chatterbox, involving restless syncopation; 119

Elgar at his most patriotic conducting massed choirs in 'Land of Hope and Glory' at the British Empire Exhibition at Wembley in 1924

Nimrod is spacious in the manner of a Beethoven slow movement, dedicated to his greatest friend A E Jaeger ('hunter' in German); and 'G.R.S.' depicts an organist friend and his playful dog. The portraits are fascinating to study, but the work stands even without this unique feature as one of the most skilful and musically satisfying sets of variations in the repertoire.

'I hold that the symphony without a programme is the highest development of art,' Elgar once declared, so it is not surprising that he waited until he was fifty-one before producing one, in 1908. He had, however, already composed a masterpiece in abstract form, the Introduction and Allegro for Strings, three years earlier. Its chief theme was inspired during a holiday in Wales when he heard a choir singing in the distance, but the main influence on the work was the Handelian concerto grosso; Elgar decided to pit a solo string quartet against the greater weight of a string orchestra. The Introduction opens with an electrifying crunch of sound, then continues in reflective mood until the Allegro, which uses the same themes with ever-increasing resourcefulness – including what the composer described as 'the devil of a fugue' – to build up into a piece unsurpassed in its field for resonance, colour and brilliance.

Long preparation made the Symphony No 1 in A flat a work of the utmost maturity and assurance, arguably the finest non-programmatic symphony since those of Brahms. It was dedicated to the composer's German champion Hans Richter, who conducted its premiere in Manchester with the Hallé Orchestra, and it enjoyed such success that it was given almost a hundred performances in the following twelve months. Though Romantic in feeling it breaks with the Classical outlines only in having an introductory march which returns with the development and coda of the first movement and again in the fourth movement. Another 'cyclic' feature of the symphony exists in the similarity between the main melodies of the second and third movements. The second, marked Allegro molto and really a Scherzo, contrasts an impetuous *perpetuum mobile* theme with a Trio which introduces a section in march rhythm. The Adagio has a nobility reminiscent of the Beethoven slow movements which Elgar so enjoyed discussing with his friend Jaeger, and is indeed worthy of the Viennese master he so admired. After a slow introduction the Finale breaks into a lively Allegro which is ingeniously developed to a climax which sees the return of the opening march and then builds up to a sumptuous close. Some have complained that Elgar uses the marking *nobilmente* too freely, to which one can only reply that many of his themes really *are* noble.

Appreciation of the Symphony No 2 in E flat has been bedevilled by its dedication to the memory of Edward VII (it was in fact planned as a tribute to the king while he was still alive), and by the quotation on the score of Shelley's lines, 'Rarely, rarely, comest thou, Spirit of Delight'. These have led commentators to search for a programme to the symphony, even though Elgar emphasized that he had no such thought when composing the music. It is a dramatic work, but in the purely musical sense of the Classical symphony, creating tension through thematic contrast and changes of key. The spirit of delight, contrary to Shelley's statement, appears frequently in the symphony, though feelings of doubt and sorrow lie just beneath the surface, always ready to take over. There is no motto theme, as in the earlier symphony, but again Elgar makes effective use of a variety of short phrases treated in an almost Wagnerian way; and although there is no thematic link between movements the work has a clear sense of unity. The sheer energy of the first movement gives way to broad solemnity in the second, and the somewhat sinister power of the third is similarly balanced by the spirit of acceptance which characterizes the finale.

Between the two symphonies Elgar composed the Violin Concerto in B minor, one of the most substantial in the repertoire, in 1910. He had planned a concerto some twenty years earlier, but had been dissatisfied with his sketches, and even when he took up the challenge for the second time he felt the need to seek constant advice from his friend William Reed. It was Reed who first played the concerto, with Elgar at the piano, to a private gathering of friends, and it was eventually given in its full form at the Queen's Hall in London with Fritz Kreisler as soloist and the composer conducting. It is at once highly virtuosic and elaborately symphonic in construction, belonging rather to the category of the Beethoven and Brahms concertos than to the easier-going display pieces by Mendelssohn and Bruch. The first movement follows sonata form, with one main subject made up of a number of motives and the other more expansively melodious; it excludes the usual solo cadenza. The second movement is a glowing Andante revealing Elgar in his most lyrical form. It is the third movement, the longest and most elaborate, which is the most original, for after a closely argued development the composer springs his biggest surprise, a lengthy accompanied cadenza. One might feel that an accompanied cadenza is a contradiction in terms, but it works here to the advantage both of the soloist and of the symphonic design of the whole work, allowing the violin to recall earlier moments from all the movements of the concerto.

When Elgar came to *Falstaff* in 1913 he produced his only work with a detailed programme, which he called a symphonic study. It does indeed fall into four movements, but there is no slow one as is usual in a symphony. It is carefully constructed musically as well as being pictorial in the manner of, say, the *Don Juan* of Richard Strauss (to whose style Elgar comes closest in this work). Elgar chose to portray the ebullient boaster of the *Henry IV* plays rather than the diminished Falstaff of *The Merry Wives of Windsor*, so there is plenty of swagger in the music, which fully reveals the composer's mastery of orchestration. Various themes are employed to show facets of Falstaff's character, and the transformation of Prince Hal from playboy to the stern soldier-king is clearly established by a change of character motives. It is a happy, extrovert work for the most part, but at the end, with the rejection of Falstaff by his one-time drinking companion, there is a keen sense of Elgar expressing his regret of the passing of the old order throughout Europe.

Personal sorrow finds more direct expression in the Cello Concerto in E minor of 1918, whose wistful character reflects Elgar's near-despair over the war which had cost so many lives and destroyed so many of the human values in which he believed. It is in no way a depressing work, for though it is austerely scored it has great melodic warmth and allows the soloist many opportunities for virtuoso display. Typically of the composer, it opens with a powerful *nobilmente* flourish, a motto which returns in two of the other three movements. The first movement presents the soloist largely in soliloquy, the second has the fleet-footed characteristics of a scherzo, the third is in the nature of an elegiac song without words, and the fourth alternates between swagger and tragic resignation. The concerto ranks with Dvořák's both in musical interest and the challenge it poses to the soloist, and as Elgar's last major work makes an impressive swan-song.

When Elgar died on 23 February 1934, he had been honoured with the Order of Merit and a baronetcy, and held the appointment of Master of the King's Music but more importantly he had proved that an English composer could produce a body of work comparable in quality and originality to that of his contemporaries anywhere in the world. That his music, so widely played at home, should be largely neglected abroad cannot easily be explained. He is not in any real sense a nationalistic composer (for he had no interest in folk music and never incorporated any into his work), but rather a follower of the grand German tradition. Perhaps the dismissal of Britain as a land without music, once so justified, has so prejudiced musicians abroad that they have refused to recognize genius where it so patently exists. Whatever the reason, the neglect of Elgar abroad has been Europe's loss.

Delius

To turn from Elgar to Delius is to encounter an entirely different musical personality. Although claimed as an English composer, Frederick Delius was the son of a wealthy Prussian industrialist who had settled in Bradford for business reasons. Born there on 29 January 1862, Frederick was intended to follow a business career too, but travels in Europe, especially Scandinavia, during his teens awoke thoughts of an entirely different way of life. When he was sent to Florida in 1882 to manage an orange plantation his 121

Augustus John sketch of Delius, who created a style of his own from his belief that 'music is simply the expression of poetical and emotional nature'

encounter with black song confirmed his resolve to make music his career, and he studied there for some months with a local musician before taking up more formal training at Leipzig. He rejected the Leipzig school of composition, however, and the main influence on his future was his friendship there with Grieg. Neither Germany nor England appealed very strongly to him, so he settled first in Paris from 1888 until 1897, then for the rest of his life at the little village of Grez-sur-Loing some forty miles from the French capital. There he composed in a style completely his own, one which nobody had even hinted at before. Several composers, notably Grieg and Wagner, influenced his music, but only as starting points for his own imaginative development, and he was generally most happy when dispensing with established forms. 'Learning kills instinct,' he wrote in an often quoted statement of his musical beliefs. 'Never believe that one must hear music many times to understand it: that is the last refuge of the incompetent. Music is simply the expression of a poetical and emotional nature.' There is no refuting the fact that his own music was essentially poetic and emotional, but it would be quite wrong to think that he did not work hard to give it form, even though this was never conventional.

Many of the titles of his orchestral pieces, which are usually quite short, suggest an Impressionistic approach similar to Debussy's, but whereas the French composer aimed to capture the essence of the scene itself Delius was more concerned with expressing the emotions the scene would inspire in the onlooker. His Nocturne, for example, subtitled *Paris, the Song of a Great City*, makes no attempt to create a sound-picture of Paris, but reflects the composer's own memories. It is one of his most attractive early works, cast in several sections, an opening night piece followed by dances and contrasting song-like movements. *Appalachia*, designed as a prologue followed by a theme with fourteen variations and a choral finale featuring a baritone soloist, is more objectively descriptive: it mirrors the moods of tropical nature in the swamps bordering the Mississippi and recalls the slave songs he had heard as a young man in Florida. The better-known English Rhapsody *Brigg Fair* is also in variation form, in four sections running continuously. Here Delius employs an unusually large orchestra, yet the textures are always clear, and the rhapsody is a magical nature piece of impressions recollected in tranquillity.

The drifting harmonies favoured by Delius cast a dreamy haze over much of his music, notably in the short pieces which are perhaps his most popular. 'Certain passages of *In a Summer Garden*,' wrote his friend Philip Heseltine (the composer Peter Warlock), 'suggest a kind of *pointillisme* as though the luminous effect of the whole were attained by a thousand little points of light and colour.' This is an apt description, and it makes the important point that Delius was a consummate craftsman, who exerted the utmost discipline on his imagination so that his music, however free, always moved step by logical step in the highly individual patterns he created. Endless fastidious care went into the writing of melodies which seem to float along with careless ease, as in *Summer Night on the River* and *A Song before Sunrise*, not to mention the deceptively simple *On Hearing the First Cuckoo in Spring* with its Norwegian (*not* English) folktune. Another favourite concert piece, *The Walk to the Paradise Garden*, an intermezzo from the opera *A Village Romeo and Juliet*, is unique in its mood of impassioned tenderness. In all these works the opulent harmonic writing is Delius's own, so that any of his music can be recognized from the first few bars.

Forays into traditional forms, such as the piano, violin and cello concertos, proved less satisfying, for the genius of Delius was to make his own way rather than to tread paths already made by others. In his larger works he was most successful with his operas and the *Mass of Life*. He was too original to win immediate recognition, Germany taking to him first, England holding back until a Delius champion emerged in the person of Thomas Beecham, and France, where he had chosen to live, virtually ignoring him. In later years, overtaken by blindness, he was fortunate to find a perfect amanuensis in Eric Fenby, who not only took down his work but himself realized a number of uncompleted scores. When he died on 10 June 1934, Delius left no stylistic followers, remaining a solitary yet infinitely fascinating figure in musical history.

Vaughan Williams

The most essentially 'English' of this first group of composers was Ralph Vaughan Williams, a fact which accounts for the special affection with which he was regarded by the British public throughout his long life. He was born in the Gloucestershire village of Down Ampney on 12 October 1872, the son of a clergyman but connected on his mother's side with families which had produced such distinguished men as Charles Darwin and Josiah Wedgwood. While still in his teens his Trio in G major was given before an audience of staff and fellow-pupils at Charterhouse, and he was fully determined to make a career as a composer. Having completed his musical studies under Parry and Stanford, he did not allow the luxury of a private income to distract him from the pursuit of this career: no man who combined a honeymoon in Berlin with attending performances of *The Ring* could be accused of lack of dedication. His visits to Germany brought him temporarily under the spell of Wagner, and he also studied briefly with Max Bruch, but he tempered this Teutonic influence with further formal instruction from Ravel. It might be thought that these experiencies would turn him into a cosmopolitan composer, but in fact he reacted against the German-dominated musical language of his time, and from his studies in France he retained only the skill in orchestration he had learned from Ravel.

Two factors combined to give Vaughan Williams his particular 'English' qualities. In the first place, he drew inspiration from English folksong, English hymnody, the music of the Tudor period and from his interest in the early English poets. He served as musical editor of the new *English Hymnal* from 1904 to 1906, which, as he wrote many years later, 'was a better musical education than any amount of sonatas and fugues'. Secondly, he was firm in the belief that 'the composer must not shut himself up and think about art; he must live with his fellows and make his art an expression of the whole life of the community'. For this reason he gave the same care

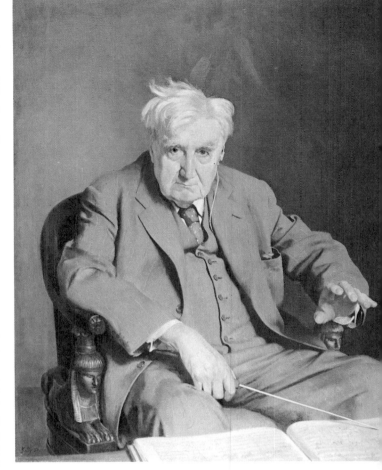

Vaughan Williams, whose musical idiom was strongly influenced by English folksong and the style of Tudor church music

to music designed for amateur singers and players and to his many film scores as to his symphonic works. It was quite natural for him to draw upon the English choral tradition for his *Sea* Symphony (1910), which in addition to the settings of Whitman poems combines traditional sea-songs in its Scherzo. Similarly, the *London* Symphony of four years later incorporates the Westminster chimes and the sounds of mouth organ and hansom cab bells within the conventional four-movement form. Neither, however, is nearly so impressive as an earlier work, the *Fantasia on a Theme of Thomas Tallis* for string orchestra divided into three sections – a full body of strings, a small orchestra of nine players and a solo quartet. These three groups are used in various ways, sometimes playing as one body, sometimes antiphonally, and sometimes accompanying each other. The music may conjure up for the listener the England of the Tudors, 123 but apart from the 'borrowed' theme it is a wholly modern work, and a most original one, even though it adopts the fantasia form current in the time of Tallis and later revived by Purcell.

Vaughan Williams's next symphony was his *Pastoral* (1921), of which he wrote: 'The mood of this symphony is almost entirely quiet and contemplative; there are few fortissimos and few allegros. The only really quick passage is the coda to the third movement, and that is all pianissimo.' It is in no way programmatic, however, despite its title: there are no bird-calls as in Beethoven's *Pastoral*, for it is an expression of moods rather than an attempt to depict nature. One of its many unusual features is the introduction of a soprano soloist into the last movement to sing a wordless recitative, another the dependence on changing orchestral colours. It is clear from these first three symphonies that Vaughan Williams was not a man either to follow established patterns or to climb on to any fashionable bandwagon, and in his three central and most successful symphonies he shows the same spirit of independence.

The Symphony No 4 in F minor appeared in 1934, when the composer was sixty-two, and marked a new direction in his development. It bears no title, has no programme and is purely orchestral: even more unusual, its tone is one of violence, even bitterness. It also has a motto within the first main theme of the first movement which plays an essential role in the work as a whole, and while this movement has a very short development section and an irregular recapitulation, its scheme is more purely symphonic than anything in the earlier essays in the form. Because of the militant nature of the music, this symphony has been interpreted as the composer's prophetic vision of the war that was to break out five years later, and it is possible that the march of world events, with which Vaughan Williams was always concerned, may have inspired a new dissonance in his music. (*Job*, a masque for dancing inspired by Blake's *Illustrations to the Book of Job*, had already shown his involvement with matters of moral conflict in 1931.) Curiously, during the actual war years he wrote a symphony expressing thoughts of peace: in No 5 in D major, dedicated to Sibelius. It returns to modal harmony and the polyphonic textures of the *Pastoral* Symphony. With some justification it has been described as a vision of peace, for the music does suggest the calm mind and resignation of spirit which might be expected of a man entering his seventies. Any thought that he was bidding farewell to the world, however, was dispelled four years later when he startled audiences with the savagely disturbing Symphony No 6 in E minor (1947), a work of violently contrasted moods and conflicting textures. This remains his most powerful work, even though its concluding section is a ghostly fugue played pianissimo throughout.

Three more symphonies followed, including the *Antartica*, which was built largely from the music he composed for the film *Scott of the Antarctic*, and the light-hearted No 8 in D minor; but the three central ones remain his most substantial. In all the symphonies, however, and in his other orchestral works, Vaughan Williams combined musical conservatism with unpredictable originality. He avoided the excesses of Romantic rhetoric, and the strong mystical streak in his creative personality was balanced by a very practical outlook on the composer's place in society. Even in his eighties he was regularly seen at leading musical events in London, where he had finally made his home after a lifetime's residence in the country. He retained so much energy that on his last visit to the United States in 1954, he insisted after a hectic day's sight-seeing on staying up to watch the sunset from the top of the Empire State Building. His music may not have made any great impression outside Britain and the United States, but it bears the hallmark of a composer of vivid individuality and integrity and seems likely to endure where already established. When he died in London on 26 August 1958, a day on which he was to have attended a recording session of his last symphony, he was mourned by British music-lovers not only as a genius who had helped to create a new and healthy climate for younger composers to inherit, but also as the friendliest of national figures.

Holst

Although he was of Swedish descent, Holst belongs quite firmly to the English tradition. Born into a musical family at Cheltenham on 21 September 1874, he was drawn into musical activities in his youth, playing the organ at a local church and conducting a choral society. At the Royal College of Music in London, where he studied composition, his main teacher was Stanford, and he increased his ties with English music by becoming a lifelong friend of a fellow-student, Vaughan Williams. He was a shy, rather remote person, whom poor health drove into increasing withdrawal from public activities into the society of a few close friends. His daughter Imogen, a conductor later associated with Benjamin Britten and the Aldeburgh Festival, noted in her biography of him that his occasional moods of despair drove him into a 'grey isolation'. From 1903 onwards he taught at various London music colleges, apparently caring little for the fame his steady stream of compositions won for him, though he seems to have been gratified by the invitations to visit the United States and the warmth with which he was received there.

Unlike Elgar and Delius, Holst took a keen interest in English folk melody, which plays a considerable part in his *Somerset Rhapsody* and the Shakespearean opera *At the Boar's Head*, just as his love of poetry was reflected in his *Ode to Death*, inspired by Whitman, his tone-poem *Egdon Heath*, a tribute to Thomas Hardy, and his settings of Keats in the Choral Symphony. It was his lifelong interest in astrology and Eastern mysticism, however, which prompted the work by which he most widely known, the orchestral suite *The Planets*. This occupied him between 1914 and 1917, and he leapt to prominence with its first performance the following year conducted by the young Adrian Boult. Its seven movements are widely contrasted in mood, melody and instrumental colour, the whole work constituting an orchestral *tour de force* which appeals to all conductors and has gained enormous popularity with audiences everywhere. It calls for a huge orchestra, including an organ, two harps and a whole battery of percussion, but these forces

Holst, a composer firmly established in the English tradition in spite of his Swedish descent, and a close friend of Vaughan Williams

are used with the utmost discrimination, Holst drawing from his resources only what he needs for each movement and throwing in their full weight only when the occasion demands.

'Mars, the Bringer of War' opens the suite with music of elemental power, its menace relentlessly increasing in power to the final reiteration of brutal chords which emphasize that Holst did not share the delusion, so common at the time, that there was something glorious about war. 'Venus, the Bringer of Peace' has a calmness and sense of distance that are almost unearthly, while 'Mercury, the Winged Messenger' moves into another world of fantasy, one of Mendelssohnian lightness. 'Jupiter, the Bringer of Jollity' shows an unexpected extrovert side to the composer, with a swaggering big tune reminiscent of Elgar, whereas 'Saturn, the Bringer of Old Age' builds up fragments of elusive melody until they eventually achieve a majestic flow. 'Uranus, the Magician' blends humour with mystery, culminating in an eerie organ glissando, and then the final movement, 'Neptune, the Mystic' carries the listener in his imagination right out into space, the orchestra playing with 'dead tone' (the composer's own words), and the wordless women's chorus at the end giving an impression of a limitless universe. Holst never achieved the originality and brilliance of *The Planets* again, though he continued to write music until his death in London on 25 May 1934; but this one masterpiece ensures him an enduring place in the concert repertoire.

Bax, Rubbra, Walton

Although they have not enjoyed anything like the success of Vaughan Williams, several British composers have followed him along the symphonic path. The most neglected has been Havergal Brian (1876–1972) whose thirty-two symphonies include the massive *Gothic* of 1919 which remained unperformed until 1961. Most of them have still never been played. Arnold Bax (1883–1953) composed seven symphonies, some of which were frequently performed in England during his lifetime but which have since fallen by the wayside, temporarily at least. He was greatly gifted, becoming a writer of stories and poems as well as a composer, and because he had independent means he was free to indulge his gifts in any direction he chose. His style is Romantic, his musical language Wagnerian, and the tensions in his symphonies arise from mood rather than thematic and tonal contrasts. His rhapsodic approach is perhaps better suited to the tone-poem; his evocative *Tintagel* and *The Garden of Fand*, still occasionally played, seem more likely to survive. Edmund Rubbra (*b* 1901) is also unlikely to see his seven symphonies find a place in the repertoire even at home, distinguished though they may be. He has developed an individual style diverging from the Classical concept of the symphony, but it is one which has not appealed to a wide public, and like Bax he has secured only a few enthusiastic followers.

William Walton (*b* 1902) adopted a more Continental style from the beginning, and was even regarded as something of an *enfant terrible* for a time, so his work has enjoyed a much wider appeal. His music for *Façade*, originally designed to accompany the recitation of poems by Edith Sitwell, was subsequently arranged in the form of two concert suites which won great popularity through their melodic appeal and astringent wit. His Symphony No 1 in B flat (1932–5) achieves dramatic tension in a Classical rather than Romantic manner, and reveals an architectural mastery rare in twentieth-century symphonies. A second

Walton, more Continental in style than other English composers, has developed from enfant terrible *to Establishment figure.*

symphony, composed more than twenty years later, is a less substantial work, though an accomplished one. The Viola Concerto of 1929 and the Violin Concerto of ten years later are the most successful examples of Walton's gift for warm lyricism spiced with a dash of bitters, works which have some of the qualities of Prokofiev. Smaller pieces like the *Scapino* and *Portsmouth Point* Overtures have found a regular place in concert programmes, while his music for *Henry V* and *Hamlet* established him as the one of the finest composers of film scores.

Tippett

An unusually self-critical composer, Michael Tippett (*b* 1905) has not allowed us to form any idea of his youthful works. In 1930, while a teacher at a school in Surrey, he reacted so sharply to a local concert devoted to his compositions that he destroyed everything he had written and returned to college for further study. He was thirty-four before he produced an orchestral work that satisfied him, the Concerto for Double String Orchestra. One of the most beautiful pieces for string orchestra composed this century,

eloquently lyrical and sumptuous, it immediately established his reputation. The Symphony No 1, which followed six years later, is based in traditional sonata style, and its textures are rich in the manner Tippett adopted at the time. This richness also characterizes his first opera, *The Midsummer Marriage* (1955), which took him seven years to write; the stylistic changes in his instrumental music have subsequently run parallel to the new directions his operas have taken. His Symphony No 3, for instance, includes three blues numbers for solo soprano in its final movement, a reflection of the blues ensemble which closes the first act of *The Knot Garden* (1970), just as the spare, tough style of his Concerto for Orchestra had resulted directly from his earlier opera *King Priam*. His concentration on opera tended to draw him away from purely orchestral music, though he composed his Symphony No 4, a one-movement work constructed along unusual yet symphonically logical lines, in 1977. Never a composer whose next move can be predicted, he reverted to a more warmly lyrical mood in 1980 for his decorative Triple Concerto for violin, viola and cello.

Britten

Although most celebrated for his operas and other vocal works, Benjamin Britten (1913–76) first made his international mark with his *Variations on a Theme of Frank Bridge* in 1937. These variations on a lilting melody by his first teacher explore every aspect of string technique, and have tuneful appeal spiced with clever parodies of other composers. This light side of his genius is also in evidence in the two suites he made from music he had originally composed for films, *Matinées Musicales* and *Soirées Musicales*, both based on melodies from Rossini. Each suite has been used for ballet. Britten never attempted a true symphony, even though three of his works bear the title. The *Simple Symphony*, an engaging piece for string orchestra in four movements is really a suite, as indicated by descriptive numbers such as 'Playful Pizzicato' and 'Sentimental Sarabande'. The *Sinfonia da Requiem* bears as little relationship to the symphony as it does to the Requiem, its sombre, intense music simply suggesting the atmosphere of the Mass. It was commissioned by the Japanese government to celebrate the country's royal dynasty, and so it seems like a deliberate joke by the pacifist composer to give Christian liturgical titles to its three movements.

The best known of Britten's orchestral works is *The Young Person's Guide to the Orchestra*, composed in 1945 for a film on the different instruments of the symphony orchestra. It consists of a set of thirteen

variations on a piece of incidental music by Purcell, each showing off the characteristics of particular instruments, after which a fugue brings them all back one by one. Far more than a simple guide, this work is so ingenious and inventive that it is a valid item for the concert hall; for Britten, like Mozart, was a wholly practical music-maker who worked with the utmost fastidiousness at every commission he undertook.

Tippett and Britten may be said to represent the last great traditional British composers. There are, of course, other composers who have made worthwhile contributions to English music. They have not made the same impact, however, and their works are only encountered from time to time. Among older composers are Arthur Bliss (1891–1975), Lennox Berkeley (b 1903), Constant Lambert (1905–51) and Alan Rawsthorne (1905–71); while the younger generation which has kept in touch with traditional styles includes Richard Rodney Bennett (b 1936) and the Australian-born Malcolm Williamson (b 1931).

Tippett and Britten, the outstanding British composers of the twentieth century who admired each other's work with no sense of rivalry

THE UNITED STATES

The composer in the United States during the nineteenth century found himself in an even more difficult position than his British counterparts. British music at that time was dominated by Continental forms and styles, despite the legacies of folk music and the tradition of the Elizabethans and Purcell. American composers, lacking even these influences, scarcely knew where to start. It is often claimed that there is a body of American folksong, but in the usual sense of the term this is not justifiable. Negro spirituals, for instance, though they may have developed from an earlier type of folksong which has been lost, are already sophisticated in the form we know them. They cannot be considered as truly national, moreover, since they have so much in common with older folk music from other parts of the world. The songs of the Appalachian mountaineers, once believed to be of purely local origin, are just as suspect, for many of them are concerned with the sea, which these inland people would never even have glimpsed, let alone been familiar with. Then the American settlers, when they had any musical background, simply took European music with them. When a public for concerts and operas finally made its appearance in the latter half of the nineteenth century, it was made up of people who had gone to the new 'land of promise' from Central Europe.

MacDowell

Leaving aside a few now forgotten names, Edward MacDowell ranks as the first American composer, yet although he was born in New York on 18 December 1861 and died there on 23 January 1908, he was almost completely Europeanized. He was taken at the age of sixteen to study in Paris, and subsequently to Wiesbaden and Frankfurt. He became a professor at the Darmstadt and at the age of twenty-one, encouraged by Liszt, he appeared at Zürich as soloist in his own first piano concerto and at once established his name. Even after his return to the United States in 1888, however, he remained a composer in the German Romantic tradition. Other European influences are indicated by the titles of works such as the *Norse* and *Celtic* sonatas. He did, on the other hand, break away from these influences to some extent in his *Indian Suite*, which draws on Indian melodies, and his music, from whatever source it derives its style, is attractive and ably constructed. His best-known work, the Piano Concerto No 2 in D minor, represents all that is best in a composer of talent and melodic inventiveness.

MacDowell, whose short career put America on the musical map for the first time although his music followed the European tradition

Ives

The composer who first expressed the American spirit in music was wholly eccentric as well as wholly original. Charles Ives, born in Danbury, Connecticut, on 20 October 1874, was the son of a bandmaster who encouraged him to experiment with musical sound from an early age. He later tried to absorb an academic training at Yale, but simply could not conform to standard musical practices, and on leaving university he began selling insurance in New York. He must have had a more conventional head for business, for in 1906 he became co-founder of an insurance firm which gave him a lifetime's financial security. For more than twenty years he led a double life, working in his office every day and at the same time composing a considerable amount of orchestral and chamber music of which his colleagues knew virtually nothing. The onset of diabetes and heart disease made him give up composition in 1928 and his official work two years later. Most of his music remained unknown until the 1950s, just before his death, though in 1947 he had been awarded a Pulitzer Prize for his Symphony No 3. He wrote four symphonies in all, the first of which owes something to Dvořák and Tchaikovsky, but which are otherwise completely individual in conception. Regarded from a conventional standpoint they are uneven works; Ives's quirky style is better suited to his shorter pieces in freer form, and it is these which made him something of a cult figure after his death in New York on 19 May 1954.

His music constantly evokes memories of the town bands, church choirs, dance and theatre orchestras of his New England youth, these memories being recalled with greater sophistication and complexity as his style developed. He was a nationalist composer in that he set out to express the American character in the spiritual and moral sense as well as the cultural. Unaffected and without pretension, he gathered the material for his works – dances, hymns, marching songs – and welded them together, sometimes clumsily but at other times with remarkable cohesion. It would be wrong to think of him as a

Ives, an eccentric and original genius, whose music drew its inspiration from material growing out of the American way of life

naive craftsman; on the contrary, he was composing atonally several years before Schoenberg. His experiments had no influence simply because none of his music was performed until long after it had been written, by which time similar techniques had been evolved by other composers. He did not adopt new techniques to advance a theory, as Schoenberg did: they happened incidentally as he sought a new way of composing that would correspond more closely than any European style to the American way of life. It is remarkable that later American composers have not taken up his pioneering work but have left him an isolated, enigmatic figure.

Gershwin

Even more curious than the neglect of Ives is the fact that the name of George Gershwin should be the first to come to most people's minds at the mention of American music. He was, after all, primarily a composer of 'popular' rather than 'serious' music. But this very distinction is a problem that has increasingly bedeviled music in the twentieth century. Certain forms of music have always appealed to wider audiences than others: during the nineteenth century, for example, more people knew melodies from the operas of Rossini and Verdi than themes from a Beethoven or Brahms symphony. On the other hand, no territorial lines were drawn between them, and nobody would think of arguing as to whether a Johann Strauss waltz was popular or serious. It is only during the present century that this distinction has been made and that a regrettable cultural snobbery has developed with it.

Gershwin, who was born in New York on 26 September 1898, was acutely aware of this new situation. He took lessons in his youth with the vague intention of becoming a concert pianist, but when he left school at the age of fifteen he took a job as a staff pianist with a song-plugging firm in Tin Pan Alley. Two years later he had his first song published, and he began writing others for use in Broadway shows, finally making his name with 'Swanee', written for Al Jolson. Then in 1924 he was invited by Paul Whiteman to compose a work for piano and orchestra, involving the jazz idiom, for a concert to be given at the Aeolian Hall in New York. The result was the famous *Rhapsody in Blue*, which won almost unanimous public approval but was given a mainly unfavourable critical reception, partly because it was known that Gershwin had needed Whiteman's arranger to orchestrate it for him. On its own terms it is an attractive work saved from sentimentality by its jazzy tang and energy. It is important to stress that 129 the music is jazzy rather than being true jazz, a qualification which applies to most other jazz-inspired works written for the concert hall; for there is no improvisation as in real jazz.

Undeterred by adverse criticism, Gershwin continued along the 'serious' path and produced his Piano Concerto in F minor in 1925, having learned the principles of orchestration so that he could compose the whole score himself. This does not attempt sonata form, Gershwin relying for variety in the opening Allegro by re-statements of its two main themes, one in Charleston rhythm and the other more gracious, interspersed with snatches of new melodies. The syncopated piano style changes to chromaticism in the course of the movement, with the composer glancing over his shoulder from time to time in the direction of Grieg and Rachmaninov. The Andante contrasts a blues-style theme for muted trumpet with a perkier melody for the piano, while strings and woodwind introduce yet another theme in a central section. There is tremendous vigour in the final Allegro agitato, so that the three movements follow traditional sequence. Gershwin made every effort to

Gershwin, a composer of popular music whose ventures into the symphonic style have won wider favour than any by his more 'serious' compatriots

establish himself as a serious composer, and during a tour of Europe he asked both Ravel and Nadia Boulanger to take him as a pupil. They both refused, not because they doubted his ability to master more traditional and advanced procedures but because they felt it wrong to interfere with a talent that was so original and valuable in its own way.

While devoting most of his energies to composing Broadway musicals, Gershwin found time to compose the opera *Porgy and Bess* (1935) and the descriptive *Cuban Overture* and *An American in Paris* which virtually complete his orchestral works. He had plans for a symphony and a string quartet, but his career was cut short by his sudden death in Hollywood on 11 July 1937 at the age of thirty-eight. His popularity with the public has endured, though his reputation has come under heavy fire from critics both of serious music and of jazz, prejudice being rampant in both these camps. He holds an unassailable position as a songwriter, a field in which he reflects his age as accurately and sensitively as Schubert did his.

Copland

Like Gershwin, Aaron Copland was born in Brooklyn, on 14 November 1900, and though the two men were to follow very different paths they both looked for inspiration in their country's roots and felt the need to bridge the ever-widening gap between composer and audience. Copland, of course, has always been a 'serious' composer, but apart from a brief period at the beginning of the 1930s he has avoided the dry intellectualism that has produced this culture gap. It is perhaps surprising that he should be so immediately recognizable as an American composer, as his parents were Russian Jews who emigrated to the United States, where the authorities misspelt their real name of Kaplan. They had no particular interest in music, and no doubt this helped the young Copland to grow up without any bias in favour of a Russian style. He began his serious studies at the age of seventeen, and four years later went to Paris to become the first American pupil of the influential teacher Nadia Boulanger. He returned to New York with 'modernist' tendencies, his earliest compositions showing a percussive, astringent character similar to that of Prokofiev. This gave way to jazz influences in *Music for Theatre* (1926) and the Piano Concerto, which he played with the Boston Symphony Orchestra under Serge Koussevitzky's baton in 1927. Unconventionally cast in two contrasted movements which are thematically linked, it was described by the composer as an experiment in symphonic jazz, but it is an austere work which has nothing in common with Gershwin's concerto. The piano Variations composed three years later carry austerity and intellectualism even further.

Copland, clearly concerned by the reaction to these early works, re-thought his whole approach to composition a few years later and made a remarkable about-turn with *El salón México*. In the autumn of 1932 he had made his first visit to Mexico and conceived the idea of writing an orchestral piece based on some of the country's folk tunes. It was fortunate that he did not actually compose it immediately, as it otherwise might have been a far less colourful and engaging piece. In the meantime he had begun to feel that American composers, himself included, had leaned too heavily towards European influences and also towards an arid avant-garde style. In *El salón México* his aim was simply to create the atmosphere of a Mexican dance-hall. 'All that I could hope to do,' he wrote, 'was to reflect the Mexico of the tourist, and that is why I thought of the Salón México, because in that "hot spot" one felt, in a very natural way, a close contact with unaffected Mexican people.' This was to be a frankly popular piece, based on folksongs, that could readily be appreciated by audiences wanting lively tunes and local colour, and fittingly it was first performed in Mexico conducted by the country's leading composer Carlos Chavez. A year later it enjoyed an enthusiastic critical reception at a concert put on by the International Society of Contemporary Music in London.

Copland pursued his popular approach in his music for the ballet *Billy the Kid* (1938); the *Outdoor Overture* and *Quiet City*, a suite drawn from his incidental music for a film, and he tried to bring himself closer to the community by writing an opera for schoolchildren. As he had once been criticized for being too intellectual, Copland began to be admonished in the 1940s for being too facile and light-weight, to which his response came in the form of the ballet music for *Appalachian Spring* (1945). In this he did not sacrifice either American flavour or open-air melodic appeal, but added to these qualities an almost symphonic breadth. The following year saw the appearance of his Symphony No 3, a more ambitious work yet still an accessible one. In its lightness of textures and directness of style it is closely related to *Appalachian Spring*. If it disappoints, this is

Top right: *Copland, whose music is decidedly American in spirit—often drawing on the jazz idiom*

Bottom right: *Nadia Boulanger, the influential teacher of composition who numbered several leading American composers among her pupils*

because Copland is a composer to whom the expression of drama does not come easily, one who responds more naturally to the rhythmic propulsion of the dance than to the tensions of the symphony. It is significant that his Clarinet Concerto, written for Benny Goodman in 1947–8, was used by Jerome Robbins for his ballet *The Pied Piper* in 1951. Copland's music does not accompany this ballet, but *is* the ballet, the dancers falling under the spell of the on-stage clarinettist and becoming his puppets. Although he later returned to a more austere style with *Connotations* (1962) and *Inscape* (1967), Copland remains best known for his ballet music with its outdoor liveliness and bright orchestral colours. Strangely, he has not returned to this type of work in his seventies, having chosen instead to pursue an active life as a conductor.

Harris, Piston, Barber

There has been no lack of accomplished composers in the United States, but they have all been unfortunate in growing to maturity in an age when music no longer crosses frontiers as easily as it did in the Classical and Romantic periods. Every country in the world today is producing a great deal of new music, yet few composers win any wide acceptance at home and scarcely any have their music played regularly abroad. This has applied for many years even in Europe, where countries are close neighbours sharing similar cultural traditions. The United States is cut off from Europe, geographically, historically and to a large extent culturally, so it has always been particularly difficult for American composers to get a foothold across the Atlantic, even when their music belongs to the European tradition. Roy Harris, for example, though he composes along traditional European lines as a symphonist, has not succeeded in

establishing his name as widely as he deserves. Born in Oklahoma on 12 February 1898, he had already established himself as a composer at home before going to Paris in 1926 to study with Boulanger. Impeccably qualified, he returned to the United States to produce a steady stream of works in the standard forms of symphony, concerto and string quartet. His symphonies are based on precise thematic statements, logically developed and scored with text-book clarity. This does not mean that he belongs to the European past in the creative sense: on the contrary, he is as resolutely American in the tone of his musical voice as Tippett is English, and his one-movement Symphony No 3 deserves more than the occasional airings it is given abroad. He was composer-in-residence at the University of California for many years before his death at Santa Monica on 1 October 1979.

A symphonist of similar stature, Walter Piston (1894–1976) was also a student of Boulanger and composed a large number of works in established forms. His most popular work is the suite he made from his music for the ballet *The Incredible Flutist*, but his remarkable gifts, of lyricism above all, are best illustrated in the Symphony No 4, which with the Harris mentioned above ranks as the best any American composer has yet produced.

Samuel Barber (1910–81) became more widely known than Harris or Piston, partly because he ventured with some national success into opera, partly because he never strayed from a middle course. His music is unashamedly Romantic, and the ardent melody of his Adagio for Strings, an orchestrated version of an earlier quartet movement, has gained a place in the repertoire denied to more assertively contemporary works. He did not entirely fulfil the early promise he showed in his twenties, yet he remains one of the most distinguished musical figures to have emerged from the American scene.

Harris

Piston

Barber

THE SECOND VIENNESE SCHOOL

With the work of the three Vienna-born composers Arnold Schoenberg, Alban Berg and Anton Webern, the tradition of Western music became so fragmented that it is difficult to trace any continuity in the works they and their followers have produced. Baroque, Classical and Romantic styles have all shared certain basic principles and a musical language rooted in tonality. A single key has tended to dominate a whole work, even though the music would modulate in the course of any section of the work into other keys related to it either closely or remotely before returning to the home key. There were exceptions, of course, such as Nielsen's use of 'progressive tonality', ending a symphony in a key different from that in which it began. The chromatic style of Liszt and Wagner strayed from this course, but their music retains an underlying sense of tonality. Important composers have always broken new ground, but after some initial lack of comprehension audiences have been able to come to terms with their 'irregularities'. But the works of the 'Second Viennese School' (so named in contradistinction to the Classicism of Haydn, Mozart and Beethoven) continue to present a problem to the majority of concert-goers after half a century, even though an enthusiastic minority finds them as acceptable as the masterpieces of Bach and Beethoven.

Schoenberg

Schoenberg, who was born on 13 September 1874, began his musical career modestly enough as a chorus master with amateur societies, receiving his only formal lessons from the composer Alexander von Zemlinsky (1872–1942). He then earned his living for a time by orchestrating operettas. His first important composition, *Verklärte Nacht* ('Transfigured night'), written for string sextet in 1899 and later revised for string orchestra, has a chromatic idiom stemming from Wagner's *Tristan and Isolde*, while his symphonic poem *Pelléas and Mélisande* (1903) is as clearly influenced by Richard Strauss, who championed Schoenberg during his stay in Berlin. The Chamber Symphony No 1, scored for fifteen solo instruments, showed him freeing himself from Romanticism in 1906, stretching tonality to its limits and reducing orchestral forces to a minimum. With the Five Orchestral Pieces of 1909 he moved completely into atonality – the music gives no sense of prevailing key. There followed a period when he devoted himself to piano and vocal rather than orchestral music,

a period when he developed his twelve-note system of composition. This was a system he devised in the belief that the traditional systems of harmony and tonality had reached a state of anarchy in the late Romantic idiom, and that a new system of organization was needed. It treats all twelve notes of the chromatic scale as having equal value, no longer subject to the hierarchical relationships that had been established by the tonal system. In twelve-note music the composer arranges the notes in a series, or fixed sequence; they may then be used successively (as melody) or simultaneously (as harmony), in inverted or retrograde form; but all twelve are normally heard before any one of them recurs.

This system, which in practice is not necessarily the music-by-numbers recipe that it looks at first, was employed by Schoenberg in his Variations for Orchestra (1928) and Violin Concerto (1936). The ear alone, which can discern changes of key under the

Schoenberg, leader of the 'Second Viennese School', broke with the traditional system of tonality to change the whole face of music

traditional tonal system, cannot register the twelve-note procedure: only by following a printed score during performance can the listener spot the mechanics of the music. It is this which makes such music difficult to take in, and impossible to comment on without resorting to technical language. It should be stressed, however, that a considerable amount of twelve-note music can make a positive emotional impact on a listener who is blithely unaware of the almost mathematical complexities of its structure. Nevertheless, Schoenberg and his followers have only themselves to blame if their music does not win wide understanding and popularity. Every creative artist has the undisputed right to express himself in whatever way he thinks fit, and as his inspiration drives him, but whether or not he communicates his vision depends on the degree of receptivity of his audience. The artist who is ahead of his time has to wait for the public to catch up with him, as happened with Beethoven in respect of his late string quartets. There can be no doubting the sincerity of Schoenberg, or his importance in the evolution of Western music. His works are still 'caviare to the general', but as new generations of concert-goers arrive who have not been weaned on the tonal tradition, the music may well be accepted as readily as that which belongs to the Classical and Romantic traditions.

Schoenberg remained a somewhat isolated figure to the end of his life. In 1933, when he held a directorship of composition at the Prussian Academy of Arts in Berlin, the Nazi edicts against Jewish citizens forced him to resign his post and seek refuge in the United States. He taught for a time in Boston and New York, but after a year ill-health caused him to move to Hollywood, where he gave private lessons and was for a period a professor at the University of California, Los Angeles. He became an American citizen in 1944 and died in Hollywood on 13 July 1951, having composed comparatively little during his last years.

Berg, Webern

Schoenberg's most famous students and disciples were Berg and Webern, highly individual composers who followed very different paths. Berg, born on 9 February 1885, had a strong Romantic streak and became the best known of the three. He was drawn to opera, and his *Wozzeck* and *Lulu* gradually established themselves in the international repertoire to secure him a far wider public than he or his colleagues have ever enjoyed in the concert hall. He had already composed a few songs before he began a period of five years as a pupil of Schoenberg, whose

Berg, whose music represents the more Romantic brand of atonal music and who is the most accessible member of the new school

music he admired and in honour of whose fortieth birthday he planned his first large-scale work, which appeared belatedly as the Three Orchestral Pieces. These pieces have a weighty, late Romantic character revealing Berg's admiration for Mahler. Work on *Wozzeck* occupied him for several years, and when that was completed in 1920 he turned again to small-scale works with the Chamber Concerto for violin, piano and thirteen wind instruments, followed by the Lyric Suite for string quartet, though he enjoyed one orchestral success with a concert suite of music from *Wozzeck* in 1924. He adopted the twelve-note system for two movements in the Lyric Suite, but in general he used it only intermittently, giving rein rather to his lyrical inspiration. His major orchestral work, the Violin Concerto of 1935, employs serial techniques with such discretion that the Romantic elements in the music ultimately predominate. It is a lyrical and dramatic concerto rooted in the tradition of Brahms, while at the same time looking to the future. This was to be his last completed work, for he developed blood poisoning as the result of an insect bite and died in Vienna on 24 December 1935.

Whereas Berg clung to Romanticism, Webern developed the atonal style to the extremes of austere economy and concentration, composing pieces which sometimes run to seconds rather than minutes: his complete works are accommodated on four long-playing records. He was born on 3 December 1883 and like Berg he began by writing songs before becoming a pupil of Schoenberg, under whose influence he had composed several pieces by 1910. Most of his works are written for small numbers of players. He progressed, like Schoenberg, through phases of chromaticism and free atonality to the twelve-note system. In his few works for full orchestra he still produces music of delicate textures, employing only a few instruments at any one time, distributing the tenuous melodic line among different instruments and even making silences a part of his musical structures. Although he was regularly invited to conduct his works abroad, the degree of concentration his music demands on the part of the listener won him only small audiences at the time, full recognition of the value of his work coming towards the end of his life. Since he earned little from performances of his music he was obliged to take on various conducting posts between 1908 and 1934, and he suffered real poverty after the Nazis banned his works in Germany and Austria for being 'culturally Bolshevist'. By a stroke of tragic irony he died on 15 September 1945 at Mittersill after being shot accidentally in the dark by an American soldier on patrol duty.

NEW TRENDS

The three members of the Second Viennese School had all, in their different ways, respected tradition even while they had evolved revolutionary techniques, but many subsequent composers among the avant-garde have carried their example to a point where established musical values have been virtually eliminated. As these composers of the second half of the twentieth century have remorselessly pursued the ideal of complete freedom of expression they have tended to produce music so esoteric in character that only a small minority of music-lovers are able to

Webern, who carried the twelve-note system to such extreme lengths of economy and concentration that some of his pieces take only seconds to play

comprehend it. This is something new in the history of music, which has never before witnessed such a wide division between the contemporary composer and his public, a development which is paralleled in the world of painting and sculpture to some extent, but which has not affected literature and drama. Not only have formal and harmonic systems been thrown aside, but the whole conception of melody has radically changed, and although melody is only one element of music, it is the one which exerts the most immediate impact on most listeners. It is for this reason that new music continues to bewilder and alienate the concert-going public. The situation is made even more difficult because there is no one 135

Stockhausen, one of the most controversial figures in avant-garde *music, in whose work a large part is played by chance techniques and improvisation*

contemporary style, nor even a handful of predominant ones, but virtually as many as there are individual composers.

Schoenberg's twelve-note system has been adopted by many composers, who have extended and adapted it in different ways, and even those who have rejected it have still subscribed to the idea that lay behind it and had brought it into being – the idea that the tonal conception of music has served its purpose and is no longer valid. This has led to experiments in aleatoric music, in which the composer leaves chance events to play a part in either its composition or performance; to *musique concrète*, which employs sounds of all kinds, from actual music to traffic noises, which are recorded and then manipulated; and to many other compositional procedures. It is impossible to say where these experiments will lead, firstly because we are too close to them to assess them, and secondly because the composers who are making them are liable to change direction at any moment in search of something new. It takes time,

too, for any new system of composition to settle down, and many composers have done no more than try to formulate a new musical language and produce new sounds. They are like writers, to attempt a rough parallel, who have invented a vocabulary of new words but have not yet managed to order them into sentences which convey any clear meaning to their readers.

Of course, some composers have succeeded in writing progressive music which the public has found more acceptable, the chief among them being Paul Hindemith (1895–1963), Olivier Messiaen (*b* 1908), Elliott Carter (*b* 1908), Witold Lutoslawski (*b* 1913), Hans Werner Henze (*b* 1926) and Krzystzof Penderecki (*b* 1933), whose works are encountered more and more frequently in the concert hall. Others, like Karlheinz Stockhausen (*b* 1928), have made a great impact on the musical scene by their force of personality and through their writings and other activities, even though their public remains specialized. Only time will decide whether these composers have blazed a new path which others will profitably develop or whether their experiments will be looked back upon as passing fads in a period of fragmentation and lack of direction.

THE CHAMBER ORCHESTRA

We are accustomed today to hearing all symphonic music played by the modern symphony orchestra, which grew gradually to its present size over more than a century. Classical symphonies, however, were originally written for considerably smaller forces. It is valuable to hear these works played from time to time by what we now call a chamber orchestra, though even this contains more players that would have been available to Haydn, Mozart and the young Beethoven. The normal maximum scoring of such symphonies was for pairs of flutes, oboes, clarinets, bassoons, horns and trumpets, with strings and timpani; though Beethoven added a third horn to the *Eroica*, piccolo and double-bassoon and trombones to No 5, piccolo and trombones to the *Pastoral*, and all these extra instruments plus percussion (triangle, cymbals and bass drum) to the 'Choral'. With such modest woodwind and brass forces, the number of strings was less than that required when the Romantic composers, led by Berlioz, began to extend the size of the orchestra to the proportions with which we are now familiar in the concert hall. The majority of Haydn's symphonies, for instance, were composed for the orchestra at Esterház which would normally consist of about twenty-five players in all, while even at the end of the eighteenth century orchestras in Vienna itself boasted less than forty.

Orchestral music before the evolution of the symphony was even more modestly scored, so the Baroque suites, concertos featuring harpsichord, violin or some other soloist, and works in the concerto grosso style should always be played by chamber orchestras if we are to appreciate their special qualities of crispness, buoyancy and freshness of inspiration. (The concerto grosso is a type of composition in which a small body of soloists play in alternation and combination with a larger body of orchestral strings, the former known as the *concertino* and the latter as the *ripieno*.) These works were turned out in enormous numbers from the late seventeenth century onwards, especially by the Italian composers Arcangelo Corelli (1653–1713), Giuseppe Torelli (1658–1709) and Tomaso Albinoni (1671–1750). They and many other prolific practitioners of the time produced music which was always expertly constructed and full of agreeable melodies. They happily followed established patterns, aiming to please the cultivated tastes of the day, rather than concerning themselves with deep emotions or personal expression. The outstanding music in this style, and the most popular, was contributed by Bach, Handel and the almost alarmingly prolific Vivaldi.

Vivaldi

Not a lot is known with any certainty about the early life of Antonio Vivaldi except that he was born some time during 1678 in Venice, where his father was a violinist in St Mark's Cathedral, and that he was ordained priest in 1703. He gave up saying the Mass after a few months, complaining that a chest ailment frequently compelled him to leave the altar during its celebration, but this was probably only an excuse, as he was never afflicted in this way when playing the violin or directing an orchestra. The church's loss proved music's gain, for there has never been a more industrious composer-performer. He became at twenty-five the director of music at a famous orphanage for girls in Venice, the Ospedale della Pietà, with which he was associated almost all his life. He was so brilliant a violin teacher that crowds of visitors came to admire the playing of the girls, modestly hidden behind screens during the performance. His duties cannot have been too onerous, however, as he found time to compose some forty operas and some five hundred concertos; it is possible that another hundred concertos have been lost. Vivaldi travelled widely, establishing his fame throughout Europe, playing for the Pope and being granted several audiences with Emperor Charles VI. It was said that Charles spoke more with Vivaldi in two weeks than with his ministers in two years, which says a good deal for the emperor's sense of values. Vivaldi finally fell foul of the church on account of his liaison with the soprano Anna Girò, and in 1738 he was dismissed from his post at the Pietà. Two years later he left Venice for Vienna, where he died in July 1741, having squandered a fortune, and was buried in a pauper's grave.

Vivaldi is known chiefly today for his concertos, of which the great majority are for violin, though he wrote others for cello, various wind instruments and even mandolin. The violin concertos are short by later standards, though in the familiar three movements, two Allegros with a central Largo or Adagio. He brought to the form a rare rhythmic vitality, a fine sense of structure and a sure feeling for the capability of the solo instrument, the natural result of his own skill as a violinist. The best known are the four concertos collected together under the title *The Four Seasons*, their popularity owing a good deal to this descriptive title. They do not constitute programme music in any Romantic sense, but suggest pictorial images of the countryside during the course

Overleaf: *Venice's Sala dei Filarmonici, one of the oldest centres of opera and orchestral music*

of the year. The usual design of the fast outer movements is to begin with an orchestral statement of the main theme (or 'ritornello'), then follow with two or three solo episodes alternating with further orchestral sections. The slow movements are shorter and simpler in form, weaving a gentle, aria-like melody.

It seems that these concertos were designed round the poetic content of four sonnets, probably by Vivaldi himself, whose lines were printed in the solo violin part. The 'Spring' concerto opens with an Allegro suggesting the awakening of nature, complete with the singing of birds (violin trills). The Largo is accompanied by lines of verse describing a goatherd resting in the field, the violin representing the sleepy workman and the viola the barking of his dog. A gay pastoral dance constitutes the Finale. The first movement of 'Summer' suggests a sultry afternoon, with the voices of cuckoo and dove, until rapid scales warn of an approaching storm. Its central movement, which uncharacteristically alternates between Adagio and Presto, reflects lines of the sonnet depicting loneliness and fear of the storm, which is unleashed in the lively Finale. In the first movement of 'Autumn' Vivaldi reveals that he must have been familiar with Monteverdi's *Il coronazione di Poppea*, for he quotes a jaunty tune from the maidservant's aria. Its Finale has the character of a hunting song, with shuddering strings at the end which tell us the huntsmen have killed their prey. The music for 'Winter' is indicative of a frozen landscape, with short, sharp tuttis in the Finale to indicate unwary village folk falling down on the ice. No extra-musical effects are used in the descriptive passages, and the listener does not need to be aware of Vivaldi's illustrative intentions, for the music stands on its own as a splendid example of Baroque style.

Bach

Although sacred music makes up the greater part of his work, Johann Sebastian Bach (1685–1750) made equally important contributions to keyboard and instrumental composition. The 'musician's musician', he reached absolute perfection in everything he did: every bar of his music is fired by genuine inspiration, and his musicianship was so prodigious that he always found the ideal form and style for the expression of his ideas. Prominent among his instrumental works are the concertos for violin and harpsichord, and the celebrated 'Brandenburg' Concertos. These last were composed during the period 1718–23, when Bach was Kapellmeister at the court of Cöthen to the music-loving Prince Leopold; they were dedicated to a prince of Brandenburg who most probably never

Johann Sebastian Bach, whose best known instrumental works are the concertos for harpsichord and violin and the 'Brandenburg' Concertos

had them played. Leopold was more appreciative (at least, until he married an unmusical wife), so they were frequently performed at Cöthen. Six in number, the concertos are each unique in scoring. Bach explored new instrumental possibilities, systematically testing the potential of all his players. The concertos vary in the number of movements, four in the case of No. 1, two in No 3, and three in the others, and also in character and mood. The Concerto No 1 in F major is the most festive, bright with the sounds of hunting horns and strengthened by oboes and bassoon. No 2, in the same key, has the ringing call of the high F trumpet. No 3 in G major is for strings alone, with only two chords dividing the joyous Allegro movements (a slow movement from one of the composer's other works is sometimes inserted in performance). No 4 in G major has a *concertino* made up of violin and two recorders while No 5 in D major is a triple concerto for violin, flute and harpsichord, the last dominating in a way that looks forward to Bach's later harpsichord concertos. This work is in fact the earliest keyboard concerto. No 6 in B flat features pairs of violas, violas da gamba with a cello and double bass, resulting in music of dark colour.

Almost as familiar as the 'Brandenburgs' are the

two concertos for solo violin, in A minor and E major, and the Concerto in D minor for two violins, all three of which Bach later arranged for harpsichord in place of violin. Both concertos for solo violin have lively, essentially sunny outer Allegros framing a central slow movement of darkly expressive meditation. The double concerto follows a similar pattern, with the added fascination of the lively and subtle interplay between the two soloists. Its beautiful slow movement is especially popular. Bach's keyboard concertos came into being for practical reasons: as director of the Leipzig Collegium Musicum (music society) in 1729, he wished to play as soloist with them, and accordingly arranged many of his earlier works as harpsichord concertos. He also drew on Vivaldi, transcribing a concerto for four violins for four harpsichords. These concertos have little in common with the later piano concerto, for there is nothing symphonic in their construction and little dramatic contrast between soloist and orchestra. Only the Concerto in D minor (arranged from a lost original for violin) is played regularly today, and more frequently on the piano than the harpsichord, which is too intimate an instrument for even a medium-sized concert hall. The sound of the piano and its performing technique are so alien to the music, however, that the concerto is best heard on recordings made with a harpsichord soloist accompanied by very small orchestra. It is a truly great concerto, its outer movements having tremendous energy and its Adagio a miraculous air of melancholy.

The four orchestral suites by Bach emphasize the international character of the music of his time. Although he was a man of stolid Germanic virtues who had no wish to travel abroad, he was a composer who accepted influences from any quarter. He happily took the Italians as his model for the sonata and concerto, and his suites all open with a French *ouverture* in the style established by Lully. The dances of the suites come from Italy (Forlane), Spain (Sarabande) and Poland (Polonaise) as well as France (Gavotte). Bach's genius transfigures all these dances, revitalizing their characteristic charm and exuberance. The Suite No 2 in B minor, which features a solo flute with string orchestra, concludes with a Badinerie, a dazzling piece which belies the usual idea of Bach as a wholly straight-faced music-maker. The other suites call for more wind instruments, with timpani added in the case of No 3 in D major, whose slow movement is familiar as the 'Air on the G string'. The music of these orchestral suites is so sunnily engaging that concert-goers may well regret that Bach devoted so much of his life to composition for the church.

Handel

First and foremost an opera composer, George Frideric Handel (1685–1759) nevertheless wrote a number of orchestral works of distinction and individuality which have maintained their place in the repertoire. One of the most popular is the *Water Music*, originally played at a concert on the Thames for George I by some fifty players, including a strong complement of trumpets and horns. Three suites from this music have been preserved, and their tuneful festive appeal remains irresistible, especially when performed by an orchestra approximating to the original forces Handel employed. (Arrangements for the modern symphony orchestra, made by musicians old enough to have known better, make the music sound more appropriate to 1812 than 1717.) His organ concertos, which he composed as interludes between the sections of his oratorios for himself as soloist, are intimate in style and afford the utmost scope for virtuosity. The writing for the organ in these works is as delicate as any harpsichord music,

Handel, though most famous for his operas and oratorios, is frequently represented in the concert hall by the Water Music *and the organ concertos*

calling for playing of real refinement. They are enchanting works designed to please a theatre audience, with no solemn pretensions. Also engaging in fairly light mood is the first collection of six Concerti Grossi, Op 3, scored for recorders, oboes and bassoons as the *concertino*.

The most important of his orchestral works are the twelve Grand Concertos, Op 6. The solo parts, two violins and a cello, are not as markedly set off from the *ripieno* as in a strictly constructed concerto grosso. Handel follows the usual four-movement pattern in principle (slow-fast-slow-fast with one of the Allegros in fugal style), but he often adds a movement or two in dance rhythm. The style is predominantly contrapuntal, at times serious and dignified, at times frisky; but in keeping with the character of a composer who was never pedantic, a love of melody for its own sake wins over formalism.

AFTER THE BAROQUE

Even after the growth of the symphony orchestra as the chief medium of the late-Classical and Romantic composer, music continued to be written for string or chamber orchestras. It consists of suites and other works cast in a more intimate, less ambitious mould than that of the symphony, and like the music of the Baroque, it is free from the large gestures and rhetoric which the larger orchestra encouraged composers to indulge in. The Serenades by Tchaikovsky and Dvořák are prime examples, as are Grieg's *Holberg* and Holst's *St Paul's* suites. British composers, especially those like Britten who have been influenced by Purcell, have favoured the string orchestra, and writers of lighter music such as Percy Grainger (1882–1961) have naturally worked most happily with the chamber orchestra. The neo-Classical movement, typified by middle-period Stravinsky, inevitably revived interest in ensembles smaller than the modern symphony orchestra.

The music of Schoenberg often calls for forces even smaller than those of the chamber orchestra proper. Many of his works, and those of his followers, fall into a special category, for while they involve more than the nine performers representing the maximum number for chamber music, they are not scored for the traditional chamber orchestra. The contemporary composer has continued this procedure of scoring for small and, from the conventional standpoint, oddly assorted groups of instruments. So while the chamber orchestra continues to flourish, and has even increased its hold in the concert hall on account of the revival of interest in Baroque music and a movement towards authentic performances of Haydn and Mozart, a smaller and more flexible kind of ensemble has also come into being.

A chamber orchestra playing in an elegant and intimate setting well suited to Baroque music

THE OPERA

When the learned Dr Johnson, who admitted to being completely unmusical, ridiculed opera as 'an exotic and irrational entertainment which has always been combated and always has prevailed' he was being rather wiser than he thought. He was referring specifically to the Italian opera of the late eighteenth century, but opera has ever since been regarded as exotic and irrational by the majority of people, even by many who understand and enjoy music in its other forms, and yet two centuries later it still prevails. The reason is quite simple: the very extravagance of opera which offends its critics is precisely what its *aficionados* find so irresistible. Everything about opera is extravagant, from its conception in the first place as a combination of drama, music and spectacle to its grandiose manner of stage presentation, even to the opulence of the theatres in which it is given and the behaviour of the public which flocks to see the same works over and over again.

The case against opera is argued on two levels, of which the one put forward by the prosaic Dr Johnson can be easily dismissed as philistine sniping. It merely reflects an unthinking personal prejudice, and it may just as readily be applied to any form of entertainment, sport or other human activity which the individual sceptic finds boring. The more serious argument against opera is that in attempting to combine drama and music it inevitably debases both. The play-goer finds that the demands of music destroy dramatic flow and pace, holding up the action when it most needs to move forward, while the music-lover more accustomed to instrumental and orchestral works sees something vulgar in the theatrical element. Most of all, the musical purist is offended by the applause which breaks out after show-stopping arias in mid-scene, interrupting the course of the music as a whole and even tempting some singers to step out of character to take a bow. Regular opera-goers are themselves split into two camps over the question of the balance between music and drama, a question which has plagued opera since its very beginnings. Works which make music the dominant or even the exclusive issue are generally referred to as 'singer's operas', and they constitute the larger part of the Italian repertoire. The danger here is that such operas encourage singers to turn them into vehicles for vocal display at the expense of any dramatic or even truly expressive musical considerations.

The most important fact to note about opera is that it combines drama and music into a new form of art which cannot be judged on the terms we would apply to either separate component. As it was originally conceived, opera is *dramma per musica*, and the emphasis here is on the expression of drama *through* music, not merely drama *with* music. The addition of music to words goes back thousands of years and has taken many forms, from the simplest kinds of song to the masque, the oratorio, the operetta and the modern musical. Opera, however, is quite different from any of these other forms in that it does not just add music to words, but fuses them together. An opera libretto rarely if ever stands on its own as a play; it does not necessarily read well by itself, nor would it provide much entertainment or satisfaction if acted out on the stage. Similarly, the music of an opera would convey very little in the concert hall if it were played without the words being sung to it. (Overtures, however, certain entr'actes and purely orchestral numbers from operas often do make satisfying concert pieces.) The music and words of an opera make sense only in combination one with the other in a stage realization. Operas may be seen in concert performance, without settings or action, or they may be listened to on gramophone records, but neither of these affords a true operatic experience.

The reason that a good opera, when successfully performed, provides a uniquely thrilling experience is that its music touches emotions which lie too deep for words alone. There is an element of drama in all music, whether it is the tonal conflicts created in the abstract form of the Classical symphony or the programmatic content of a tone-poem. When words are given dramatic expression through music they take on a more powerful dimension. The meeting of Mimì and Rodolfo in the first scene of *La Bohème* is a commonplace situation which no exchange of spoken words could make more than moderately touching in a sentimental way: expressed through Puccini's music, their encounter is magical and has deservedly become one of the immortal scenes in opera.

Opera at Court

A group of scholars and amateur musicians known as the *Camerata* began to meet at the home of Count Giovanni de' Bardi in Florence some time about 1580 with the high-minded object of reviving the Classical drama of the Greeks and Romans. These Renaissance enthusiasts knew that music had been featured in performances of the tragedies of Sophocles and Euripides, because the philosopher Aristotle refers to them in his *Poetics* as employing 'pleasurable language that has the embellishments of rhythm, melody and metre'. It is indeed imperative that some kind of musical declamation was used, for this would help to carry the words across to the audience of thousands seated in an open-air theatre, and there is evidence to suggest that the choruses were not merely declaimed, but actually sung. Aristotle obviously approved, for he wrote that music was 'the most delightful of all the pleasurable accompaniments and embellishments of tragedy'. The problem for the *Camerata* was that they did not know, any more than we do today, how this music actually sounded. Only one mutilated fragment of a unison melody from a chorus in Euripides' *Orestes* has survived, and the Florentines did not even know of this.

The men who met under their aristocratic patron were a motley crew, headed by the theorist and composer Vincenzo Galilei, father of the famous astronomer Galileo, the poet Ottavio Rinuccini and the tenor and composer Giulio Caccini. They seem to

First Intermezzo in La Liberazione di Tirreno, *from an engraving showing the splendour of Italian court entertainment*

have spent most of their time together theorizing rather than producing any music of note, coming to the conclusion that polyphonic vocal music, in which various voices sang different melodic lines at the same time, should give way to a monodic style in which a soloist singing a melody with light instrumental support would be able to make the words clear to the audience. No practical progress was made by the *Camerata* until 1592, when Count Bardi left Florence for Rome and his place was taken by another nobleman, Jacopo Corsi, who brought with him Jacopo Peri, a tenor-composer like Caccini but with greater creative talent. Five years later the very first opera, *Dafne*, was performed in Corsi's house, Rinuccini having written the text and Peri the music (with the addition of a few numbers by Caccini). It was given several times over the next two or three years, apparently with considerable success, but most of the music has disappeared. A second opera, *Euridice*, performed in Florence on 6 October 1600, has survived complete, the text again the work of Rinuccini, set to music by Peri apart from the few choruses supplied by Caccini.

Because it was composed for a joyful occasion (a royal marriage), Peri's version of the story of Orpheus and Euridice has a happy ending, which removes most of the dramatic tension. The action is carried on by solo voices singing a melodic line adhering faithfully to the natural rhythms and inflections of the highly poetic words. There are no arias in the modern sense. There were originally at least four accompanying instruments, harpsichord, lyre and two lutes.

Opera spread rapidly once it had started, though it remained for its first few years a private form of entertainment given in ducal palaces. The Duke of Mantua, for example, had been present in Florence at the premiere of *Euridice,* which so impressed him that he decided to establish opera at his own court. He was particularly fortunate in this venture, for his *maestro di cappella* was none other than Claudio Monteverdi, the first composer whose operas have stood the test of time.

Although he had been born at Cremona, Monteverdi was employed as a musician in various capacities at the Mantuan court from 1591 until 1612, and it was there that he composed his *Orfeo* in 1607. In principle he followed the plan established by *Euridice* seven years earlier, but his opera made Peri's effort pale into amateurish insignificance. The differences between the two works are due to the fact that Monteverdi was a professional composer of genius, soundly trained in technique, applying real creative imagination to *dramma per musica*, whereas Peri was 145 a dilettante experimenting with antiquarian theories. Monteverdi called for an orchestra of thirty-eight instruments, including harpsichords and organs as well as wind and strings, using these forces to achieve a wide range of dramatic colouring. He also drew on a variety of vocal styles, the florid strophic aria which repeats the same bass line with different embellishments in the voice part, the three-part aria in *da capo* form, recitative with new expressive intensity, and choruses in polyphonic madrigal style. By combining all the diverse methods of musical expression current at the time, Monteverdi produced in his *Orfeo* the only opera in the Florentine idiom which has enjoyed twentieth-century revivals, not only as a festival rarity, but as an occasional repertoire piece in London, New York and many European cities. Of *Arianna*, his other Mantuan success, only the elegiac song known as *Lamento d'Arianna* has survived. When first heard in the opera house this aria is reported to have moved the entire audience to tears, and became what might be called the first operatic hit song.

Opera Goes Public

Venice, when the first public opera house was opened in 1637, had lost much of its former power as a city-state, but it was still a place of unique beauty and fascination and a centre of international fashion. Its carnivals were unsurpassed anywhere else in Europe, and it attracted hordes of tourists just as it does today. Its great families competed with one another to display the magnificence of their palaces, their extravagant clothes and personal jewellery and the parties they gave. There was another side to the Venetian coin, however: mortal feuds were common among the ruling families, and similar bloodshed was rife in humbler circles too. Professional assassins lurked for hire in all the dark alleys, so that Verdi's Rigoletto would have found a dozen Sparafuciles in as many minutes' walk. Life in Venice, in fact, was like an opera itself, the ideal environment for it to develop into a popular form of entertainment for all. The change began when some of the aristocratic families decided to put on sale a number of seats at their otherwise private performances for their guests. It was the Tron family who finally presented the first real public performance at their Teatro Tron di San Cassiano in 1637, with such immediate success that others quickly followed suit.

Once the craze for opera had started there was no stopping it. By the end of the century Venice boasted almost a dozen theatres exclusively devoted to opera, an astonishing number for a city of some 125,000 inhabitants, and nearly four hundred operas had

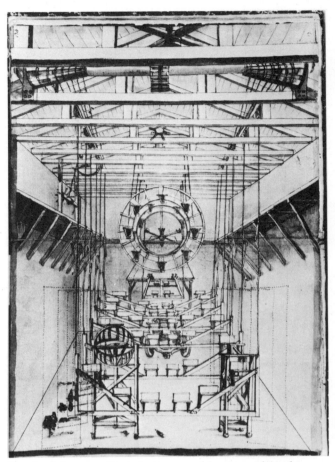

Sketch of the complicated stage machinery used in the presentation of opera to the Venetian public in the seventeenth century

been given. At first performances were restricted to the three-month carnival period, between Christmas and the end of March, but eventually two further annual seasons were added. The theatres were built on the lines familiar today, but while the seats in the stalls were sold for each individual performance the boxes which rose in tiers above were hired for the whole season by the wealthier families.

Catering for a large public brought changes in styles, not always for the best in the artistic sense. Over the years the demand increased for elaborate staging, even more important, for star singers. The first to arrive on the scene were the sopranos, who conquered the public as they developed ever-increasing vocal agility; many of them made conquests in society as well. The castratos came next, only too eager to escape from the church choir to display their artificially preserved male soprano voices. Their remarkable voices, which combined a woman's natural

Scene from Monteverdi's Il ritorno d'Ulisse in patria *at the Glyndebourne Festival with Frederica von Stade as Penelope, the wife of Ulysses*

range with a man's lung-power, quite captivated their new audiences, and because they were in relatively short supply, these singers were able to demand enormous fees. With the rise of the solo performer the chorus declined in importance, a complete reversal of the *Camerata*'s ideals. By the end of the seventeenth century Venice had reduced opera to an entertainment which simply afforded the star singers opportunities to show off their vocal athleticism. Before the decline set in it had allowed one very great composer to show what could be achieved with the facilities it provided – Monteverdi, who had already won distinction at Mantua.

Monteverdi

The conditions under which Renaissance composers had to work are exemplified in the long and varied career of Claudio Monteverdi, who was born at Cre-

mona in May 1567, the son of a barber-cum-surgeon with something of the versatility of Rossini's Figaro. He studied so profitably with the *maestro di cappella* of the city's cathedral that some of his short church pieces were published when he was only fifteen. He next turned his creative gifts to the madrigal, at the same time earning a more regular living as a string player. When he was almost twenty-four he gained an appointment with the ducal court of Mantua, where he won considerable fame with his *Orfeo*. By the age of forty he had composed several books of madrigals, no less original in style than *Orfeo*; they made his name known throughout Europe. The sudden death of his wife in 1607 sent him into a state of depression for several years which dried up his flow

147

of composition and drove him to quarrel with the Mantuan court, whose new duke finally dismissed him. Fate smiled on him unexpectedly in 1613 with an invitation to become *maestro di cappella* at St Mark's in Venice, where he spent the rest of his life.

As yet there was no operatic activity in Venice, but Monteverdi was fully occupied in administrative work and writing a certain amount of church music. He was free to travel from time to time, going to other cities to supervise productions of his operas. He still composed dramatic works for Mantua and other Italian courts, but only two of the eighteen works he produced between 1613 and 1642 have been preserved. These are the late Venetian operas, *Il ritorno d'Ulisse in patria* ('The return of Ulysses to his homeland') and *L'incoronazione di Poppea*, ('The coronation of Poppea'), which reveal such genius that we can only feel the most profound regret that the others, which might have been equally fine, have been lost for ever.

The ultimate miracle of Monteverdi's art was that, after the opening of the first public opera house in Venice, he was able to give the world its first indisputable masterpiece in the form. He achieved a considerable advance on what had gone before with *Il ritorno d'Ulisse in patria* (1641), in which recitative is no longer a mere heightened form of declamation of the words but takes wing to become of truly musical interest. Maximum emotional effect is exploited as serious and comic scenes alternate, yet everything is most skilfully organized to maintain a just dramatic balance. The stage was set for Monteverdi to produce his masterpiece, *L'incoronazione di Poppea*, the following year, when he was seventy-five, a triumph in old age which only Verdi has equalled since. This opera has established itself in the standard repertoire, no less than four British companies taking it up within a few years of Glyndebourne's staging of 1962. The work has to be edited for performance, because the score, like many of its time, does not give exact instructions for instrumentation. Of the many different 'realizations' the one by Raymond Leppard is the most exotic; some scholars have criticized him for going too far in the search for colour and contrast.

The first notable thing about the opera is that it presents characters with whose joy or sorrow we can identify. Earlier operas had tended to deal with figures from Classical mythology – gods, goddesses and heroes for the most part – who were utterly unreal, while the simpler pastoral stories concerned equally unreal nymphs and shepherds. Here, for the first time, are recognizable human beings whose behaviour can readily be understood. Whether their behaviour is condoned is another matter, for Monteverdi

Monteverdi, who brought opera to its first flowering

chose the story of the emperor Nero and his love for Poppea. In order to marry Poppea, Nero banishes her husband Ottone and divorces his own wife Ottavia, also ordering his ex-tutor Seneca to commit suicide for having dared to oppose the imperial marriage plan. It might seem impossible for any composer to win our sympathies for such a reprehensible couple, yet the love music, especially in the closing duet, has such voluptuous grace and passion that moral scruples are swept aside by the happiness of Nero and Poppea. The other characters are also made flesh and blood by their music, Ottone in the noble resignation of his aria mourning the loss of Poppea's love, Ottavia by the infinitely touching grief of her lament over her humiliation by her husband. The death scene of Seneca is richly inventive, his pupils imploring him not to take his life as he affirms his intention of proving in deed the stoic principles he has always taught. All is not tragic, however: two young servants have a love duet which is at once skittish and endearing, while Arnalta, Poppea's old nurse, sings a deliciously witty aria in which she contrasts her present humble state with her future glory. *Poppea* achieves the perfect balance between the rival claims of music and drama, and in its expression of human emotion marks the birth of modern opera.

Monteverdi passed the remaining year of his life in retirement, honoured and respected. In the early part of 1643 he visited Cremona and Mantua, and on 29 November died in Venice, the city that provided the conditions for his genius to flower.

SERIOUS OPERA

It might logically be supposed that opera, having produced a resounding masterpiece some forty years after it first ventured on to the stage, would then go steadily forward from strength to strength. This was sadly not to be the case, for after *L'incoronazione di Poppea* its fortunes changed by fits and starts so that little of lasting value appeared until the works of Handel and Gluck about seventy years later. There was one exception, Purcell's 'chamber' opera *Dido and Aeneas*. Not that there was any lack of effort on the part of hundreds of composers. The new art-form became the most fashionable kind of entertainment in all the countries of Europe, invariably carried there by Italians or modelled by native composers on the Italian pattern. Many of them contain attractive or original music, but virtually all of them fail in the primary objective of opera – the expression of drama through music. They became showcases for the virtuosity of the singers. History may perhaps have been unfair to these composers, though periodic attempts made to exhume their works have usually proved that their neglect is deserved. A few composers, however, merit a brief mention here.

Prominent among the Venetian composers was Monteverdi's pupil Pier Francesco Caletti-Bruni (1602–76), who took the name of his patron, Cavalli. He made the overture bear a closer relation to the opera itself than the brief, usually ceremonial measures of the earlier Venetian-style introduction, and gave greater importance to arias (as distinct from recitative) than Monteverdi had done. He also designed them as dramatic scenes rather than self-contained solo numbers. Two or three of his operas have enjoyed modern revivals in Raymond Leppard's arrangements, notably *L'Ormindo* at Glyndebourne in 1967. Another follower of the Venetian style, was Pietro Antonio Cesti (1623–69), whose style is more graceful and tender than Cavalli's. His best-known work is *Il pomo d'oro* ('The golden apple'), written in Vienna in 1667 for a royal wedding; a spectacular opera appropriate to such an occasion, it has several ballets and a variety of arias from the elegiac to the comic.

By the end of the seventeenth century Venice ceased to be the centre of opera, though composers such as Antonio Vivaldi and Tomaso Albinoni carried on the tradition. The new centre was Naples, at that time the largest city in Italy, where Alessandro Scarlatti (1660–1725) led the way. By 1700 he had established the new three-movement Italian overture, or sinfonia. His music has a considerable range of emotional colour, from sensuousness through tender melancholy to gentle playfulness, all controlled with aristocratic elegance. He made much use of the type of three-part aria known as *da capo*, in which the third part is a repeat of the first after a contrasting middle section. Scarlatti kept his arias relatively short, but the later Neapolitan composers extended them to wearisome length, which largely accounts for the fact that their names are now restricted to footnotes in history books.

Opera flourished throughout Italy at this time, so it is surprising that so little of lasting value should have been composed in the field of *opera seria* during the late seventeenth and early eighteenth centuries. The main reason was that opera might have been called *seria* but it was taken anything but seriously by the audiences. Although it was a social necessity for any family of wealth or noble descent to have a box at the opera, whether in Rome, Milan, Naples or Venice, few of these patrons went there with any intention of actually listening to the music, and even when they occasionally did turn an ear it was not in the pure spirit of the idealistic *Camerata*. Contemporary accounts of a night at the opera rival anything in the Marx brothers' film with that very name. The grand folk in their boxes played cards and other games, and as the English musical historian Dr Burney discovered on his travels: 'Chess is marvellously well adapted to filling in the monotony of the recitatives, and the arias are equally good for interrupting a too assiduous concentration on chess.' It is hardly surprising in these circumstances that the singers resorted to virtuosity to attract attention. Evenings at the opera were not occasions likely to encourage the development of opera as a dramatic art.

France

Despite its strong cultural ties with Italy, France resisted the craze for opera longer than most countries. The French have always prided themselves on being rationalists, and at first they scorned opera much as Dr Johnson was to do later. Furthermore, they could boast the finest drama and ballet anywhere in the world at this particular time. Paris did not see an Italian opera until 1645, and even then was not impressed. Some of the elements necessary for opera were nonetheless available (such as the court orchestra which had grown from the *Violons du Roi*, and the ballet-pantomimes which combined dances with plays portrayed in mime); and in 1669 the opera enthusiast Louis XIV granted permission to the composer Robert Cambert and his librettist Pierre Perrin to build a public opera house. The Académie Royale de Musique, the official name of the Paris Opéra, 149

opened two years later with their *Pomone*. In 1672 they were summarily replaced by the Italian-born, rags-to-riches Lully.

The Florentine Giovanni Battista Lully (1632–87) entered the service of a French noblewoman as a scullery boy, but from his arrival in Paris as a boy he rapidly proved he was destined for greater things; at twenty he became director of the court orchestra and court composer a year later. He composed a whole series of ballets over the next decade, also arranging the music into orchestral suites, a novelty at the time, and throughout the 1660s collaborated with Molière on numerous comedy-ballets. Lully's great opportunity came with his securing control of the Académie Royale, which gave him a monopoly of theatre music in Paris. He threw his whole energies into the creation of a national style of French opera, contributing nineteen operas to the repertoire of the Académie Royale between 1673 and his death.

150   In some ways Lully was a forerunner of Wagner,

A scene from Cavalli's L'Ormindo *in the Glyndebourne Festival production of 1967, with the music arranged by Raymond Leppard*

not for his musical style, but because he considered the libretto of equal importance to the music and also concerned himself with every detail of settings, costumes, production and choreography. He had at his command a large, rich and disciplined orchestra. The drawback with even his best works, such as *Thésée* and *Armide*, is their weighty seriousness. Lully was completely the king's man, and they have irrelevant prologues glorifying Louis, while the dramas themselves are devoid of any comic element or reference to ordinary life. However, they did establish certain admirable qualities which characterize most subsequent French opera.

Lully's most important successor was Jean Philippe

Above: *Decor for* L'Armide *by Lully, the Florentine composer who made his career in Paris*

Right: *Rameau, Lully's successor in Paris, who came to opera late in life*

Rameau (1683–1764), a contemporary of Bach and Handel and in some respects their equal. He came late in life to the opera (at fifty-one), having made his name first as an organist, instrumental composer and theorist. His style is more Italianate than Lully's, and his more fully developed arias look forward to Gluck. He used instrumental episodes to depict scenes such as natural landscapes, sunrises or, in *Les Indes galantes* (1735), an earthquake. His first opera, *Hippolyte et Aricie* (1733), displayed a new intensity and richness. His most famous work is *Castor et Pollux* (1737), which was a favourite with audiences for a number of years before new styles came along and swept it aside with the other operas in the Lully tradition.

151

Sandra Browne and Christian du Plessis in the title-roles of Purcell's Dido and Aeneas

England

Whereas French composers successfully developed opera from dramatic ballet, their English counterparts met with only sporadic success in a parallel attempt to develop a national form of opera from the masque. This form of entertainment was a lavish stage spectacle involving spoken dialogue, songs and instrumental music that enjoyed its heyday under James I and Charles I and continued as a private diversion during the Commonwealth. It was the Puritans' opposition to the theatre which caused the first English opera, *The Siege of Rhodes* (1656), to be passed off as a concert work. It appears to have been well received and to have won some popularity, but with the return of Charles II in 1660 and the consequent reopening of theatres, the English happily went back to their plays and opera took a back seat. The failure of English opera to develop was perhaps inevitable in view of this general lack of interest, though the story might have been different had not Purcell, the only composer fully equipped to compose dramatic music, died at such an early age. It is sad too that John Blow (1649–1708) did not follow up his fine pastoral opera *Venus and Adonis*. Its occasional performances make one wonder why Blow, having tried this form around 1682, did not compose anything else for the stage.

Henry Purcell, born in London in 1659, was a chorister at the Chapel Royal, where he studied under three fine composers: Henry Cooke, Pelham Humphrey (who had studied with Lully in Paris) and Blow. He made good progress and at the age of eighteen was appointed composer to the Chapel Royal. In 1680 he was invited to write incidental songs for a play to be given in Dorset Garden, the first of more than forty such commissions. These were to provide valuable experience for his only true opera, *Dido and Aeneas*. The manner in which it was commissioned and presented suggests that however irrational the whole idea of opera may be, no Englishman has ever had the right to say so. Where, other than in England, would the country's leading composer be asked to write an opera for amateur performance at a boarding-school for 'gentlewomen'? And where else would such a work remain the country's only successful one for two and a half centuries?

Only in its scale is *Dido and Aeneas* less than great: everything else shows mastery. Within an hour of drama the Virgilian story of Dido's love for the Trojan prince is represented not in formal splendour but in intimate human terms. In particular, Dido's music is expressive and faithful to the accents of the language to a degree rarely achieved by any opera composer before or since. The work is crowned by her lament, 'When I am laid in earth', as she dies of a broken heart. In emotional grandeur, in drama perfectly expressed through music, this aria stands alone in the music of its time.

Purcell's other theatre music, though considerable and varied, is of an incidental nature. The best of his songs and instrumental numbers for *Dioclesian* (1690), *King Arthur* (1691) and *The Fairy Queen* (1692) establish beyond any doubt that he was potentially a major opera composer denied the opportunities he would have been given in Italy or France. He did not lack the appreciation of his countrymen, however, for his death on 21 November 1695 was widely mourned, and he was buried in Westminster Abbey to the music he had himself composed for Queen Mary's funeral the previous year. His passing removed any hope for English opera, public taste moving towards Italian *opera seria* as if in preparation for the arrival of Handel.

Germany

There was no unified German nation until 1870. In the seventeenth century more than a thousand separate states and independent cities were loosely bound together under the Holy Roman Empire, and after the havoc of the Thirty Years' War little general sense of German identity remained. The innumerable courts of the area fell completely under the sway of Italian opera, Munich, Dresden and Hanover quickly following the example of Vienna, where Cesti had settled. Opera moved to the public domain in 1678 with the opening of the first opera house at Hamburg, a free city, where German composers were able to make some contributions of their own to the Italian-dominated repertoire. None of their operas is of anything more than academic interest, however. It may seem strange that Germany, which has produced so many leading composers, and which was to rival Italy in the operatic field throughout the nineteenth and early twentieth centuries, should be so slow to develop any opera of its own. However, before Bach's time music in Europe had been dominated by composers from Italy, France and the Netherlands (England having enjoyed a period of early glory), so that most music in Germany was either imported or written under foreign influences. Then Germany also suffered because Handel left to work in London as a composer in the Italian tradition; while Gluck chose first Italian and then French for his reform operas. Even Mozart was to concentrate on *opera seria* and *opera buffa* for his mature works, giving to German opera only *Die Entführung aus dem Serail* and *The Magic Flute*. It was not until Weber's *Der Freischütz* of 1821 that a wholly national style was established.

COMIC OPERA

So far it might seem that opera was a very serious affair, with the characters, to quote that marvellous phrase of Lucian's, 'melodizing their calamities'. This could scarcely have been so with any form of entertainment dominated by the laughter-loving Italians, and comic scenes were soon introduced into otherwise serious operas – brilliantly in the case of Monteverdi's *L'incoronazione di Poppea*, but mostly in a clumsy, rather slapdash manner. It was not until the eighteenth century that comic opera achieved full independence. In Italy there was *opera buffa*, in France *opéra comique*, in England the ballad opera, in Germany the *Singspiel*, and in Spain the *zarzuela*. Their plots were light or farcical, involving characters drawn from everyday life; their singers were often relatively unskilled; and most included spoken dialogue. Within about fifty years, however, comic opera had become sufficiently sophisticated to have won itself a place alongside serious opera, quite different in style yet equal in esteem, reaching its pinnacle with Mozart.

The earliest Italian comic operas were no more than 'low-brow' intermezzos played between the acts of serious operas as light relief, and were derived from the *commedia dell'arte*, the national improvised comedy full of robust dialogue and visual horseplay. Several hundred turned out by about 1750 are only of academic interest – with one exception. A highly talented young composer produced a gem which has remained famous and is still occasionally performed today.

Pergolesi

Giovanni Battista Pergolesi was born in 1710, and thanks to the generosity of a noble patron was sent to Naples for his advanced studies. After composing various now-forgotten operas, in 1733 he wrote *Il prigionier*, an *opera seria* remembered solely because of its association with the intermezzo *La serva padrona* ('The maid mistress'). The music of this minor masterpiece has melodic grace as well as comic verve, and what might have been a cynical story (of a maid trying to marry her master for his money) has sufficient warmth to become a genuine comedy of manners. Typical of *opera buffa* are the mock-serious arias which make fun of the more pretentious heroic operas then in vogue.

Pergolesi never capped this success in his later stage works, though he composed a *Stabat Mater* which has always been highly regarded. Even so, he established with *La serva padrona* a style which was 153

to remain basic to Italian comic opera for two centuries. His clever matching of music to text, so that song comes naturally to the characters; his juxtaposition of beguiling melody with rapid patter; his making the bass a prominent figure of fun; his use of parody – all these features, extended and refined upon, survive in the comic operas of Rossini and Donizetti, in Verdi's *Falstaff* and Wolf-Ferrari's *I quattro rusteghi*. Sadly, Pergolesi died from consumption in 1736. His work, fortunately, was carried on by two other gifted Italians who helped to pave the way for Rossini.

Paisiello

Some idea of the number of comic operas produced in Italy during the late eighteenth and the nineteenth centuries may be gathered from the fact that almost a hundred were composed by Giovanni Paisiello, who was born at Taranto in 1740. He was sent to a musical conservatoire in Naples at the age of fourteen and started his creative career in church music. He

Opposite: *'Intermezzo', a painting showing an early opera buffa*

Below: *Paisiello, the Italian composer whose early version of* The Barber of Seville *delighted the court of the Empress Catherine of Russia*

quickly discovered that his real talent was for opera, partly serious but predominantly comic. He won success quite early, and in 1776 turned down offers from Paris and London in order to take up the post of court composer in St Petersburg in the service of the Empress Catherine.

Practical like all composers of the eighteenth century, Paisiello settled himself down to the dual task of composing the serious operas his patroness expected of him, and of selecting singers from the company who could be trained for comedy. Gradually he introduced a few comic operas into the court repertoire, preparing the ground for what was to be his own masterpiece, *Il barbiere di Siviglia*, in 1782. His choice of subject was extremely astute, because the Beaumarchais comedy had been presented there several times in recent years. Already familiar with the play, the nobility would have no problem in following *The Barber of Seville* even with an Italian libretto. Paisiello had some cuts made, however, because as he explained in the preface 'the Empress does not like to stay in the theatre for more than an hour and a half'. The opera was an immediate success. Seeing or hearing this masterpiece today, one cannot help feeling history has been unfair to the composer. It is true that he could not throw off tunes as memorable as those in Rossini's later *Barber* – who could? – but the musical characterization is masterly, the music flows with a Mozartian elegance, and his orchestral writing is more inventive, colourful and subtle than that of any of his Italian contemporaries.

Paisiello never equalled this success again, even though he returned to Naples to become *maestro di cappella* to Ferdinand IV with tremendous prestige. He was something of an opportunist, and his temporary move to Paris, where he composed the music for the coronation of Napoleon, with whom he enjoyed a friendship based on mutual admiration, aroused the hostility of the despotic Ferdinand. His last years in Naples, where he died in 1816, were passed in comparative obscurity.

Cimarosa

There could be no greater contrast than that between the personalities of Paisiello and his shorter-lived rival Domenico Cimarosa, who was born in 1749. Whereas the older man was malign and unlovable, Cimarosa was a charmer who wore his success as easily as he earned it. He was born into a poor family, but had the good fortune to be recognized as precociously gifted and sent to the finest teachers in Naples. He repaid his benefactors' faith in him by scoring an immediate triumph with his first opera, *Le*

Cimarosa

stravaganze del conte, at the age of twenty-two. *Opera buffa* was his natural speciality, for his music bubbles with simple, direct inventiveness, and while the orchestra is always deftly and delicately handled, its chief attraction lies in the rewarding vocal writing. In 1791 Leopold II offered Cimarosa the post of Kapellmeister to the Austrian court in Vienna, and it was there that his most enduring work, *Il matrimonio segreto* ('The secret marriage'), was first given at the Burgtheater in 1792. This opera is still regularly staged today, thanks to its spontaneity and tunefulness, qualities which makes Cimarosa come close to Mozart, though he lacked the latter's depth of feeling and power of musical construction. The Emperor enjoyed *Il matrimonio segreto* so much that he invited all the participants to supper and then commanded an encore of the whole opera. On his death later in the year there were changes at court, leading to Cimarosa's dismissal. He was compensated on his return to Naples by seeing *Il matrimonio segreto* enjoy an unbroken run of fifty-seven performances and by being appointed *maestro di cappella* to Ferdinand IV and music teacher of the princesses. A stream of successful comic operas and less successful serious ones flowed smoothly from his pen. He met his downfall in 1799 through his support of the French republican army which had marched into Naples. Only his fame and popularity saved Cimarosa from the executioner. After a period of imprisonment he left Naples for St Petersburg but died in Venice in 1801, on the first leg of his journey.

France

It took a considerable time for comic opera to develop in France, though comedy-ballets, entertainments in which spoken dialogue was enlivened by songs and dances, were produced by Molière and Lully during the 1660s. The establishment of an Italian Theatre in Paris led to a mongrel form of musical comedy, which took over from the comedy ballet with the death of Molière in 1673. The 'Italian' company gave an inferior brand of farces in French, with incidental songs, and then towards the end of the century the foreigners were replaced by French companies presenting little vaudevilles. During the 1740s the standard of these shows was greatly raised by Charles-Simon Favart, a librettist and impresario who became director of the Opéra-Comique, the opera house in Paris which is colloquially called the Salle Favart to this day. The return of an Italian company to present seasons of *opera buffa*, notably *La serva padrona*, finally paved the way for native French comic opera. An early example was *Le Devin du village* ('The village soothsayer') by, of all people, the philosopher Jean-Jacques Rousseau. It is Italian in form – musically continuous with sung recitatives – but French in melodic style. It was first given in 1752 at Fontainebleau for Louis XV and his court, ironically in that the last great absolute monarch was full of enthusiasm for a work by a principal architect of the approaching Revolution. Rousseau, it is recorded, sat unshaven in a box facing his royal admirer, whom he refused to meet.

True *opéra comique* followed quickly on the heels of Rousseau's hybrid. A word of explanation is needed for the term *opéra comique*. It does not mean 'comic opera', but implies any opera in which spoken dialogue is used in place of sung recitative, and so includes works with tragic endings such as Bizet's *Carmen* and, for the French, Beethoven's *Fidelio*. The earliest composer of *opéra comique* to have any real importance was the Belgian André Ernest Grétry, who brought a variety of romantic elements into comic opera and a new sentiment absent in Italian *opera buffa*. He was born in Liège in 1741, completed his studies in Rome, and with the encouragement of Voltaire made Paris his home. He wrote some fifty

operas, of which the most successful are *Zémire et Azor* (1771) and *Richard Coeur de Lion* (1784). The latter has a 'rescue' plot, a subject much in vogue for a time and which is familiar to us through *Fidelio*. Grétry remained a leading figure right up to his death near Paris on 24 September 1813, but outside France is now virtually forgotten. His importance was in establishing the basis of *opéra comique*, which later composers would refine and develop in the most popular French masterpieces.

England

Just as the British lagged behind all other nations in producing any serious opera of their own, they made a poor showing in the comic field. However, Italian opera had taken over so completely that a reaction inevitably set in, and a form of ballad opera grew up which both gave expression to native song and ridiculed the foreign style. The earliest and the most imaginative was *The Beggar's Opera*, a masterpiece by any standards, and in reality the first musical rather than a comic opera. Whereas later attempts at English comic opera by such composers as Arne and William Shield died early deaths, *The Beggar's Opera* has remained successful to the present day. Its author, John Gay, was born at Barnstaple in 1685, and was fortunate enough to receive a legacy which allowed him to

Gay, whose savagely satirical Beggar's Opera *proved so popular in London that it drove the Italian opera from the stage for a time*

Hogarth print of a performance of The Beggar's Opera, *a ballad opera which matched his own gift for caricature*

take up residence in London 'as befitted a private gentleman' – which meant indulging his three chief interests, women, good food and fine clothes. In 1720 the publication of his collected poems brought him the sum of a thousand pounds, a fortune in those days, but he promptly lost everything by buying the South Sea stock whose bubble burst and ruined thousands of investors. Friends came to his rescue, so that he was able to live on their generosity until 1728, when *The Beggar's Opera* ran for sixty-two nights at Lincoln's Inn Fields in London and created a sensation. It satirized Italian operas so effectively that it drove them from the London stage for some time, and its political lampooning so offended Parliament that the Drama Censorship Act was passed. It made Gay such a celebrity that until his death on 4 December 1732, he lived in luxury as the guest of the Duke and Duchess of Queensbury.

Gay was not a composer, and for the sixty-nine short songs in *The Beggar's Opera* he chose familiar English, Scots or Irish airs that would fit his lyrics. Tongue in cheek, he also included a few operatic melodies, including a march from Handel's *Rinaldo*. Audiences were delighted, after years of *opera seria*

sung in a foreign tongue, to hear tunes they knew incorporated into a wickedly satirical comedy. Gay's method is unusually subtle: he presents a picture of life among the lowest criminals, highwayman and prostitutes, whom he shows by a series of witty analogies to be quite as dishonest and immoral as people of fashion. When Macheath, the highwayman hero, sings of the two girls fighting over him, 'How happy could I be with either/Were t'other dear charmer away', he was clearly pointing to the current scandal concerning the prime minister, Sir Horace Walpole, his wife and his mistress. The quarrels between Macheath's Polly and Lucy were also recognized as reflecting the similar hair-pulling antics of the two rival prima donnas Francesca Cuzzoni and Faustina Bordoni. As a comprehensive satire on opera, politics and social hypocrisy all at the same time, *The Beggar's Opera* has never been equalled, and the sheer abundance of its pleasing songs has secured immortality for the work. Revivals have included the Nigel Playfair presentation in London which ran for close on fifteen hundred performances, and composers who have made more sophisticated arrangements of the music include Arthur Bliss and Benjamin Britten. It was also the inspiration for *Die Dreigroschenoper* ('The threepenny opera') by Kurt Weill and Bertolt Brecht, premiered in Berlin in 1928.

Germany

Curiously enough, the German *Singspiel* sprang from a now forgotten English ballad opera, *The Devil to Pay* by Charles Coffey, which was produced in London in 1731 and in Berlin twelve years later in a German translation. It was subsequently given in Leipzig, but this time with new music by the obscure J C Standfuss. The new entertainment caught on, and a whole series of ballad operas quickly followed. The English influence waned quickly, the *Singspiel* taking up the pattern of the French *opéra comique* and in the process becoming sentimental and cosy, set in either rural or middle-class society and with virtue always triumphant. The outstanding composer in this style was Johann Adam Hiller (1728–1804) whose melodies have simple, gentle appeal. His most successful work is *Die Jagd* ('The hunt'), first performed in 1770, which remained the most popular of all German operas until Weber's *Der Freischütz* of 1821. Hiller's rival Georg Benda (1722–95) trod an unusual path in his 'melodramas', stage pieces in which the characters speak their lines accompanied by or alternating with orchestral playing.

In the south of Germany the public found such works too sedate: the Viennese in particular wanted livelier music and more Italianate vocal display. The kind of *Singspiel* first put on there was more farcical, and if anything of the supernatural crept into the texts it was made to look deliberately ridiculous. Not until the Emperor Joseph II gave orders that musical entertainments should be sung to German words, and a national opera theatre was founded, did the *Singspiel* establish itself in the Imperial capital, with Karl Ditters von Dittersdorf its leading figure. Haydn composed one, but the music has unfortunately been lost, and other composers produced attractively tuneful pieces in the *genre* which have lapsed into obscurity. The importance of the *Singspiel* rests on one great composer: here, as with *opera buffa*, all roads seem to lead to Mozart.

Spain

The seventeenth century was a golden age for the drama in Spain, dominated by its virtual founder,

Felix Lope de Vega (1562–1635), an astonishingly prolific genius who wrote more than two thousand plays. In 1629, two years after the Italian opera had been introduced into Spain, he became the librettist of the first Spanish opera, *La selva sin amor* ('The forest without love'), of which the music – by an unknown composer – has not survived. Even before this, however, ballads and other songs had been incorporated into plays, so the time was clearly ripe for some new form of drama in which music could be given a greater part. The man who created it was Lope de Vega's distinguished successor, Calderón de la Barca (1600–1681), who brought music and poetry together in a form that has ever since remained exclusive to Spain, the *zarzuela*. The two earliest *zarzuelas* were given in Madrid, both with texts by Calderón, *El jardín de Falerina* and *El laurel de Apolo*. The subject matter of these early pieces was drawn

Goya painting of a majo, *the typical gallant of Madrid whose amorous adventures provide plots for so many Spanish operettas*

Goya painting of two majas, the vivacious ladies of Madrid who are featured in zarzuelas *and* tonadillas, *Spanish forms of comic opera*

from Classical legend and drama. Rustic and popular elements were also included, as was the *seguidilla*, a popular song-and-dance form which came, like Don Quixote, from La Mancha.

The increasing interest in Italian opera pushed the *zarzuela* into a decline about 1780, only a few years after Classical subject matter had given way to scenes of popular life and humbler characters in *Las labradoras de Murcia* ('The workwomen of Murcia') and similar works. For fifty years its place was taken by the *tonadilla escénica*, a sort of comic opera lasting no more than twenty minutes. In Madrid alone some two thousand of these *tonadillas* were given at two theatres. They dealt with characters drawn from everyday life, above all the gallants of Madrid and their vivacious ladies, the *majos* and *majas* familiar to us from Goya's paintings. They were essentially ephemeral, however, and when the *zarzuela* returned to popularity in the nineteenth century they simply faded away – though they gave an enduring national flavour to Spanish music.

Handel

No composer has ever been more completely the product of his time than the man we know as the Great Mr Handel. He was born a German, Georg Friederich Händel, at Halle on 23 February 1685; he chose to become a British subject in 1726; and he brought the Italian *opera seria* of the eighteenth century to its full flowering. It would be wrong to think of him as German, English or Italian: he was cosmopolitan in personality, outlook and profession. He could live happily wherever the right conditions existed for him to get on with his work, and politics made the decision for him with the Hanoverian succession to the English throne. Free of nationalist ideals, he was able to incorporate into his musical style whatever he found suitable. He was astute and knew how to play the musical market, securing royal pensions on the one hand and managerial fees on the other so that he ended up a man of considerable substance. He could turn his hand to orchestral music, opera and oratorio, always working at high speed, and was a sensational keyboard virtuoso. All this suggests that he could carry his inborn practicality and realism to the point of opportunism, yet his genius was such that whatever he composed to suit the fashion of the moment was always genuinely inspired. Historians of music have berated him for taking what they have seen as the easy path to success; but Beethoven, in artistic outlook the very opposite of Handel, showed more perception. When asked towards the end of his life whom he considered to be the greatest composer who had ever lived, Beethoven replied without hesitation: 'Handel; to him I bend the knee'.

Whereas Bach, who was born less than a month later in the same year, had a musical family background, Handel was actively discouraged by his father, a barber-surgeon, from taking up such an unstable career as that of a musician. His organ playing at the age of nine or ten so impressed a local nobleman, however, that his father was persuaded to let him study with a Halle organist, Friedrich Zachau. The young Handel received a solid training in composition as well as playing the organ, harpsichord, violin and, his favourite instrument at the time, the oboe. He still paid heed to his father's concern for a stable future, continuing his general studies as the University of Halle even after the latter's death, and it was not until 1702, when he was seventeen, that he took up an appointment as organist. A year later he moved to Hamburg, where there was a public opera house; there he met Johann Mattheson, a competent composer, and the two men became friends, despite a quarrel leading to the fighting of a duel in which Mattheson's sword fortunately broke on a button on Handel's coat. They went together to Lübeck to apply for the post of organist there in succession to the famous Buxtehude, but they backed down quickly on discovering that the prize was conditional upon marrying the old master's daughter, whose years outnumbered her charms.

Handel realized his ambition to become an opera composer when his *Almira* was staged in Hamburg on 8 January 1705, and proved popular enough to enjoy about twenty performances. *Almira* had a typical Hamburg libretto, with its arias in Italian to suit the singers' taste and the recitatives in German so that the audience could follow the plot. Encouraged by this whiff of success, Handel decided to move on to Italy, the home of opera. His exact movements there remain uncertain to this day, though we know that in Rome he engaged in a famous keyboard contest with Domenico Scarlatti, proving equally accomplished on the harpsichord, and outright winner on the organ. His opera *Agrippina* was staged in Venice and showed that he could compete with the Italians on their own ground; it became the triumph of the season. It was as something of a celebrity that he returned to Germany in 1710 to become Kapellmeister to the Elector of Hanover. Within a few months he was given leave of absence to go to London, a visit which was to prove the turning point in his career. Handel, who must have realized the possibilities open to him in London, was given immediate encouragement in the form of a commission to write an Italian opera. *Rinaldo* was composed in two weeks, the 'borrowing' of arias from earlier works helping to meet this deadline, and presented to great acclaim on 24 February 1711.

Duties in Hanover demanded his return, but within a year he had begun to find it rather tame after the splendours of London. He applied for a further leave of absence, which was granted 'on condition that he engaged to return in a reasonable time', but when he returned to London towards the end of 1712 he made it his permanent home. In 1713 he pleased Queen Anne with a *Birthday Ode*, and so impressed her with his *Te Deum* that she granted him a royal pension of £200 a year. Her death in the following year caused initial embarrassment for Handel, because the Elector of Hanover, whom he had so conspicuously neglected to serve as Kapellmeister, was proclaimed George I of England. Reconciliation came easily, however, the good-natured monarch confirming his pension and adding a further £200 a year himself. Handel enjoyed financial security for the rest of his life.

Joan Sutherland in Alcina, *an opera complete with the magical elements in its libretto which Handel often favoured*

For a few years Handel achieved little in the field of opera. With his instinct for survival, he found a new patron in James Brydges, who as Paymaster General of the armies abroad had managed to line his own pockets with money that should have gone to the troops. He built an Italianate palace for himself at Canons a few miles outside London, where he installed Handel as composer in residence. Two dramatic works were staged at Canons, the masque *Acis and Galatea* which includes two of Handel's most celebrated songs, 'Love in her eyes sits playing' and 'O ruddier than the cherry'; and the first English oratorio, *Esther*.

Opera was given a fillip early in 1719 with the foundation of the Royal Academy of Music, named after the Académie Royale de Musique in Paris, and Handel was sent abroad to find suitable singers for this new opera company. For the next eight years his activities were centred on the King's Theatre in the 161

Handel, whose many successful operas and oratorios in London made him the most celebrated composer of his time

Haymarket, where the opera seasons were given, for he was director of the orchestra as well as composer of a dozen operas presented between 1720 and 1728. These included some of his finest works, *Radamisto*, *Ottone*, *Giulio Cesare* and *Rodelinda*. By 1728, however, resistance to Italian opera was building up, so that the success of *The Beggar's Opera* was enough to whisk

its audience away to the less exotic delights of pungent satire laced with simple English songs. The Royal Academy went bankrupt, and for the next few years Handel busied himself with other opera companies, doubling the duties of composer and impresario.

When these ventures finally failed in 1737 he had lost a considerable amount of his own money, a setback which turned out in the end to have been a blessing in disguise, for it made him take up the oratorio, a form to which he had previously paid only intermittent attention. With the obvious exception of *Messiah*, Handel's oratorios are really operas in all but name: their subject matter may be biblical, but the music is as dramatic as that of his operas. The best of the oratorios, such as *Saul*, *Samson*, *Semele* (unusual in that its subject is not biblical) and *Jephtha*, present characters more dramatically convincing than are those of the operas, and it is not surprising that they have frequently been given full operatic production.

With *Rinaldo*, his first opera for London, Handel showed his rich melodic gift in a profusion of arias which are remarkably varied in their dramatic colouring. The solo aria was all-important in the operas of the first half of the eighteenth century: it constituted the aesthetic basis of *opera seria*. Composers sought to present the state of mind or feeling of a character at a given moment, as it were suspended in time. The plot was not in itself of major importance, nor did either composer or public expect it to present 'natural' action on the stage. The plot was the means by which the characters were placed in a series of situations in each of which an aria would crystallize their thoughts or feeling at that moment. (After each aria, in fact, the character would make his or her exit, having made the dramatic point.) What put Handel head and shoulders above his contemporaries was his inborn dramatic sense, which enabled him to give his characters such vividly expressive arias that their thoughts and feelings are made very real to an audience prepared to accept the convention.

A fine example of Handel's imaginative and vital use of the *opera seria* is *Giulio Cesare*. The characterization of Cleopatra, here a young girl, is remarkably subtle, revealing the various facets of her nature in different arias, her awareness of her powers to charm in 'Tutto può donna vezzosa', her warm seductiveness in 'V'adoro, pupille', her deeper feelings in two outbursts of the utmost poignancy, 'Se pietà di me non senti' and 'Piangerò, la sorte mia', and her sensuous rapture in the final duet with Caesar, a worthy companion-piece to Monteverdi's duet for Nero and

*Janet Baker as Caesar in the English National Opera
production of Handel's* Giulio Cesare *at the London
Coliseum*

Poppea. Caesar also is brought out as a fully three-dimensional figure. Cornelia, Pompey's widow, is throughout a tragic character, yet her noble music is varied, while her son Sextus rejoices in two vengeance arias and a tearful duet with his mother. The orchestral writing is superbly inventive, its colouring reinforcing the drama at every turn, and with skilful use of key changes to prepare shifts of mood.

It should be noted that we can never hear most of Handel's dramatic works sung as he intended them, for the age of the castrato has long departed. Tenors and basses do not have the range or flexibility of the castrato voice, while the substitution of a female mezzo leads to the incongrous sight of a woman striding round the stage with helmet and sword in the manner of a principal boy of English pantomime. This above all has made opera-goers reluctant to accept Handel's operas, though the revivals of interest in the works in Germany during the 1920s and in England during the 1950s have produced many converts. In other respects the formality of style should not prevent anyone from enjoying a wealth of glorious music.

Although the popularity of Italian opera was clearly declining, Handel continued to bring out new works in the form until 1741, but the sensational success of *Messiah* the following year finally persuaded him to devote all his energies to the oratorio. He remained active as composer, performer and manager until 1753, when his eyesight, which had begun to fail two years earlier, went altogether. He continued to attend performances of his works, and it is recorded that many of the audience were in tears as the blinded hero of *Samson* sang the aria 'Total eclipse' while Handel sat sightless by the stage. Handel was a celebrated musical figure all his adult life, a widely travelled man of sophistication with friends in high places, and a genius who knew his worth and was determined never to let anyone forget it. His death in London on 14 April 1759, was a matter of national concern, three thousand people attending his funeral at Westminster Abbey, where his body was buried in Poets' Corner.

Gluck

Opera was in a melting-pot during the working period of the man considered to be its first great reformer, Christoph Willibald Gluck, whose career highlights many of the conflicting ideas of his age concerning the proper qualities of the opera libretto, the kind of music best suited to works for the stage, 163 and the relative importance of words and music. The operas by which he is remembered, and which are still performed, *Orfeo ed Euridice*, *Alceste*, *Iphigénie en Aulide* and *Iphigénie en Tauride*, broke new ground and were highly controversial in their day, yet many of his other works continued to follow the very Neapolitan style which his reforms set out to destroy. Gluck's early life is not well documented: we know that he was born at Erasbach on 2 July 1714, but nothing is certain regarding his education. He worked in Prague between 1732 and 1736 before moving to Vienna to become a chamber musician in an aristocratic household. After a year there he found a patron who took him to Milan for further studies, and so it was in Italy that his first operas were staged. They were successful enough for him to be invited to London in 1745, where he had an opera produced the following year which drew from Handel the unkind comment that 'he knows no more about counterpoint than my cook' (though Handel's cook, Waltz, was in fact a composer). The two composers nevertheless became friendly, and even appeared together in a concert at which Gluck played the glass harmonica. The London visit was scarcely a success, so he returned to Germany to become conductor of a travelling Italian opera company which went as far afield as Holland and Denmark. In 1749 he was back in Vienna on a visit during which he met the daughter of a wealthy banker. He asked to marry her but was refused the consent of her father, and that might have been the end of the matter had not the latter died the following year, enabling Gluck to marry Marianne and become financially independent for the rest of his life, thanks to the generous dowry she brought with her. From this date he was free to compose only such operas as appealed to his own taste.

The original creators of opera had concentrated on words and music as being the equally important chief elements of their new form of *dramma per musica*, but within a hundred years this ideal had been lost. By the end of the seventeenth century the most important element had become stage machinery, which was combined with scenic painting to create elaborate spectacles for the audiences to marvel at. Second in importance was the composer, who was required to write for the gratification of the castrato and the prima donna. The librettist occupied the lowest rung on the ladder. Two Italian poets finally came to the rescue, first Apostolo Zeno (1668–1750) and then Pietro Metastasio (1698–1782), who restored the librettist to his original place of honour. Both wrote neatly turned verse of a heroic nature, and both concentrated exclusively on characters of impossible nobil-

Gluck, the composer considered to be opera's first great reformer

ity. Genuine human emotion rarely came into the drama, which was wholly artificial in form and feeling. It is because Italian *opera seria* was so completely conditioned by Metastasio's librettos that it became equally rigid in form. It was against the style of Metastasio that one of Gluck's librettists, Ranieri Calzabigi, rebelled. *Orfeo ed Euridice* by Calzabigi and Gluck was produced at the court theatre on 5 October 1762 and marks a new epoch in opera. Gluck avoided the usual coloratura aria in his search for a new style that would use the simplest yet most expressive means to make its points, faithfully following the example of his librettist, who had reduced the action to a series of tableaux.

It is appropriate that this first of Gluck's reform operas should have had the same subject as the earliest surviving work of the Florentines, for his aim was the same as theirs, *dramma per musica*. His *Orfeo ed Euridice* treats the story very differently, however, starting after the death of Euridice and showing Orfeo and the chorus lamenting round her bier. Left alone, Orfeo sings, not an aria, but a strophic song,

human being. Then there is the conventional, dramatically inappropriate happy ending, which can only be excused on the grounds that a tragic one would not have been acceptable to eighteenth-century taste, and quite out of the question in the case of an opera being given its premiere on the Emperor's name-day. Most surprising of all is that Orfeo's 'Che puro ciel' in Act II, though it sounds wholly appropriate in its context, was actually 'borrowed' by Gluck from an aria he had used twice before – and in operas with librettos by Metastasio! Nobody, it would seem, can be completely consistent.

If *Orfeo* set Gluck apart from his rivals, he still competed with them in the traditional field as well, for he was no revolutionary zealot who pursued a fixed course. Prominent among these rivals was Niccolò Jommelli (1714–74), a Neapolitan who worked for sixteen years at the court of Stuttgart, who was something of a reformer too. Another popular composer at the time was Niccolò Piccinni (1728–1800), whose comic *La buona figliuola* (1760) is still revived in Italy occasionally. All the works produced in the traditional *seria* style by Gluck, Jommelli and Piccinni have vanished into limbo, but the three operas by Gluck which continued the style of *Orfeo* have made their way into the repertoire. *Alceste*, produced in Vienna in 1767 and revised for Paris nine years later, went further along the path of reform than *Orfeo ed Euridice*, its aims clearly stated in a preface to the published score two years later: 'I have striven to restrict music to its true office of serving poetry by means of expression, and by following the situations of the story without interrupting the action or stifling it with a useless superfluity of ornaments.' Such ideals were not entirely new, but Gluck was the first publicly to nail them to his aesthetic mast.

The most notable feature about *Alceste* is not the quality of its individual arias and choruses, impressive though these are, but the gradual progress of the whole drama in carefully constructed scenes. This musical continuity was something Gluck developed even more skilfully with his two finest works for Paris, in which his music, kept subservient to the poetry in the reform operas he composed for Vienna, was raised to a position of equality. His move to Paris was perhaps inevitable, for he had failed to make an international reputation in Vienna and needed a more prestigious launching platform, such as the French capital then afforded. Paris, though not the operatic centre it was to become in the nineteenth century, was the most cultured capital in Europe, and Gluck knew he had a friend there in his one-time singing pupil, Marie Antoinette, wife of the Dauphin.

Kathleen Ferrier in the title-role of Orfeo, *the first of Gluck's reform operas*

its three strophes interrupted by short recitatives. The second act opens with the scene of the Furies guarding the gates of the underworld, who allow Orfeo to pass only when he has won them over by the magic of his singing, then moves to the Elysian Fields, where the celebrated Dance of the Blessed Spirits is followed by Orfeo's aria 'Che puro ciel'. The third act includes the aria 'Che farò senza Euridice' ('What shall I do without Euridice') and concludes with general rejoicing after the couple's final reunion. There is only one other soloist, Amor the god of love, but the chorus play a positive part, and while the action is stately it has intense inner emotional freedom. The music has remarkable richness despite it simplicity, and a modern audience can respond to it as to any true masterpiece, for it transcends its time.

In a few respects the opera may be thought less radical than Gluck and Calzabigi claimed. The casting of Orfeo as a castrato role appears to be contrary to the spirit of reform, but the character is after all a symbol of the musician's art rather than an ordinary

A group portrait including the poet/librettist Metastasio and the castrato Farinelli, who became a favourite with London audiences

In 1773, at the age of fifty-nine, Gluck paid a visit to Paris and set his plans in motion, his chief concern being not to upset French susceptibilities by presuming to write operas in that language. He had already prepared the libretto of *Iphigénie en Aulide*, based on Racine's tragedy, and by means of several highly diplomatic moves he had it accepted by the Paris Opéra. In a Paris journal he had published a letter declaring his belief in the suitability of the French language for operatic purposes, which supporters of Italian opera led by Jean-Jacques Rousseau had hotly disputed. All this, with the backing of Marie Antoinette, was sufficient to win the day so far as the staging of *Iphigénie en Aulide* was concerned: it remained only for him to live up to his claims. He did so on 19 April 1774, when the opera was hailed as a masterpiece by his champions and attacked just as enthusiastically by his opponents.

The action of *Iphigénie en Aulide* moves far more rapidly and decisively than in any of Gluck's earlier operas, its musical units being shorter and more closely integrated one with another in the general scheme. It begins with a programme overture (often played in the concert hall) which presents the forces of the drama. The music has a new freedom, so that Agamemnon is able to give voice to his conflicting thoughts in a way not possible in the traditional aria designed to express only one mood or state of mind at a given moment in time. His monologue at the end of the second act establishes Gluck as a dramatic composer of uncommon power. Clytemnestra is drawn in equally graphic music as she turns from unsuccessful pleading with the Greeks to denunciation of them as she calls upon the wrath of Jove. Iphigénie's farewell in the last act, 'Adieu, conservez dans votre âme', has been described as one of the most perfect emotional utterances of the eighteenth century. Gluck did not only extend the expressive possibilities of the voice: he used the orchestra beyond the point of accompaniment to evoke ideas which words could not convey, an almost Wagnerian principle.

Gluck thus became a celebrity overnight, a man to be interviewed and an opera composer whose rehearsals had to be made public events. It is likely that he looked somewhat cynically on his belated appointment as Imperial court composer in Vienna later the same year: the honour he should have been accorded long before. His decision to devote his energies exclusively to French opera is not therefore surprising, and it was for the Opéra that he composed his undoubted masterpiece, *Iphigénie en Tauride*, an opera in which all the best elements of his previous works were combined. This was produced on 18 May 1779. Nicolas-François Guillard, the young poet who wrote the libretto as a mark of his esteem for Gluck, showed the same respect for the original play by Euripides. Although its flavour is French in many respects, the libretto is true to the ideals of Greek tragedy, giving the composer his finest chance to put his own ideals into practice. He triumphed on two levels, in creating whole scenes as homogeneous units and in supplying the characters with arias and recitatives of remarkable inventiveness. The music was a revelation at the time, and it still affords an experience of searing intensity to a modern audience which has grown up with the dramatic works of Verdi and Wagner designed to stimulate the senses far more directly and freely. Indeed, Gluck seems to anticipate Wagner when Oreste sings an aria in which the orchestral accompaniment gives the lie to his words. Individual moments stand out in the opera, but the most important thing about *Iphigénie en Tauride* is that the whole is greater than the sum of its parts.

The failure of a slighter work, *Echo et Narcisse*, later in the year turned Gluck's love for Paris into bitter dislike at a stroke, and he decided to return immediately to Vienna. He had usually accepted such setbacks more stoically, and it is probable that his bitterness on this occasion had much to do with his failing health. He was sixty-five, suffering from frequent minor strokes, so was in no fit state to cope with the rigours of operatic life at the top. In Vienna, though he retired from public life, he continued to take an interest in the musical activities around him, even planning to compose some operas for Naples. In 1782 he invited Mozart to dinner, after being enchanted by the younger composer's *Die Entführung aus dem Serail*, which he must have admired for its spontaneity and lyrical ease. Deteriorating health caused Gluck to spend his last three years quietly at home, where he died from a stroke on 15 November 1787. Ironically in the case of a composer of such austere style, this was brought on by indulging in the forbidden pleasure of a glass of liqueur.

Mozart

Looking back on the eighteenth century from the vantage point of today, we can see that opera lacked a sense of direction, various different types having developed to a certain extent but in each case having reached what can only be considered something of a dead end. The *opera seria* had been carried by Handel to a purely musical peak in a style which he himself knew to be fatally outmoded, while Gluck had restored the dramatic element to its rightful place without managing to escape from the confines of a formal straitjacket. The *opera buffa*, while it enjoyed an earthier freedom, still dealt only with types, the stock figures of *commedia dell'arte* which dominated French as well as Italian comic opera, rather than real three-dimensional characters. The German *Singspiel*, the most recent form, was largely based on folksong and was more of a play with music than opera proper. All these problems were resolved with the arrival on the scene of that most miraculous of geniuses, Mozart, who turned everything he touched to gold. The mature operas Mozart composed two centuries ago have defied the passage of time. When we see tragic operas by Handel and Gluck, or comic ones by Cimarosa and Paisiello, we cannot hope to appreciate them unless we try to adjust our minds to the period in which they were written. There is no such necessity in the case of Mozart, whose *Don Giovanni* and *Figaro* are just as 'modern' in their treatment of human behaviour and relationships as any operas composed more recently.

The Vienna Burgtheater where both The Marriage of Figaro *and* Così fan tutte *were first performed*

It is something of a miracle that Mozart was able to succeed as he did, because he worked in the same conditions which bedevilled all opera composers of the period. The audiences for which he wrote chattered and played cards during the performance, making even the worst of today's chocolate-eating, bangle-rattling opera house pests seem paragons of virtue by comparison. Then the singers, who ruled the operatic roost, demanded music tailored to their individual capabilities and tastes. Mozart was able to overcome these handicaps. There were several things in his favour. He was a born dramatic composer, having a fine sense of theatre and also the insight into human nature, revealed in his letters, which enabled him to understand rather than attempt to judge his fellow men. Then he had been taken on wide-ranging tours as an infant prodigy, which allowed him to see operas of all kinds performed in Vienna, Paris, Rome, London and other important centres. Finally, he was unique among composers in that he was commissioned between the ages of twelve and fourteen to write *Bastien und Bastienne* (1768), a simple *Singspiel*, *La finta semplice* (1769), an *opera buffa*, and then in yet another style *Mitridate* (1770), an *opera seria*, which gave him valuable experience in all the current forms of opera. Over the following ten years he produced only three more prentice works for the stage, not because he had lost interest in opera but simply because it was his lot to provide whatever kind of music happened to be demanded of him at any time.

The chance to show what he was really capable of came with a commission to write an *opera seria* for Munich in 1780 on the story of Idomeneo, the king of Crete who vows during a storm at sea that if Neptune spares his ship he will sacrifice the first living creature he meets on dry land. True to Classical convention, the first person Idomeneo sees on his arrival is Idamante, his own son. It might seem that *Idomeneo* could not possibly be the kind of opera to inspire Mozart to his best, and indeed it was only revived once during his lifetime after the Munich premiere on 29 January 1781, and subsequently suffered the same general neglect as most other *opere serie*. It was not staged professionally in England until the Glyndebourne production of 1951, but has since entered the repertoire of both London opera houses. Its first performance in New York took place the same year, but only in a concert version. Seen in the opera house it comes as a revelation, for Mozart transformed the rigid style of *opera seria* to create a work that stands alone, a tragedy (despite its happy ending) of great dignity filled with the most intense expression of human passions. The characters are drawn from ancient mythology, but the music makes them as real, though inhabiting a loftier plane, as those of his ever-popular comic operas. With this remarkable work Mozart truly poured new wine into an old bottle.

Later in the year which had seen the launching of *Idomeneo*, Mozart turned to the very different world of *Singspiel* for *Die Entführung aus dem Serail*, a masterpiece which continues to delight audiences everywhere. Since this is a German comic opera, the action is carried on almost exclusively in dialogue, the characters bursting into song chiefly at moments of high emotional tension. The whole confection might have been just another popular entertainment for a season or so, but the sublime music lavished on Belmonte and, above all, Constanze, has given it immortality. It might be argued, in fact, that the heroine's arias are too long and too elaborate for their context, especially 'Martern aller Arten' with its four obbligato instruments, sophisticated orchestration and fiendishly difficult vocal writing, but in practice it works in the theatre with stunning effect. The arias for the other characters are shorter and simpler in style, though all are perfectly suited to the dramatic situation, and Mozart gave Osmin two of the best comic bass numbers in the whole repertoire. The *Singspiel* had never risen to such heights before, and would do so again only when Mozart came to write *The Magic Flute*. It is interesting too that while he was composing it the young composer wrote the letter to his father which included the now famous statement that 'the poetry must be altogether the obedient daughter of the music'.

This declaration by Mozart has given rise to a great deal of misunderstanding, when in fact it is a remark of admirable common sense. On the face of it, Mozart appears to be directly opposed to the reforming ideas of Gluck, whose ideal was 'to restrict music to its true office of serving poetry', and also to the much-publicized later theories of Wagner, who declared that opera was 'cursed' because 'a means of expression [music] had been made the end, while the end of expression [the drama] has been made a means'. When composers turn theorists, alas, their pronouncements are often suspect, and they are saved from becoming bad composers only when they do not put their theories fully into practice. Whatever their composers might have argued in print, it is Gluck's music, not Guillard's verse, which has kept *Iphigénie en Tauride* alive, just as it is Wagner's music for *Tristan and Isolde*, and not the 'poem' he wrote himself, which makes us happy to sit for such an unconscionable time in the opera house. Wagner even went to the length of berating Mozart for being prepared to set 'any and every opera text offered to him, almost needless whether it were a worthwhile task for him as a pure musician', a criticism, incidentally, which is just not true. Mozart certainly accepted texts without complaint in his earliest operas, when he was a mere teenager, but once he had matured he revised them as and whenever he thought fit, such being the case with *Idomeneo* when he was still only twenty-four. Had Wagner read the letters Mozart wrote to his father concerning his dealing with the librettist of *Die Entführung aus dem Serail*, he could never have made such an elementary mistake. Mozart and Da Ponte collaborated very closely on the preparation of the three comic masterpieces they produced together, and it is sad that there is no record of the discussions they had, for it would surely have made fascinating reading. The point of Mozart's remark about poetry being the 'obedient daughter' of the music is that he realized, with an instinct that was wiser than all Gluck's and Wagner's intellectual theories, that the literary quality of a libretto in itself is not a virtue: its value lies in its suitability for musical treatment and in the inspiration it gives to the composer. By the same token, the quality of the music in an opera cannot be judged solely on its own merits, but according to the way in which it faithfully expresses and extends the dramatic ideas of the text.

There may be room for minor reservations about Mozart's operatic mastery in these early works, but admiration is completely unqualified when it comes to the three Italian *opere buffe* he composed to texts by Lorenzo da Ponte. In each case the libretto was ideal for Mozart's purpose, an 'obedient daughter' but also an uncommonly lively one, and from beginning to end the elegantly nimble verse is clearly tailor-made for musical setting, marvellously fluid in the case of the ensembles. The expertise of Da Ponte is made very clear in the case of *Le nozze di Figaro* ('The marriage of Figaro'), his first libretto for Mozart. In the first place, he was obliged to take the edge off the political tone of the original play by Beaumarchais (*Le Mariage de Figaro*, a sequel to his *Le Barbier de Séville*), which would never have passed the Austrian censors. Then it was necessary to reduce the original sixteen characters to eleven and cut several scenes and satirical exchanges. 'For these,' Da Ponte explained in his preface, 'I have had to substitute *canzonette* [songs], arias, choruses, and other thoughts and words susceptible of being set to music – things that can only be handled with the help of poetry and never with prose.' In the final outcome he completely transformed the play, transplanting it, in the words of Alfred Einstein, 'into a new, purer, richer and more ideal soil – that of music'. There are elements

Ruggero Raimondi as Don Giovanni in the Joseph Losey film of Mozart's opera with a cast of internationally celebrated singers

of *commedia dell'arte* in Susanna and Figaro, while Don Bartolo and Marcellina are simply *buffo* figures, but the characterization of Cherubino, the Count and, above all, the Countess, carry *Figaro* beyond the limits of *opera buffa* into something utterly new, a *commedia per musica* as the title-page described it. This is not immediately apparent when we see the opera, because it opens in *buffo* style with Figaro and Susanna in a typically lively scene for a servant couple. With the entries of first Cherubino and then the Count, however, the whole artistic atmosphere changes, and with the introduction of the Countess in her poignant aria at the opening of Act II we have left *opera buffa* far behind in favour of comedy in the sense of Shakespeare's *Twelfth Night*. Da Ponte's and Mozart's concern is not merely a stock situation in which wily, resourceful servants pull the wool over 169 the eyes of their betters, but a sensitive study of human relationships. The Countess is drawn to Susanna – who starts out as a conventional likeable comic character and then grows into a lovable woman of real substance – across the social barriers that would never be breached in *opera buffa*. Most important of all, when the complicated plots and counter-plots have been resolved on the surface, the opera ends, not with a full stop but a question mark. Whereas Rossini's *The Barber of Seville* implies that Count Almaviva and his Rosina will live happily ever

Geraint Evans as the comically scheming and flamboyant Figaro in a Covent Garden production of The Marriage of Figaro

after, *Figaro* leaves us with the certain knowledge that this now married couple will continue to be faced by uncertainties and infidelities, as most probably will Figaro and Susanna as well. And what of Cherubino? Will he grow out of his adolescent calf-love for every pretty woman he meets, or will he meet the fate of Don Giovanni?

Some of the subtleties here are inherent in Da Ponte's libretto, but ultimately it is Mozart's music which penetrates to the hearts of the characters, reveals the depth of feeling behind their words, and makes them real men and women we feel we have learned to understand and identify with by the end of the performance. It is difficult to think of any other opera comparable to *Figaro* in this respect. Many composers since have emulated Mozart, and there are indeed many operatic characters who engage our sympathy across the footlights as though they were real people; yet is there another single opera which presents so many characters in such revealing depth and with such complete conviction? Verdi's Violetta is a fully developed character, and so is the Marschallin of Richard Strauss, but the other characters in *La Traviata* and *Der Rosenkavalier* do not have anything like the same substance. Puccini's Rodolfo and Mimì are credible characters, and evenly matched, yet they are shallow figures beside the Count and Countess, through whom Mozart explores so many of the complexities of love and marriage. Wagner probes into the whole psychology of love in *Tristan and Isolde*, though in such a symbolic way that audiences do not see themselves reflected in such larger-than-life characters. (This is not meant as a criticism of Wagner, whose purpose was manifestly different from Mozart's and was uniquely fulfilled.) The most remarkable achievement of *Figaro* is not the way in which the composer illuminates the human condition through his music, but the fact that he does so in a work designed primarily to entertain. Mozart never set out to teach or edify his audience, only to please them, and the miracle, to use that term again, is that his music reveals so many truths without his apparently being aware of it. This is why his is a 'pure' genius unlike any other.

Another unusual fact about Mozart's operas is that no two of his mature works are at all alike. With *Don Giovanni* he turned to a different world altogether, but one which he explored with the same blazing imagination. The extent of his originality is all the greater when we consider that the subject was chosen out of mere expediency, not because he had any artistic compulsion to treat its theme. Vienna had received *Figaro* on 1 May 1786, quite respectfully, though not with any particular enthusiasm: the

Scene from the Covent Garden production of Così fan tutte *showing the colourful Neapolitan setting of this highly artifical comedy*

Viennese, as the story of music makes clear over and over again, were not nearly so cultured as they professed to be, and they simply could not appreciate the opera Mozart had given them. A few months later it was given in Prague, Mozart's favourite city, where the more receptive public greeted it with unprecedented enthusiasm. The composer, wishing to enjoy the triumph, accepted an invitation to Prague during the following January, when he was commissioned to write a new opera for the coming season. Having no time to waste, Mozart and Da Ponte picked on one of the oldest of European adventure stories which had just been given at Venice in a new operatic version. The original play, *El burlador de Sevilla y convidado de piedra* ('The deceiver of Seville and the stone guest'), was the work of a Spanish priest, Gabriel Terrez (1571–1648), who wrote a number of risqué plays under the pseudonym Tirso de Molina. (It is charitably assumed that his detailed knowledge of the seamier side of erotic life was acquired in the confessional rather than through any personal experience.) The 'deceiver of Seville' was Don Juan, of course, and the 'stone guest' the statue who accepts

his supper invitation. The story was adapted by dramatists in many countries, Molière in France, Goldoni in Italy, Shadwell in England, but the basic idea was always retained. Da Ponte drew largely on the libretto written for Venice by Giovanni Bertati, but composed far wittier verses and added a considerable amount of new material to fill out Bertati's one-act comedy into two acts. In effect, the *Don Giovanni* he prepared for Mozart contained in the second act a series of dramatically irrelevant postponements of the final scene of retribution, all of which fortunately inspired the composer to some of the finest music in the score.

Don Giovanni, called a *dramma giocosa* (playful drama), does not fall easily into any conventional category. Even the music of the overture is ambivalent, both menacing and mocking, and then the opera opens with Leporello, who is more than the stock comic servant, impatiently complaining that he en- 171 dures waiting in the wind and rain while his master enjoys his debauchery indoors. Suddenly all is violence and tragedy, as Don Giovanni callously murders the father (the Commendatore) of the woman he has just violated or at least attempted to violate – we cannot be sure which. After a duet for Donna Anna and her betrothed, Don Ottavio, in which she calls on him to avenge her father's death, the spirit of the opera switches to a comic vein with Leporello singing his famous catalogue of his master's conquests. There is, however, an enigmatic quality about everything in this opera, which has Donna Anna and Don Ottavio central to it, yet at the same time set apart from the other characters by virtue of the grand manner of their arias. Donna Elvira is dramatically complex, hating the man who has made love to her and then deserted her, yet still infatuated with him, and she too has arias close to the spirit of *opera seria*. The 'simple' couple, Zerlina and Masetto, are not just foils to the nobility, for Mozart gives them music of unusually tender quality. Most enigmatic of all is Don Giovanni himself, whom Mozart makes charming and courageous to such an extent that we cannot help admiring him in spite of our moral scruples, niceties which would not have worried Casanova, who was present at the first performance. We can see *Don Giovanni* any number of times without growing tired of it because it intrigues and stimulates the dramatic imagination as much as it gratifies the musical appetite.

No less enigmatic, though it inhabits a very different world, is the last Da Ponte-Mozart opera, *Così fan tutte*. It is, at first sight, the ultimate in heartless *opera buffa*, with a plot as carefully worked out as a chess problem. Two young officers, engaged to two sisters in Naples, are persuaded by a cynical older friend to test their fiancées' fidelity by pretending to go off to war only to return disguised as Albanians and each woo the other's prospective bride. They accept the wager, and to their mortification both succeed in overcoming the ladies' initial protestations, resulting in the condemnation of the whole opera by successive generations of moralists and, more recently, feminists, who cannot accept the cynical Don Alfonso's assurance at the end that the young men should not worry unduly because 'all women are the same'. The more sensible opera-goer will ignore this po-faced moralizing and simply enjoy some of the most melodious and gracious music ever composed, arias and ensembles overflowing with wit and charm enhanced by brilliantly effective orchestration. *Così fan tutte*, like *Figaro* and Verdi's *Il trovatore*, is one of those rare operas in which every single number is a highlight. The tantalizing aspect of *Così fan tutte* is the question as to how the two men and two women should be paired off at the end. Da Ponte's libretto suggests that they forget the charade which has taken place and return to their original partners, but Mozart's music makes the perceptive listener wonder. The music for the early scenes presents two couples who are happily in love in a somewhat unthinking way, whereas the music for the scenes in which the men are disguised has greater sensuousness, as though the characters have matured and discovered a new, more understanding affection. It is this final question mark which makes one begin to think that Mozart, perhaps unconsciously, was commenting on human relationships more deeply than the surface gaiety of the work implies.

Even more controversy is aroused by *Die Zauberflöte* ('The magic flute'), a *Singspiel* composed in 1791, the last year of his life. Written at the request of his friend Emanuel Schikaneder, a comedy actor and manager with his own small theatre just outside the city walls of Vienna, it was an immediate success and has remained one of the composer's most affectionately regarded works. Its evolution, however, was extraordinary, even in the irrational world of opera. The work began as a fairytale about a fairy queen whose daughter Pamina is carried off by an evil magician and eventually rescued by a princely hero with the aid of a magic flute. Then half way through Mozart and Schikaneder changed their minds: both were Freemasons, and they decided to turn the original wicked magician into Sarastro, the benevolent high priest of a virtuous order clearly modelled on Masonic ideals. The good fairy of the first act was accordingly transformed into the villainous Queen of the Night, and the princely Tamino conveniently transferred his allegiance from her to Sarastro. The symbolism of the second act, including Tamino's ritual initiation into the Masonic order, as well as the curious duality of the work as a whole, has prompted all kinds of interpretations of *The Magic Flute*. These are fascinating and often rewarding to study, though it has perhaps better for our understanding of Mozart simply to laugh with his engagingly comic Papageno, marvel at the way the music depicts Tamino and Pamina gradually maturing into wisdom, and relish the simple yet sublime trios of the Three Ladies and the Three Boy Spirits. If the wicked Queen of the Night excites us with her scintillating coloratura arias more than Sarastro with his solemn hymn-like songs, this is just another example of the rule that the devil has all the best tunes. As always with Mozart, the music speaks to us more clearly than do the words which are set to it, and the emotional response we make to it is more important than an intellectual one.

Scene from The Magic Flute *at Covent Garden with the Three Boys borne aloft in a wholly appropriate Baroque manner*

Mozart composed another opera at the same time, *La clemenza di Tito*, commissioned as part of the celebrations in Prague for the coronation of Leopold II as King of Bohemia. This was a wholly unexpected reversal to *opera seria* with a libretto by Metastasio which had been set several times before. (The text, incidentally, was drastically revised by Caterino Massolà.) It is true that Mozart did not this time infuse the old operatic form with the vitality and imagination he had brought ten years earlier to *Idomeneo*, but *La clemenza di Tito* does not merit the harsh judgments so many scholars have passed on it. The magnanimous Roman emperor and the other characters are all so formally conceived in the text that not even Mozart could bring them to life, yet he wrote truly magnificent arias and duets for them which make their sentiments expressively convincing. And what

majestic music they contain! Considered in purely musical terms, Sesto's 'Parto, parto' and 'Deh per questo istante', the former with clarinet obbligato, are on the highest level of nobility, while Vitellia's 'Non più di fiori', with its basset horn obbligato, portrays in hair-raising style a woman crazed with hatred. Tito's 'Se all'impero' is rich alike in feeling and vocal bravura, and in an outstanding accompanied recitative the emperor meditates like Shakespeare's Henry VI on the sorrow and loneliness of kingship. Of special interest too are the short yet vivid choruses. *La clemenza di Tito*, the first of Mozart's operas to be given in London (1806), remained one of his most popular for some forty years, but then fell into neglect until a series of revivals in the 1960s proved that it was not such a mistake on the composer's part as had been believed, but a work which has a great deal to offer an audience prepared to meet its conventions half-way. That it should be the work of the same hand as *Figaro* and *The Magic Flute* only adds to one's sense of wonder at the versatility of Mozart's genius.

NINETEENTH-CENTURY GERMANY

Beethoven

It is curious that so many regular concert-goers are prejudiced against the whole idea of opera, regarding it as musically inferior to the kind of works heard in the concert hall. Indeed, they seem to think that the theatre, with its glamorous trappings, is no fit place for a self-respecting composer to be seen in. Composers themselves, of course, have always thought otherwise, with a few exceptions amongst whom Bach and Brahms are the most notable. Some of the great symphonists, like Mozart and Tchaikovsky, have been equally successful in the opera house, while others, such as Schubert, Schumann and Mendelssohn, have failed because they did not have the necessary dramatic sense. Beethoven wrestled so hard that eventually, though he cannot be considered a great opera composer, he managed to produce one very great opera, *Fidelio*. He valued it so highly that he spent more time on it than on any of his other works, two early versions being staged in 1805 and 1806 before it was finally given on 23 May 1814, in the form in which we know it today. In the course of these revisions no less than four overtures were written for it. The composer referred to the opera as his 'crown of thorns' yet he believed in it so much that when he looked back over all his work as he lay dying he declared that of all his 'children' it was the one most dear to him, because he held it 'worthy of being possessed and used for the science of art'. He considered many other subjects for further operas, including Part I of Goethe's *Faust*, which he must surely have been the only composer fitted to tackle; Shakespeare's *Macbeth* and *Romeo and Juliet*; and the historical characters Alfred the Great (later taken up by Donizetti) and Attila (eventually tackled by Verdi). All these plans make it clear that Beethoven took a lofty view of opera. Indeed, he openly declared: 'I could not compose operas like *Don Juan* and *Figaro*! They are repugnant to me. I could not have chosen such subjects, for they are too frivolous.'

The reason why *Fidelio* appealed so strongly to him was that Leonore, who takes on a man's guise and risks her own life in order to save her husband's,

Alberto Remedios as Florestan in the English National Opera production of Fidelio, *the opera in which Beethoven expressed his ideas of freedom*

represented for Beethoven the ideal, heroic woman, the female counterpart to the male ideal of the *Eroica* Symphony. Having found his subject, where was he to look for guidance in the style of his opera? Mozart, as he had made plain, he rejected as 'frivolous', even immoral. He did, however, adopt the *Singspiel* form insofar as *Fidelio* employs spoken dialogue instead of recitative to carry the action forward; but style is a different matter from form, and for this he turned to the followers of Gluck. These were mainly Italian composers who had found fame and fortune in Paris as leaders of French opera, and included Spontini (1774–1851) and Cherubini (1760–1842). The latter exerted the greater influence on Beethoven by virtue of his opera *Les Deux journées*, a 'rescue opera' using a kind of plot which was much in vogue during the French Revolution and the Reign of Terror. The ideals of humanity were expressed by the virtuous characters and, in particular, by means of important choruses, as Beethoven does with such moving effect in the Prisoners' Chorus in the first act of *Fidelio* and in the joyous finale of the second. It is interesting that Beethoven should have turned to a libretto by Jean Nicolas Bouilly, who had also been responsible for the text of *Les Deux journées*. This original French libretto, which had been set to music by Pierre Gaveaux in 1798 as *Léonore, ou L'Amour conjugale*, and subsequently made into Italian operas by Paër and Mayr, was first adapted for Beethoven by Joseph Sonnleithner but completely revised by Georg Treitschke for the final version of *Fidelio*. Beethoven himself always wanted his opera to be entitled *Leonore*, but he was persuaded not to do so as it might have been confused with the earlier ones.

In spite of all the care lavished on it, and at the risk of offending those who regard *Fidelio* almost as a way of life rather than an opera, one must admit that the result is a flawed masterpiece. The libretto is chiefly to blame, for in order to make a full-length opera it introduces two secondary characters, Marcelline, the daughter of the gaoler Rocco, and her lover Jaquino, who attract most of the attention in the first scene (almost a third of the entire work) only to be brushed aside when the drama eventually gets into its stride. Beethoven, whose mind was fixed on the moral conflict involving Florestan, the just man wrongfully persecuted, his wholly faithful wife, and the irredeemably wicked Pizarro, appeared not to realize the weakness of the opening scene, even though he agreed happily to have it shortened in the final version. His music for it – Marcelline's aria, her duet with Jaquino, Rocco's song in praise of gold, the four-part canon 'Mir ist so wunderbar' – is attractive in itself, yet strangely at odds with the gran-

The final scene of rejoicing in the English National Opera production of Fidelio *with Josephine Barstow as Leonore*

deur of what is to follow. There is a total change of mood with the brief march which signals the entry of Pizarro, whose powerful aria is intensified by the use of the whole orchestra for the first time and the music of which portrays his character indelibly on the listener's mind. From this point onwards Beethoven maintains a secure grip on the work, matching each successive dramatic moment with music of searing imagination.

It has been said that Beethoven does not so much express the actual words of *Fidelio* in his music as the ideas behind them, his own ideas rather than the librettist's. In the revised form, Leonore's recitative and aria 'Abscheulicher! . . . Komm Hoffnung' first gives vent to her loathing of Pizarro, then calls on hope for guidance, and finally explodes into an affir-

mation of her resolution to save Florestan. She becomes transformed from a heroic woman into a symbol of heroism itself. The earlier version had remained on a more womanly level, decorated with more *fioriture*, and the change is significant in showing how the composer's whole conception of the opera had grown deeper and more intense the more he had thought about it. The later version is still florid enough in its final section to daunt all but the most gifted of sopranos, yet there is no feeling of bravura for its own sake; the demands made on the singer, often in lines which sound instrumental rather than 175 vocal, reflect the demands made on Leonore herself to find more than ordinary human courage. Similarly, the chorus sung by the prisoners as they emerge from their cells into the air of day transcends the particular situation: their quiet song of joy, embraced by tender orchestral phrases, is symbolic of mankind's search for spiritual light. The beginning of Act II returns to the personal level as Florestan, fettered in his dungeon, reflects sombrely on his fate, rises to an outburst of ecstasy as he experiences a prophetic vision of Leonore coming to save him, then faints from exhaustion. The entrance of Rocco and Leonore leads to a section of spoken dialogue, a 'melodrama' in fact, which has a compelling urgency here in contrast to the routine conversation of the opening scene. The action culminates in Leonore's revealing her true identity and confronting Pizarro with a pistol when he comes to kill Florestan, a situation resolved by one of the most memorable of all *coups de théâtre* as the sound of an off-stage trumpet announces the arrival of the Minister of State, a friend of Florestan. A vigorous quartet and a rapturous duet for the reunited wife and husband pave the way for the only possible resolution of the drama, a finale in which the chorus first celebrate the dawn of a new era of liberty and then, joined by the main characters, offer up a hymn of praise to womanhood as personified in Leonore.

Besides being Beethoven's only opera, *Fidelio* is the only opera of its kind. The weakness of the opening scene, as well as the fact that the demands made on the voices of Leonore and Florestan are sometimes virtually impossible to meet, pale into insignificance when the total effect of the work is considered. The choruses make an overwhelming impact on the human level, but even more important, they carry us into the rarefied atmosphere of the choral finale of the Ninth Symphony. Its spiritual qualities, or its 'message' if that much-abused term may for once be used with justification, are timeless. Uncannily, time has a habit of catching up with *Fidelio*. After World War II, for instance, Rocco was seen as representing the countless people who had served a tyrannous regime yet excused themselves on the grounds that they were only carrying out orders. More recently, and as an equally terrible indictment of human society, we see Florestan as representing the prisoner of conscience. It is not surprising that Beethoven struggled so hard to make *Fidelio* match his ideals and was then unable to find sufficient inspiration for a second opera. Perhaps he knew that he could never repeat such a remarkable achievement, and certainly no composer since has produced an opera comparable to *Fidelio* on its own terms.

Weber

The Romantic movement born with the dawn of the nineteenth century spread quickly from literature to music, inevitably affecting opera to a greater extent than instrumental works since the former deals with the thoughts and actions of characters in dramatic situations. Whereas composers of Baroque and Classical opera had remained somewhat aloof from the feelings of their heroes and heroines, the Romantics used them to express thoughts and ideals of their own. Romanticism and nationalism were brought together in the operas of Weber, whose *Der Freischütz* was hailed as the first truly German opera. Before Weber appeared on the scene, opera had been international, Handel composing his works in the Italian tradition, Gluck finally switching his allegiance from the Italian to the French style. (The use of Italian librettos and the Italian style was not nationalism, but simply a reflection of the fact that opera had begun in Italy and had been copied everywhere else.) It was Weber's deliberate intention to change opera from an international form of art, with texts often based on Classical legends, to a national form employing stories from German folklore and music with something of the quality of German folk melody.

It took some time, however, for Weber to give his whole attention to opera – which is the more surprising as his childhood was spent with a theatre company. Carl Maria von Weber was born on 18 November 1786 in the small town of Eutin, near Lübeck, where his father was Kapellmeister to the local prince bishop, and where his mother was a noted singer. He was only a year old when his father set up a company of actors, and the boy's first ten years were spent travelling from one theatre to another. His father was determined from the start that his son should be an infant prodigy like Mozart, and Carl Maria learnt the piano from the age of four. He later studied with Michael Haydn, brother of the famous symphonist, for a time in Salzburg, and it was there that the eleven-year-old Weber's first compositions were published. Soon afterwards he began his career as a concert pianist, and in 1800 he saw his first opera produced in Freidberg, a romantic-comic confection entitled *Das Waldmädchen*. This was subsequently given in Vienna but except for two fragments it has since disappeared. It is possible, even, that the composer destroyed the copies himself, for he once declared that 'puppies and first operas should be drowned', a suggestion that must appal admirers of *Fidelio* as much as it does dog-lovers. Between 1801 and 1816 he held various musical directorships in Breslau, Stuttgart and Prague, where

René Kollo as Max in Der Freischütz, *the opera with which Weber launched the German Romantic movement and paved the way for Wagner*

he supervised the presentation of more than sixty operas by more than thirty composers, though none of his own. During this period he also made successful concert tours and found the time to compose the bulk of his orchestral works, the two symphonies and various concertos, as well as the two operas *Silvana* and *Abu Hassan*.

Der Freischütz was composed from 1817 onwards and premiered in Berlin in 18 June 1821, with immediate and overwhelming success. There were no less than thirty productions in other German cities by the end of the following year. *Der Freischütz* ('The freeshooter') is based on the legend of the marksman who enters into a pact with the forces of evil to obtain magic bullets which will always find their target, a rather naive legend which took its strongest hold in central Europe where there were vast forests. The forest itself, provider of food and work and at the same time a place of darkness and danger, dominates here as the spirit of the sea permeates the music of Wagner's *The Flying Dutchman*. Bound up with the forest are the customs and superstitions of the village folk whose lives are presented so vividly by Weber in music that is unmistakably German. The hero is a forester who desperately needs to win a shooting contest in order to marry the girl with whom he is in love, and who allows himself to be tempted to cast magic bullets in the Wolf's Glen, a place feared by everyone. This scene, filled with every ingredient of Gothic terror, a precursor of the twentieth-century horror movies involving vampires and werewolves, was entirely new to opera, Weber writing music evoking a spine-chilling atmosphere which had never been attempted before and which has never been surpassed since. It is the more effective for its complete contrast to the simple, open-air charm of the folklike dances and choruses of huntsmen and bridesmaids, the Gluck-like expressiveness of the heroine's arias and the amusing *soubrette* songs of her livelier cousin.

Several of the unforgettable melodies from the opera itself appear first in the overture, which is also a deservedly popular piece in the concert hall. Weber achieves his Romantic effects largely by his imaginative orchestration, using chords of the diminished seventh, string tremolos and pizzicato bases to suggest the menace of the dark forces of evil, expressive woodwind to create the magical beauty of the woodland setting. He also gives continuity to the score by means of recurrent themes that anticipate Wagner's leitmotif technique. At a single stroke *Der Freischütz* established a new style of opera that challenged the dominance of Italian opera in theatres throughout the German states. Even Weber himself was surprised by the extent of its success, writing prophetically in his diary after conducting a performance in Vienna: 'Greater enthusiasm there cannot be, and I tremble to think of the future, for it is scarcely possible to rise higher than this.'

His next opera, *Euryanthe* (1823), was more ambitious, dispensing with spoken dialogue and more highly developed musically so that within the same scene accompanied recitatives would merge imperceptibly into arias or symphonic developments. It was unfortunate that he chose an absurd story of medieval chivalry in the first place, and his choice of librettist, Helmina von Chézy, was positively disastrous. The music is splendid in itself, notably the overture and several elaborate and powerful arias comparable to those in *Fidelio*. Weber's handling of the orchestra and use of leitmotifs anticipate Wagner remarkably, as does his exploration of chromatic writing. (Chromaticism introduces notes alien to the prevailing key, thus tending to break down tonality.)

The comparative failure of *Euryanthe* was followed by a considerable deterioration in Weber's health. It was in 1812, when he was only twenty-five, that he had first shown symptoms of tuberculosis, and during the remaining fourteen years of his life he suffered bouts of severe pain and weakness. There was

177

A depiction of the Wolf's Glen, which in Der Freischütz *is the setting for the casting of the magic bullets with supernatural help*

then no cure for the illness, which in his case was no doubt aggravated by his constantly having to travel in the course of his work, and by the heavy demands made on his energies by the post of Kapellmeister at Dresden, which he held from 1817 until his death. He drove himself hard towards the end of 1825 to complete the score of *Oberon*, an English opera he had been commissioned to compose for Covent Garden. He finished it in January 1826, and the following month set out for London against all his friends' entreaties. 'Whether or not I go,' he argued, 'I shall be a dead man in a year. But if I go, my children will eat when their father is dead, and if I stay they will starve.' When the door slammed on his departure, his wife Caroline ran to her room crying, 'I have heard the lid close on his coffin'. Despite his weakness he was able not only to supervise and conduct *Oberon* but also to give a number of concerts in London, which he appeared to like even though he complained of all English food being served with the same sauce. Above all, he was gratified by the success of *Oberon*. This last of his operas has unfortunately passed out of the repertoire, not because of any musical shortcomings, but on account of its clumsy libretto. Performances are rare, though the magnificent overture must open more orchestral concerts than any other, and dramatic sopranos find the aria 'Ocean, thou mighty monster' an irresistible challenge.

Weber stayed in London as a guest of Sir George Smart, a distinguished organist and conductor, at his house in Great Portland Street, and it was there that he died alone in his room in the early hours of 5 June. He was buried in London, his body remaining there for eighteen years until a committee at Dresden, where Wagner had become his successor as Kapellmeister, arranged for the transfer of the coffin to Germany. When the body of the originator of German Romantic opera was finally buried in Dresden, the graveside speech was appropriately delivered by Wagner, the man who was to carry his work to its ultimate fulfilment.

The death of Weber robbed German opera of its sense of purpose, for he had no immediate successor. The interest in the supernatural was pursued by Heinrich Marschner (1795–1861), whose *Der Vampyr* ('The vampire', 1828) and *Hans Heiling* (1833) were widely popular in Germany for a period. He had quite a gift for comedy, which he interpolated even into his serious operas, sometimes disconcertingly. Another composer who followed the *Singspiel* tradition was Gustav Lortzing (1801–51), who aimed less high than Weber or even Marschner, and hit his popular target fair and square. His two best comic operas, *Zar und Zimmermann* ('Tsar and carpenter') and *Der Wildschütz* ('The poacher'), first produced at Leipzig in 1837 and 1842, respectively have remained hugely popular in Germany but have not travelled very successfully. He made a single more ambitious attempt with *Undine* (1845), a noteworthy Romantic opera on the theme of the water-sprite who lures her unfaithful mortal husband to his death.

Chance has always played a considerable part in determining the fate of operas which fall into the category of good second-rate works, and this accounts for the far greater success of *Martha* (1847), a sentimental light opera by Friedrich von Flotow (1812–83). Its setting is English, with the subtitle 'The Richmond Market', and it includes the Irish folk song 'The last rose of summer'. The seal of international success for *Martha* was provided by Caruso's choosing to sing the part of the tenor hero and making his aria 'Ach, so fromm' a world-wide hit in Italian ('M'appari'). Musically, however, *Martha* is inferior to the best of Lortzing's operas. Another German composer whose most popular opera has an English setting is Otto Nicolai (1810–49), who succeeded in giving a Romantic flavour to Shakespearean comedy in *Die lustigen Weiber von Windsor*. A decade later, Peter Cornelius (1824–74), a friend of Liszt and a champion of Wagner, composed a sophisticated oriental comedy, *Der Barbier von Bagdad*, in which the systematic use of leitmotifs and the importance given to the orchestra owe much to the influence of early Wagner. Like all Weber's followers, however, he has been eclipsed by the towering, revolutionary genius of Wagner, who changed the whole course of dramatic music.

Wagner

To do justice in this single section to Richard Wagner's contribution to music, let alone his influence on the conception of art in general, is almost as hopeless a task as trying to climb Everest in slippers. His operas and mature music-dramas are arguably less perfect works than the finest operas of Mozart, and one may prefer the emotionally more direct operas of Verdi – or even not like Wagner's music at all – but it is impossible not to marvel at the magnitude of the artistic revolution he set out to achieve. As writer of his own librettos he regarded himself as poet and dramatist as much as composer, believing that poetry and music grew organically from the need for true dramatic expression and constituted two aspects of one and the same creative process. Even this union was not enough for him: all matters of stage production, movement and design, were to be embraced in his grandiose view that the individual arts could only be fully realized in a single 'total artwork'.

Only too aware that neither the public nor the vast majority of other creative artists were ready to accept his radical ideas, Wagner felt obliged to explain and justify them and accordingly wrote a series of books and essays. These finally amounted to several formidable volumes comprising more than a million words. In response, he became the subject of some ten thousand books and articles during his lifetime, some attacking and others defending his music and the ideas which lay behind it. Even today there exist

The Festspielhaus at Bayreuth which Wagner had especially built for the performance of his ambitious music-dramas

more books about Wagner than any other historical figure apart from Jesus and Napoleon; and he may well have overtaken the latter as a subject for controversy. He is all the more fascinating and disturbing for his philosophical and political views, and also for the complexity of his own personality. He was a dictatorial and often devious man who demanded utter devotion and obedience from anyone who fell under his personal spell or shared his artistic beliefs. He was so confident of his genius that he expected the world to bow before it – and so ruthless that he succeeded.

Success did not come easily, however, and his early life was bedevilled by false starts and failures. He was born at Leipzig on 22 May 1813, and it is most likely that he was not the son of his mother's husband, Karl Wagner, but of the actor Ludwig Geyer whom she married when Karl died some months after the child's birth. This fact troubled the composer in later life, not because of the trifling matter of illegitimacy, but because he had grown violently anti-Semitic and feared that Geyer might have been of Jewish descent. Geyer, however, was a benevolent and understanding man, and seems to have encouraged the boy's precocious interest in music and the theatre. The young Wagner was given a sound general schooling, first at Dresden, where he showed an obsessive enthusiasm for Greek tragedy, and then at Leipzig, where he studied music for about a year. As a musician, however, he was almost entirely self-taught, having learned the piano at the age of eleven in order to play tunes from the operas he had heard, and having taken a few lessons in composition at fifteen so that he could provide music for a Shakespearean tragedy he had written. He thus revealed the ambition to become both poet and theatre composer. His progress may have been haphazard, but his prodigious natural talent is proved by his appointment at nineteen (with a symphony and three concert overtures to this credit) as chorus master of the opera at Würzburg. He became conductor of another company based in Magdeburg a year later.

Wagner completed his first opera, *Die Feen* ('The fairies') in 1834, and its projected production at Leipzig was abandoned only because the theatre director did not favour its imitation of Weber's style. It remained unperformed until 1888, since when it has rarely been revived. A second opera, *Das Liebesverbot* ('The ban on love'), secured a single performance at Magdeburg in 1836, and was closer to the style of Bellini and Auber, suggesting that though Wagner had decided to become an opera composer he was uncertain as to which tradition to follow. The reason for his attraction to the Italian style at this time is made clear in articles he contributed to several journals. In these, the earliest of his theoretical writings, he gave due credit to German composers but cast serious doubts on their ability to compete with the Italians when it came to opera. 'We are too intellectual,' he argued, 'to create warm human figures. Mozart could do so because he enlivened his characters with the beauty of Italian song. Since we have come to despise this, we have strayed further and further from the path that Mozart made for the salvation of our dramatic music. Weber never knew how to handle song, and song is the instrument through which a human being can communicate himself musically, and so long as this is not fully developed he lacks genuine speech.'

He was to change these views radically in later years, but for a time he remained under the spell of Bellini in particular. He favoured the Italian style, for practical reasons also, since as conductor at various minor German opera houses and at Riga (1837–9) he had discovered that audiences preferred it to the German. With his eye on Paris, then the operatic capital of the world, he realized that stage spectacle was as important as attractive vocal writing. Thus it was natural that he should also look for an example to Meyerbeer, who had been astute enough to take the Italian and French schools as his models and beat both of them at their own games. The result of all this for Wagner was the composition of *Rienzi*, a grand opera inspired by Bulwer Lytton's novel, which after its premiere at Dresden in 1842 came to be known as 'the best Meyerbeer opera that Meyerbeer did *not* compose'.

During the composition of *Rienzi* Wagner conceived the work which foreshadowed some of his later stylistic innovations and set him on the road from opera to music-drama – *Der fliegende Holländer* ('The Flying Dutchman'). The idea of an opera on this story first came to him in 1838 in Riga, but he was at that time too occupied with his directorship of the opera house to pursue it, and it was not until two years later, during his unhappy stay in Paris, that he made the first sketch of the libretto. In 1841 he wrote the 'poem' in its final form and composed the music in the space of only seven weeks. A story connected with its composition illustrates some of his personal traits and the kind of trouble which they could lead to. Having gone with his wife Minna to Riga (then under Russian rule) to escape his creditors in Germany, he was again up to his ears in debt after two years, and forced to take flight. After crossing into Prussia he decided to travel to Paris by sea because he felt a long coach journey would cause in-

Wagner with Cosima, the daughter of Liszt who became his second wife and supported him as he struggled to achieve his ambitions

course even if he has to keep sailing for ever. Taken at his word, the Dutchman is condemned to an eternity on the sea with only one faint hope of salvation: every seven years he is allowed one day ashore to look for a woman prepared to remain faithful to him to death. After many unsuccessful attempts he finally meets Senta, who has long been obsessed by a portrait of him and whose favourite ballad recounts his unhappy fate. She agrees to marry him at first sight. A few hours later, mistakenly believing that she has betrayed him, the Dutchman sets out on his restless voyaging again, but Senta proves her fidelity by throwing herself from a cliff into the sea and releases him from the curse.

This story introduces an ideal which was to recur in Wagner's later works, the redemption of man through a woman's love. Musically it is also prophetic of his future development in its imaginative use of leitmotifs, each representing a particular person, object, emotion or idea. For example, Senta's ballad – the very heart of the opera, composed before any of the other music – presents the Dutchman and Redemption motifs as well as others related to the spirit of the sea. The overture, a superb sea-picture in music, includes nine which feature prominently throughout the work. The score contains a variety of 'set pieces' – arias, duets and trios – such as the composer professedly scorned at the time; but they are conceived in a new style, more psychologically apt and musically continuous. Because of these operatic 'numbers', and because it is dramatically compact and of normal length, *The Flying Dutchman* makes the ideal introduction to Wagner.

The premiere of *The Flying Dutchman* at Dresden on 2 January 1843 was far less successful than that of *Rienzi*, given at the same theatre ten weeks earlier. Wagner was mortified, laying the blame on the poor production and some weak singers among the cast. He was able to draw comfort from his appointment as musical director of the Court Theatre, which allowed him to lead a comparatively settled life in Dresden for the next six years. It was during that period that his work began to become known throughout Germany. It aroused as much hostility in some quarters as idolatry in others, for there were never any half-measures where Wagner was concerned. As well as this growing interest in his compositions, he won considerable respect in Dresden for his conducting and his choice of repertoire. He did much to promote neglected operas of the past, like Gluck's *Iphigénie en Aulide* which he arranged, conducted and produced. The next of his own operas was *Tannhäuser*, which he directed on 19 October 1845. It was received with little enthusiasm at first,

tolerable discomfort to the family pet, a Newfoundland dog. On the first leg of the voyage the ship ran into a heavy storm and took refuge in a Norwegian fiord, giving him first-hand experience of the seascapes that are so important a part of *The Flying Dutchman*.

The so-called 'Legend of the Flying Dutchman' does not actually belong to the realm of legend at all, but began life almost simultaneously in various European countries early in the nineteenth century. Its simple plot concerns a ship's captain who swears during a terrible storm that he will continue on his

but with each successive performance audiences reacted more warmly and it soon gained wide favour. The initial confusion arose from its transitional character, combining the dramatic idea of redemption (as in *The Flying Dutchman*) with the spectacular elements of grand opera employed in *Rienzi*. However, its music is more flexible and continuous than anything he had composed before though still including occasional set numbers.

The story of *Tannhäuser* is based on the legend of the medieval knight who falls under the spell of Venus and later makes a pilgrimage to Rome in search of papal absolution, which is refused. Salvation finally comes for him through the virtuous Elisabeth, his earlier love, who dies of a broken heart. Its theme, the relationship of profane to sacred love, is treated with remarkable imagination, apart from the occasional slide into moral censoriousness. The overture poses this dramatic conflict by contrasting a stately pilgrims' march with the erotic music of the Venusberg, the mountain retreat to which the goddess and her nymphs lure and captivate unwary passing knights. Taking part in a song contest to win the hand of Elisabeth in marriage, an idea which anticipates *The Mastersingers*, Tannhäuser extols the sensual delights so generously bestowed by Venus in a song which arouses the moral indignation of the other knights. (A modern audience, however, is inclined to think that envy rather than piety prompts their animosity.) In his subsequent audience with the pope he is told that the papal staff is more likely to burst into flower than he to be pardoned for his offence. In the final scene, when Tannhäuser meets Elisabeth's funeral procession, the staff does in fact flower, a symbol of redemption and renewal. The opera is rich in expressive solos – Elisabeth's Greeting and Prayer, Tannhäuser's song in praise of Venus, Wolfram's song to the Evening Star – and also in choruses; but these are completely integrated into the flow of the score as a whole. Similarly, the spectacular scenes serve a serious dramatic purpose as well as providing feasts for the eye.

During the next three years, in addition to fulfilling his official duties, Wagner composed *Lohengrin* and wrote the poem of *Siegfried's Death*. His future appeared settled and secure. In 1848, however, the Year of Revolution throughout Europe, he threw himself into political activities with intellectuals and students, so giving his enemies and his many creditors the opportunity of branding him as a dangerous

Wagner's Parsifal *at Covent Garden with Peter Hofmann in the title-role being tempted by Kundry and the Flower Maidens*

radical activist. Eventually, after the unsuccessful rebellion in Dresden, he was compelled to flee to Weimar, where he became friendly with Liszt, who had just presented *Tannhäuser* there. His life took a new turn when news came from his wife that a warrant for his arrest had been issued in Dresden, which meant he could no longer live in safety in any of the German states. In desperation he sought political asylum in Switzerland, where he spent most of the next ten years. He was unable to attend the premiere of *Lohengrin* on 28 August 1850, which was conducted by Liszt, now one of his foremost disciples.

Lohengrin can be regarded as the last, and greatest, of German Romantic operas. It resembles Weber's *Euryanthe* in many respects – in plot and characters, in its declamatory style, and in the use of leitmotifs. It represents an advance on *Tannhäuser* in that it is concerned less with dramatic events themselves than with their symbolic significance, the characters accordingly becoming the agents of superhuman forces rather than human beings whose actions should be taken at face value. The idea of Elsa becoming the bride of the knight who has vindicated her innocence on the strict condition that she never

Karan Armstrong and Peter Hofmann in Lohengrin, *the opera in which Wagner blends the legend of the swan knight with the myth of the Holy Grail*

asks his name is risible on the everyday level, for no woman could be expected to go through life just calling her husband 'darling'. It makes sense only on the symbolic level, where Lohengrin represents divine love seeking unquestioning faith and Elsa represents human nature incapable of meeting such a demand. The drama's chivalric trappings also strike an absurd note to twentieth-century audiences, yet the spell of the often sublime music results in a willing suspension of disbelief. *Lohengrin* moves further from the traditional division into separate numbers, recitative and aria merging into a style of free declamation which, after a period of several years during which he rested from composition altogether, was to result in the revolutionary music-dramas.

Wagner was far from idle during those years: he first set out to clarify and organize his new ideas on the nature of music and drama, in a series of lengthy essays giving a systematic account of both the philosophy and the technical means which would govern his future music-dramas. He then decided that his projected *Siegfried's Death* should be developed into a cycle of music-dramas combining the story of Siegfried with the downfall of the gods of German mythology. He spent almost two years on the four librettos of *Der Ring des Nibelungen* ('The ring of the Nibelungs' – usually known in English simply as *The ring*), writing them in reverse chronological order. In 1853 he began composing the music, and had completed more than half of it by August 1857, when he laid it aside for twelve years. His work on *The Ring* was not interrupted for any artistic reason, but because he was involved in an extra-marital love affair. He had become friendly in Zurich with Otto Wesendonck, a wealthy silk merchant, and his wife Mathilde. Wagner had no scruples about seducing the wives of his close friends – indeed, he made rather a habit of it – and he was only too ready to respond to Mathilde's passion for him. This led on the personal level to open quarrels between Mathilde and his own ill-used Minna, and on the creative level to the expression of his new feelings in *Tristan and Isolde*. He finished the opera in Lucerne in 1859, but the difficulties of having it staged to his satisfaction delayed its premiere for six years. In the meantime a series of changes took place in his fortunes, beginning in 1860 with his being granted permission to return to Germany. At last he was able to see *Lohengrin* on the stage, in Vienna, and he took on conducting engagements as far afield as Moscow. The most important event was his meeting in 1864 the young King Ludwig II of Bavaria, who became infatuated with Wagner and his works, and who was to give him financial support on a truly royal style for many years. For a time Wagner settled in Munich, where *Tristan* was finally presented on 10 June 1865, conducted by his friend and fervent disciple Hans von Bülow.

It is entirely due to Wagner that the Celtic story of Tristan and Isolde has become universal. The lovers are fixed in the popular imagination as vividly as Romeo and Juliet, romantic characters which have become household names even to people who have never seen Wagner's opera or Shakespeare's play. The musical treatment of the drama is unique in that external events are reduced to the minimum, all the action taking place within the minds and through the emotions of Tristan and Isolde. So completely does the music take over that words almost cease to have any importance: the ideas of love and death, or rather death-in-love, encompassed in the idea of night, are created in pure musical expression. There are relatively few musical motifs, and they melt one into the other to produce a web of magical sound so skilfully spun that it is difficult to say where the lovers' greeting turns into their duet 'Descend upon us, night of love', or where the love duet of Act II, which builds up gradually into an almost unbearable intensity of passion, actually begins. There are no set numbers, the score being conceived as a seamless flow of what has become known as 'endless melody'. The writing is essentially chromatic throughout, though kept within the tonal (key) system of the eighteenth and nineteenth centuries. Wagner differs from earlier composers, who had resorted to chromatic passages as a means of effective contrast, in using chromaticism consistently. *Tristan and Isolde*, which unlike his earlier operas was an immediate success, changed the course of Western music: it influenced both operatic and orchestral composers throughout Europe, finally leading to the twelve-note system of Schoenberg which broke with the tonal tradition.

The inspiration of *Tristan and Isolde* had been one love affair: the events leading up to its first performance involved another. This time, however, it was no passing infatuation, but a perfect union of spirits. Wagner persuaded Ludwig to bring Hans von Bülow to Munich to collaborate with him, for he believed him to be the ideal conductor of his works. He was also in love with Bülow's wife Cosima, the illegitimate daughter of Liszt, whom he knew had reciprocated his feelings when they had first met some years earlier. The affair progressed so swiftly that three months before the premiere of *Tristan* Cosima gave birth to his daughter, Isolde, whom Bülow accepted, officially at least, as his own. Then, when Ludwig's political advisers had Wagner banished from Munich in December 1865, Cosima waited only a few months

before joining him in Switzerland. Bülow, who was fully aware of their relationship and had to endure the humiliation of listening to the constant gossip to which it gave rise, nevertheless continued to champion Wagner the composer whatever he might have thought of him as a man. With Cosima at his side to encourage him, Wagner was able to compose *Die Meistersinger von Nürnberg* ('The mastersingers of Nuremberg') comparatively quickly and with ease, but for the sake of appearances she returned to live with her husband for the premiere he was to conduct on 21 June 1868. Matters came to a head after the performance, which was given a hostile press, with Cosima returning to Lucerne with Wagner, now estranged for ever from Bülow and for several years from Liszt. They were able to marry two years later when Bülow divorced Cosima, and the marriage proved a perfect one in every sense. Wagner had at last found a wife who fully understood his genius as well as worshipped him. (Minna had separated from him in 1861 and died in 1866.) She shared his life and work completely, took down his autobiography at his dictation and also wrote her own diaries, which were published in 1976 after a long family embargo was lifted.

The Mastersingers is Wagner's only comedy, the most warmly human of all his works, though deeper than the usual comic opera in every sense. Its story sets the love of Walther and Eva against the background of the mastersinger guilds of sixteenth-century Nuremberg and their song contests. Hans Sachs, the central character, was a historical shoemaker-composer who lived from 1494 to 1576, and it is upon him that Wagner lavishes his most affectionate and characterful music. The opera returns to the use of set numbers, such as Walther's Prize Song, the two monologues of Sachs, the very beautiful Quintet and the grand finale of dances and choruses. Comedy is introduced by the spiteful Beckmesser, a caricature of the critic Eduard Hanslick who attacked Wagner's later music, and it must be admitted that the humour is cruel as well as crude. The opera presents a tremendously vivid picture of the life and manners of the times, its genial music ranging from the almost cheeky Dance of the Apprentices to the majestic Entry of the Mastersingers, and not even the outburst of somewhat unsavoury nationalist sentiments towards the end can mar the feeling of spiritual well-being generated by a good performance. It affords an uplifting experience that no other opera can match, not because it sets out to preach, but because it expresses the joy of life in music of the utmost richness.

In the winter of 1868 Wagner was at last able to return to *The Ring*. The first two works of the cycle 185 were performed individually at Munich, *Das Rheingold* ('The Rhine gold') in 1869 and *Die Walküre* ('The valkyrie') in 1870, but the whole tetralogy was not staged until 1876. The intervening period was one of feverish activity for the composer, for in addition to completing *Siegfried* and *Götterdämmerung* ('The twilight of the gods') he was busy with the formidable task of having a special festival theatre built for the performance of *The Ring* and his other works. He gave concerts to raise funds, persuaded his devotees to rally to the cause and finally, with assistance again from Ludwig, the Festspielhaus was built at Bay-

reuth. Wagner was without doubt a ruthless man, arguably a megalomaniac, but without his relentless drive and singleness of purpose he could never have achieved such seemingly impossible objectives; for he devoted his life unstintingly to art. *The Ring* was first given in his ideal theatre from 13 to 17 August 1876 with immense artistic success; and it has remained a landmark in music ever since.

It is in *The Ring* that Wagner put all his theories of music-drama into practice, resulting in a work of unparalleled complexity which nevertheless holds the listener's attention through the sheer power of

Berit Lindholm as the doomed heroine of Tristan and Isolde, *Wagner's revolutionary music-drama of love and death*

Gwynneth Jones and Yvonne Minton in a scene from Götterdämmerung, *the last of the four operas of* The Ring of the Nibelung

the music. Its plot, too complex to give in detail here, centres on the theft from the Rhine of the precious gold which brings destruction to all who possess it in turn: human beings, the gods and even the hero created to return it to the waters. Wagner's plot sets forth a myth concerning the relationships of men to God, to nature and to their fellow-men in society, encompassing religion, philosophy and sociology. To present such an all-embracing story, Wagner inevitably resorted to the use of symbols, and because symbols are by their very nature subject to different interpretations, The Ring can be interpreted many ways. The music involves nearly a hundred leitmotifs associated with particular characters, objects or ideas, which are played singly or in contrapuntal combination, developed and transformed, so forming a symphonic pattern corresponding exactly to the inner action of the drama. They appear constantly in the orchestra, but only occasionally in the vocal parts; Wagner said that the words 'float like a ship on the sea of orchestral harmony'. (The voice parts, however, are always melodic, also making heavy demands on the singers.) All this may make The Ring sound a highly complicated, 'difficult' work, but in performance it is enjoyable on the most exhilarating level, so that the uninitiated can happily revel in the splendour of the music. Scenes such as the gods' entry into Valhalla in The Rhine Gold, the love duet for Siegmund and Sieglinde and Wotan's farewell to his daughter Brünnhilde in The Valkyrie, the forging of the sword and the forest scene in Siegfried, and the more 'operatic' choruses, death of Siegfried, funeral march and Brünnhilde's immolation in The Twilight of the Gods are among the most thrilling experiences to be encountered in the opera house. Familiarity with The Ring, its drama and all the subtleties behind its surface magic, breeds ever-increasing enjoyment.

During the remaining seven years of his life Wagner composed only Parsifal, first performed at Bayreuth for patrons only on 26 July 1882. Based on the legend of the Holy Grail, this is the most difficult of all his works to appreciate, owing largely to its slightly dubious religiosity. However, much of the music is intense in feeling and exceptionally rich in harmony and orchestral colour, so that it affords considerable rewards to the seasoned Wagnerite; and even to the unconverted its Grail music is sublime. It was to be the final testament of 'The Master', who was already in declining health. For three years he had spent much of his time in the kinder climate of Italy, and it was in Venice that he died on 13 February 1883. Five days later he was buried with due pomp at Bayreuth, where the theatre remains today an active monument to his genius.

NINETEENTH CENTURY ITALY

Rossini

'Give me a laundry list and I will set it to music.' This quip by Rossini is indicative both of his wit as a man and his almost incredible facility as a composer. Unfortunately it has also helped to create the mistaken idea that he was simply a minor composer who happened to have hit the jackpot once in his life with The Barber of Seville. Of course, his comic operas have always been more popular than his serious ones. Even if this were the whole story, however, it would not lessen his claim to genius, any more than the stature of Aristophanes, Molière and Jane Austen is diminished because they are essentially comic writers. But this is not the whole story: William Tell, Semiramide and Le Siège de Corinthe form a sufficiently strong basis for arguing a case for Rossini as a major composer of opera seria. The problem with these works is that they were written according to the conventions of the period, which were to fall into disfavour even during Rossini's lifetime and which are not readily acceptable today.

Gioacchino Rossini was born at Pesaro on 29 February 1792, so that he could only celebrate his birthday every four years. His father was a local 'character', town crier, theatre horn player and inspector of public slaughter-houses. The young Rossini inherited his father's irresponsible nature and his mother's ability to sing. His musical studies began when the family settled in Bologna in 1804, and by the age of fourteen he was in some demand as chorus master at minor theatres. Then came two years as an official student at the Liceo Musicale. His first modest taste of operatic success came in 1810, when he was invited to provide a one-act comedy for the Teatro San Moisè in Venice, a work which already showed his sparkling wit.

One has to listen to a great deal of the world's music to find its few precious grains of wit. There is a wide repertoire of comic operas, of course, but their wit springs from their librettos rather than from their music. Mozart frequently raises a laugh with his music, as in the limping accompaniment to Figaro's claim that he has hurt his foot in the second act of Figaro; but only Rossini has ever produced constantly witty music. One of the best examples is The Italian Girl in Algiers first produced at the Teatro San Benedetto on 22 May 1813, whose score dances along in a fit of mad frivolity. The words cease to matter at all in the finale to its first act, the singers simply expressing their astonishment by making noises such as 'din-din', 'tac-tac' and 'cra-cra' while the music

187

Rossini photographed in 1860, thirty years after he had retired from composing operas to live in Paris and be courted by the famous

brings tears of laughter to the audience's eyes.

Rossini worked at tremendous speed. In 1812, for instance, he completed five operas, one of which, *La pietra del paragone*, was given fifty performances during its first season at La Scala, Milan. Its success made the young composer a fashionable celebrity and also won him exemption from military service – 'a clear gain to the army' was his own typical comment. The year 1813 provided the real turning-point in Rossini's career, its four operas including *Tancredi*, premiered at the Teatro la Fenice in Venice on 6 February. Based on Voltaire's tragedy of the same name, it is an *opera seria* which reveals the romantically expressive side to Rossini's music that has so often been overlooked. There is the utmost tender-

ness, for example, in the aria 'Di tanti palpiti', which became so popular in Venice that a judge was forced to interrupt a court action to admonish the public for humming the tune. Equally important in *Tancredi* is the handling of the orchestra, which is more elaborate and imaginative than had been the case in earlier Italian operas.

The pleasure-loving Venetians were even more delighted by *L'italiana in Algeri* ('The Italian girl in Algiers'), which has remained the most popular of Rossini's early operas. The score contains three memorable arias in the composer's most graceful style, the tenor's suave 'Languir per una bella', the mezzo's coquettish yet elegant 'Per lui che adoro' and martial 'Pensa alla patria'. It is Rossini's melodic fluency which places him above all other Italian composers of comic opera, and second only to Mozart in the whole field. On the other hand, melody arguably came too easily to him, as his very facility encouraged him to throw off in a matter of weeks operas which might have endured had he taken more trouble over detail. When he made his astonishing decision to retire from the theatre in 1829 he had composed thirty-eight operas over a period of nineteen years – yet less than a dozen of these works are worth remembering. This figure exceeds the number of successes achieved by most other composers, but it is difficult not to feel that Rossini could have done more with his prodigious talent.

In 1813, however, at the age of twenty-one, there could have been no fears or doubts in his mind. He had just proved his mastery of both serious and comic opera, and was in demand all over Italy. He chose Milan at first, writing for La Scala the unsuccessful serious *Aureliano in Palmira*, and the comic *Il turco in Italia*, which was received with some resentment because the Milanese felt he was fobbing them off with a mere pendant to the *Italian Girl in Algiers*, underestimating what is in fact a frothy opera of considerable originality. Rossini was scarcely more fortunate with his new opera for Venice, *Sigismondo* (1814), a near-disaster from which he later salvaged a couple of numbers for *The Barber of Seville*. The occasional failure did not trouble him very greatly: after all, he could always knock out another opera in a few weeks which might well be a hit. Three comparative failures in a row, however, made him grateful for an offer from Naples commissioning a series of operas for the Teatro San Carlo. Not only was this a fresh field to conquer, but it brought him into contact with two people who were to exert a considerable influence on his future.

The first was Domenico Barbaia, an incredible figure even in the crazy world of Italian opera. He was an illiterate who had started life as a waiter, in which capacity he won fame by inventing the mixture of whipped cream with coffee or chocolate which is still popular in Naples and Vienna. He speculated in army contracts during the Napoleonic Wars and gambled in Milan, making such profits that he was able to set up as an impresario, becoming the all-powerful manager of both La Scala and the San Carlo. He had the utmost faith in Rossini, and later was to be Bellini's first benefactor. The other important encounter in Naples was with the prima donna Isabella Colbran, who as Barbaia's mistress virtually ruled the San Carlo. A Spanish beauty of undoubted musical ability, she was also on far more than nodding terms with the King of Naples. She deserted both men for Rossini, recognizing his personal appeal and genius as promptly as he appreciated her beauty and talent. It was a notable working relationship, for she created

Richard Van Allan (seated) as Mustafà in L'Italiana in Algeri, *the scintillating comic opera with which Rossini conquered Venice when he was twenty-one*

the leading coloratura mezzo roles in no less than seven operas that he composed for her, the first of them being *Elisabetta, regina d'Inghilterra*, which set a fashion for operatic portraits of England's most famous queen and the Tudors in general. This opera, first produced on 4 October 1815, immediately established Rossini as a favourite with the Neapolitans.

Elisabetta typifies some of the problems relating to Rossini's serious operas. It was dismissed by Francis Toye in his book of 1934, *Rossini: a Study of Tragi-Comedy*, a standard work ever since. In Toye's day Rossini was represented in actual performance by only two or three operas; the rest of his work was judged from the printed scores alone. But the merits of an opera can only be properly assessed in performance, and the recording of the opera reveals the strength of the recitatives, expressive arias and powerful finales. The drama, concerned with the love of Elizabeth for the Earl of Leicester, involves only four main characters, and the action is highly concentrated and the music correspondingly taut. Rossini gave new sophistication to the scoring, providing full

instrumental accompaniment to the recitative. Another novel feature is the use of the chorus as active participants in the drama. *Elisabetta* thus anticipates the grand operas Rossini would later compose for Paris.

Taking a few months' leave of absence from Naples, Rossini went to Rome for his next two operas, the first of which, *Torvaldo e Dorliska*, was perhaps his greatest fiasco, the second his most famous work, *Il barbiere di Siviglia* ('The barber of Seville'). The latter was dashed off in a couple of weeks, something of a miracle even when we know that Rossini took some of the music from earlier operas. The self-borrowings do not detract from the spontaneity of the score, which fizzes along as though the music came to Rossini in an unbroken flow of inspiration. The solo numbers suit the characters to perfection: Figaro's sparkling 'Largo al factotum', Rosina's high-spirited 'Una voce poco fa', the melting arias for the lovesick Count Almaviva and the arias for the unpleasant Dr Bartolo and Don Basilio. The last part of the duet for Figaro and Almaviva, in which the former explains the way to reach his barber's shop, bears out Rossini's claim that he could set anything to music. The chattering Act I finale is breathtakingly inventive, the supreme example of the ensemble in which all the characters express their individual reactions to the

Scene from The Barber of Seville, *the opera which had a disastrous first night but survived to become the most popular of all Rossini's comedies*

comic turn of events.

It is one of the great ironies of operatic history that the premiere of this masterpiece on 20 February 1816, should have been a disaster. This was due to the presence of hostile supporters of Paisiello, whose own opera on the same play had long been popular; and to a variety of stage mishaps including the Don Basilio falling through a trap-door left open by accident. Rossini showed no outward concern, but stayed at home for the second performance, pleading sickness, and only learnt of its rapturous reception late at night from friends who had hurried to congratulate him. The opera soon made a triumphal round of the major Italian theatres. Within a year or two it gained the worldwide popularity it has enjoyed ever since – not to mention the generous praise of heavyweight composers like Beethoven, Wagner and Brahms.

Rossini was now the king of the musical world, his reputation so secure that the failure of several of his later operas scarcely dented it. Of the seventeen he composed before he left Italy, only four were really worthy of him. Three of these followed in quick succession in 1816 and 1817. First came *Otello*, a travesty of Shakespeare's tragedy, yet an opera containing some of his most beautiful music and which would probably have survived had not Verdi produced his far superior version in 1887. With *La Cenerentola*, a version of the Cinderella story seen through sophisticated Italian eyes, is a gem of elegant comedy. *La gazza ladra* ('The thieving magpie') is half-comic, half-melodramatic, shifting in mood from pathos to tragedy, tenderness to gaiety. Its characters and situations are so realistic that it is surprising the Rossini revival of the 1950s did not re-establish it in the repertoire.

Before settling in Paris, Rossini indulged for a time in a wandering life. There was a brief period in Vienna, where his operas aroused the vitriolic hatred of Weber, who resented the public's preference for Italian music. A meeting with Beethoven, on the other hand, was a most cordial occasion, the Viennese master declaring that 'your *Barbiere di Siviglia* will be played as long as Italian opera exists'. Then came a return to Venice for *Semiramide* at La Fenice on 3 February 1823, a heroic opera on an impressive scale and full of virtuoso arias, duets and ensembles. Again Rossini scored a huge success, with *Semiramide* quickly taken up by opera houses in France, England and Germany as well as Italy. Basking in this latest triumph, Rossini paid a visit to London with the intention of composing an opera for the King's Theatre. The management went bankrupt, but Rossini's visit turned out to be highly profitable. He was paid large sums either for singing himself or for accompanying others, the most notable occasion being his performance as Apollo in his vocal octet *The Lament of the Muses for the Death of Lord Byron*. He also enjoyed the distinction of singing duets with George IV.

Settling in Paris in 1824, Rossini embarked on his last creative phase, composing five operas to French texts and in the French style. Two of them, *Le Siège de Corinthe* and *Moïse* ('Moses'), were actually revisions of earlier Italian operas, transformed to become prototypes of French grand opera. The music has a dramatic vigour and emotional excitement new not only to Rossini but to opera in general, and they call for spectacular staging, elements guaranteed to please the taste of the audiences of the Paris Opéra. They have a Romantic grandeur which never fails to exert its magic when lavishly staged with high-powered singers, and their recent neglect is due to the difficulty of assembling suitable casts. Rossini then turned back to comedy for *Le Comte Ory* ('Count Ory'), which crystallizes all that is best in the tradition of French light opera. Elegance and piquancy abound in a score which allows for music of tender warmth as well as comic sparkle, even hilarity.

The last of the Paris operas – for we must discount *Il viaggio a Reims* as unworthy of the mature Rossini – was *Guillaume Tell* ('William Tell'), produced on 3 August 1829. Based on Schiller's play about the fictitious national hero of Switzerland, this grandest of grand operas won unanimous approval at first but was shortly to be treated in extremely cavalier fashion. The original four-act version was first cut to three acts, and then it became the custom to present only Act II as part of an operatic evening. When a friend once told him that this single act of *William Tell* was being given at the Opéra, Rossini caustically asked: 'What! The whole of it?' The work includes much superb music and does not deserve its neglect. It is long, and there are times when inspiration deserts the composer; yet if the superfluous ballet were cut it would be shorter than several repertoire works which audiences sit through without complaint. There are first-rate arias and ensembles, including the assembly of the Swiss cantons which is positively electrifying, and the whole work is conceived as one huge dramatic sweep.

Rossini by this time was only thirty-seven and had almost forty years still to live, yet he decided to compose nothing more for the opera house. Many reasons have been put forward for this retirement while he was still at the height of his powers: the failure of *William Tell*; the decline, as he saw it, of standards of singing; the development of opera in a direction of which he disapproved; even his own tongue-in-cheek statement 'I always had a passion for idleness'. Whatever the true reason, he chose to spend his remaining years in Paris, lovingly tended by his second wife, the ex-courtesan Olympe Pélissier, and resting on his well-deserved laurels. As a celebrated raconteur and *bon vivant* he was visited by everybody who was anybody, and while he no doubt chuckled to himself from time to time over the extravagant compliments showered on him, he really enjoyed this kingly life. He composed two sacred works, the *Stabat Mater* and the *Petite Messe solenelle*, and threw off a few trifling piano pieces and satirical songs, but otherwise his muse remained silent. It was appropriate, at the end, that the superstitious wit who had been born on 29 February should die on Friday, 13 November 1868. The poet Heine should have the last word: 'A genius, conscious of having already produced his best work, is satisfied; despising the world and its petty ambitions, he goes like William Shakespeare to Stratford-on-Avon, or, like Gioacchino Rossini, strolls down the Boulevard des Italiens with a smiling face and a caustic tongue.' 191

Bellini

Just as Rossini's operas, with the exception of *The Barber of Seville*, were neglected for many years, those of Bellini were long written off as being too old-fashioned for a twentieth-century audience to take seriously; this attitude was adopted in England even towards his finest work, *Norma*. But Wagner, no lover of *bel canto* opera in general, admired *Norma* tremendously, pointing out that its music was always 'intimately bound up with the words' and even going so far as to declare that its last act constituted genuine music-drama, the term he normally used to distinguish his own works from those of lesser mortals. Thanks to the interpretative genius of Callas in the 1950s musicologists and audiences alike came to realize the true stature of Bellini, so that his other operas were also brought out of mothballs.

Vincenzo Bellini was born in Catania on 3 November 1801, into a family of Sicilian musicians. He soon developed into a child prodigy, playing the piano expertly at the age of four, writing down his own compositions two years later, and hearing his music performed in neighbouring churches at nine. His first opera, *Adelson e Salvini*, was given in 1825 at the Conservatorio San Sebastiano in Naples while he was still a student there. It revealed the remarkable gift for flowing melody that was to characterize all his music, and attracted the attention of Domenico Barbaia. The result was a commission to compose an opera for the San Carlo, *Bianca e Gernando*, which was presented in 1826, with a fine cast. Its success led to the young composer being invited to compose an opera for La Scala.

Up to this time Bellini had been influenced on the one hand by Rossini and on the other by his teacher at the conservatoire, Nicolò Zingarelli. With his new opera, *Il pirata*, he began to find a style of his own, bringing a quality of gentle, elegant lyricism to Italian opera like that which Chopin was introducing into piano music. His vocal line is less florid than Rossini's, more expressive of the emotions it was designed to convey, and the flexibility with which he handled declamation enabled him to explore new depths of feeling. These new developments coincided with Bellini's collaboration with Felice Romani, the most sought-after librettist of the time. Their six-year partnership proved valuable to them both, each bringing out the best in the other. *Il pirata* was such a triumph that it was promptly taken up for production in London, Vienna, Madrid and other cities, making Bellini an overnight celebrity.

He continued to refine his idiom with his next two operas, *La straniera* and *I Capuleti ed i Montecchi* (based not on Shakespeare's *Romeo and Juliet* but on one of the several earlier versions of the story). Writers of the time commented on his 'avoiding flowery ornamentation and substituting a melody that is too syllabic' and choosing 'a method which we hardly know whether to describe as declaimed song, or sung declamation'. Today these notions seem strange, for we think of Bellini's vocal writing as highly elaborate and far from 'syllabic'. To his contemporaries, however, Bellini's style was remarkably restrained, compared with the other composers turning out operas to meet the insatiable demand for what were the popular entertainments of the day. Today we rarely if ever hear any of these works, so we do not realize how much of a reformer Bellini really was.

Bellini took full advantage of his physical elegance, 'wandering from one beauty to the next' in his own smug words, until he fell in love with Giuditta Turina, who remained his mistress from 1828 until 1833, when her hitherto complaisant husband started legal action for a separation. Bellini at once dropped her like a hot brick and began looking around for a wife who would bring with her a dowry large enough to give him financial independence. His letters concerning this plan reveal a despicably calculating side to his nature. His jealousy of Donizetti and his suspicion that Rossini might be favouring his rival at his own expense also show him in a highly unfavourable light. But his ambition and egotism gave him the single-mindedness to impose his will on the star singers who generally exerted greater power and earned far more money than their composers. We should perhaps be grateful that the 'sigh in dancing pumps' (Heine's description) could be more ruthless than his appearance suggested.

The year 1831 saw the production of two of his fully mature masterpieces, *La sonnambula* ('The sleepwalker') and *Norma*, both starring the legendary soprano Giuditta Pasta. At first Bellini and Romani had decided on an adaptation of Victor Hugo's *Hernani* as an ideal subject, but the all-powerful censors stepped in, fearing that its theme was too inflammatory. So many alterations were demanded that the composer and librettist decided to give up the project. They turned from political tragedy to pastoral romance. The story of Amina, a village girl who walks in her sleep into the wrong man's bedroom, is as slender as it is sentimental; but the sweetness and gentle charm of Bellini's melodies, and the delicate subtlety of his writing for the voices, struck a new note of pathos which audiences took to their hearts. Bellini's dramatic mastery and the wisdom of his decision to restrict the use of *fioriture* are made stunningly clear in the final scene of the sleep-walking heroine's simple cavatina lamenting the loss of her lover followed by her joyous, ornamental cabaletta on being awakened to find him repentant at her side.

From the idyllic *La sonnambula* Bellini turned to the heroically tragic *Norma*. It was to prove his most impressive work, a high point in Italian opera. The story of *Norma*, based on a play by Alexandre Soumet, is rich both in dramatic tensions and opportunities for strong characterization. Romani and Bellini worked together as with a single mind so that words and music should be perfectly combined, even inseparable. The drama is admirably direct, and the music is conceived in long scenes which mount steadily in tension, giving the whole work remarkable grandeur. More than ever Bellini uses *fioriture* for dramatic expressiveness, never as vocal display for its own sake.

Joan Sutherland in I Puritani, *Bellini's last opera, produced in Paris with great success just nine months before his death*

He also employs conventional forms with such imagination that they seem the most natural method of developing a dramatic situation.

The first night of *Norma* at La Scala on 26 December 1831, was not the success that Bellini had anticipated, due largely to the off-pitch singing of Pasta. Pasta could have her off-nights, and the dramatic intensity with which she threw herself into her roles inevitably emphasized any flaws in her singing. There is a detailed study of her artistry occupying a whole chapter in Stendhal's *Life of Rossini* which vividly describes the overwhelming impact she made on her audiences, yet which hints at the jarring effect her voice could produce when occasionally out of control. Fortunately she recovered her form at subsequent performances, establishing *Norma* as the triumph it deserved to be. *Norma* proved to be the kind of opera which depends in performance on its leading protagonist: staging it without an inspired soprano singing at her best is a case of *Hamlet* without the Prince. The

golden age of *bel canto* singing did not last long, and with its decline the fortunes of *Norma* and other operas by Bellini suffered accordingly, flourishing only when a Lilli Lehmann, Rosa Ponselle or Maria Callas arrived on the scene.

Bellini was less fortunate two years later with his next work, *Beatrice di Tenda*, falling out with Romani as a result. He received some comfort, however, on his visit to London, where he spent the summer of 1833 being lionized by society and seeing four of his operas enthusiastically received by the public. In a letter to one of his friends he reported: 'I know all London, and therefore they all invite me – so much so that I am suffocated by so many diversions. So you see I naturally find myself in the midst of beautiful women.' He seemed by this time to have decided to remain a bachelor after all, for he went on to confess that he 'put more value on friendship than upon love, so as not to run the risk of acquiring a wife.' In August he crossed the Channel with the intention of visiting Paris just long enough to secure

Shirley Verrett in the title-role of Bellini's Norma, *the most refined of* bel canto *operas. This is probably the most taxing of all soprano roles*

a contract for the Opéra. In fact, his last opera was produced at the Théâtre des Italiens instead, and he was destined never to leave Paris. He renewed the acquaintance of Rossini and found a circle of friends at the house of the exiled Princess Belgioioso which included George Sand, Alexandre Dumas, Victor Hugo, Heine, Chopin and Liszt. There, too, he met Count Carlo Pepoli, a liberal Italian patriot and poet whom Bellini chose as librettist for *I puritani*.

Pepoli, alas, was no Romani, so Bellini was saddled with verses of inferior quality concerning a far-fetched story of Roundheads and Cavaliers. The score as a whole does not match those of *La sonnambula* and *Norma*, though there are some fine individual numbers. Its reception on 24 January 1835 was ecstatic. The future must have looked rosy indeed for the composer, who had also made up his quarrel with Romani and looked forward to collaborating with him again. He returned in May from Paris to the nearby village of Puteaux, where he had composed *I puritani* in peace and quiet, full of ideas for two new operas, but he was taken ill towards the end of August, and died on 23 September, a few weeks before his thirty-fourth birthday. The news of his death shocked the musical world, which turned out in Paris to give him a spectacular funeral. The four pall-bearers were Rossini, Cherubini, Paër and Michele Carafa, a Neapolitan then teaching at the Paris Conservatoire; and an adaptation of 'Credeasi misera' was sung after the Mass. Bellini was buried in the cemetery of Père Lachaise, where fourteen years later the body of Chopin, with whom he had so often been compared as an exquisite melodist, was laid to rest close by.

Donizetti

Outside its native country, early nineteenth-century Italian opera has been the victim of much scholarly snobbery, from which no composer has suffered more than Donizetti. Even after the reluctant rehabilitation of Rossini and Bellini by the critical establishment, Donizetti is still largely written off except for *Don Pasquale* and *L'elisir d'amore*. The doyen of opera historians, Donald Grout, dismisses Donizetti as a composer who 'understood his theatre and audiences with *cynical* clarity' (my italics), and goes on to condemn his music as 'suffering from an almost

Katia Ricciarelli as the tragic Walter Scott heroine in Donizetti's Lucia di Lammermoor *at Covent Garden in 1980*

inconceivable poverty of harmonic, rhythmic and orchestral interest'. But there is nothing cynical about a dramatist or a composer understanding his theatre and his audiences – both Shakespeare and Mozart plainly did so – and the other strictures are demonstrably unjust. Donizetti's harmony and rhythm conform to the style of his time, yet achieve considerable flexibility; while his orchestration is as elegant as that of any of his contemporaries. He was, however, content to work traditionally to produce operas which would please the public, just as Handel had done. There is a need for reformers and innovators if music is to progress: but that does not mean that the works of more conventional composers are of no account. Another reason for the disparagement of Donizetti is the sheer size of his output, which includes some seventy operas, more than four hundred songs and sacred pieces, and a variety of orchestral, chamber and piano works. It would be senseless to claim for most of these works more than routine charm, but it is equally absurd to suggest that only three of his operas claim any serious attention. In addition to *Lucia di Lammermoor*, his operas *Poliuto*, *Anna Bolena*, *Lucrezia Borgia*, *La Favorite*, *Maria Stuarda* and *Roberto Devereux* deserve regular revival.

Gaetano Donizetti was born in humble circumstances at Bergamo on 29 November 1797, the son of an unsuccessful tradesman. The composer was later to describe his home in unflattering terms: 'You went down cellar steps to the basement apartment, where no glimmer of light ever penetrated. I was born underground, and like an owl I took flight.' Gaetano's progress was brought about almost exclusively by the kindly interest taken in him by Johann Simon Mayr (1763–1845), a composer remembered today only as a footnote to his pupil's life story, and as the originator of the orchestral crescendo exploited so successfully by Rossini. Mayr brought from his native Bavaria knowledge of Classical chamber music, which encouraged Donizetti to try his hand at some twenty string quartets and quintets. When he realized he had taught his pupil all he could, Mayr arranged for him to study further in Bologna.

At Venice in 1818 Donizetti saw his first opera to be produced, *Enrico di Borgogna*. Although no triumph, it was received well enough to impress his name on managements dealing with dozens of busy composers; other commissions followed, leading to a decisive breakthrough with *Zoraida di Granata* at the Teatro Argentina in Rome in 1822. Over the next eight years he composed twenty-five operas which established him throughout Italy but which are scarcely known today; though the titles *Alfredo il grande*, *Emilia di Liverpool* and *Elisabetta, o Il castello di Kenilworth*, once heard, linger in English minds. It was with another Tudor opera that Donizetti reached international fame; *Anna Bolena* was premiered at Milan's Teatro Carcano on 26 December 1830, with Pasta in the title role. One of the finest of his operas, it is unusually rich in inspired ensembles – three duets, a trio, a quintet and a sextet, as well as the splendidly developed finale. A string of arias for the distraught queen on her way to the block use the chorus, as throughout the opera, to focus sympathy upon her innocent suffering. Donizetti's dramatic sense is shown by the absence of arias for Enrico (Henry VIII), who instead sings recitative of powerful intensity.

The whole work is so carefully wrought in detail that one might think it was composed over a long period; yet it was actually completed within four weeks of receiving the excellent libretto by Felice Romani. Donizetti's letters reveal his wholly practical attitude towards deadlines and the need to provide arias tailored to the leading singers' vocal abilities. But he was liable to jocular exaggeration; some of his statements must be taken with a pinch of salt, especially his claim that *Don Pasquale* had cost him 'ten days of effort' when in fact he worked on it over about ten weeks. He always composed with great facility; why, then, do we find a genuinely inspired opera followed by several which show little more than competence? *Anna Bolena*, for instance, was followed by eight undistinguished works, Donizetti not returning to good form until *L'elisir d'amore* (1832), as brilliantly successful in the comic field as *Anna Bolena* in the tragic. Unlike Verdi and Wagner, who progressed consistently after achieving maturity, Donizetti continued erratically even after freeing himself from the influence of Rossini and developing a style of his own. It seems that his imagination was simply fitful, for which there is no explanation even in his voluminous correspondence.

Never did Donizetti's muse smile more benignly on him than during the three or four weeks in 1832 when he composed *L'elisir d'amore* ('The elixir of love'), one of the most popular and original of all comic operas. All too often Italian *opera buffa* is concerned with heartless stories in which cruel revenge is taken on silly, harmless characters, frequently old men trying to win young wives. In *L'elisir d'amore* there is plenty of wit and deception, but neither spite nor malice play any part in the behaviour of its four delightfully drawn main characters. The butt of the jokes is Nemorino, a lovesick village lad who is no buffoon, though misdirected producers have sometimes made him appear so. Donizetti treats him with the warmest affection, giving him two of the most tenderly beguiling love songs in the tenor repertoire. Adina, though a flirt, is shown clearly to be in love with Nemorino even when she provokes his jealousy. Conceited military men have often made absurd characters in comic opera – they are absurd in real life – but none so hilarious as Belcore, who introduces himself as 'handsome Paris' in an aria of magnificent swagger. As for Dulcamara, the quack doctor, he is an irrepressible and irresistible rogue. The opera preserves the most delicate balance, never surpassed, between comedy and sentiment. *Don Pasquale*, which followed eleven years later, is generally regarded as a finer work, the most successful comic opera between Rossini's *Barber* and Verdi's *Falstaff*, and it certainly sparkles like a diamond; yet *L'elisir d'amore* is more original and more heart-warming.

Most of Donizetti's serious operas are based on historical characters belonging to later periods than those figuring in the works of Rossini and others. Elizabeth I became an obsession with Donizetti, who portrayed her in three operas. Betrayed by her lovers in two of these, and taunted by Mary Stuart in the other, she was made to measure for Donizetti's coloratura sopranos, hell having no *fioriture* like a woman scorned. Donizetti's first flirtation with her was in *Elisabetta*. He produced a deeper study in *Maria Stuarda* (1834), contrasting her ruthless sense of duty to the state with Mary's more tender yet devious nature. The final scene, Mary's preparation to meet the executioner, is as imaginative as the corresponding scene in *Anna Bolena*. Donizetti's musically most effective portrait of Elizabeth came with *Roberto Devereux* in 1837. He was fortunate in that the libretto by Salvatore Cammarano, who had already collaborated with him on *Lucia di Lammermoor*, is unusually compact, involving four strongly contrasted characters. Apart from Elizabeth and the Earl of Essex (the title role), there are the Duke and Duchess of Nottingham, he a friend of Essex, she a confidante of the Queen. The score reveals Donizetti's acute response to dramatic situations, most powerfully expressed in the electrifying duets. Elizabeth herself is presented in music of thrilling, self-tortured majesty, her best scenes standing comparison with Bellini's *Norma* and the operas of Verdi's middle period. The success of the first performance prompted Donizetti to write to his publisher in typically urbane style: 'It is not for me to tell you now how it went. I am more modest than a whore; therefore I should blush. But it went very, very well.'

Roberto Devereux was completely neglected for a century before its rediscovery at Naples in 1964. The realization that this and several other revived operas are of the high quality of *Lucia di Lammermoor*, has

José Carreras (left) with Geraint Evans in L'elisir d'amore, *Donizetti's opera buffa filled with uncommonly tender and elegant melodies*

caused a reappraisal of Donizetti's works. From being rated as the poor man's Rossini, he is now put in the front rank of late *bel canto* opera and as the link between that school and the more robust style of Verdi.

Donizetti began to show distressing signs of mental and physical breakdown in 1844, and at the end of January 1846 he was forcibly and by all accounts illegally confined in an asylum at Ivry, a few miles from Paris. There he languished until the summer of the following year, when he was finally released after a great deal of diplomatic and legal pressure. Even then he was forced to remain in an apartment in Paris for another three months before the Préfecture agreed to his return to Bergamo. There, with the 1848 Revolution raging in the streets outside, the city's most famous son dragged out a living death until 8 April. It was a gruesome end to a brilliant career.

197

Verdi

Italian musical genius came to its highest point in the nineteenth century with the operas of Verdi, just as the German genius culminated in the music-dramas of Wagner. The two men were born in the same year; but in most other respects they had nothing in common. While Wagner broke with the past to create a revolutionary musico-dramatic style, Verdi accepted the tradition that had developed from Monteverdi through to Bellini and made it more virile and dramatically powerful. Today we recognize the two composers as equals, occupying twin peaks of achievement, but this has not always been the case. Wagner was generally misunderstood and even violently attacked, so a spate of learned studies appeared in order to explain his ideals and methods and convert the public to the Wagnerian cause. But, because the public needed no such inducement to see *Rigoletto*, *La traviata* and *Otello*, musicologists virtually ignored Verdi, and it was not until the Istituto di Studi Verdiani was set up in Parma in 1959 that his works began to receive serious attention. It says a lot for Verdi that he came to dominate the operatic repertoire without any outside help.

It would be wrong, however, to imagine that Giuseppe Verdi, who was born at the village of Le Roncole near Parma on 10 October 1813, enjoyed an easy journey to success. His father, the village innkeeper, saw to it that his talented son was taught the rudiments of music by the local church organist, and then sent him to the small town of Busseto for further tuition. There he was soon composing music for the town band and for the church, which so impressed his benefactor, Antonio Barezzi, that money was raised to send him to Milan at the age of nineteen. He hoped to be admitted to the Milan Conservatoire, but the examiners refused to bend their rules, which stipulated fifteen as the maximum age for a student to be accepted. This was a slight which Verdi never forgot or forgave. Fortunately he was able to study privately for two years, after which he went back to Busseto to become director of the Philharmonic Society. In 1836 he married Margherita Barezzi, the daughter of his benefactor, and began to work on his first opera, *Oberto*, which was accepted for performance at La Scala, Milan, and warmly received there in 1839. A series of personal tragedies then befell the composer, the deaths of his two children being followed by the sudden death of his wife in 1840, while he was somewhat reluctantly engaged in writing the comic opera *Un giorno di regno*. This was a failure at La Scala later in the same year, and Verdi, grief-stricken, decided to give up composition. Nobody knows what his future might have been had not the impresario of La Scala handed him the libretto of *Nabucco* by Temistocle Solera and made him promise to read it. Verdi later recounted that he threw the manuscript violently on to a table; it fell open at a page including the verses of 'Va, pensiero, sull'ali dorate', in which the Hebrew slaves in Babylon express their longing to return to their homeland. This immediately impressed him for two reasons. In the first place, the lines were almost a paraphrase of the Bible, which with Shakespeare constituted his most constant reading. Secondly, he was strongly sympathetic to the liberal nationalist cause which sought a united Italy freed from Austrian rule, and the patriotic nostalgia in the poem paralleled his own feelings. He began writing the music for the opera slowly, but gradually his interest was aroused and he completed the score during the autumn of 1841.

Nabucco, a drama of power politics, deals with the blasphemy, madness and final conversion to Christianity of Nabucco (Nebuchadnezzar), and much of its music is composed in a grand, ceremonial style. It has some fine arias and magnificent choruses, while the scene of Nabucco's recovering his sanity establishes the young Verdi's remarkable insight into dramatic characterization. It was a riotous success at its premiere on 9 March 1842, largely because the Milanese audience was quick to seize on the nationalist implications of 'Va, pensiero', but also because the overwhelming intensity of the music proved that a potentially great composer had arrived. *Nabucco* also introduced something new into Italian opera, the identification of the composer with his characters; whereas Rossini, for example, stands outside his heroes and heroines, observing and describing them from a distance, Verdi enters into them, rejoicing and suffering with them. (This is something he shared with Shakespeare, a quality which makes his *Macbeth*, *Otello* and *Falstaff* the most satisfying of Shakespearean operas. *Nabucco* was given seventy-five times at La Scala before the end of year, then in Vienna the following year conducted by Donizetti, and reached London in 1846 and New York in 1848.

Verdi found himself in demand all over Italy, and between 1843 and 1849 he composed twelve operas, counting the revision of *I Lombardi* (Milan, 1843) as *Jérusalem* (Paris, 1847). He was later to refer to this period as his 'years in the galleys', for he did not have the facility of Rossini or Donizetti, who could turn out three or four operas a year without feeling

A portrait of Verdi, the venerable master of Italian opera after a lengthy career of slow but steady artistic progress

199

Maria Callas as Violetta in La traviata, *a role she made her own by virtue of her gifts for vocal characterization and dramatic interpretation*

Three operas stand out in this first period of his career. *Ernani* (Venice, 1844) has a wealth of glorious melodies expressing human emotions at white heat, to remain unequalled until *Il trovatore* nine years later. *Macbeth* (Florence, 1847, revised version Paris, 1865) ranks as Verdi's first great opera, introducing a musical style which probes into the psychological depths of its characters. We may smile indulgently over the witches, as indeed we do in Shakespeare's play, but elsewhere the music matches the drama so perfectly that the tension created with the entrance of Macbeth never slackens. There are several breaks with Italian tradition: only Lady Macbeth introduces herself in the usual cavatina-cabaletta form; there is no love interest iń the plot whatever; and the scheme of the sleep-walking scene is without precedent. The guilt-ridden Lady Macbeth, instead of singing the kind of showpiece which Donizetti or Bellini would have given her, reveals her mental torment in free arioso, with melody concentrated in the orchestra. *Luisa Miller* (Naples, 1849) marks another development in Verdi's style, introducing a domestic, intimate tone into his music which would later give such individuality to *La traviata*. There is a new tenderness in the musical portrait of Luisa, inspired by the idealization of her relationship with her father, while her scenes with her lover, Rodolfo, have a gentle poetry which touches the heart more than comparable scenes in the earlier operas, where the heroic note tends to dominate.

Since the death of his wife, Verdi's life had been one long round of work on a succession of operas, with the inevitable financial wrangles, and he had found little time to think about a more settled private life. His fortunes changed in the summer of 1847 when he paid a visit to Paris, for it was there that he renewed his acquaintance with Giuseppina Strepponi, who had created the leading role of Abigaille in *Nabucco*. She had since retired from the stage and settled in Paris as a teacher. It was undoubtedly because of her that Verdi spent nearly two years in Paris, apart from one brief visit to Italy. Within a few months they became lovers, living together for twelve years before finally marrying. She made the perfect companion, for in addition to her loving and understanding disposition her musical experience helped his work. The main reason for Verdi's tardiness in making an 'honest woman' of her was his respect for the feelings of Barezzi, his first benefactor and father-in-law. This delay caused much ill-feeling when Verdi and Giuseppina left Paris to settle at the Villa Sant' Agata near Busseto, where the scandalized townspeople resorted to a campaign of ill-natured gossip. Their bigoted moral outlook is portrayed,

overworked. He worked within an established style, but he placed too much importance on dramatic truth to produce music according to a set pattern. It is easy to point to a lack of sophistication in these operas, to note a roughness in the orchestral technique and to complain of a lack of harmonic variety. Even in the most conventional of them, however, there is always an indication in some aria or ensemble, sometimes in a whole scene, that Verdi was feeling his way towards the powerful originality of his more mature works. His use of orchestral colour, for example, is highly imaginative in the final scenes of *I due Foscari* (Rome, 1844) and *I masnadieri* (London, 1847). Like Rossini and Bellini, he always gave the voice first priority, but whereas they indulged the singers by expanding arias to allow maximum virtuoso display, Verdi condensed them to make their dramatic values more effective.

consciously or otherwise, in the character of Germont *père* in *La traviata*, where Verdi's sympathy for Violetta strikes a personal note.

Having developed his style over the years, and having found this new happiness in his private life, Verdi was all set for the three operas which established his reputation beyond any doubt. The music of *Rigoletto* (Venice, 1851) throws a remarkable light on the psychology of the characters, its title role constituting one of the most subtly drawn portrayals in all opera. The score is splendidly integrated from first to last, its arias and, above all, duets carrying the action forward at every point. Its famous Quartet is a stroke of genius, allowing the characters to express their individual feelings in different themes which combine into a uniquely satisfying whole. Verdi also handles the orchestra with unprecedented skill and brilliance. *Il trovatore* (Rome, 1853) suffers from a complicated plot which is never made clear in the text, and the characters are not presented with the psychological depth of those in *Rigoletto*, but the sheer prodigality of melody and the concentration of emotional expression in every number sweep all such reservations aside. The vitality and passion of the score, which moves at tremendous pace, give it an almost elemental quality. By contrast, *La traviata* (Venice, 1853) is the most intimate, tender and appealing of all Verdi's operas, dominated by a heroine whose heart is magically laid bare by her music in one masterly scene after another. Violetta, whose character in the play *La Dame aux camélias* by Alexandre Dumas *fils* was based on that of a famous Parisian courtesan, is made a wholly credible woman by the music for her pleasure-seeking brilliance in Act I, her magnanimous self-sacrifice in Act II and the death-scene of Act III, so miraculously does Verdi's humanity and compassion shine out. Not since Mozart's *Figaro* had an opera created a character with whom an audience can so warmly identify. Surprisingly it was a failure at first, though Verdi surely had the last word. In a letter to a friend after the first night he wrote: '*La traviata* was a fiasco; my fault or the singers'? Time alone will tell'.

From then on, Verdi went from triumph to triumph. He composed six highly successful operas as against only two which did not quite hit the target. *Les Vêpres siciliennes* (Paris, 1855) contains a good deal of splendid music, but suffers from being cast in the outdated form of French grand opera. *Simon Boccanegra* (Venice, 1857) is an altogether different case, a work which was ahead of its time. It disappointed audiences of the day, and even today has won popularity only in Italy and Britain. It is a dark, austere work with fewer arias than the composer had

Leontyne Price in the title-role of Aida, *the most spectacular of Verdi's operas which is nevertheless an intimate story of love and jealousy*

lavished on the other middle-period scores. The central character of the historical Boccanegra, Doge of Venice, is magnificently characterized, constituting what the baritone Tito Gobbi has happily described as 'Italian opera's answer to Boris Godunov', and the theme of political power is compellingly treated. The Council Scene, which involves the opposing patrician and plebian factions, is a triumph of taut, dynamic construction.

The international stature of the composer in latter life is indicated by the cities in which the next four operas were premiered. *Un ballo in maschera* ('A masked ball', Rome, 1859), dealing with the assassination of Gustav III of Sweden, is the most elegant of Verdi's operas, the music for its royal hero having all the aristocratic virtues of charm, grace and wit. Its production marked the last time that Verdi had to cope with the Austrian censors, who forced him to 201

change the locale from Stockholm to Boston, Massachusetts, and to transform Gustav into Riccardo, Earl of Warwick, the English colonial governor. *La forza del destino* ('The force of destiny', St Petersburg, 1862) may be considered a regressive step only because of its libretto, a Romantic farrago of implausible coincidences surrounding the pursuit of a personal vendetta across Spain and Italy during the eighteenth century. With such a melodramatic subject Verdi was unable to bring any great subtlety to his characterization, but on its vast canvas produced a series of vivid scenes of military and monastic life.

The world had to wait almost five years for a new opera, while Verdi gave most of his time to travel, business and the pleasures of country life at Sant' Agata with Giuseppina. He had married her in 1859, becoming an even more respectable figure two years later as a member of the first parliament of the newly independent Italy. Quickly tiring of parliamentary duties, he had no doubt welcomed his two visits to St Petersburg, and he spent more time abroad, in Madrid, London and Paris. Composing for the Opéra was not easy for Verdi, who found its conventions alien to his musical temperament, but with *Don Carlos* (Paris, 1867) he succeeded in producing a grand opera which is never merely grandiose and whose characters are vibrantly alive. The lonely Philip II harried by the Grand Inquisitor and saddened by his loveless marriage; Carlos and Elizabeth caught up in a hopeless love affair; Eboli torn by jealousy and Rodrigo a victim of the ruthless Inquisition; all are portrayed with sympathy in music of astonishing melodic and expressive richness. Verdi was not too dismayed by its cool reception, having no high opinion of French taste, and he returned to Busseto with some relief. The period before *Aida* saw him more occupied with his land and his domestic affairs than with musical commissions. No subject appealed to him until he was sent a synopsis of a drama set in Egypt, originally intended for an opera to mark the opening of the Suez Canal. Although the canal was already open when the synopsis reached Verdi, he was still invited to compose the opera for the Cairo Opera House, where *Aida* was eventually premiered in 1871 after further delays caused by the Franco-Prussian War. Verdi did not attend the Cairo performance, choosing to stay in Italy to prepare the singers for the production at La Scala six weeks later. The opera was a huge success with the public and the critics, though a few of the latter irritated the

Sherrill Milnes in the title-role with Kiri Te Kanawa as his daughter in Verdi's sombre yet magnificent Simon Boccanegra

Victor Maurel as Falstaff, the role he created in the comic opera with which Verdi, at the age of seventy-nine, astonished the world

composer by accusing him of using Wagnerian devices. *Aida*, of course, is pure Verdi, melodically radiant and most imaginatively scored, an opera without equal in its skilful balance of intimate and public scenes. The Triumphal Scene of Act II is deservedly famous as epitomizing the idea of grand opera, yet it is the Nile Scene with its magical atmosphere which reveals the composer's inspiration at its peak.

For a long time after the success of *Aida* it seemed that Verdi had exhausted his energies and would never compose another new work for the stage, though he wrote his *Requiem* in memory of the poet and novelist Alessandro Manzoni and extensively revised *Simon Boccanegra*. Then in 1884, after five years' scheming by his publisher, Giulio Ricordi, the old fire was re-kindled in the composer, now aged seventy-one, and he began work on the music of *Otello*. He had already been collaborating on the libretto for some time with Arrigo Boito, a man of letters as well as a composer, and he continued to 203

Verdi's funeral in Milan, where it seemed the entire city came out to honour the memory of Italy's greatest composer

take his time. Not until 5 February 1887 did La Scala finally present *Otello*, the first new opera from Verdi's pen for fifteen years and arguably the greatest of all tragic operas. His melodic gift blazes throughout the score to produce one wonderful highlight after another, the love duet which so rapturously recalls the courtship of Otello and Desdemona, the hero's marital 'Ora e per sempre addio' and heart-broken 'Niun me tema', the heroine's Willow Song and Ave Maria, Iago's sinister Dream and god-denying 'Credo'. Each of these is a model of musical characterization, and each is woven into the continuous texture of the score, which from its stormy opening to the hushed close as Otello 'dies upon a kiss' reveals a miraculous sense of orchestral colour. The first-night audience recognized *Otello* for the masterpiece it is, giving the composer an ovation that even he had not expected. When he left the theatre an enthusiastic crowd pulled his carriage to his hotel.

It must have looked as though Verdi had played his last card, for he was seventy-four and busily engaged with local matters including a new hospital he had built near his home. In 1889, however, he showed considerable interest in a new libretto Boito had sent him – *Falstaff*, based on Shakespeare's *Merry Wives of Windsor* with a few ideas culled from *Henry IV*. He could never resist the English dramatist, whose *King Lear* he had considered for years but never taken up. He began work on the score the following year, insisting that he was composing to

pass the time, and refusing to discuss any plans for a production. Despite periods of depression he completed the music in 1892. In January 1893, with an energy astonishing in a man in his eightieth year, he began rehearsals at La Scala, where the premiere was given on 9 February. It proved as great a revelation as *Otello* had been, for nobody had expected the composer of so many high-powered tragedies to display a gift for comedy that is the equal of Mozart's. The score, like chamber music in its mercurial grace and translucence, bubbles along its witty course, a seamless flow of brief yet telling melodies which are thrown aside as quickly as they are brought into view. It shows an incredible zest for life and laughter, ending with a stroke of absolute genius as the characters join in a dashing fugue to declare that all the world's a stage.

Verdi's eight last years were spent in retirement, though he still threw himself into projects like the Rest Home for Musicians which he set up in Milan and arranged to be financed from his royalties. After the death of his wife in 1898 his time was divided between his home, Genoa and Milan, where he died on 27 January 1901. He was mourned as a national hero by the country whose spirit he had so perfectly distilled in his music.

OPERA IN FRANCE

Paris was a flourishing centre of opera throughout the nineteenth century, but before 1859, when Gounod arrived on the scene with *Faust*, the successes in serious opera were scored by foreign composers, who proved the best judges of French taste. Berlioz never received recognition by his own countrymen: his *Benvenuto Cellini* was given twenty-nine rehearsals but only seven performances at the Opéra in 1838, while his masterpiece *Les Troyens* ('The Trojans') was not performed complete during his lifetime. Italian composers ruled supreme, with Cherubini and Spontini making their careers in Paris and leading composers such as Rossini, Donizetti and Verdi setting French texts to secure favour with the most fashionable, if not the most discriminating, of European audiences. French composers, however, developed a national style at the rival Opéra-Comique, where a lighter type of work was staged. The term *opéra comique* is misleading, for operas which fall into this category have not always been comic. The term eventually came to be applied to any opera which include spoken dialogue, so that it embraces Bizet's *Carmen*, which not only has a tragic ending but is basically serious throughout. Technically, even *Fidelio* is an *opéra comique*. Many fine operas were produced in this form during the early nineteenth century, but they have not established themselves in the repertoires of opera houses outside France.

Two composers of *opéra comique* deserve a brief mention; their overtures are frequently performed and it is possible that their operas might return to favour. François Boïeldieu (1775–1834) is still celebrated in France for *La Dame blanche*, a romantic comedy based on Walter Scott's *Guy Mannering* and *The Monastery* which was given a thousand performances in Paris alone within seven years of its premiere in 1825. His numerous other operas have fallen by the wayside, though in the course of a busy career he enjoyed many successes in Russia as well as in Paris, where he taught composition at the Conservatoire. An even more prolific composer was Daniel Auber (1782–1871), though he was so timid that he is believed never to have attended a single performance of any of his fifty operas. His historical tragedy *La Muette de Portici* ('The dumb girl of Portici') enjoyed a great success at the Opéra in 1828, and a performance at Brussels two years later precipitated the outbreak of the Belgian revolution which led to the country's independence; it also won favour too at Drury Lane in 1829. *Fra Diavolo* (1830) continues to be revived from time to time, mainly because its title-role makes a strong appeal to leading international tenors. Like other Auber operas it is most widely known for its overture in the Rossini tradition.

Cherubini

When Ingres painted his famous portrait of Luigi Cherubini in 1841 he achieved more than just a good likeness of the composer: he cunningly conveyed the academic correctness of his nature. Born in Florence on 14 September 1760, the son of a musician, the teenage Luigi revealed outstanding gifts as a composer of masses and other church music. His talents were best suited to ecclesiastical works, but opera offered greater rewards and he began writing for the theatre when he was twenty. In 1788 he decided to settle permanently in Paris. He worked by fits and starts, sometimes producing a steady stream of operas or church works, then composing nothing at all. He gained the respect of his fellow-composers and secured recognition from the successive rulers of France. He was regarded almost with awe by Haydn and Beethoven, while his work was honoured equally by Napoleon and Louis XVIII. Only two of over twenty operas are remembered today, due mainly to his repressing his native gift for flowing melody, in his constant striving towards the Classical restraint of Gluck. *Médée* alone has retained its place in the world repertoire, though his 'rescue opera', *Les Deux journées*, is still occasionally seen in France. His inspiration dried up after 1800 so far as opera was concerned, and he composed mainly church music from that time until his death in Paris on 15 March 1842.

Médée, better known in its Italian version as *Medea*, was originally given with spoken dialogue, but this was soon replaced by recitatives composed by Franz Lachner to emphasize its Gluckian dignity of conception. It is indeed a work of lofty inspiration, its impressive solos, duets and concerted numbers welded together with consummate mastery in ever-mounting tragic intensity. The role of Medea – made wholly credible by Cherubini's music – offers a wonderful challenge to the great soprano who is also a powerful actress (as Maria Callas was); she has had her brother cut to pieces before the action begins, and takes her revenge on the faithless Jason at the end by murdering their children as well as her rival in love. *Les Deux journées*, generally known in English as *The Water Carrier*, is a melodrama in which the humanity of the music softens the chilling suspense of the story, Cherubini supplying arias and choruses more beguilingly melodic than those in any of his other operas. It is less ambitious than *Médée*, at once less uncompromising and more immediately appealing; 205

Ingres's portrait of Cherubini, a good likeness which also brings out the stern character of the composer of Medea

in its extolling of heroism and self-sacrifice it stands as a forerunner of *Fidelio*.

Spontini

Like Cherubini, Gasparo Spontini enjoyed his greatest successes in Paris, where he spent twenty-four years of his life in two periods separated by twenty years as Kapellmeister at the court of Frederick William III of Prussia. He saw little of his native Italy, where he was born on 14 November 1774; he left at the age of twenty-eight and returned to his birthplace only a year before his death there on 24 January 1851. Again like Cherubini, he possessed great talent which rarely flowered into genius, the result of attempting to please a fickle public rather than pursue his own convictions. It was thanks largely to the championship of the Empress Josephine that he became established in the French capital, where the deserved success of *La Vestale* ('The vestal virgin') in

1807 finally gave him supremacy over his rival Cherubini. He rode the crest of the wave with *Fernando Cortez* two years later, but *Olympie*, an epic on the life of Alexander the Great's mother, over which he had laboured for several years, met with failure in 1819. He was comforted two years later when the opera was presented in revised form in Berlin, with unprecedented lavishness involving thirty-eight trumpeters and several elephants in its processional scenes. Even this triumph was short-lived, German audiences soon succumbing to the charms of Weber's *Der Freischütz* and forgetting the more conventional Italian. Spontini became embittered, melancholic and quarrelsome, and though he was respected (he was greatly admired by the young Wagner) and had amassed considerable wealth, he composed nothing of value during his last twenty years.

His place in operatic history rests firmly on *La Vestale*, a compelling drama of a priestess of the Temple of Vesta who is condemned to death for neglecting her duties in the pursuit of mortal love but is saved when a flash of lightning rekindles the sacred flame on the altar. The masterly libretto presents a passionate love story with the solemnity of genuine tragedy, and Spontini rose to the occasion with music of Gluckian dignity which blazes out at climaxes into arias and ensembles of overwhelming power. The work has all the spectacular qualities of French grand opera, complete with elaborate ballets, and represents all that is best in the *genre*. Sadly, the opera has been revived only when there is a Rosa Ponselle or a Maria Callas to ensure that Spontini's heroine is worthily portrayed.

Grand Opera

The term *grand opéra* was used initially as a contrast to *opéra comique*, the former employing accompanied recitatives where the latter used spoken dialogue. From about 1830, however, the adjective 'grand' took over with a vengeance, operas being composed on a huge, heroic scale with stage spectacle given priority. Gluck and his immediate followers had turned to Greek antiquity for their subject matter, but the composers were now attracted by medieval or more recent history. Grand opera had a Romantic basis that reflected the novels of Walter Scott and the dramas of Victor Hugo, drawing on nationalistic and religious themes and treating them in a melodramatic, often violent style. Many of these operas have great entertainment value, and the best, such as *William Tell* and *Don Carlos*, are works of genius. At worst, however, grand opera was simply grandiose.

French composers had little enduring success in

grand opera. Auber's *La Muette de Portici* was quickly forgotten, and the only work by a French composer to have held the stage is *La Juive* ('The jewess') by Jacques-François Halévy (1799–1862). Its story of Christian persecution of the Jews is set in fifteenth-century Switzerland, ending on a horrendous note typical of grand opera as Rachel and her father Elé-azar are thrown into a cauldron of boiling water. Its choruses and ballets are weak but the music for the principal characters is melodically inspired and dramatically expressive. But it was in the work of Meyerbeer that grand opera reached its peak.

Meyerbeer

No composer has ever suffered such an extreme and humiliating change of fortune as Giacomo Meyerbeer. For three decades after the premiere of *Robert le diable* in 1831, he dominated the whole of Europe, contemporary opinion extolling him even above Beethoven as 'the Michelangelo of music'. Yet within twenty years of his death in 1864 he was despised and rejected by the musical establishment – although his operas continued to delight and thrill the public

A scene from L'Africaine, *the last of Meyerbeer's four spectacular grand operas tailored to fit popular Parisian taste*

into the second decade of the twentieth century. His best operas do not begin to compare with the mature masterpieces of Verdi and Wagner; but both these more distinguished composers owed a great deal to his pioneering work. And his four Opéra successes, *Robert le diable*, *Les Huguenots* (1836), *Le Prophète* (1849) and the posthumously produced *L'Africaine* (1865) all contain so much fine music that one cannot help suspecting that the pendulum of taste has swung too far against the fallen idol.

There are many curious features about Meyerbeer both as man and artist. To begin with, his very name was revised almost as conscientiously as his meticulously prepared scores. He was born in Berlin on 5 September 1791 as Jakob Liebmann Beer; to secure a legacy from a relative called Meyer he was obliged to extend his surname to Meyerbeer. During a ten-year stay in Italy, he dropped both his forenames in favour of Giacomo. He spent the best years of his creative life in Italy and France, but remained essentially Ger- 207

man. Being Jewish meant little to him in any spiritual sense, for he seems to have had no religious leanings, though it might have contributed something to his lifelong feeling of insecurity.

Inheriting wealth from his father and culture from his mother, Meyerbeer was ideally set for an artistic career. He won acclaim as a virtuoso pianist in Berlin at the age of nine; but his sights were already set on becoming a composer. After a period of study in his native city he went on to Darmstadt to become a pupil of the eccentric Abbé Vogler, idealized and immortalized in a poem by Robert Browning. Meyerbeer frequently gave the other members of the Vogler circle money to go out in search of wine and women while he stayed behind in the laborious search for song. This typifies Meyerbeer's character. Thanks to his private wealth he had no need to work; but he chose to become one of the most dedicated of all composers, endlessly revising his work until it met the high technical standards he had set himself. Abstemious by nature, he was the complete antithesis of Rossini, with whom he became friendly during his Italian sojourn. Rossini, the *bon vivant* of all time, made fun of Meyerbeer's preferring sauerkraut to spaghetti and solitary walks to the indoor charms of

The scene in Meyerbeer's Robert le diable *where the ghosts of dead nuns rise from their graves to dance—the first Romantic ballet*

the salon, yet despite his mockery he fainted when he heard of his friend's death.

Meyerbeer began his career as a good German, but his first opera, *Jepthas Gelübde* ('Jeptha's vow'), was unsuccessful in Munich in 1812 and *Wirt und Gast* ('Host and guest') came close to disaster in Vienna two years later. In desperation the young composer turned for advice to Antonio Salieri, who suggested that he would learn more about the art of vocal writing in Italy, so in 1815 he paid the visit to Venice which was to prove a turning-point in his life. Casting aside the tradition in which he had been brought up, Meyerbeer set out to become an Italian composer, and his six Italian operas succeeded through combining fluent melodic style, learnt from Rossini, with the harmonic and instrumental techniques that he had mastered during his German studies. His fame spread throughout the country, and he returned to Germany confident of receiving a hero's welcome. But his friend Weber expressed distaste that 'a composer of creative ability has become an imitator in order to win the favour of the crowd'. Meyerbeer had reckoned without the sudden upsurge of German nationalism.

As always he reacted in the most sensible way: he went back to Italy. There he quickly vindicated himself by writing for La Scala *Margherita d'Anjou* (1820), which was his first international success. He extended his fame even more widely with *Il crociato in Egitto*, composed for Venice in 1824. The following year Rossini invited Meyerbeer to produce it in Paris, and unwittingly caused him to turn his back for ever on Italy. He found great favour with Paris audiences, but even more important was his meeting with Eugène Scribe, the most indefatigable 'manufacturer' of plays and opera librettos. Scribe could provide Meyerbeer with the grand subjects he was now seeking, subjects involving magnificent spectacle and every kind of breathtaking stage novelty. Grand opera was well suited to Meyerbeer, whose weakness was a lack of melodic spontaneity, and whose strength lay in his breadth of music structure.

It was six years, however, before the Meyerbeer-Scribe partnership bore fruit, with *Robert le diable* finally produced after five months of rehearsal at the Opéra on 22 November 1831. Its immediate success with the Parisian public may have contributed to Rossini's decision to retire from the opera stage. *Robert le diable* is indeed a remarkable work, cunningly contrived to dazzle the spectator by combing all the elements of French grand opera as never before. 'I don't know whether there has ever been such magnificence in the theatre,' enthused Chopin after seeing the opera. With the scene in which the ghosts of dead nuns rise from their graves to dance, a stunning *coup de théâtre*, this opera inaugurated the Romantic ballet. (*La sylphide* appeared during the following year, 1832, and *Giselle* nine years after that.) Musically Meyerbeer displayed the best of his talent.

Having become the leading figure in French grand opera overnight, he took five years to compose *Les Huguenots*, an epic demanding seven star singers for its leading roles and presenting the spectacles of a ballet of bathing beauties and the Massacre of St Bartholomew. After a further gap of thirteen years, *Le Prophète* included several visual feasts: a skaters' ballet, a coronation and finally an explosion which destroys everything on the stage. The last of Meyerbeer's grand operas, *L'Africaine* calls for a full-scale shipwreck in its third act. It is a measure of Meyerbeer's ingenuity that he was able to compose music on a scale to match these theatrical extravagances. The criticism that he was a facile composer is as inaccurate as it is unfair: had he really been facile he would have followed up the success of *Robert le diable*

with the speed of a Donizetti. He was still revising *L'Africaine* when he died on 2 May 1864. The problem with Meyerbeer's operas is that they make such fiendish demands: only the most lavish productions with carefully chosen casts of the greatest international singers can hope to do them justice. When these requirements are met, however, they provide unusually exhilarating and satisfying experiences. They are of historical importance, for they showed the way for Wagner and Verdi.

Berlioz

It is a sad reflection on French taste that Paris audiences venerated Meyerbeer so completely as to ignore totally their own far greater genius, Berlioz, who composed four dramatic works between 1838 and 1862. To be fair to the public of the time, it must be remembered that Meyerbeer calculated to give it precisely what it wanted, whereas Berlioz remained true to his artistic principles even when this would lessen

Caricature of Berlioz, the most distinguished of all French composers

HECTOR BERLIOZ

his chance of winning popular success. It must also be admitted that his operas, present considerable practical difficulties in performance. The same is true, of course, of Wagner's later works, but the German composer had such powerful personal charisma and ruthless determination that he was able to overcome all opposition. Berlioz, though he had supporters including Franz Liszt, lacked this kind of fighting spirit and was therefore powerless in the face of public indifference and critical hostility.

His first surviving opera, *Benvenuto Cellini* (1838), is a robust comedy in the tradition of Auber, and is relatively straightforward. It includes two impressive scenes in the Roman Carnival (the music of which was later used in the overture of that name) and the casting of the Perseus statue. It disappoints, however, in that its only outstanding vocal numbers, Cellini's aria and his love duet with Teresa, do not occur until the last act; this lack of lyrical highlights has told against a work of strong imagination and dazzling orchestral virtuosity. *La Damnation de Faust* (1846) is often given as an opera, though it was composed as a concert work, a dramatic cantata based on episodes from Goethe. There is no action at all in some of the scenes, leaving their staging to the producer's individual imagination; the work as a whole has little dramatic shape or balance. After the *Symphonie fantastique*, however, it is perhaps Berlioz's most popular score, embracing attractive numbers in a variety of styles, the orchestral Dance of the Sylphs, Minuet of the Will-o'-the-Wisps, Faust's Invocation to Nature and Marguerite's hauntingly beautiful 'D'amour, l'ardente flamme'. *Béatrice et Bénédict* (1862), based on Shakespeare's *Much Ado about Nothing* but leaving out the sinister aspect of the drama, is a predominantly lyrical work of exquisite craftsmanship – so exquisite, in fact, that it is almost too intimate for the opera house and seems to work best in the concert hall.

When we come to the composer's masterpiece, *Les Troyens* ('The Trojans'), there are no reservations to be made. At first glance it may appear to belong to the tradition of grand opera, for it is made up of set numbers and includes elaborate choral and ballet scenes, but in its conception it is something far greater. Berlioz himself wrote the libretto, which is based on Books I, II and IV of Virgil's *Aeneid*, and into which ideas and events from other parts of the epic poem are woven. Unable to have the work performed complete, Berlioz split the opera into two smaller works, *La Prise de Troie* (Acts I and II) and *Les Troyens à Carthage* (Acts III, IV and V). Cassandra is the dominant figure in the first and the lovers Dido and Aeneas the chief protagonists of the second.

Where *The Trojans* differs fundamentally from grand opera is in being not a personal tragedy but a cosmic one, in which the characters, though powerful and convincing in themselves, are agents of the epic idea of the founding of Rome. (The idea that Rome was of Trojan origin is a fable, but it was adopted by Virgil for his *Aeneid*.) Cassandra meets her death with a cry of 'Italie!', Dido with 'Rome immortelle!'; Berlioz makes his opera a true epic as Wagner made his music-dramas true myths. *The Trojans* may be regarded as the Latin counterpart of *The Ring*.

The two parts of the opera are contrasted so skilfully and subtly that they complement each other to perfection. The first, which deals with the capture of Troy by means of the wooden horse, is austere in its musical colouring and Classical in the manner of Gluck (whom Berlioz revered above all other composers). The second, with its pastoral Carthaginian setting, has sensuous, lyrical music for the love story of Dido and Aeneas – though it ends on a note of heroic resignation when Dido, deserted by Aeneas, kills herself. For the noble acceptance of fate by the leading characters Berlioz composed music that is remarkably true to the spirit of Virgil, a poet he had read and re-read with growing enthusiasm since boyhood. The richness of his invention seems also to owe something to Shakespeare, the other great influence on his dramatic thinking; indeed, the great love duet in Act IV uses words from *The Merchant of Venice*. Berlioz's ability to reveal through his music the innermost private feelings of men and women caught up in public action gives a special grandeur to the opera. Miraculously, Berlioz achieves this grandeur without sacrificing any of his customary fire and vitality, and the whole score is virtually a series of highlights, wonderfully flowing melodies for the singers and such dazzling orchestral numbers as the Trojan March and the Royal Hunt and Storm ballet.

The long history of neglect of *The Trojans* is difficult to explain. Berlioz never saw the first part staged at all, and the Paris production of the second in 1863 was far from complete. The complete work is the same length as *Tristan and Isolde*, and therefore shorter than *The Mastersingers*, so it cannot be considered over-taxing. It also contains all the ingredients which appeal to the opera-goer; a strong story-line, vivid characters and glorious spectacle, as well as its musical wealth. It was not until 1957, at Covent Garden, that *The Trojans* was given virtually complete, to warm public and critical acclaim. This not-

Berlioz's The Trojans *at Covent Garden in 1957, the first complete version ever given in a major opera house*

able production, which made the musical world appreciate the full worth of a masterpiece that had been ignored for a century, has since been followed by stagings at many opera houses elsewhere. Yet the opera is still regarded as a work to be performed as a special event rather than as a standard repertoire piece. One reason is that French operas have a distinctive style which singers trained for the Italian and German repertoires find difficult to master; and France has not itself produced many outstanding singers since the early part of the twentieth century.

Gounod

Whereas Berlioz suffered from neglect, Gounod's reputation has been spoiled by the phenomenal success of *Faust*, which for several decades was the most popular of all operas throughout the world. Inevitably reaction set in, and his music has become seriously underrated. It became the fashion to dwell on the weaker aspects of the operas and to ignore their many attractive qualities, taking advantage of the fact that his work was as uneven as his personality was unstable.

Charles Gounod was born in Paris on 18 June 1818 into a cultured family environment, his father being a painter of some distinction and his mother a piano teacher. As a boy he showed gifts in both arts; he could as easily have become a painter as a composer, just as he had later to choose between the church and the theatre. For a long time he wished to become a priest and at twenty-eight, having served as an organist and choirmaster, he enrolled at the seminary of Saint-Sulpice. He yearned for the peace of the cloister, but on other hand could not resist pretty women or the glamour of the opera house. Although he renounced the spiritual life for the material in 1848, he never resolved the conflict within himself and suffered as a result from frequent nervous breakdowns.

He won the Prix de Rome at twenty-one, but this early promise did not produce any important results for a considerable period. In Italy he was influenced above all by hearing Palestrina's masses in the Sistine Chapel. On returning to Paris after a stay in Germany, he was almost unique among French composers in his knowledge of the latest music outside France. Yet when, as the result of meeting the singer Pauline Viardot, he brought out his first opera, *Sapho* (1851), his style owed most to the French works of Gluck. When this and a subsequent serious opera failed, Gounod turned to comedy and won a resounding success with *Le Médecin malgré lui* (1858), a work which caught the authentic flavour of Molière's play.

The turning-point in his career came in 1859, with *Faust* which at first appealed more strongly to fellow composers and professional musicians than to the general public – a fascinating fact when we consider how it eventually came to be loved by the masses but sneered at by the experts. Surprisingly, the most favourable review of the premiere was written by Berlioz, whose own *Damnation of Faust* had been mauled by the critics. It is not difficult to see why it attracted both hostility and affection. Gounod was quite incapable of translating into music the spirit of Goethe's drama of philosophical inquiry into the nature of good and evil, and it is significant that Marguerite is really the principal character. (*Faust* has always been given in Germany under the title *Margarethe*.) Gounod reduced Goethe's cosmic tragedy to a love story with a few superficial diabolic effects to give undemanding audiences an enjoyably mild shudder from time to time. On the other hand, it is impossible to resist the lyrical numbers that Gounod showers so liberally on the singers. The Garden Scene remains unsurpassed in its sustained melodic inspiration: Faust's 'Salut, demeure chaste et pure' is followed by Marguerite's ballad of the 'Roi de Thulé' and Jewel Song, then the act is concluded by the quartet and love duet. There are other justly popular numbers, the Serenade for Méphistophélès, the aria for Valentin and the final trio, all of them revealing the composer providing his best music to fit character and situation. *Faust* is almost certain to survive its temporary lack of favour.

After *Faust*, the composer returned to the lighter style of comedy for *Philémon et Baucis* and *La Colombe*, both premiered in 1860, but he did not appear to put his heart into them as he had done for *Le Médecin malgré lui*, and their inevitable failure served to strengthen his resolve to break into the world of grand opera in the manner of Meyerbeer. This was a fatal decision, because the 'grand' elements in *Faust* constitute its weakness. *La Reine de Saba* (1862), a dramatically risible version of the meeting between the Queen of Sheba and King Solomon, was a humiliating flop. Even Berlioz, who had championed *Faust*, dismissed it out of hand. He commented, 'how can one support something which has neither bone nor muscle?'

Of the five operas which followed only *Roméo et Juliette* (1867) has proved to be of lasting quality, and the reason is that the composer and his librettists wisely concentrated on the intimate scenes for the lovers and ignored the greater part of Shakespeare's plot. Just as *Faust* has survived on account of the exquisite music for its Garden Scene, *Roméo et Juliette* is frequently revived on the strength of the four duets

Mirella Freni with Stuart Burrows in Faust, *the opera by Gounod which for many years was the most popular work in the international repertoire*

for the lovers. Youthful passion and youthful tragedy brought out all that was best in Gounod, and here he was afforded every opportunity to shine. Even a composer with his gift for melody faced the danger of monotony in writing four duets for the same couple, but he achieved remarkable variety: the first is a stylized 'duetto galant', the second an outburst of exultant passion, the third an expression of rapture darkened by anguish, and the last an affirmation of love in death. There are also four solo numbers in the composer's happiest vein: Juliet's waltz song, Mercutio's quicksilver Queen Mab aria, Romeo's cavatina in the Balcony Scene, and the Page's provocative Italianate chanson which leads to the fateful duel. With its fluent, attractively coloured orchestral writing, *Roméo et Juliette* is arguably Gounod's most consistently successful score.

Gounod passed his last twenty years as the revered patriarch of French music. On his death on 18 October 1893, he was widely mourned and given a state funeral. He deserved no less, for however uneven his large output of music might have been, his two finest operas freed the national style from foreign influence. Ravel provided the most perceptive comment on his work: 'The musical renewal which took place with us towards 1880 has no more weighty precursor than Gounod.'

Thomas

In addition to Gounod, several other French composers threw off the yoke of Italian influence in the mid-nineteenth century, but most are noted only for a single operatic success. Ambroise Thomas (1811–93), though exceptionally talented, never fully realized his early promise. He is remembered chiefly for *Mignon* (1866), an adaptation of Goethe's novel *Wilhelm Meister* which, while of undeniable charm, reduced the stature of the German writer's work even more than *Faust* had done. Accepted on its own terms, however, *Mignon* can be enjoyed for its easy lyricism, at its best in the aria 'Connais-tu les pays', and for the brilliance of the soprano's 'Je suis Titania'. Thomas was less successful with his *Hamlet* (1868), which offends Anglo-Saxon audiences because of the way the librettists treated Shakespeare. Hamlet indulges in a drinking song – an excellent number in its own right – and Ophelia goes mad in waltz time. Ironically, Thomas would probably have succeeded better if he had chosen less ambitious subjects.

Saint-Saëns

Saint-Saëns was a more gifted composer than Thomas, but had no theatrical flair. Betwen 1872 and 1895 he wrote thirteen operas whose music has substance but rarely gives off the whiff of greasepaint. His goals were formal perfection and stylistic polish rather than the expression of strong emotion, so it is hardly surprising that his operas are deficient in human warmth at a time when other French composers were reaching heights of sentimentality. It is for this reason that Saint-Saëns, a highly respected figure, could not secure a performance in Paris of *Samson et Dalila*, on which he had worked so meticulously between 1868 and 1872. Thanks to the kindly influence of Liszt, the opera was premiered at Weimar in a German translation on 2 December 1877, when it was enthusiastically received. The opera made its way to Paris by way of Rouen, but the Opéra did not stage it until 1892: the management must have kicked its collective self for waiting twenty years to accept a work with a box-office appeal almost equal to that of *Faust*. Having chosen a Biblical subject, Saint-Saëns

Agnes Baltsa as Giulietta in the voluptuous Venetian scene of Offenbach's Tales of Hoffmann *at Covent Garden in 1980*

inevitably fell into a somewhat oratorio-like style, especially in its first and third acts, but he was inspired to a rare height of passion with the music for Delilah in the second. Her aria 'Amour, viens aider ma faiblesse' has one of the most voluptuous melodies ever composed, while her 'Mon coeur s'ouvre à ta voix' conquers not only Samson but also audiences everywhere. For once the composer had found a libretto which allowed him to give the public the erotic and visual elements it craved for without sacrificing his own ideals of Classical balance.

Offenbach

Although his reputation ultimately rests on his success in the field of operetta, Jacques Offenbach always nursed the ambition to be taken seriously. This ambition was finally realized with *The Tales of Hoffmann*, an opera which many far more distin-

214

A set design for the first act of Carmen, *Bizet's celebrated opera which shocked the public with its new realism*

guished composers would have been proud to have written. Sadly, he did not live to complete it; the work was orchestrated by Ernest Guiraud for its premiere at the Opéra-Comique on 10 February 1881. Its libretto follows the German poet E T A Hoffmann as he lives through three of his typical fantasies. Each finds him pursuing a new love, and in each he is thwarted by his evil genius in a different guise. In the true spirit of fantasy Hoffmann falls in love with a mechanical doll, a singer and a Venetian courtesan, roles which should be sung by the same soprano. A piece of excellent theatre, *The Tales of Hoffmann* is rich in memorable melodies.

Delibes

Léo Delibes (1836–91), remembered today for his splendid ballet scores *Coppélia* and *Sylvia*, and for the successful opera *Lakmé*, was a prolific composer in various forms, from sacred works to operettas. He was happy to work in any musicial capacity almost in the manner of an eighteenth-century composer. Operatic success came with the production of *Lakmé*

at the Opéra-Comique on 14 April 1883, when he suddenly found himself a celebrity. This exotic opera, of high workmanship and lyrical charm, enjoyed international vogue for several decades, but is rarely given outside France. It is one of those neglected operas which come into favour only when there is a singer who can do full justice to the principal role.

Bizet

The French composers of the mid-nineteenth century who found favour with the public had all written skilful operas and at their best achieved a sensitive balance between words and music, yet none of them rose to the heights of Verdi or Wagner. However much one may enjoy *Faust* or *Samson et Dalila*, one would not class them alongside *La traviata* or *Tristan and Isolde*: the former are the products of high talent, the latter of genius. Even in the best French operas 215

Ann Howard as Carmen, with Geoffrey Chard as Escamillo, in the masterpiece by Bizet which set a new style of operatic realism

of this period, characterization tends to be two-dimensional: Gounod's Marguerite, for example, could be any young girl in love, a pale figure beside Verdi's Violetta. It was left to Bizet to contribute the first indisputable masterpiece after *The Trojans*, for *Carmen* is a complete and almost perfect work of art, its two principal characters drawn with complex, wholly convincing truthfulness. We can only speculate about the greater heights Bizet might have reached, for he died at the age of thirty-six just three months after *Carmen* had bewildered and outraged its first Paris audience. To appreciate Bizet's achievement, it should be remembered that by their mid-thirties Verdi had only reached *Luisa Miller* and Wagner *Tannhäuser*: operas which scarcely indicate the full scope of their genius.

216 Georges Bizet, who was born in Paris on 25 Octo-

ber 1838, appeared at first to have everything in his favour. His father was a singing teacher and his mother a gifted pianist; his precocious talent secured his entry to the Conservatoire at the age of eleven; and the Symphony in C which he composed at the age of seventeen ranks him with Mozart and Mendelssohn as a youthful master. As winner of the Prix de Rome in 1857 he responded to Italian influence by composing *Don Procopio*, which not only has a plot almost identical with that of Donizetti's *Don Pasquale* but slavishly follows the Italian style. Bizet confided to Gounod that he was worried by his facile ability to write music tailored to an existing style, which helps to explain why he took so long to develop a style of his own. There is much beautiful music, for example, in *Les Pêcheurs de perles* ('The pearl fishers', 1863), but there are also too many echoes of Gounod, Verdi and even Meyerbeer. The opera continues to be revived thanks to some fine numbers and many passages of supple, piquant scoring, but as a whole does not bear a very individual stamp. Bizet made little advance with his next opera, *La Jolie fille de Perth* (1867), a clumsy adaptation of Walter Scott's novel, but the one-act *Djamileh* (1872), though a failure with the public, finally showed the composer freeing himself from Gounod's influence and finding a voice. Also in 1872 came another mature score, the incidental music for Alphonse Daudet's play *L'Arlésienne*, twenty-seven numbers of which many are very brief but none is negligible. The composer made an orchestral suite from a selection of the numbers, a delightful work which was immediately successful and has remained a concert-hall favourite ever since.

Bizet was not equipped to write an opera of true originality, and by the happiest of chances his interest was aroused by the short novel *Carmen* by Prosper Mérimée. It is difficult to imagine a subject better suited to his particular gifts – or to imagine *Carmen* set by any other composer. Bizet seems to have known from the first that Mérimée's story was the ideal for which he had searched so long, for his enthusiasm never wavered during the two years that elapsed between his starting the work and finally seeing it performed at the Opéra-Comique. The difficulties began when his librettists, shocked by the violence of the story and the raw passions of its characters, tried to soften everything down. Bizet, on the other hand, was only prepared to make minimal changes in the process of translating the novel into dramatic form.

He must have known that audiences would be outraged by the seamy realism of *Carmen*, but he had never been a man to betray his convictions to win popular acceptance. It was this independence, in fact, which had always made him something of an outsider and which forced him to waste much of his time giving lessons to earn a living. His marriage was far from ideal, and in 1874 he separated from his wife for a time. To these pressures were added attacks of quinsy, which led to his early death, and the hostility of the opera house management.

No opera previous to *Carmen* had depicted scenes and characters with such realism or attempted to give tragic stature to a man and a woman of such lowly nature. Carmen herself is a wild creature, shamelessly flaunting her sexuality at Don José in the street, ready to start a fight with other girls in the cigarette factory, always on the look-out for a new lover. The miracle of Bizet's music is that it wins for Carmen the sympathy and admiration of the audience, admiration for her pride and her willingness to die rather than be untrue to herself. José, who is really the central figure of the opera, is portrayed with uncanny musical subtlety. We follow every step in his downfall from simple, loyal soldier to desperate victim of his fatal love for Carmen. The illumination of character by means of music has never been accomplished more successfully, and it is this which makes *Carmen* such an advance on other French operas of the period. As well as bringing the characters such vivid life, Bizet's music creates a wonderful sense of place and atmosphere. It not only evokes the colour and vitality of Seville, but it also portrays the brooding fatalism below the exotic surface, preparing for the gripping final scene in which Carmen is killed by José.

It seems incredible today that the opera was a failure at first. That the audience was shocked by the story is understandable, but the accusation that *Carmen* was too 'Wagnerian' and lacked melody is so patently absurd that it can only be put down to the general hostility towards the composer. José's Flower Song, Escamillo's Toreador Song, Carmen's Habanera, Sequidilla and Card Scene, the Quintet in Act II with its Mozartian wit – all these prove Bizet to be a melodist of the highest order. The opera's cool reception on 3 March 1875 probably contributed to the composer's early death at Bougival just three months later (3 June). By a terrible irony he died only a few hours after the curtain had fallen on a performance of *Carmen* during which Célestine Galli-Marié, overwhelmed by foreboding, had fainted in the wings after singing the ominous Card Scene. The crisis in Bizet's health is considered to have been largely psychosomatic, the result of his feelings of personal and artistic insecurity. He was not to know that *Carmen* would be recognized within a matter of three years as one of the greatest operas of all.

Massenet

Only a few French opera composers of note followed Bizet, and of these only one contributed a considerable body of work. Jules Massenet was born at Montaud on 12 May 1842, and like Bizet gained entrance to the Paris Conservatoire at an early age. While in Italy as winner of the Prix de Rome he met Liszt, through whom he was introduced to the girl who became his wife and who helped to give him a more stable life than most composers have enjoyed. He was a tireless and conscientious worker and, combining a brilliant talent with determination to please his public, was consistently successful. He arrived on the Paris scene at just the right time, scoring a triumph with *Le Roi de Lahore* at the Opéra in 1877, two years after the death of Bizet. This spectacular opera established his reputation abroad as well as in Paris, and within five years had been produced in Rome, Milan, Munich, Budapest, Prague, St Petersburg, Madrid,

Massenet, who combined his work as a prolific composer with teaching at the Paris Conservatoire

217

Buenos Aires and Rio de Janeiro – a success that no composer today could hope for.

Massenet is a difficult composer to categorize because his many operas cover a wide range of styles. Like *Le Roi de Lahore*, *Hérodiade* (1881) is a grand opera, but this time with a Biblical setting instead of the former's more exotic India of Hindu legend. The libretto is based on Flaubert, and deals with the vindictive Herodias persuading her daughter Salome to dance for King Herod and then demand the head of John the Baptist as a reward. Massenet had Salome transformed into a tender-hearted heroine genuinely in love with the prophet, an interesting change suggesting that Massenet realized the need for a strong love interest. His music, in fact, is always at its best when portraying women in love and suffering for it. Not surprisingly, Prévost's story of Manon Lescaut and the Chevalier Des Grieux inspired his most successful, virtually flawless opera.

Manon is a work of exquisite balance and refinement, and perhaps even more important, it portrays its central character with the utmost persuasiveness

Valerie Masterson as Manon, the heroine of Massenet's most popular opera, the kind of vulnerable young woman he portrayed so delicately in his music

and credibility. Manon comes alive in music as vividly as Carmen does, though they are very different characters. When Manon sings 'N'est-ce plus ma main' she becomes irresistible, and in all her music is revealed as a woman with far more heart than the empty-headed character in Prévost. It was never difficult for Massenet to give this kind of vulnerable charm to his heroines – even when they are far from virtuous – because his melodic style has a quality all of its own, tender and sweetly sensuous. In the case of Manon he found a character ideally suited to his dramatic style. Massenet's treatment of the story is thoroughly French in style, just as Puccini's *Manon Lescaut* is unmistakably Italian. A sensational success on its first appearance at the Opéra-Comique on 19 January 1884, *Manon* has remained the most popular of the composer's operas.

Further proof that Massenet understood his limi-

tations came with *Werther* eight years later. Like Gounod and Thomas he turned to Goethe for a dramatic subject, but whereas they had aimed too high he chose the intimate, domestic drama of *The Sorrows of Young Werther*. This novel has always held a special fascination because it was based on Goethe's own experience when he fell deeply in love with a married woman. Fortunately for posterity he broke off the affair in good time, unlike his fictional hero who is driven to suicide. The novel made a remarkable impression on the over-romantic German youth of the day, thousands of whom adopted Werther's distinctive style of dress, a yellow waistcoat and blue jacket, and a considerable number of whom even took their own lives. Massenet shows consummate skill in translating into musico-dramatic terms a story with little outward action. The opera begins with idyllic scenes of family life in which we are shown Werther's first meeting with Charlotte, who is engaged to another man, then builds up gradually yet inevitably to the final tragedy. The music makes both characters stronger and more positive than they

Alfredo Kraus in the title-role of Massenet's Werther, *which was based on Goethe's partly autobiographical novel*

appear in the novel, Massenet even managing to give charm and allure to a predominantly bourgeois heroine. His opera has held the stage ever since its first performance in Vienna on 16 February 1892.

Massenet was equally successful when working on a broader canvas. His technique, whether writing for voices or for the orchestra, was so assured that he could turn with complete ease from one style to another, Wagner-influenced medievalism for *Esclarmonde* (1889), *verismo*-type violence for *La Navarraise* (1894), the miracle play for *Le Jongleur de Notre Dame* (1902). As he produced one success after another he must have been the despair of all his rivals, though really he had so little to fear from them that the anxiety with which he checked the box-office receipts was unnecessary. He has often been criticized for trying too deliberately to please the popular taste: a more balanced view might be that his natural style 219

– delicately crafted, fluently melodic, sweetly erotic in flavour – happened to suit the taste of the audience. He continued to work right up to his death on 13 August 1912, his last operas being produced posthumously at Monte Carlo.

Chabrier, Chausson, Charpentier

Like Gounod and Bizet, Massenet resolutely followed the French tradition, never significantly influenced by developments in Italy or Germany. In this he proved wise, for those of his contemporaries who fell under the spell of Wagner met with no success. Emmanuel Chabrier (1841–94), for instance, having made a reputation with two light operas of typical Gallic vivacity, changed course completely after visiting Bayreuth. His *Gwendoline* (1886) showed that he had sacrificed much of his natural verve in the process of absorbing Wagner's influence. Ernest Chausson (1855–99) admitted that he was haunted by 'the red spectre of Wagner' while he was at work on *Le Roi Arthus*, and when it was produced four years after his death its curious blend of Wagnerian and grand opera elements damned it to oblivion. Gustave Charpentier (1860–1956), a pupil of Massenet, enjoyed one resounding triumph with *Louise*, which he described as a 'musical novel'. This work of startling realism, in which the composer expressed his liberal social outlook, is a celebration of his Bohemian view of Paris. Charpentier was fascinated to the point of obsession by the workpeople of Paris, so he chose to make his heroine a seamstress whose love affair with a young painter is destroyed by her demanding parents. The romantic side of Paris is represented by the scene in which Louise is crowned as the Muse of Montmartre, the city's pleasures by the symbolic character of the Night-prowler. When first seen at the Opéra-Comique on 2 February 1900 the realistic aspects of *Louise* aroused great controversy, but today the opera is appreciated more for its tuneful and affecting score. *Julien* (1913), the sequel to *Louise*, was a surprising failure, and none of Charpentier's other music is of any note.

Debussy

Although performed at the Opéra-Comique only two years after *Louise*, Debussy's *Pelléas et Mélisande* seems to belong to a different age. One of the most revolutionary of all operas, it is nevertheless like no opera composed before or after it. When he saw Maurice Maeterlinck's symbolist play of the same name in 1892, Debussy immediately decided to write incidental music for it. He soon changed his mind and began

Teresa Stratas and Raymond Gibbs in the title-roles of Pelléas et Mélisande, *Debussy's uniquely elusive yet hypnotic opera*

to use almost the whole text as the libretto of a five-act opera. The Impressionist in him was uniquely and irresistibly attracted to the elusive story of Prince Golaud, who marries the mysterious Mélisande whom he has found wandering in a forest, only to suspect that he is losing her to his brother Pelléas. His fierce jealousy drives him to ill-treat Mélisande, even though his suspicions of her are not proved, and then to kill Pelléas. The drama is so tenuous, and the characters so reluctant to express their feelings fully, that everything seems to be happening in a dream-world. The music matches this curious drama, throwing a veil of shadowy orchestral sound over the text and confining the vocal writing within a narrow range which keeps as close as possible to the rise and fall of speech. Debussy manages to suggest suspense and suppressed violence that must inevitably break through.

Everything about this discreet, magical score makes it clear that Debussy was avoiding Wagner's influence and developing an alternative style of music to Wagnerism. The full orchestra is scarcely ever used apart from the interludes which link the various scenes within each act, and there are only a handful of loud passages in the entire score. Debussy employs leitmotifs, but he does not develop them in a symphonic way. When Mélisande finally confesses that she loves Pelléas, she simply sings 'Je t'aime aussi' in a low voice on a single note. Nothing could be less 'operatic', yet the effect is overwhelming. The orchestral writing is an imaginative *tour de force*, creating as it does a magical web of delicately coloured harmonies and half-suggested melodies.

Even before it was first presented on 30 April 1902, *Pelléas et Mélisande* had created a newspaper scandal. Maeterlinck had stubbornly insisted that the role of Mélisande should be sung by his common-law wife, the star of the play, but the manager of the opera house had overruled him and given it to Mary Garden, whom Debussy had been coaching for months. Rival musical factions broke into fisticuffs on the first night, and some of their anger spilt over into the reviews, one of which described this most gently haunting of operatic scores as 'a blistering assault on the ears'. It is oddly fascinating that this thoroughly French opera was launched by two Scottish sopranos, Maggie Teyte following Mary Garden in the role of Mélisande. When Debussy met the latter for the first time he reacted with typical reserve, simply murmuring, 'une autre écossaise?' He was, as his music shows, the master of understatement.

Ravel

As might be expected, Maurice Ravel's contribution to opera was delicate, witty and completely off-beat. *L'Heure espagnole* (1911) is a typical comedy of the Spanish character as seen through French eyes, dealing with the antics of the flirtatious wife of a clock-maker who takes advantage of his absence to entertain a couple of her lovers. Ravel's music simply points the stage action, expanding into lyrical numbers only in the case of the lover who is a poet and for the final Habanera quintet. His other one-act opera, *L'Enfant et les sortilèges*, is a setting of a libretto by Colette, a fanciful story about a selfish child who smashes the furniture and torments the household pets as his boredom explodes into anger, and who is suitably punished when his victims finally turn on him. Ravel was just the man to provide witty music to fit this fantasy, a rare example of genuine musical fun. It was taken all too seriously in 1925 by its first audience, which expressed noisy hostility to the foxtrot sung by the Wedgwood cup and teapot and the love duet for two cats.

Poulenc

If Ravel's *L'Heure espagnole* was naughty, Francis Poulenc's *Les Mamelles de Tirésias* struck the public as being positively outrageous. Guillaume Apollinaire's libretto presents a feminist girl whose balloon-like breasts float away when she decides to leave her husband and become a man. The deserted husband, in retaliation, finds a way of producing thousands of babies each day by means of an incubator. This musical farce is typical of a period in which composers took up any novel idea for an opera, a silly season which quickly passed away. The more serious side of Poulenc is revealed by *Les Dialogues des Carmelites*, a deeply religious opera about a community of nuns who are driven out of their convent during the French Revolution to suffer martyrdom under the guillotine. First produced in 1957 at La Scala, Milan, this conservatively lyrical work was rapidly taken up by the Paris Opéra, Covent Garden and the Metropolitan to become one of the few international successes of recent times. Poulenc's music shows here the qualities which have characterized most French opera from Gounod's time – fastidious treatment of words, an interest in spectacle, careful choice of subject and, above all, refinement.

David Hockney design for Les Mamelles de Tirésias, *the almost farcical opera by Poulenc with a surrealist libretto by Guillaume Apollinaire*

OPERA IN RUSSIA

Russian composers established a distinctive style of opera remarkably quickly once the nationalist movement took hold in the nineteenth century. Opera did not arrive on the scene until the mid-eighteenth century, when Italian operas were occasionally presented at court. Catherine the Great was an opera enthusiast, and it became a more regular feature of royal entertainment after her accession in 1762. The repertoire, however, remained exclusively Italian. Amateurish operas with Russian texts, sometimes making use of national melodies, came into vogue towards the end of the century, but no real progress was made in setting up a Russian school. It was left for Glinka, the first of the nationalist composers, to create single-handed an essentially Russian style, in two operas which influenced all the composers who came after him.

Glinka

Ironically, the man who established the vigorous nationalist Russian school of opera was a thoroughly cosmopolitan dilettante with none of the personal qualities usually associated with an artistic trail-blazer. Mikhail Glinka, who was born at Novospasskoye on 1 June 1804, was described accurately, if unkindly, by Tchaikovsky as 'a talented Russian gentleman of his time, pettily proud, little developed, full of vanity and self-adoration.' But he was also 'the acorn from which the oak of Russian music sprang'.

Glinka suffered all his life from a childhood spent in the care of his maternal grandmother, who brought him up, physically and morally, in an enervating hothouse atmosphere. He lived through a period of tremendous political, social and intellectual upheaval, yet made no positive response to any of the changes taking place around him. He enjoyed financial security all his life. He was attracted to teenage girls, the more empty-headed the better; and the one he married, to whom he was frequently unfaithful, turned the tables on him by taking a new husband without troubling to divorce him first. He suffered from poor health, which he exaggerated to justify regular travel to warmer climates. As his memoirs reveal, he was in many ways a rather pathetic figure.

He began to take an interest in music during his early school days in St Petersburg, though it was some time before he took formal lessons; only when he went to Italy in 1830, at the age of twenty-six, did he begin to study in earnest. He later studied in Berlin. But the more he worked with Italian and German teachers, the more he became determined to develop a revolutionary style, as free of their influence as possible. Within two years of his return home he completed the first truly Russian opera, *A Life for the Tsar* (known in the Soviet Union as *Ivan Susanin*), which was premiered in St Petersburg in 1836. It proved a wild success, admired for its freshness and patriotic appeal, while more perceptive critics and fellow-musicians also appreciated it as fulfilling their nationalist aspirations. The vocal writing owes a good deal to Italian models (not surprisingly, since Glinka had admitted to shedding 'copious floods of tears' over Bellini's *La sonnambula*), but the orchestration is more imaginatively varied than any Italian opera of the period, and was to be emulated by all later Russian composers. Glinka pioneered the use of leitmotifs. Susanin's final recitative, the most imaginative stroke in the opera, is made up of no less than eight motifs from earlier scenes.

Glinka carried his revolutionary ideas much further in his second opera, *Russlan and Ludmilla*, a farrago of magical plot and counter-plot adapted from a poem by Pushkin. Curiously, he abandoned the leitmotif system but in other respects he established further precedents for the style of Russian opera. Heroic declamatory writing is combined with more lyrical, unmistakably national passages, anticipating Mussorgsky. It also abounds in unusual harmonies which effectively express the supernatural elements of the story, as well as incorporating authentic Oriental themes to create the atmosphere of fantasy which Rimsky-Korsakov was later to favour. Finally, there are colourfully scored dances and choruses which must surely have inspired Borodin in his *Prince Igor*.

Russlan and Ludmilla, first given in 1842, was rather too novel for the conservative St Petersburg public and the opera was not a success. Even the warm praise of Liszt, who was visiting Russia, could not console Glinka, who sank into despair and composed nothing more of importance. He felt, with some justification, that his countrymen did not appreciate the importance of his work, and lacking the courage to fight back he took refuge in constant travels through Europe. He returned to Russia occasionally, but the more sophisticated West always lured him back, and he died in Berlin on 15 February 1857.

Mussorgsky

It was some time before Glinka's experiments were followed up, a delay caused by the curious status of Russian composers. They were amateurs in both senses of the word: full of enthusiasm but with little formal training. Indeed, many of their operas were

put together so clumsily that Rimsky-Korsakov took it upon himself to tidy them up. He edited the score of *A Life for the Tsar*, completed Dargomizhsky's *The Stone Guest* and Borodin's *Prince Igor*, re-orchestrated Mussorgsky's *Boris Godunov* and completed his *Khovanshchina*. The first of Glinka's successors, Alexander Dargomizhsky (1813–69), developed in *Russalka* (1856) and *The Stone Guest* (1872) a form of melodic recitative in which the vocal line exactly (and tediously) followed the inflection of the words. But this ideal of dramatic and semi-melodic recitative was carried to a height of inspiration by Mussorgsky, the erratic yet powerful genius of Russian opera.

Born at Karevo on 21 March 1839, Modest Mussorgsky was the son of a wealthy landowner, and therefore set for a life of leisure. He did not consider music as a career, choosing instead to enter a military academy; at seventeen he joined a regiment whose officers devoted most of their energies to heavy drinking, a pastime which was to cause his early death. It was during his brief period of military service that a meeting with Balakirev, who became his teacher for a time, turned his attention to composition. A few early songs indicate that he had an original talent, and his progress might have been orderly and more productive had not the liberation of the serfs in 1863 impoverished his family. He was suddenly forced to work as a government clerk in Russia's unwieldy bureaucracy, an environment which he found so boring that he turned to the bottle in earnest. He subsequently suffered from frequent alcoholic breakdowns, and it was remarkable that he succeeded in composing at all, let alone that *Boris Godunov* should emerge as the greatest Russian opera. The work has a curious history: Mussorgsky composed it in 1868–9, then rewrote it in 1871–2. Since it proved too sombre in its orchestral colouring for contemporary taste, Rimsky-Korsakov made a revised version in 1896 which not only brightened the sound but cut and reordered several scenes; a further version of 1908 restored the deleted scenes. This second Rimsky-Korsakov edition made its way into the international repertoire, and only more recently has Mussorgsky's own second version come into its own. Even so, opera-goers are still more likely to see the opera in Rimsky-Korsakov's version than Mussorg-

Above: *Sketch of the decor for a scene in Glinka's* A Life for the Tsar *(known in the Soviet Union as* Ivan Susanin*)*

Right: *The powerful death scene from Mussorgsky's* Boris Godunov *in the 1976 production at the Bolshoi Theatre in Moscow*

sky's. There is no doubt that on artistic grounds the latter is to be preferred, for its bold imagination far outweighs any lack of polish; yet we should be grateful to Rimsky-Korsakov, for without his well-meaning intervention the score might now be lying in some obscure music library gathering dust.

Mussorgsky prepared the libretto himself, drawing on Pushkin's drama of the same title and on Karamzin's *History of the Russian Empire*. Boris, the guilt-ridden tsar who can never forget that he gained his throne through the murder of the rightful heir, Dimitri, so dominates the drama that his presence is felt even in the scenes in which he does not actually appear, more than half the total number. The secondary characters include the 'false' Dimitri, a young monk who aspires to the throne with the help of the Polish princess Marina, whose scene together provides the love interest in music of Italianate style, at odds with the rest of the opera. Comic relief is afforded by two drunken monks, while touches of tenderness are provided by Boris's children, whose music derives from folksong. More important overall is the chorus, vividly representing the Russian people. In its scope *Boris Godunov* has affinities with Tolstoy's *War and Peace* and Shakespeare's *Henry IV*, presenting the broad sweep of history with the spotlight focussed from time to time on the central character. The most forceful feature of the music is melodic declamation concentrating emotion with electrifying directness, so that the heart and nerve-ends of Boris are completely bared in his Act II monologue and in the Farewell and Prayer of his death scene.

Khovanshchina, alas, remained an unfinished opera, though Mussorgsky worked on it for almost ten years. *Boris Godunov*, rejected, at first, was premiered in 1873 and despite some hostile criticism was revived subsequently every year, which should have encouraged the composer; but his frequent bouts of drunkenness sapped his creative energies. Even in the form we know it, so largely the handiwork of Rimsky-Korsakov, *Khovanshchina* can be recognized as even more intensely national than *Boris Godunov*. The choruses for the Old Believers capture the essence of Russian church music. However, the opera lacks the dramatic concentration of *Boris* and lacks a powerful central character. Mussorgsky's last years make a pitiful story of a genius destroyed by personal weakness: he was dismissed from his clerical post and was obliged to take up the menial job of accompanist in classes for singing students. Thrown out of his lodgings in February 1881, he lived on only for a few weeks in a military hospital, dying on 28 March a few days after his forty-second birthday.

Borodin

It was not alcoholism which prevented Borodin from completing *Prince Igor*, but the rival demands made on his time by science and music, the former always gaining the upper hand. He first conceived the opera in 1870, and though he kept laying it aside in favour of other projects he had outlined all the music before he died seventeen years later. There were loose ends, including much orchestration, which a more professional composer would have wanted to tidy up. The indefatigable Rimsky-Korsakov, with the help of Alexander Glazunov, took on the task of editing it. The story of *Prince Igor*, from a medieval Russian epic, is little more than an excuse for a patchwork of

Scene from Prince Igor, *unfinished on Borodin's death and completed by Rimsky-Korsakov*

scenes, some comic and others romantic, with pride of place given to spectacular dances and choruses. It is less a drama than a series of *tableaux* with predominantly lyrical music often in Italianate style. The most potent Russian flavour, tinged with an oriental element, comes with the Polovtsian Dances of Act II which have an almost barbaric splendour. They range from soft, seductive melody to climaxes of harsh vigour.

Although regularly performed in Russia, *Prince Igor* has been surprisingly neglected in the West. There is exquisite love music for Vladimir (Igor's son) and Kontchakovna, daughter of his captor, and Borodin sustains a yearning lyricism through her languishing nocturne, his tender aria and their passionate duet. The final insult to the composer was the wholesale plundering of his opera for the successful musical *Kismet*.

Tchaikovsky

Although not one of the nationalist group of composers, Tchaikovsky nevertheless gave strong Russian character to his cosmopolitan operas through his basically Slavonic temperament. He did, in fact, experiment in the nationalist style with two early operas, but he was quick to realize this was not suited to his talents. In May 1877 he hit on the fortunate idea of an opera based on Pushkin's *Eugen Onegin*, a subject that might have been made to measure for him. This peom, which Pushkin described as 'a novel in verse in the manner of Byron's *Don Juan*', deals with two characters with whom Tchaikovsky readily identified: in their different ways, they are both defeatists, doomed to frustration in love. Indeed, life and art went hand in hand during the opera's composition; Tchaikovsky succumbed to the charms and tantrums of Antonina Milyukova, and married her. Within three weeks the marriage broke up and he took refuge first in Switzerland and then in Italy, where he completed *Eugen Onegin* in January 1878. Rarely have despair and frustration brought about the composition of such a masterpiece.

The story of *Eugen Onegin* is simple in outline, however subtle its implications. Onegin is a cynical dandy in the Byronic manner who not only rejects Tatyana's declaration of love with supercilious sermonizing, but goes on to flirt openly with her younger sister, Olga, whose lover Lensky challenges him to a duel and is killed. Some years later Onegin again meets Tatyana, now wife of a retired general. Realizing that he has loved her all the time, he arranges to see her privately, but though she confesses to returning his love she declares that honour binds her to her husband, and leaves him to despair.

Apart from the duel scene, this is an intimate, domestic drama far removed from the usual run of operatic subjects. 'How delightful,' Tchaikovsky wrote to his brother, 'to get away from all the commonplace pharoahs, Ethiopian princesses, poisoned chalices, and all the stories about puppet creatures. What poetry is to be found in *Onegin*! I am not blind to its faults. I quite see that it doesn't give scope to full operatic treatment; but the richness of the poetry, the simple, human subject to be found in Pushkin's inspired verse will compensate for whatever it lacks in other ways.' If Tchaikovsky at first felt that *Eugen Onegin* did not 'give scope to full operatic treatment', the libretto, which he adapted himself, nevertheless works splendidly. It affords plenty of opportunities for his special vein of graceful melody, and there are two scenes in which dance music is dramatically justified. He would have been out of his depth with 225

Scene from the Bolshoi production of Eugen Onegin, *Tchaikovsky's opera based on the Byronic 'novel in verse' by Pushkin*

heroic characters, but here they are all of the sensitive, reflective kind to which he could respond with appropriate music.

The first performance of *Eugen Onegin*, given by students at the Moscow Conservatoire on 29 March 1879, was only modestly successful, and it took many years for the opera to establish itself in the international repertoire. Four subsequent operas, *The Maid of Orleans* (1881), *Mazeppa* (1884), *The Enchantress* (1887) and *Iolanthe* (1892), have never become well known outside Russia, but he scored a second international hit with *The Queen of Spades*, another Pushkin setting, this time adapted by Tchaikovsky's brother, Modest. Its melodramatic story concerns a poor officer, Herman, who becomes a gambler in the hope of making a fortune. Learning that an old countess, grandmother of the girl he loves, possesses the secret of three lucky cards which will win every time, he breaks into her house to learn the secret, but so terrifies the old lady that she dies of fright before she can divulge it. Her ghost later visits him and names the three cards, but when he tries his luck at the tables the third card, the ace of hearts, changes before his eyes into the queen of spades.

Tchaikovsky began the opera in January 1890, composed most of it during a visit to Italy, and completed the score within a few months. It opens with an idyllic scene of children playing in a park as the townspeople stroll about gossiping, but from the entrance of the moody Herman the tension mounts steadily through his meeting with Lisa and the Countess, a friend telling of the latter's phenomenal gambling success and the outbreak of a violent storm. There is a ballroom episode that allows the composer to indulge his love of ballet music, before the fateful scene in which Herman enters the Countess's bedroom, culminating in her death. The terrifying scene in which her ghost appears to Herman is perhaps the most dramatic Tchaikovsky ever conceived, and hardly less forceful are those of Lisa's suicide and the tragic finale in the gaming room. The composer had a more powerful sense of theatre than he is usually given credit for. There are also lyrical moments, and the way that these are balanced against declamatory passages on the one hand and *divertissement* music on the other makes *The Queen of Spades* a deeply satisfying work. Like *Eugen Onegin*, it was not an immediate success, but within a few years was acclaimed throughout Europe and the United States and has never lost its popularity.

Rimsky-Korsakov

Composers are rarely the best judges of the durability of their own works, as is shown by Rimsky-Korsakov. Throughout his life he set the greatest store by his operas, rating them far higher than his orchestral music. Outside Russia, however, he figures more prominently in the concert hall than the opera house. He was above all a master of orchestral writing, but there is another, equally important reason. His operas are based on fairytale or magical subjects with a strong leaning towards the oriental, giving them a particular flavour which is not to the taste of Western audiences. They are staged from time to time, but none has made its way into the repertoire, for while they are intriguing as rarities, their lack of human interest prevents our wanting to see them very often.

Stage curtain design by Natalia Gontcharova for The Golden Cockerel, *the best known of Rimsky-Korsakov's satirical operas*

All his operas nevertheless contain a great deal of original, arresting music, as we know from the orchestral suites that Rimsky-Korsakov made from them.

The Golden Cockerel (1907), the last of his operas, has proved the most popular, with its curious blend of the spectacular and the satirical. It includes the coloratura Hymn to the Sun, sung by the young Queen of Shemakha, which like the Song of the Hindu Merchant from *Sadko* is among the world's most famous melodies. All too often, however, Rimsky-Korsakov's vocal writing is superficially brilliant rather than dramatically expressive, more demanding than rewarding to the singer. It is always possible, of course, that tastes will change.

Stravinsky

As might have been expected, Stravinsky took a highly individual approach to opera, changing style between one work and the next and rarely concern-

ing himself with the practical matters of their staging or fitting into the general repertoire. His first venture was *Le Rossignol* ('The nightingale'), produced in Paris during the Diaghilev season of 1914. It is an exotic, fairytale work influenced to some extent by Rimsky-Korsakov. Then came *Mavra* (Paris, 1922), a one-act comic opera in *opera buffa* style complete with arias and other set pieces. A much more impressive work is *Oedipus Rex* (Paris, 1927), a cross between opera and an oratorio which nevertheless stages very effectively. Soloists and chorus all wear masks, and there is no movement, the drama all being carried out in the music. Although Stravinsky seemed determined to keep personal involvement at arm's length, even having Jean Cocteau's text translated into Latin, the emotions of the listener are engaged by the music through which the characters express themselves so vividly. The self-confidence of Oedipus, for example, is made clear by his almost arrogantly florid vocal line, while the gentler character of Jocasta is established by more flowing music. Stravinsky captures the austerity of Greek drama in his writing for the male chorus, its relentless rhythm

A scene from the Glyndebourne Festival production of The Rake's Progress *designed by David Hockney*

suggesting the working of the pitiless gods.

The Rake's Progress (Venice, 1951) represents the peak of the composer's neo-Classical style, and is based on Hogarth's famous series of paintings. It follows a Mozartian pattern of recitative and aria and is scored for a Classical orchestra with harpsichord accompaniment for the recitatives. But its idiom is modern, and this duality of character tends to make the opera too self-conscious. Brilliantly inventive as it is, *The Rake's Progress* remains somewhat heartless.

Prokofiev

Like Stravinsky, Prokofiev ran true to form in his approach to opera, swinging from one stylistic extreme to another. His *The Love for Three Oranges* (Chicago, 1921) is a riotous farce which allows him to exploit his keen sense of irony, while *War and Peace* (Leningrad, 1946) is an epic work with a strong and patently serious sense of patriotism. Based on Tol-

228

stoy's novel, the later opera is divided into two parts, the first dealing with the social activities of its main 'private' characters in times of peace, complete with Tchaikovsky-like ballroom scenes and a strong love interest, the second concerned with the 'public' theme of the defence of Russia against the Napoleonic invasion. The music has directness and power, warmed by enchanting breadth of melody in the first part, and *War and Peace* affords a rewarding experience in performance. Only its length and its heavy demands of its staging have prevented it becoming a repertoire work in the West. An earlier opera, *The Angel of Fire* (Venice, 1955), is widely considered to be Prokofiev's masterpiece, but the violence and unpleasantness of its subject have prevented its becoming a popular work.

Sketches of hussars' costumes for Prokofiev's satirical opera The Love for Three Oranges, *commissioned by the Chicago Opera in 1921*

Shostakovich

Violence is also a stumbling-block in the case of Shostakovich's *Katerina Ismailova* (also known as *Lady Macbeth of Mtsensk*; Leningrad, 1934), a crude yet melodramatically effective study of adulterous passion. The opera won notoriety when two years after its favourable reception it was officially condemned as decadent and offensive. It seems that Stalin himself disapproved. Today, and with all political considerations laid aside, it can be seen as a work of originality and remarkable vitality, which ultimately fails because it is an undigested mixture of styles, even mannerisms. Only in the gloomy convicts' choruses in the last act does the music express any genuinely deep feeling. An earlier opera based on Gogol's grotesque story *The Nose* (Leningrad, 1930) is a witty and inventive satire, but as with many such works is fun when first seen but too slight to return to. Shostakovich had an undoubted talent for opera, but the storm he created at twenty-six with *Katerina Ismailova* made him reluctant to develop it.

Andreyeva as Katerina Ismailova, the heroine of Shostakovich's opera of the same name

CZECH AND HUNGARIAN OPERA

Smetana

The distinctive style of Czech opera was the creation of one man, Bedřich Smetana (1824–84), who showed his nationalist colours with his first work for the stage, *The Brandenburgers of Bohemia* (Prague, 1866). Only a handful of operas had been written in Czech, since German was the official language of what was still a province of the Austrian Empire. (Smetana himself had not attempted to write a letter in Czech until he was thirty-two.) His first opera was a revelation in that it was in the native tongue, introduced a new national music flavour and expressed nationalistic sentiments. Its success confounded his critics in the opera house and led to his being appointed chief conductor at the Provisional Theatre in Prague. The work had been completed three years earlier, and in the meantime Smetana had composed a comic opera which was produced less than four months after *The Brandenburgers*. *The Bartered Bride* did not immediately set the Vltava on fire; but the

muted response was due to the unsettled political situation at the time of the premiere, and within a few weeks this comedy of Bohemian village life had become a resounding success. It has remained a favourite with audiences in Prague, where it reached its two-thousandth performance in 1952. Its simple characters are drawn in the most skilful musical terms, its high spirits never descend into farce, and the score combines warmth with sparkle, vigour with refinement, and includes passages of Mozartian grace. The composer keeps the pulse of Czech folk music racing through the score, though he never draws on actual folk materials.

Dalibor (Prague, 1868), a tribute to a legendary Czech patriot, was less successful, as its progressive music bewildered an audience expecting another lively comedy. The opera was rarely given during his lifetime, but two years after his death it returned to the Prague repertoire and has held a place of honour

Scene from Dalibor, *the opera by Smetana which pleased the patriotic sentiments of the Czech audience of the time but which they found too progressive*

there ever since. In spite of continuing hostility from his colleagues and the deafness that overtook him in 1874, Smetana completed five more operas whose different styles reveal his considerable virtuosity. Of these *The Two Widows* (Prague, 1874) is a conversation-piece of great charm and originality which was later to have an influence on Richard Strauss. *The Bartered Bride* became a popular work with audiences everywhere, and though Smetana's operas have lost some ground to those of Janáček since the 1950s, it is unlikely to lose the public's affection.

Janáček

It might have been expected that Dvořák would become Smetana's operatic heir, and he did in fact compose ten operas. A superb melodist, he unfortunately lacked the ability to give shape and thrust to his dramatic ideas. There are fine moments in the comic *The Devil and Kate* (Prague, 1899) and the romantic *Russalka* (Prague, 1901), but the operas ultimately disappoint, and they are rarely performed outsice Czechoslovakia. Smetana's work was carried on instead by a man who must have seemed the most unlikely candidate until he reached the age of fifty. Leoš Janáček, born on 3 July 1854 in the Moravian village of Hukvaldy, worked for a time as a schoolteacher and choirmaster before he was able to afford advanced music studies in Prague and then, briefly, in Vienna. He disagreed with the academic authorities, holding highly unorthodox theories of his own, including the view that music should follow the rhythms and shapes of the human voice. At twenty-seven, fired by the ambition to found a new style of national music, he embarked on a varied career, teaching, studying folk music and writing choral works and a couple of operas which revealed little individual character. Up to his late forties he made almost no progress as a composer.

Then in 1903, he finally completed *Jenůfa*, which was produced in Brno the following year with considerable success but was not taken up anywhere else. Another twelve years went by before the opera was given in Prague, making the composer, by then sixty-two, an overnight celebrity. The story is set in a Moravian village, but its stark *verismo* treatment of action and characters make it very different from *The Bartered Bride*, and the folk dances introduced into the opera have a rougher quality than those of Smetana, while the music is more astringent and modern in idiom. Janáček's use of Czech speech rhythms result in a short-phrased melodic idiom that is remarkably trenchant yet now and again takes wing in

Marie Collier with David Hillman (centre) and Raimund Herincx in Janáček's The Makropoulos Affair, *a drama of near-immortality*

flights of memorable lyricism. His vocal melodies and their accompanying orchestral figures evoke and sustain a tensely exciting atmosphere. *Káťa Kabanová* (Brno, 1921) is a logical development of *Jenůfa*, its music even more economical and compressed. Its juxtaposition of warm lyrical passages with terse dramatic ones makes the opera satisfy on all levels, placing it among the most impressive works of the twentieth century and securing for it an ever-increasing popularity all over the world. Just as *Káťa Kabanová* reveals the composer's love of humanity, so *The Cunning Little Vixen* (Brno, 1924) expresses his love of nature, not only in its wonderful portrayal of country landscapes and activities, but in its caring yet unsentimental treatment of the animal characters which make up more than half the cast. Two later 231 operas, *The Makropoulos Affair* (Brno, 1926) and *From the House of the Dead* (Brno, 1930), inhabit very different worlds. The first is a study of a woman who has lived for more than three hundred years after drinking a magic potion, has found near-immortality more of a burden than a cause of happiness, and greets her death in the final scene as a welcome release. There is an unattractive dryness about the music of the first two acts, but ample amends are made by the beautiful transfiguring lyrical outburst of the final scene. *From the House of the Dead*, based on Dostoyevksy's novel, offers an unforgettable series of character studies expressed in music which probes deep into the hearts and minds of the wretched prisoners. The subject is gloomy, even harrowing, yet Janáček defiantly proclaims in the music his unshakable faith in human goodness, which prompted him to write at the head of the score: 'In every human being there is a divine spark'. This opera, like the songs and chamber music he composed during the same period, proved that he had not lost the drive and energy of his youth. His health, like his creative powers, showed no sign of decline until he died suddenly in Prague on 12 August 1928, from pneumonia.

Bartók

Hungary has never developed a school of opera which has established itself abroad, the only work in the international repertoire being Bartok's one-act *Duke Bluebeard's Castle* (Budapest, 1918). Although composed before the composer's full maturity, the opera shows originality and a sure sense of dramatic purpose. Derived like *Pelléas et Mélisande* from Maeterlinck, it bears some influence of Debussy, but it has sufficient individuality to cause regret that Bartók never returned to opera. The drama is completely static, with singing parts only for Bluebeard and his new wife Judith, the three former wives being mute roles. The theme is loneliness, which is treated in a symbolic, psychological manner: Bluebeard's tragedy is that his happiness depends on those he loves, whom he is unable to hold except in his memory. The vocal line is directly conditioned by the inflections of the Hungarian language, rendering translation a practical impossibility. Fortunately the drama is basically so simple that it can be appreciated with the aid of a synopsis. But the work makes a genuinely dramatic impact through its expressive music. It has kept its place in the repertoire remarkably well considering that it plays for just under an hour and is difficult to pair with another short opera for a complete evening's programme.

A portrait of Bartók, whose Duke Bluebeard's Castle, a study of loneliness, makes a dramatic impact in the theatre in spite of its static character

GERMANY AFTER WAGNER

One cannot help feeling sorry for the German composers who followed Wagner: how could they possibly hope to approach, let alone rival, masterpieces of the order of *Tristan and Isolde*, *The Mastersingers* and *The Ring*? Those who slavishly took up his methods and style only produced pale carbon copies of the real thing, yet it was difficult for any composer to remain unaffected by the revolution he had brought about. By a curious irony the most sucessful of his disciples found international fame by writing a fairytale opera for children. Engelbert Humperdinck (1854–1921) won a Mendelssohn Prize in 1879 which gave him the funds to travel to Italy to continue his compositional studies, and it was there that he met Wagner. The older man was so impressed by him that he invited him to Bayreuth to assist in the preparation of *Parsifal*. A few years later, after he had returned home, Humperdinck was asked by his sister to supply music for a play she had written for children based on the Grimm story *Hansel and Gretel*. He did so with some reluctance, but later he became so fascinated by the subject that he extended the simple music he had already composed into the three-act opera which has established a place in the world repetoire as the only really sucessful opera for children, especially as a Christmas entertainment. The style of the orchestral writing is both Wagnerian and symphonic, but the score is lightened by simple children's songs which give it an easy charm. Humperdinck's later operas were relative failures, leaving it for Richard Strauss who had arranged for the premiere of *Hansel and Gretel* at Weimar in 1893 to bring German opera back into the limelight.

Strauss

Before even considering his first opera, Richard Strauss was famous for the tone-poems *Don Juan* and *Death and Transfiguration*, which provoked considerable controversy in 1889. He was born in Munich on 11 June 1864, son of Germany's foremost horn player, Franz Strauss, and composed his first song at the age of six. Although he had secured a conducting appointment and presented his first orchestral works to the public by the time he was twenty, two early operas met with little success; it was not until 1905 that *Salome* created a sensation in Dresden. Its libretto, a German translation of Oscar Wilde's play,

Scene from Hansel and Gretel, *a favourite opera for children composed by Humperdinck, one of Wagner's keenest disciples*

deals with Salome's dancing for King Herod so that she may demand the head of the John the Baptist, which she fondles and kisses in a final scene of neurotic horror. Strauss matched this gruesome action in music of dissonant harmonies and almost sensual richness of textures which runs an unbroken course in one act of mounting tension. Though no longer shocking, *Salome* continues to fascinate by virtue of its rhythmic drive and colourful orchestration. It makes heavy demands on the singers, Salome's part involving an unusually wide range with huge leaps from one one note to another, and all the voices have to compete against mammoth orchestral forces.

The next Struass opera, *Elektra* (Dresden, 1909), introduced as librettist Hugo von Hofmannsthal, a dramatist of the utmost poetic refinement who collaborated with the composer over a number of fruitful years. As with *Salome*, the music makes a direct onslaught on the emotions, though this time there is a greater sense of genuine tragedy. The opera is based on Sophocles's play, concerned with Elektra's obsessive desire for revenge on her mother, Clytemnestra, for her complicity in the murder of Agamemmon, a Classical theme which had assumed new significance as a result of Freud's analysis of ancient mythology. Strauss makes effective use of leitmotifs and carries

Anja Silja as Salome, the degenerate character so vividly portrayed in Richard Strauss's opera which created a scandal in 1905

his harmonic idiom to the point of becoming virtually atonal, his complex score alternating lush melodic warmth with harsh distance. No opera is more dramatically condensed and compulsive than *Elektra*, which has its audience emotionally stunned by the time the curtain falls.

Strauss must have felt he could proceed no further along the path of violence, and he made a most dramatic *volte-face* in *Der Rosenkavalier* (Dresden, 1911), a sentimental comedy of manners set in eighteenth-century Vienna. The story concerns a Marschallin giving up her lover Octavian (the 'Knight of the Rose'), a mezzo trouser-role, so that he can marry the young girl of his choice. Strauss, no less than Puccini, was in love with the soprano voice, and *Der Rosenkavalier* gave him the ideal chance to indulge himself. The trio of the third act must surely contain the most sublimely blended music for women's voices ever composed, and the duets for the young lovers are simply exquisite. Musical characterization reaches its peak with the Marshallin, especially in the monologue in which she recalls her innocence when she married and muses over the time to come when she will no longer attract new young lovers. (Though often misrepresented, she was intended by Strauss to be no more than thirty-two.) The comedy element is provided by Baron Ochs, a character who lacks all the Marschallin's sensitivity and whose clumsy lechery leads him to humiliation in the last act. In its combination of comedy with genuine feeling, *Der Rosenkavalier* ranks alongside *Falstaff* and *The Mastersingers*. The music is less complex than that of *Salome* or *Elektra*, returning to a more diatonic idiom, and relies on a flow of engaging, often erotic melody. The voluptuous floating soprano line became a hallmark of his later operas.

The ingenious Hofmannsthal next thought up *Ariadne auf Naxos*, a one-act opera designed to be performed after Molière's comedy *Le Bourgeois Gentilhomme* in place of the concluding ballet. This extravagant work was premiered at Stuttgart in 1912, and productions followed in other cities including London, where the Molière was given in a translation by Somerset Maugham. Two things mitigated against its becoming an established repertory piece. First, opera-goers were likely to be bored by the play, while theatre-goers would not necessarily enjoy watching an opera. Secondly, having to engage both a company of actors and a company of singers for one evening's entertainment was found to be monstrously expensive. Strauss and Hofmannsthal accordingly concocted a splendid Prologue to replace the play which would explain *Ariadne auf Naxos* and provide a full evening of opera. In the Prologue, an

Josephine Barstow in the title-role with Norma Burrowes as Zdenka, dressed as a boy, in the English National Opera production of Arabella

opera company and a troupe of *commedia dell'arte* players are told that their entertainments are to be presented simultaneously so as to be over in time for a firework display, causing an outbreak of fury from the idealistic Composer (soprano trouser-role). Creating a character to extol the value and power of music appealed strongly to Strauss, who repeated the device in his last opera, *Capriccio* (Munich, 1942). The second act is a remarkably skilful concoction of high drama and broad comedy presented side by side. For this unique work Strauss uses a chamber orchestra of thirty-six players, a far cry from the huge forces he had demanded before. His style was to change in other respects too: he wrote significantly to Hofmannsthal, 'I have now cast off the whole armoury of Wagner for ever'.

He was fifty-two and universally acknowledged as a leading composer, with thirty-three more years to live. But he did not develop any further, and though inspiration fired a few of his later works, others had less distinction. Strauss had to face the problems that come to all composers who achieve maturity and success early in their careers. He never needed to seek advice, and even if he had, nobody would have dared offer any; and since he was not a man of vision like Wagner, there was no force within him to drive

Elisabeth Schwarzkopf as the Marschallin in Der Rosenkavalier, *a charming comedy of manners showing Strauss at his most romantic*

that although he was hounded to some extent by the Nazi regime after 1935 he stayed on in Germany and continued with his work regardless. There is no reason to blame him for this: the world to which he and his music belonged had vanished years before.

He managed to overcome the pretentious text of *Die Frau ohne Schatten* (Vienna, 1919) and fill it with some of his richest music, so that it still holds the stage, and in *Arabella* (Dresden, 1933) he recaptured a fair measure of the glamour and melodic warmth of *Der Rosenkavalier*. For *Intermezzo* (Dresden, 1924) he wrote his own libretto, drawing on incidents from his own domestic life. His final work for the stage, *Capriccio* (Munich, 1942), will always fascinate opera-goers, because its subject is a dramatization of the argument as to whether words or music are of greater importance in opera. A young countess, portrayed in exquisite music as Strauss's ideal woman, tries to choose between two rivals for her affections, a poet and a musician, but at the end she still cannot make a decision. The work is the most sophisticated of all operative conversation-pieces, culminating in a scene for the countess alone in which she sings the last of the rapturous arias which Strauss lavished on the soprano voice. It is surely the most fitting end to his career as an opera composer, though before his death on 8 September 1949 he found inspiration for the no less impressive *Four Last Songs*.

Schoenberg, Berg

The only German composer to have made a lasting impact after Strauss is Alban Berg (1885–1935), whose two operas have established a place in the international repertoire even though they concede little to conventional taste. His mentor, Schoenberg, has been less fortunate, though the practical problems of staging his operas are largely to blame. *Erwartung* ('Expectation'), a psychological melodrama which simply shows a woman searching for her lover in a dark wood and finally stumbling over his dead body, is a short work that is difficult to slot into an operatic evening, great though its dramatic impact may be. Composed in 1909, it had to wait fifteen years for its first performance. *Moses and Aaron* presents even greater difficulties, for it is so static that it comes closer to oratorio than opera; and though Schoenberg had written two acts by 1932 he laid it aside for almost twenty years and then died in 1951 before making any progress with the projected third act. Composed in the twelve-note manner its music had unexpected emotional power, yet it is difficult to imagine it ever becoming a repertoire work.

Berg's *Wozzeck* was conceived in 1914, but com-

him forward. He married in his early twenties, and though his temperamental wife was responsible for some stormy domestic scenes, he had so much affection for her that the marriage survived. A practical, sociable man, he arranged his business affairs well and took his relaxation in simple pleasures such as the card game of Skat, which is featured in the opera *Intermezzo*. He was not an intellectual, and the sophisticated ideas of Hofmannsthal mostly passed right over his head. Nor was he a political man, so

position was interrupted by the war and the score was not completed until 1921. Even then, the apathy of managements was such that the opera did not have its premiere until 1925, in Berlin. Expressionistic and neurotic, it presents in the character of Wozzek a universal figure representative of all poor and oppressed victims of human society. The mostly atonal music is continuous throughout each of the three acts, each of which is cast in a specific musical form. Act I consists of five 'character-pieces', a rhapsody, a passacaglia and so on; Act II is a symphony in five movements; Act III is a set of six 'inventions'. There is no need, however, for the audience to be aware of this structure, for the music has such dramatic power that it rivets the attention on the characters and action. The voice parts are written in a flexible declamatory style known as Sprechgesang, or 'speech-song', and the principal characters have leitmotifs. *Wozzeck* affords a rewarding, unforgettable experience in the opera house, if not a very comfortable one.

Berg's second opera, *Lulu*, remained incomplete at his death, and for forty years it was only seen in this two-act form. The third act, however, was complete except for some of the orchestration. It was the composer's widow who stood in the way of its being prepared for performance, imposing a complete ban on the material and even refusing scholars permission to study it. Only after her death in 1976 was the way clear for *Lulu* to be given complete in a version by the Austrian composer-conductor Friedrich Cerha. The world premiere was presented in Paris in 1979, to be followed by productions in many other cities, including New York in 1980 and London in 1981. *Lulu* is musically more advanced than *Wozzeck*, employing the twelve-note technique and having a symmetrical dramatic and musical structure whose point of balance is the orchestral interlude between the two scenes of Act II. Its complexities are too great for the ear to take in during performance, but fortunately *Lulu*, like *Wozzeck* before it, exerts a compulsive dramatic spell. Where it may be considered less satisfying than *Wozzeck* is in its subject matter, for whereas Wozzeck arouses sympathy and pity, Lulu is not a character who touches the feelings. She is presented as a *femme fatale* or, more pretentiously, the 'eternal feminine', but since her sole attraction is her sexuality, and she is devoid of charm and intelligence, she is a passive, lifeless figure when compared to, say, Carmen or Manon Lescaut. She is made interesting, both in Berg's opera and the two plays by Frank Wedekind on which it is based, only through the characters who surround her. Despite this flaw, Berg's *Lulu* is one of the most successful attempts to bring a radically new musical style into opera.

Henze

Since Strauss and Berg the most successful German opera composer has been Hans Werner Henze (b 1926), whose operas combined traditional and novel elements in a sometimes uneasy alliance. His first full-length opera, *Boulevarde Solitude* (Hanover, 1952), an updated version of the Manon Lescaut story, showed his remarkable skill and ingenuity, which he exploited in a number of subsequent works in a variety of styles. One of the most satisfying is *Der junge Lord* (Berlin, 1965), which allows full rein to his gift for satire, directed in this case against social snobbery and bourgeois hypocrisy. More ambitious in scale and richer in tone, *The Bassarids* (Salzburg, 1966) reveals the inconsistencies which so often accompany too ready a facility. Henze gives the impression that he has never been too seriously committed to his work, and in 1970 he confessed that he believed opera was 'finished'. He even called *We Come to the River* (London, 1976) 'actions for music' as distinct from an opera, and sadly it contained more actions than music of apparent value. His earlier operas, however, deserve to survive for their freshness and imaginative flair.

Overleaf: A scene from Berg's Lulu, *with Karan Armstrong in the 'eternal temptress' title-role*

Henze, who brought novelty and flair to his early operas but now believes that opera is 'finished'

ITALY AFTER VERDI

Opera in Italy was so dominated by Verdi that the other composers who occasionally emerged from the shadows inevitably appeared second-rate. Furthermore, they were next faced by the arrival of Puccini, whose *Manon Lescaut* was produced in 1893 just eight days before the old master's *Falstaff* and immediately established him as the most likely successor. The composer who suffered most by these cruel comparisons was Amilcare Ponchielli (1834–86), who was born five years before Verdi launched his first opera and who was to be eclipsed a few years after his death by the younger man who had been one of his pupils. He was a worthy man who rose from a poor background to become the respected professor of composition at the Milan Conservatoire and to produce nine more than competent operas. He achieved lasting success with only one, *La Gioconda* (Milan, 1876), which is one of those operas that survives in spite of criticism that it is crudely scored and old-fashioned in conception. It does lack subtlety, for Ponchielli ignored the literary pretentions of the libretto by Boito, providing music of vigorous, lyrical abandon to drive on its melodramatic plot. It is difficult, however, to resist the generous flood of show-stopping arias it affords the five principals.

A man of the utmost cultural refinement, Arrigo Boito (1842–1918) was not cut out for the tough practicalities of Italian opera. He embarked on a career as a writer and critic, even attacking fellow composers for ignoring progressive movements evolving in other countries. His *Mefistofele* (Milan, 1868) led to fights inside and outside La Scala as traditionalists and progressives gave vent to their feelings, and the opera was withdrawn after three performances by order of the police. However, after revision the opera enjoyed a huge success in Bologna seven years later. It is based on both parts of Goethe's *Faust*, and is more faithful to its spirit than any other operatic version; it also includes fine arias in the best Italian tradition, so it is surprising that it has not enjoyed greater popularity. In addition to his composition, Boito will always be remembered for having persuaded Verdi to compose *Otello* and *Falstaff*, for which he wrote librettos of unsurpassed quality.

Another composer remembered for only one of several operas, Ruggiero Leoncavallo (1858–1919) based the libretto of *Pagliacci* ('clowns') on a sensational murder trial at which his father was judge. Prior to this he had composed two operas which failed to secure production, one of them on the story of the ill-fated English poet Thomas Chatterton. The immediate success of *Pagliacci* (Milan, 1892) led to the hope that he would make a considerable career, but none of his subsequent operas and operettas won any favour, though his version of *La Bohème* (Venice, 1897) might have established a place in the repertoire if Puccini had not produced his superior opera on the same theme a few months earlier. *Pagliacci* belongs to the *verismo* school, an effective slice of real life which brings its character to life in highly emotional arias supported by vivid orchestral writing. Fate at least smiled on Leoncavallo in giving *Pagliacci* a companion piece, Mascagni's *Cavalleria rusticana*, to make up a double bill which looks like enduring for ever.

Like Leoncavallo, Pietro Mascagni (1863–1945) was a prolific composer who hit the jackpot only once, and with his first opera. 'It is a pity,' he once remarked, 'that I wrote *Cavalleria* first; I was crowned before I was king.' He was a pupil of Ponchielli at the same time as Puccini, with whom he shared lodgings for a period, the two young men indulging in pranks which Puccini later incorporated into the libretto of *La Bohème*. He entered the one-act *Cavalleria*

Mascagni's Cavalleria Rusticana *in the Zeffirelli production at Covent Garden starring Placido Domingo as Turiddu*

rusticana (Rome, 1890) for a competition sponsored by the publishing house of Sonzogno, emerging an easy winner. Its story of Sicilian village life is passionate and violent, expressed in music which makes a direct onslaught on the emotions. The score is alive with warm-hearted melodies whose directness immediately appealed to audiences weary of post-Wagnerian grandeur. It is the epitome of *verismo*; the low-life characters it portrays are all too true to life. Aware of his limitations as a composer, Mascagni embarked on a successful conducting career. His greatest mistake was to embrace fascism when Mussolini came to power, composing all manner of choral and orchestral works to celebrate the new regime. Most of his fellow musicians rejected him, and when the dictator was overthrown he was stripped of his property and honours. It was a sad end for a man who had given the world one of its best-loved operas.

A more admirable side of Mascagni's character was shown by his championship of a slightly younger rival composer, Umberto Giordano (1867–1948), whose reputation rests similarly on a single work, *Andrea Chénier* (Milan, 1896). Based on the life of the famous poet of the French Revolution, this opera affords yet another example of direct, virile melody giving memorability to a score in which subtlety and refinement have no place. Boldness of characterization and orchestral colour are again the ingredients of success. *Fedora* (Milan, 1898), a Romantic drama which provides a Cook's tour of Paris, Switzerland and St Petersburg, gives much rewarding music to the singers but has never enjoyed the popularity of *Andrea Chénier*.

The last of these 'one-work' composers who worked in the shadows of Verdi and Puccini, Francesco Cilèa (1866–1950) was the odd man out. A man of gentle disposition, he lacked the force of character to cut his way to the top in opera and, having achieved success at thirty-six with *Adriana Lecouvreur* (Milan, 1902), he chose the quieter life of music professor and contented himself with writing instrumental music. His renunciation of opera is to be regretted, for he sounded a note of restraint and refinement at a time when most voices were raised in relatively crude vigour and violence. *Adriana Lecouvreur*, a tragedy based with blithe disregard for historical accuracy on the life of the eighteenth-century actress of the Comédie-Française, was perfectly tailored to his gifts for delicacy of sentiment and exquisite lyricism. In addition to the poignant arias for the heroine, the score presents an ingenious flow of subtle melodies with a highly personal flavour. The role of Adriana remains a favourite with prima donnas.

Puccini

The operas of Puccini are so universally popular, and their music flows with such spontaneous ease, that one might imagine he was a man who led a charmed life and found composition easy. Both suppositions are entirely false: his personal life was far from happy, while each of his mature operas, which he laboured long and hard to perfect, was greeted with coldness by the critics and sometimes with noisy hostility by the first-night audiences. His personal problems were due to his growing up in a home dominated by women, while his artistic difficulties were the result of his having to forge a new style, having decided neither to carry on the tradition of Verdi nor take up the *verismo* manner in vogue at the time.

Giacomo Puccini was born on 22 December 1858 into the fifth generation of a musical family in the Tuscan town of Lucca. He was only five years old when his father died, leaving him and his brother Michele to grow up with their mother and five sisters. He was expected eventually to succeed to the position of organist and choirmaster that his father had held, and was given the appropriate education. His earliest compositions, written at sixteen, were organ fantasies which he played in the church, often shocking priests and congregation alike by introducing into them local folksongs and popular opera tunes. The ambition to become an opera composer came to him one night in 1876 when he had walked twenty miles to Pisa and back to see *Aida*. 'Listening to *Aida*,' he recalled,' I felt that a musical window had opened for me.' Another of his recollections is even more revealing: 'God touched me with His little finger and said, "Write for the theatre – mind well, only for the theatre!" And I have obeyed the supreme command.' While Puccini was always aware of his worth he never over-estimated his genius. He realized he could never master the broad sweep of Verdi or Wagner, but he was convinced that he had a more perfect sense of theatre than either of these musical giants. He accepted his limitations with regard to the dramatic subjects he chose and the characters they involved. The heroics of *Il trovatore* and the colossal scope of *The Ring* were not for him, nor could he ever create a character in the mould of Manrico or Siegfried.

The staging of his first opera, the one-act *Le Villi* (Milan, 1884), came about in curious circumstances. Puccini had moved from Lucca to Milan at the age of twenty-two to continue his studies, and was fortunate to have Amilcare Ponchielli as one of his teachers. Having completed his three-year course, and living in the most impecunious state, he dashed off the score of *Le Villi* in such a hurry for a competition that the judges found it too untidy to give it more than a passing glance before rejecting it out of hand. When, a few months later, Puccini sang and played some extracts from it at a private party in Milan, Arrigo Boito and other guests were so impressed that they decided to raise the money to have it put on in the city's Teatro dal Verme. It enjoyed a modest success, and the publishing house of Ricordi bought the rights and commissioned a new opera from him for La Scala. Although this was clearly the chance of a lifetime, Puccini wrestled for five years to complete *Edgar*, the work thrust upon him, because it was a subject quite unsuited to his talents and its libretto was fatally clumsy and inept. When *Edgar* (Milan, 1889) proved the expected fiasco, he determined that in future he would refuse to set any text until he was satisfied with its every detail.

It was fortunate that Giulio Ricordi was not dismayed by the failure of *Edgar* but continued to have faith in him. The choice of *Manon Lescaut* for the next opera was a daring one, for Prévost's novel had already been successfully set by Massenet, but Puccini was unperturbed: 'Massenet feels its as a Frenchman, with powder and minuets; *I* shall feel it as an Italian, with desperate passion.' There were desperate passions over the libretto, to which no fewer than five writers contributed, two of whom, Giuseppe Giacosa and Luigi Illica, were later to collaborate on the three most popular of Puccini's operas, *La Bohème*, *Tosca* and *Madama Butterfly*. The story of the frivolous Manon and her long-suffering Chevalier Des Grieux was ideal, for Puccini had a tremendous flair for portraying fragile heroines and simple love affairs in his music. *Manon Lescaut* was produced on 1 February 1893 at the Teatro Regio in Turin. It was a complete success, establishing Puccini as the strongest talent among Italy's young composers. Within a year productions were staged throughout Italy, in Germany, Russia and South America, and when it reached Covent Garden in 1894 Bernard Shaw, then London's most celebrated music critic, declared: 'Puccini looks to me more like the heir to Verdi than any of his rivals'.

Several features of *Manon Lescaut* were to remain Puccini's hallmarks. The arias are less elaborately planned than those of Donizetti or Verdi, their melodic phrases shorter though no less effective in expressing strong human emotion. They also grow out of the preceding music, so there is no feeling of their being deliberately placed as set numbers. His orchestral palette covers a wide range of delicate colour, and his harmony is suave and daring. He constantly

Maria Callas in the title role of Tosca, *Puccini's spine-chilling melodrama of politics, sexual jealousy and sadism set in Rome at the time of Napoleon*

studied new trends in such composers as Debussy and Richard Strauss, but he was too individual to be radically influenced by them. His own idiom was thoroughly Italian in its emphasis on melody.

In 1884, only a few months after the production of *Le Villi*, Puccini eloped with Elvira Gemignani, wife of a former school-friend, an indiscretion which had a lasting effect on his life and work. Unable to marry until 1904, when Elvira's lawful husband died, they lived together for twenty years in a liaison regarded as particularly scandalous in a Catholic society. Romance soon wore thin, for Elvira proved incapable of sharing in his artistic activities and after a short time developed into a jealous shrew. This unhappy do- 241

mestic situation caused a morbid obsession with moral guilt and feminine suffering, accounting for the curious blend of tenderness and sadism with which he treated the heroines of so many of his operas after *Manon Lescaut*. The first of them, however, is portrayed with pure sympathy, and there is no doubt that the character of Mimì drew him to *La Bohème* in the first place. The subject was a difficult one to handle dramatically, for the libretto had to be strung together from different episodes in Mürger's novel and affords no sense of conflict. It simply shows the first meeting between Mimì and Rodolfo and two later reconciliations after unspecified lovers' quarrels, with Mimì dying at their last encounter. They are characters new to opera, the boy and girl from next door acting out a day-to-day drama. They exert fascination through the realistic way in which Puccini presents them, which he was able to achieve only by his insistence on every detail of the libretto being right for his purpose.

La Bohème presents its characters in such a convincing setting that their behaviour always seems logical, even inevitable. The horseplay of Rodolfo and his friends is not just a good comedy scene: it establishes the irresponsibility of his character. Similarly, the scene outside the Café Momus places the lovers firmly in the context of a social group whose lighthearted philosophy does not include the possibility of marriage or even the formation of a permanent relationship. The setting of Act III, a Paris customs-gate, with the chill of a February morning conveyed by a shuddering of bare fifths from the cellos and falling snowflakes depicted by flutes and harp, forms the ideal background to the couple's reunion. Puccini's unfailing sense of theatre is revealed again in Act IV, when Mimì and Rodolfo meet for the last time in the garret where they first met, after a scene of similar skylarking. The libretto is so direct and economical that there is not a surplus word, and the music matches it by sticking to essentials and cutting out rhetoric. The score is more flexible than that of *Manon Lescaut*, the lyrical outbursts briefer and more telling, the orchestration more delicate, and the transitions from one mood to another more adroitly managed. Although the public were enchanted by *La Bohème* (Turin, 1896), the critics at the premiere failed to appreciate Puccini's subtleties and gave it a mainly unfavourable reception. One even went so far as to pronounce, 'It will leave no great trace upon the history of our lyric theatre',

Opposite: *The affecting scene from the final act of Puccini's opera* La Bohème *in which Mimì dies of consumption in front of the grief-stricken Rodolfo*

Yasuko Hayashi as Madam Butterfly, a character who develops convincingly through Puccini's most famous opera from ingénue to tragic heroine

words which one can only hope he lived long enough to eat.

From that time onwards Puccini never repeated himself, each new opera having a different locale and dramatic flavour. After the intimate *La Bohème* came the melodramatic *Tosca* (Rome, 1900) with its bloodthirsty story of politics, torture, murder and suicide. The immensely complex plot of Victorien Sardou's play is brilliantly reduced to an opera with only three main characters, in which events move at breakneck speed – so fast, in fact, that a few loose ends are rarely noticed in the excitement. Two of the characters are portrayed in most powerful music, the prima donna, Tosca, who is prepared to kill in order to save her lover, and the chief of police, Baron Scarpia, whose sadistic nature is established by the savage

243

Amy Shuard in the title-role of Turandot, *the last and most ambitious of Puccini's operas which was completed after his death by Franco Alfano*

opening chords of the opera. The music is broader than that of *La Bohème*, despite Cavaradossi's two arias and Tosca's 'Vissi d'arte', and the action allows for none of the delicate musical nuances that characterize the earlier work. Whereas Mimì's death is presented in gentle, hushed tones, those of Tosca, Scarpia and Cavaradossi are discordantly brutal and quick. Puccini's sense of theatre allows him to turn the screws to maximum effect in the off-stage torturing of Cavaradossi and his death by firing squad, and *Tosca* packs a more powerful dramatic punch than any of his other operas. Its brutality offended many of the critics at the time, and even though audiences have always found it gripping, the music is still condemned in certain quarters for its unrelenting violence and lack of subtlety.

After this Puccini made a complete about-turn, choosing for his next subject the fragile tragedy of *Madam Butterfly* (Milan, 1904). In its original form this opera was met by such outbursts of catcalls and laughter at La Scala that the composer withdrew it after the first performance for revision, notably by dividing up the long second act to produce a three-act opera. Three months after the disastrous premiere the opera was given in its revised form at Brescia and was a gratifying success. At first glance *Madam Butterfly* may seem to be exploiting sentimentality, and Puccini certainly plays on the pathos of the geisha heroine. Closer examination, however, reveals that the work has a greater stature than this, firstly because Butterfly herself is a genuinely tragic character, developing from the naive child-bride in Act I, through newly found dignity in Act II, to the self-sacrificing mature woman of Act III, and secondly because the music is on such a high level of refinement. The exoticism of the music is an integral part of the score, and steely strength lies close below the apparently easy, shimmering surface.

Puccini continued to extend his style in subsequent works, even branching out into *verismo* for *Il tabarro* ('The cloak'), and into comedy for *Gianni Schicchi*, two of the contrasted operas in the triple bill known as *Il trittico* (New York, 1918). An event in his stormy marital life influenced two of his later operas, *Suor Angelica* (the remaining work in the *Trittico*) and *Turandot*. In 1908 Elvira drove to suicide a servant girl whom she had wrongfully accused of having an affair with Puccini. She was prosecuted for defamation of character, the court found her guilty, and the affair was only resolved after an appeal and a settlement to the dead girl's family. It is surely not fanciful to see Elvira reflected as the cruel Principessa of *Suor Angelica* and the vengeful Turandot, with the unfortunate servant girl represented by Angelica and Liù. The composer found some consolation in his travels, his enjoyment of high living and his passion for fast cars and mechanical gadgets of all kinds. The most important and successful of his later works are *La fanciulla del West* ('The girl of the golden west', New York, 1910) and the unfinished *Turandot*, which was completed by Franco Alfano and first performed at La Scala in 1926. *La fanciulla del West* is notable for its vitality and the composer's brilliant evocation of the Californian setting. It shows an increasing mastery of orchestration, looking forward in this respect to *Turandot*, the most ambitious of all the operas. Here Puccini at last attempted the grand style and succeeded in producing a work that is as powerful in its achievement as it is in conception. Turandot herself is a character in truly heroic mould, while Liù is the last example of the composer's ill-fated *ingénues*. One can only conjecture what the composer would have gone on to achieve had he not died a victim of cancer on 29 November 1924.

ENGLAND

Britten

It is ironic that England, which operatically had lain dormant for two and a half centuries, should produce the most successful modern opera composer. It is also appropriate that Benjamin Britten should have been born on St Cecilia's Day (22 November) in 1913, for he was a man who lived almost exclusively for music. He was no more than seventeen when he determined to make composing his career, an ambition that there was little hope of realizing in the England of that time. He suffered many frustrations at first, including the refusal of permission to use a travelling bursary to go to Vienna to study with Alban Berg, but he managed in 1935 to obtain work supplying incidental music for documentary films and other music for radio and theatre. This, coupled with his flair for songwriting, was an early indication that his future lay largely in the opera house; though it was not until 1914 that the operetta *Paul Bunyan* was produced in New York, where he had gone to live in the summer of 1939. Disappointed by its failure, and homesick for his native Suffolk, in 1942 Britten returned to England, where he was exempted from military service on account of his pacifist principles, and spent most of the next three years on his first opera, *Peter Grimes*. Its premiere at the Sadler's Wells Theatre on 7 November 1945 established him as a major composer and put England on the operatic map. It has since become one of the most frequently performed modern operas all over the world.

There are several interesting points about *Peter Grimes*. Its central character is a social outcast in a Suffolk fishing community, reflecting Britten's own feeling of loneliness in society, caused partly by his withdrawn nature and partly by his full-time concern with his art. (This role was written specifically for his lifelong friend Peter Pears, for whom he wrote leading tenor roles in all his later operas.) *Peter Grimes* is traditional in structure, containing arias and other set-pieces though each act is continuous – rather like Verdi's *Otello*. It is also tonal; Britten's music is always rooted in the past without sounding old-fashioned. Specifically *Peter Grimes* is concerned with the sea, present in all its moods in scene after scene and treated symphonically in the so-called 'sea interludes' which open each of the three acts and connect the two scenes in each, and which are numbered among the finest orchestral sea-pictures ever composed. The opera also reveals the composer as a master of musical characterization.

Britten later tended to favour operas on a smaller scale, though he composed two further works in the manner of *Peter Grimes*. The first was *Billy Budd* (London, 1951), a tragedy of naval life with an all-male cast and a central character who represents another of Britten's preoccupations, that of human beings destroyed by their innocence. The opera has not proved so popular as *Peter Grimes*, but its music and its sense of drama are certainly not inferior. Then came *Gloriana* (London, 1953), commissioned to celebrate the coronation of Elizabeth II, a work of considerable melodic inspiration with splendid choruses. It had an unhappy launching to an audience of royalty, heads of state and political celebrities, few of whom have been noted for the musical taste of their predecessors.

Relaxing in Venice from work on The Turn of the Screw: *(foreground, clockwise) John Piper, Benjamin Britten, Peter Pears and Myfanwy Piper*

Scene from Death in Venice, *Britten's sensitive opera based on the short novel by Thomas Mann with ballet a positive element in the drama*

opera. This involves the twelve notes of the scale, but there is no recourse to twelve-note techniques in any sense, Britten merely using the theme to give unity to the score. The music is brilliant in evoking the atmosphere of the household haunted by the ghosts of two former servants who exert a powerful hold over the minds of two children, themselves highly ambiguous characters. Britten's operatic version for *A Midsummer Night's Dream* (Aldeburgh, 1960) treats Shakespeare's comedy in an unusually happy way, giving the fairies the greatest importance and placing all the action apart from the final scene in the enchanted wood. The music flows on three different idiomatic levels to differentiate the fairies, the lovers and the comic rustics, faithfully reflecting the spirit of Shakespeare's lines.

After a somewhat less felicitious experiment in television opera with *Owen Wingrave* (BBC, 1971), the composer rounded off his operatic work with *Death in Venice* (Aldeburgh Festival, 1973), a sensitive and deeply felt adaptation of the short novel by Thomas Mann. The central character is again a solitary man, this time a writer reaching the end of his life who feels that he has sacrificed too many pleasurable experiences to the pursuit of his career. He is lured to forsake his orderly ways in a search for beauty personified in a young boy, a character who expresses himself by dancing, thus introducing ballet as a dramatic element. Even in this last opera Britten was experimenting in new directions, and mastering them by virtue of his instinctive dramatic sense. He remains unique among the composers of his time for following his inspiration and trying out new methods without confusing or alienating the opera-going public. He had also worked out a new form of short dramatic work for performance in church, the 'church parable', calling for only six or seven instruments to accompany the singers, and all three of these pieces have been widely played. His ability to compose effective music for intimate or large-scale works, as the situation demanded, should ensure Britten a permanent place in dramatic music. He had seen his operas taken up all over the world before he died at Aldeburgh on 4 December 1976.

Tippett

Several years Britten's senior, Michael Tippett did not come to opera until comparatively late in life with *The Midsummer Marriage* (London, 1955), a work of mystic symbolism recalling the spirit of *The Magic Flute* yet wholly modern in its musical idiom. The score is remarkably rich and impassioned, and its failure to win immediate favour was due to the ob-

Britten's first chamber operas, *The Rape of Lucretia* (Glyndebourne, 1946) and *Albert Herring* (Glyndebourne, 1947), were written specifically for the English Opera Group, and their success both at home and abroad led to the founding of the Aldeburgh Festival under the composer's direction in 1948. Even more impressive is *The Turn of the Screw* (Venice, 1954), based on the story by Henry James and written in two acts and eight scenes which are ingeniously linked by variations on the theme which opens the

Tippett's controversial The Ice Break, *an opera dealing with contemporary issues, first produced at Covent Garden in 1977*

scurity of its libretto, written by the composer. The Ritual Dances of the second act, however, quickly became popular in the concert hall, and eventually the whole work was given the recognition it deserves, though still only in Britain. Its Romantic warmth finds no place in Tippett's second opera, *King Priam* (Coventry Festival, 1962), an austere work based on the *Iliad*. With his two later operas the composer has continued to move away from the luxuriant style of *The Midsummer Marriage*, concerning himself with contemporary human problems in a way

that may well make *The Knot Garden* (London, 1970) and *The Ice Break* (London, 1977) date all too quickly. Whereas the tragic situations of Wozzeck and Peter Grimes have a universal, timeless significance, those of Tippett's characters in his later operas do not, and this may well prevent the survival of operas that nevertheless contain much impressive music.

247

OPERA TODAY AND TOMORROW

The twentieth century has not seen the emergence of many successful opera composers, though there is perhaps a larger worldwide audience for opera today than in any other period. Puccini and the *verismo* school have produced some highly successful works which have stayed the course, as also have Strauss and Janáček, but these were all composers with their roots in the nineteenth century. Only Berg and Britten have proved successful in the sense of having their works accepted throughout other countries in Europe and in the United States as well as in their own countries. A great number of other composers have had their operas accepted at home, or have even enjoyed a wider vogue for a time, but it would be rash to predict which, if any, of these works will enjoy a permanent place in the international repertoire.

It is not only the avant-garde composers who have failed to win lasting support from the public. Gian-Carlo Menotti, who was born at Cadegliano on 7 July 1911 and made his home in the United States in 1927, has kept to the form and idiom of the Italian late Romantics, but his operas have not established themselves after enjoying initial success. His *Amelia Goes to the Ball* (Philadelphia, 1939) made it clear that he has a keen theatrical sense and the gift of melody, qualities which he developed further in *The Medium*, a macabre offspring of the *verismo* movement, which enjoyed a run on Broadway in 1947 and was well received in London, Paris and various Italian cities. His most substantial work is *The Consul* (Philadelphia, 1950), which also enjoyed a Broadway run and subsequent successful productions in Europe. Its story of repression under political dictatorship gave it topicality and an appeal to audiences which do not usually go to see an opera, but its music does not add anything to the melodramatic text. Manotti sets out to satisfy the public in the manner of a latter-day Puccini, but his operas have neither Puccini's imagination nor his musical distinction, and his well-intentioned melodies lack memorability. There is more substance to *The Rise and Fall of the City Of Mahagonny* by Kurt Weill (1900–1950), despite its deliberately 'popular' style of vocal writing. It also has the advantage of an unusually brilliant libretto by Bertolt Brecht which gives a bitterly satirical picture of degenerate capitalist society.

Many other composers have been active in the United States, where seasons of new American operas have been staged at the City Center in New York. Douglas Moore's *The Devil and Daniel Webster* (1939) and *The Ballad of Baby Doe* (1956), composed in

Scene from Porgy and Bess, *the most successful of American operas, in which Gershwin uses the jazz idiom to provide a folk basis*

folk idiom, top this list of American operas which have been praised at home but not won favour abroad. Others include Aaron Copland's *The Tender Land* (1954), and Samuel Barber's *Vanessa* (1958) and *Anthony and Cleopatra* (1966). Of more musical interest is Gershwin's *Porgy and Bess* (Boston, 1935), which uses jazz elements in a positive way for a drama about characters for whom it is the most natural form of self-expression. A wonderful melodist, Gershwin packs out the score with memorable songs. *Porgy and Bess* does not fit into any convenient operatic category, and purists have objected to its being considered an opera in the proper sense, but its music has force and character which carry it far beyond the level of the musical or most operettas.

England has seen a spate of new operas ever since

Britten won immediate success with *Peter Grimes*, but almost all have sunk without trace after an initial run of performances. Walton's *Troilus and Cressida* (London, 1954), a traditional work with big tunes and grand gestures, was taken up almost at once by New York and Milan, but interest in it quickly faded. A younger generation of composers using more advanced styles has been no more succesfful, though it is always possible that some of their works, which secured a small partisan following, may be taken up in the future. Prominent among these are Thea Musgrave (*b* 1928) for *The Voice of Ariadne* (1974) and *Mary Queen of Scots* (1977); Peter Maxwell Davies (*b* 1934) for *Taverner* (1972); and Harrison Birtwistle (*b* 1934) for *Punch and Judy* (1968). They have all tried in their different ways to bring opera into line with other musical developments, moving away from traditional harmony and the kind of melody that audiences can recognize and remember. It is this lack of tunefulness which most alienated the public from the operas of the late twentieth century, and it disturbs many singers too. The international stars who have perfected their voices and techniques to do justice to the music of Mozart, Verdi and Wagner are almost all indifferent to contemporary opera, which they feel does not offer them vocal rewards.

Opera stands at a crossroads. On the one hand, the vast majority of the public chooses to stick exclusively to the established repertoire, unwilling even to consider going to see an opera by Luciano Berio or Karlheinz Stockhausen, who for their part make no concessions to public taste. On the other hand there is a small audience, and also a few singers, prepared to go along with the avant-garde composers. The gulf between the two seems unbridgeable for a powerful reason: these composers have not just wrought changes of style and idiom within the wide limits of the established operatic form, as Wagner and even Berg succeeded in doing. They have carried their experiments to such lengths that the operatic form which developed from Monteverdi to Berg is not recognizable at all. It is possible that opera as an art-form has been exhausted, as became the case with verse-drama, and that opera-goers will have to remain content with the huge existing repertoire. This is indicated by the revival in interest over the past few decades in the long-neglected operas of Rossini, Donizetti and the young Verdi. The more recent rediscovery of Haydn as an opera composer is another pointer in this direction, which might well be followed by a long-overdue revival of interest in Gluck. This is one way over the present difficult period, while one hopes that opera will eventually be revitalized more positively.

OPERETTA

The history of operetta is a curious one, that of a form of musical entertainment which danced its way into the theatre with Offenbach in 1855, quickly spread from Paris to Vienna, London and New York, but fizzled out before the middle of the twentieth century as the musical overtook it in popularity. No artistic form arrives completely out of the blue, and operetta had its origins in comic opera. It is not easy to draw a line between comic opera and operetta, but there is one important difference. The arias which Rossini gives to Rosina in *The Barber of Seville* and Donizetti to Nemorino in *L'elisir d'amore* establishes their individual character, whereas the songs Offenbach provides for his Grande-Duchesse de Gérolstein and Johann Strauss for Rosalinde in *Die Fledermaus*, though first-rate musical numbers, do not tell us anything about them that we do not know already from the spoken dialogue. But it is mere snobbery to believe that the musical is somehow inferior to operetta: Richard Rodgers' *Oklahoma!* and Leonard Bernstein's *West Side Story* can hold their own against all but a dozen outstanding Viennese operettas.

Offenbach

If ever the right man arrived on the scene at the right time it was the composer we know as Jacques Offenbach. His family name was really Eberst, which his father had changed to that of his native town of Offenbach on the River Main, and he himself had been baptized as Jakob Levy. He was born in Cologne on 20 June 1819, and when the family moved to Paris in 1833 he studied at the Conservatoire before becoming a cellist in the orchestra of the Opéra-Comique. He made a friend of Flotow, with whom he appeared at some of the smarter musical soirées, the couple throwing off agreable trifles for piano and cello to delight *nouveau riche* ears. In 1842 he made his first foray into the satirical territory he was later to exploit so brilliantly. Setting to music six of the *Fables* of La Fontaine he turned their morals upside down and was promptly accused of bad taste – the best recommendation any satirist could hope for. The following year he arranged a concert of his own music which included a scandalous piece which simultaneously poked fun at the revered Victor Hugo, grand opera and bourgeois morality. The young composer subsequently found the doors of the Opéra-Comique closed to him.

Social climate played an important role in determining the character of operetta and accounts for the 249

Offenbach, whose sparkling operettas were the rage of Paris expressing the frivolous spirit of the French Second Empire

huge differences in the styles of Offenbach, Johann Strauss and Sullivan. Operetta requires the large-scale support of the middle classes and must therefore reflect the tastes, even the prejudices, of that section of the population. Offenbach found his ideal audience once Louis Napoléon became emperor, just as Strauss struck the right note of cosy sentimentality for the Vienna of his day and Sullivan touched the genteel chord of Victorian society in London. The French Second Empire was built on sand and could only survive by concealing its dangerous social and political realities below a show of state splendour on the one hand and frivolous entertainment on the other. In 1855, the year of the World Exhibition in Paris, Offenbach became the lessee of a tiny wooden

theatre on the Champs-Elysées and put on *Les deux Aveugles*, a skit on the tricks played by the city's resourceful beggars. The composer and his Bouffes Parisiens shot to fame overnight, and the public literally fought for seats in a theatre so cramped that it was said that if a man wanted to take off his jacket he had to open both the door of the box and the window in the corridor outside.

Most of the string of operettas he composed during the following three years are now forgotten, but at the time they played to packed houses every night as visitors from all over Europe fell under the spell of the 'Mozart of the Champs-Elysées'. The music was infectiously tuneful, while the librettos provided witty, often wicked comments on current affairs and personalities well known from the gossip columns. New dialogue was added almost nightly, and society figures returned over and over again to find out which of their friends had become the latest targets. With *Orpheus in the Underworld* in 1858 the composer turned to full-length works instead of the one-act pieces with which he had made his name. The satirical element, though no less keen, was made more general: the corruption of Olympus by Jupiter in *Orpheus* could readily be equated with Napoleon III's corruption of France, while the outrageously immoral Greeks of *La belle Hélène* (1864) were immediately recognizable as caricatures of politicians. Offenbach's music also became more substantial, many of the songs resembling arias, the ensembles taking on a greater complexity and the orchestration becoming more subtle.

It seemed that Offenbach's star would never be dimmed as one success followed another, *La Vie parisienne* in 1866, *La Grande-Duchesse de Gérolstein* in 1867 and *La Périchole* in 1868. Then Napoleon's candyfloss Empire began its rapid decline, to be overthrown in 1870, and with it died the public demand for operettas which heartlessly debunked the whole framework of French society. Offenbach travelled abroad to conduct his music, but showed little enthusiasm for composition. Then, towards the end of his life, he fulfilled his long-held ambition to compose a serious opera with *The Tales of Hoffmann* (see p.214). He died in Paris on 4 October 1880.

Johann Strauss

Although operetta in Germany developed rather differently from France, it shared many of its fundamental characteristics. It was basically a play with music, almost invariably bringing in a number of dance sequences, and because the first important composer of German operettas happened to be

Strauss these were invariably waltzes as distinct from the galop and cancan favoured by Offenbach. The main difference between the two styles was that whereas Offenbach's approach was cynically witty, dealing largely with passing sexual encounters, that of Strauss and his followers was cosily romantic, with wedding bells ready to sound for the lovers at the end. Vienna, however frivolous, was more respectable than Paris: Rosalinde and Eisenstein in *Die Fledermaus* are a typical middle-class married couple, quite the opposite of Helen of Troy and Paris in *La belle Hélène*. Strauss was a more accomplished composer than Offenbach, but most of his dozen or so operettas were comparative failures because he was prone to accept the first libretto offered to him, and with the exception of *Die Fledermaus* and *Der Zigeunerbaron* they were fatally weak and witless.

The life of the younger Johann Strauss was of the stuff that Hollywood movies are made. The first Johann (1804–80), who virtually created the Viennese waltz from the earlier Ländler, became famous throughout Europe for the concerts he gave with his own orchestra playing mostly his own works. Three of his legitimate sons followed in his footsteps, though he tried to discourage them in every way; they were able to defy him only because he spent little time at home with his family, preferring the company of a mistress. His even more successful son Johann was born in Vienna on 25 October 1825. Although the boy wrote his first waltz at the age of six, he was made to work as a bank clerk as soon as he had finished his schooling. His mother, however, had encouraged him to take violin lessons, so by the time he was nineteen he was able to form his own small orchestra and introduce his own waltzes. His fame soon rivalled that of his father, and he graduated from the ballrooms of Vienna to European tours in the course of which he was idolized like a pop star of today. His marriage brought him wealth enough to give up his orchestral work and concentrate on 251 composition, producing a host of immortal waltzes such as *The Blue Danube*, *Tales from the Vienna Woods* and *Roses from the South*. Like his father, however, Johann II had an eye for the ladies and took several mistresses and three wives, only settling down when he found himself third time lucky in marriage.

He came relatively late to operetta, and even then it was at the suggestion of Offenbach, whom he met in Vienna in 1863. After a couple of failures Strauss eventually enjoyed his first operetta triumph with *Die Fledermaus* ('The bat', 1874), which contains music of a high order. Of Rosalinde's Czardas Ernest Newman wrote with great perception: 'It shows what depths of expression there were in Strauss had he chosen to explore them more consistently. No genuine Hungarian could sing more movingly of the pain of separation from the homeland or of the fire in the Hungarian breast that drives them to the dance.' It is no wonder that *Die Fledermaus* is the operetta that most of the world's major opera houses include in their repertoire and that Rosalinde is a role which has appealed to so many leading operatic sopranos. Significantly, Strauss's other huge operetta success, *Die Zigeunerbaron* ('The gypsy baron' 1885), combines the exotic Hungarian idiom with his native Viennese style. Other operettas followed, but none reach the level of inspiration of these masterpieces. He continued to write dances with all his youthful flair almost up to his death in Vienna on 3 June 1899.

Sullivan

It is ironical that Sullivan should be remembered today exclusively for the operettas he wrote in collaboration with Gilbert, for he rather despised them, always nursing the ambition to become either the nineteenth-century Handel or the English Schumann. The good fairies seem to have gathered for his birth in London on 13 May 1842, lavishing on him the gifts of good looks, immeasurable charm and prodigious musical talent. By the age of eight he had learned to play every instrument in the band of his father, who was bandmaster at the Royal Military College of Sandhurst, and four years later he was admitted to the Chapel Royal as a chorister. In 1855, when he was only thirteen, two events pointed towards his later musical and social success – his anthem *O Israel* was accepted for publication, and the Duke of Wellington, on a visit to the Chapel Royal, patted him on the head and gave him a gold sovereign. Three years later, having won a national scholarship, he went to Leipzig to continue his studies, and it was there that he developed an enthusiasm for the music of Schumann which he championed on his

return to England in 1861. His early works include a symphony and a cello concerto, but he subsequently devoted himself almost exclusively to vocal composition, hymns and cantatas on the one hand and operettas and drawing-room ballads on the other.

Sullivan's first venture into operetta was the one-act farce *Cox and Box* (1867), with a libretto by F C Burnand, but when this failed to set the Thames on fire he turned his back on the theatre for five years. He had no more success the first time he worked with W S Gilbert, their *Thespis* running for only a month in 1871 before vanishing without trace. Then in 1875 the two men hit the jackpot with the one-act *Trial by Jury*, their only operetta to have no spoken dialogue. From then on their names were to be linked

Cartoon of Sullivan, whose collaboration with Gilbert produced a uniquely consistent and successful flow of operettas

as indissolubly as those of Rolls and Royce. Gilbert's contribution was the treatment of whimsical situations in verse of considerable wit and inventiveness, Sullivan's a quick melodic response to their lilt and patter, with a keen sense of musical parody.

The Gilbert and Sullivan operettas stand midway between the German and French schools, being less sentimental than the former and less sophisticated than the latter. There is a keen sense of fun in their sallies against the peerage (*Iolanthe*), the Aesthetic movement (*Patience*), the Admiralty (*H.M.S. Pinafore*) and the cult of *japonaiserie* (*The Mikado*), but they were careful never to offend Victorian taste. Their satire is never outrageous like that of Offenbach, who would undoubtedly have exposed every possible scandal

Trio from Patience, *the Gilbert and Sullivan operetta making fun of the Aesthetic movement which Victorian society could not understand*

concerning the members of the House of Lords if *he* had written *Iolanthe*. The so-called Savoy Operas also differ from their Continental counterparts in that not one of their characters ever hints at any sexual feelings, the words of their love songs sounding more appropriate to a boy scout teaching a girl guide to tie knots. Gilbert clearly realized that sex was taboo so far as the Victorian family audience was concerned, and Sullivan seems to have been incapable of composing emotional music in any case. There are ample compensations, however, for Gilbert's ingenuity with words and rhymes remains unequalled, while Sullivan's gift for elegant melody and vivacious patter songs comes close to that of the composers of *opera buffa*. If he had not lived in a musically backward society – and we must remember that the English musical renaissance did not begin until Elgar's *Enigma Variations*, composed a year before Sullivan's death – he might well have been encouraged to set his sights considerably higher. As it was, he turned out music neatly tailored to the national taste and which is so expertly crafted that it has not lost its sparkling appeal a century later. He was rewarded with financial success, honorary doctorates at both Oxford and Cambridge and a knighthood before he died, the most respected English composer of his time, on 22 November 1900.

THE MUSICAL

The change from operetta to the musical was a gradual process reflecting changing public attitudes throughout Europe and the United States. The earlier form continued for some decades, Offenbach being succeeded in France by composers like André Messager (1853–1929) and Alexandre Lecocq (1832–1918), Strauss by Karl Millöcker (1842–99) and Franz Lehár (1870–1948; of *The Merry Widow* fame) in Germany, and Harold Fraser-Simpson (1872–1944) whose *Maid of the Mountains* ran for a record 1,352 performances in London. In the United States the first operettas were the work of immigrants, Victor Herbert (1859–1924) from Ireland and the Czech-American Rudolf Friml (1879–1972), a pupil of Dvořák who wrote *Rose Marie* and *The Vagabond King*. Jerome Kern (1885–1945) struck a genuine American note with *Show Boat* in 1927, and Gershwin wrote many musicals as well as his opera *Porgy and Bess*. Composers of a new country, however, were not naturally attracted to the kind of Ruritanian romances favoured by the Europeans, and they had their own history, folklore and musical idiom to draw upon. The American way of life which its composers chose to reflect was vigorous, even brash, and a different style of music was

253

called for, a style which transformed the operetta into what has come to be known as the musical. The musical treats more realistic subjects, places greater emphasis on the spoken dialogue and favours a gutsier type of song. Whereas the songs in European operettas were designed for opera singers, the songs in American musicals have been written with less trained voices in mind.

The musical has not only replaced the operetta, but has taken over from opera as a musical form of theatre with mass appeal. In the nineteenth century arias from the operas by Rossini and Verdi became hit-tunes, a status rarely achieved by numbers by Benjamin Britten or Hans Werner Henze. The number and remarkable stylistic variety of musicals is too great to be considered here, and it can only be pointed out that they constitute the most vital, stimulating form of theatre to have emerged in the twentieth century. They have considerable dramatic as well as musical significance, because many of them deal with important social problems and they provide valuable comment on contemporary life. It is this new dramatic consciousness that has resulted in a special kind of musical written for actors with minimal singing ability rather than the conventional musical comedy artist. The flavour of a musical is set by the writer of the book and lyrics rather than the composer, so that the style of Richard Rodger's music, sharp and concise when setting the words of Lorenz Hart, became more gently lyrical and sentimental when he began his collaboration with Oscar Hammerstein. The musical has not hesitated to draw on literary classics from time to time, Cole Porter's *Kiss Me Kate* being based on Shakespeare's *Taming of the Shrew*, Leonard Bernstein turning to Voltaire for his *Candide* and Austrian-born Frederick Loewe adapting Shaw's *Pygmalion* for his *My Fair Lady*; but in the main it is an art-form as truly American as early opera was wholly Italian. It has developed an enormous range of subject matter in a comparatively short time, extending from the open-air naivete of *Oklahoma!* at one extreme to the urban sophistication of *The Best Little Whorehouse in Texas* at the other. Adapting as it does to the changing world, the musical seems assured of a longer life than the operetta enjoyed.

RECITALS
AND
CHAMBER
MUSIC

Manuscripts of early keyboard music go back to the fourteenth century, and keyboard instruments existed long before that. They took many forms but, apart from the organ, the harpischord is the only one earlier than the piano which is likely to be encountered by the concert-goer of today. An intimate instrument, capable of a wonderful variety of expression, it belongs to the salon rather than a public hall, but thanks to the gramophone the solo harpsichord works of Scarlatti and Bach can be enjoyed in the home through recordings. In public these works are more frequently played on the louder piano, but this changes—purists will say destroys—the music's character. The instruments produce radically different sounds, the harpischord plucking the strings with a quill, the piano hitting them with a hammer. They therefore demand different styles in composition, and it is no more proper to play Scarlatti on the piano than to play Chopin on the harpsichord. On the other hand, music was composed to give pleasure to its audiences, and it is pedantic to condemn pianists for including harpischord music in recital programmes. The authentic attitude was wittily expressed by the distinguished harpischordist Wanda Landowska, who was overheard saying to an equally famous artist who played Bach on the piano: 'Very well, my dear, you continue to play Bach your way and I'll continue to play him *his* way.'

Bach composed chiefly for the organ during his early appointments, but after his move to the court at Cöthen he concentrated on the harpischord to produce some of his best known works: the Chromatic Fantasia and Fugue, the 'English' and 'French' suites and the twenty-four preludes and fugues in all the major and minor keys known as Book I of the *Well-tempered Clavier*, completed in 1722. With the companion set which he completed in 1744, these have become known as the 'Forty-eight', and they display both contrapuntal mastery and sheer beauty of inspiration. The 'Goldberg' Variations, consisting of thirty elaborate variations on a sarabande theme, was published about 1742 and belongs completely to his later, flawlessly organized style.

Domenico Scarlatti (1685–1757), who was born only seven months after Bach, was the dominant Italian keyboard composer of the period, though he left his native country in 1721 to spend the rest of his life in the courts of Portugal and then Spain. His music is less intellectual than Bach's, though he did more to explore the expressive potential of the harpsichord. Every imaginable nuance of the instrument's sonority and every aspect of its technique are covered in his more than five hundred sonatas, the majority of which are arranged in pairs, each pair effectively

forming a two-movement sonata. They are immensely varied in style, sometimes highly virtuosic, sometimes simple and reflective, and they occasionally feature snatches of Spanish popular songs and dance rhythms.

Haydn and Mozart

It was during the careers of Haydn and Mozart that the piano came into its own, though gradually as the technicalities of the new instrument's construction were worked out. By 1760, when Haydn began to compose his fifty-two sonatas, the piano had begun to supplant the older keyboard instruments, though the harpischord was still used for accompaniment in concerted performances and in operatic recitative. The Haydn piano sonatas are so attractive that their comparative neglect seems unfair. They have never won the popularity of the symphonies, though they developed side by side with them. The last five at least, composed between 1789 and 1794, merit a place in the repertoire by virtue of their poetic and imagi-

Artur Rubinstein, one of the most versatile and brilliant of twentieth-century pianists, a lover of life as well as music

native qualities. Mozart's piano sonatas are similarly less well known, and frankly for the most part less distinguished. than his works in other forms, the piano concertos and operas in particular. Many of his sonatas were written for teaching purposes or as salon pieces, and music for solo piano meant less to Mozart than it was to mean to Beethoven. Inevitably, however, there is much grace to be found in his sonatas, and also an Italianate lyrical ease that makes the best of them more charming than Haydn's. A favourite is the Sonata in A major, K331, composed during his visit to Paris in 1778, which includes an elegant Andante with variations and a dashing Rondo in his beloved Turkish style.

Beethoven

Following Haydn's and Mozart's pioneering work in the sonata, Beethoven was to make it a major means of musical expression. We do not think of any Haydn sonata in the same way as his 'London' symphonies, nor place any of Mozart's alongside the 'Jupiter' Symphony, mature concertos or *Don Giovanni*. With Beethoven, however, the piano sonata becomes a form through which a composer can express his deepest and most personal thoughts as compellingly as in a symphony. Conveniently, his thirty-two sonatas fall into three periods, the first leading up to but not including the Sonata in A flat, Op 26, a four-movement work which reveals an inward, spiritual urge striving for outward form. This eventually led to his making a break with conventions, extending the length of a single movement beyond anything conceived before, or increasing the number of movements to four. The most popular of the early sonatas is the *Pathétique* – not a nickname, but Beethoven's own title for Op 13 in C minor – which expresses tragedy with a youthful urgency, a tragedy of love which positively glows in the central Adagio. In addition to the appeal of its heartfelt melodies, the *Pathétique* opens a whole new world of expressiveness in a form which had previously been predominantly objective. The sonatas of the second period, including the 'Waldstein' and the 'Appassionata', which introduce tensions and powers of imagination characteristic of the mature Beethoven. They date from the period of the *Eroica* Symphony and similarly reveal the way in which the composer was stretching Classical limits towards Romanticism. With the slightly earlier 'Moonlight' Sonata (a nickname which is misleading rather than just meaningless) he raised the piano's singing tone to a new height in the opening Adagio, while the Finale's explosive energy brings a keen sense of drama.

The sonatas of Beethoven's middle and final periods all have original and memorable qualities, so it is not surprising that they all feature prominently in the repertoire. The Sonata in B flat, Op 106, commonly known as the 'Hammerklavier', carries the four-movement plan to an epic scale, making it a terrifying challenge to the pianist mentally as well as technically, not least in its contrapuntal complexity. The last of all, the Sonata in C minor, Op 111, sums up much of the composer's musical character. Its first movement, after a most powerful slow introduction, plunges into a mighty Allegro with strong contrapuntal leanings, eventually subsiding into a calm coda to prepare for the second movement, an Arietta. This is a set of variations on one of the most sublime melodies ever composed, and it would seem that Beethoven felt he had reached such a peak of beauty and serenity that nothing further could be added; the sonata was left in two movements expressing to perfection his last thoughts in a medium he had exploited so richly. Of his many other works for solo piano mention must be made of the Variations and Fugue, Op 35, of which the theme is that of the *Eroica* Symphony's last movement, and the dazzling 'Diabelli' Variations which rank with Bach's 'Goldberg' Variations in ingenuity and comprehensiveness.

Schubert

In form, Schubert's sonatas are influenced by Haydn and Mozart rather than by Beethoven, though they are far more lyrical. Of the twenty he started only half were completed, and the early ones are agreeable enough though not of any great consequence. The later sonatas, however, are so rich in expansive melodies – and Schubert deserves to be called a 'divine' melodist – that the lack of any concise thematic development does not seem to matter. The last three, composed in his final year, in C minor, A major and B flat respectively, are incomparable in their lyrical inspiration, the last of all being his finest work for the piano, mysterious in its spacious first movement, superb in its sustaining of the slow melody of the second. irresistibly light of foot in the Scherzo and generous almost beyond belief in the chain of themes of the Finale. Also considerable in scale, and far more difficult to play, the 'Wanderer' Fantasia has four movements centred on an Adagio with variations. (This work is popular in Liszt's arrangement for piano and orchestra.) Schubert was a master of the miniature, his six *Moments Musicaux* and eight *Impromptus* being gems which set a model for the various types of short, intimate pieces adopted by later composers.

257

ROMANTICISM

Although composers have continued to write sonatas since the time of Beethoven, the most imaginative and interesting piano music has usually taken a freer form. This was perhaps inevitable with the rise of the Romantic movement, composers like Schumann, Liszt and Chopin naturally wanting to give full rein to their ideas in a way that a strict musical form would not allow. It would be wrong to think, however, that the sonata was discarded altogether, for there are few composers from Schumann to Boulez who have not taken up its challenge from time to time, finding that new ideas could still be given full expression within the disciplines imposed by the Classical pattern. Other changes came about as the piano itself was developed, the modern concert grand having a far wider dynamic range than the instruments available to Beethoven and Schubert. Virtuoso pianists, often the great composers themselves, have also played a part by finding ever more expressive performance techniques. When we think of Chopin and Liszt, for example, it is not their sonatas which first come to mind, but their polonaises and waltzes or works with such titles as *Transcendental Studies* and *Consolations*. Even Brahms, who tried to keep his Classical head when Romanticism ran to excess all around him, turned from the sonata to the more evocative Ballade.

Two composers who represent important aspects of the post-Beethoven period are Weber and Mendelssohn. The former projected his poetic personality into the sonata itself, his four essays in the form combining novel and conventional elements in a most attractive manner. His most famous piano piece, however, is the evocative *Invitation to the Dance*, to which he appended a bar-by-bar programme. This music has irresistible pianistic flair as

well as melodic appeal, displaying a gracefulness which reconciles the old and the new attitudes to formal style. His high spirits are heard at their best in the *Polacca brillante*, a dashing example of the bravura side to his character. Mendelssohn, also a virtuoso pianist, wrote for the instrument with more Classical restraint, notably in his sonatas and impressive *Variations sérieuses*. His best known piano works, however, are the forty-eight short pieces, composed at different times during his career and then issued under the collective title *Songs without Words*. Among the best, and only lightly touched with Romantic colouring, are the 'Gondola Song' and the 'Spinning Song'.

Schumann

The clearest indication of Schumann's extreme Romanticism is to be found in a letter he wrote to Clara Wieck when he was twenty-eight. 'I am affected,' he declared, 'by everything that goes on in the world and think it all over in my own way, politics, literature and people, and then I long to express my feelings and find an outlet for them in music.' That was in 1838, when he had been composing almost exclusively for the piano for eight years, a path he continued until his marriage to Clara two years later, after which he turned his attention to orchestral music. The piano works of these ten years represent the essential spirit of the composer, volatile and poetic. Even the titles, *Carnaval, Papillons* and *Faschingsschwank aus Wien* ('Carnival jest from Vienna'), emphasize that he was aiming to express extra-musical fancies. The idea of a carnival, which permeates all these works, appealed to him because it enabled him to project his personality in different guises, from behind different masks, which places him among the most daringly original of all the Romantics. The twenty 'scenes' which make up *Carnaval* include tributes to his friends Chopin and Paganini as well as the obviously descriptive 'Pantalon and Columbine' and the 'March against the philistines'. Schumann once described the *Faschungsswank* as a 'grand Romantic sonata' but in fact it is a piano suite, only its last movement being cast in sonata form. One of its jests in the first movement is a snatch from the *Marseillaise*, which the Austrian censors of the time (1839) forbade anyone to sing or play.

Schumann personified two different aspects of his own nature in the imaginary figures of the impulsive Florestan and the poetic Eusebius who feature in much of his piano music, sometimes openly and sometimes only by inference. *Kreisleriana* is a rather different set of musical portraits, a gallery of fantastic

Fan decorated with cartoons of the great virtuosos with their admirers in the Romantic period of the nineteenth century

characters drawn from the novels and stories of E T A Hoffmann. Half-way between these fanciful pieces and the sonatas comes the great C major Fantasy, which Schumann considered the 'most passionate' work he had ever composed and to whose three movements he first gave the titles 'Ruins', 'Triumphal arch' and 'Starry crown'. The tonality of C major dominates the outer movements to symbolize simplicity and serenity. Flights of lyricism are skilfully sustained, and the piano writing is masterly, making this one of the composer's most satisfying essays in formal style, though it is less tautly constructed than the *Etudes symphoniques*. Most of these studies in fact are variations on a main theme, a device which suited Schumann because he found it easier to construct a large-scale work in variation form rather than by thematic development. His weakness in the latter technique is shown up in his three sonatas, which feature some very beautiful melodies which he fails to develop to any purpose. It is a relief to turn from these to the unpretentious little pieces of *Kinderscenen* ('Scenes from childhood') which positively shine with spontaneous inspiration.

Chopin

When it comes to the matter of sheer keyboard poetry, all composers can only bow the knee to Frédéric Chopin, who was born at Zelazowa Wola in Poland on 1 March 1810 and who was to revolutionize piano music completely in the course of his short life. Because he was the only boy in the family his parents paid him special attention, and his musical talent was encouraged from the beginning. His development was helped by the family's move to Warsaw. By the age of seven he was playing in public and astonishing audiences with pieces of his own.

A legend has grown up that he was a sickly boy of morbid disposition, but in fact he took part in the usual sports with his school companions and was quite precocious in his enjoyment of high life. A visit to Vienna in 1829 widened his horizons, and he found Warsaw restrictive on his return, so after introducing his two piano concertos there in the following year he went back with high hopes to the Austrian capital. The Viennese, however, no longer found him a novelty, and he found them increasingly trivial. 'During supper,' he wrote in a letter home, 'Strauss or Lanner play waltzes; and if they play a potpourri of opera tunes or dances the public is so pleased that it goes off its head – it just shows you 259

Chopin, whose intimate works in the forms of preludes and nocturnes introduced a new sense of poetry into music for solo piano

how corrupt the taste of the Viennese is.' When we remember that these same Viennese had completely ignored Schubert's last symphonies, we can appreciate the justice of Chopin's criticism.

In the autumn of 1831 Chopin arrived in Paris, which was to become his permanent spiritual home. His first attempts to establish himself as a concert pianist were surprisingly unsuccessful, but he was taken up by the Rothschild and other wealthy families and enjoyed a sensational success with his playing at soirées, also earning enough, by giving lessons to the daughters of the aristocracy, to have his own carriage and a manservant. The aristocracy liked him because he was a 'gentleman' as well as a composer-virtuoso, while composers like Berlioz, Liszt and Mendelssohn admired him as a refined player. He was bemused by this adulation, joking in one of his letters, 'I have gained the entrée to the first circles; I have my place among ambassadors,

princes, ministers, but I don't know by what miracle it has happened, for I have not pushed myself forward. I'm a revolutionary, money means nothing to me.' The mention of his revolutionary feelings refers to a recent unsuccessful attempt by the Poles to gain independence, and because his country fell under complete German and Russian domination Chopin never returned. His life was soon complicated by his decline into chronic ill-health and his liaison with Armandine Dupin, a writer famous under the pseudonym George Sand. He withdrew as much as possible from public concerts and played mostly at private soirées, retiring with George Sand to her country house at Nohant so that he could compose in peace. Their tempestuous relationship did not bring him happiness, yet he could not bear living without her, and their final separation in 1847 blighted the last two years of his life as he wasted away from consumption. After his death on 17 October 1849 the French gave him a funeral of unusual splendour. A small box of Polish earth was scattered over the grave a year later.

The delicate poetry of his intimate works, the preludes, impromptus and nocturnes, has never been equalled in eloquence, refinement and subtlety. The preludes, ranging through all the major and minor keys, combine the same qualities of purity and imagination as Bach's *Well-tempered Clavier*, never distorting line and form in the expression of every imaginable mood. The nocturnes extend the form invented by John Field, bringing the singing style to perfection and exploring a vein of rich and subtle fantasy. His waltzes – never intended to be danced – are in the nature of past festivities recollected with aristocratic taste. The spirit of the dance is more vigorously expressed in the mazurkas, which make tone-poems out of this Polish country dance, and in the heroic polonaises in which Chopin seems to be stressing his Polish patriotism.

More ambitious in scale are the four scherzos, not the playful works that the title implies, but virile and passionate music in a rhapsodic, improvisatory manner. The four ballades encompass elements of various forms, sonata and variation, transformed to suit the composer's purpose with a logic of his own. The F minor Fantasy extends the boundaries of the ballade by involving a greater number of themes and striking a more Romantic note. The use of the terms 'tone-poem' and 'Romantic' does not imply programmatic music, for Chopin disliked that concept intensely; his idols, after all, were Bach and Mozart. His fastidiousness enabled him to produce masterpieces in the form of the *étude*, studies primarily concerned with a specific technical problem. His two sets of studies enshrine the soul of the piano; the listener is only aware of the magical end-product of the technical experimenting. Because he was so uniquely successful as a miniaturist his sonatas have been underrated. The B flat minor Sonata, including the famous Funeral March, has an artistic totality of its own which overcomes any formal weakness, and the later B minor Sonata has its rewarding lyrical ideas too. It is in his short pieces, however, that the genius of Chopin is most fully revealed, and it is through them that he affected the whole course of piano music.

Liszt

If Chopin was the supreme poet of the piano, Liszt was its greatest propagandist. His life was as brilliant as his music, for he rip-roared his way through the capitals of Europe with a style and panache exceeding even Paganini's. Born at Raiding on the estate of Prince Esterházy on 22 October 1811, he studied piano under Carl Czerny in Vienna and at the age of eleven began a successful career as a concert pianist. Although he became the world's most dazzling piano virtuoso, he gave up performing in public in 1848, playing thereafter only for friends and pupils or for charitable purposes – a *volte-face* typical of his dual nature. He was vain to a degree, yet also generous to everyone who came to him in need. His love affairs were as exotic as they were well publicized, ranging from ladies of high position to Marie Duplessis, the original Lady of the Camellias immortalized by Dumas and Verdi, and Lola Montez, the Irish dancer and adventuress. In Weimar, where he was Kapellmeister from 1842 to 1858, he conducted the first performance of *Lohengrin*, having become a fervent champion of Wagner. The course of his friendship with Wagner was not withouts its crises, however, the major one concerning Liszt's illegitimate daughter Cosima. In 1857 Cosima married his friend and pupil Hans von Bülow, but left him later to live with Wagner. Liszt was outraged, and it was not until 1872 that he was reconciled with his new son-in-law. In the meantime, Liszt had lived mainly in Rome, where he took minor orders in the church while he continued to be a real-life Don Giovanni, or, as he was once described, 'Mephistopheles disguised as an Abbé'. From 1871 he divided his time between Rome, Weimar and Budapest, though he was to die, on 31 July 1886, at Bayreuth, a few days after watching a performance of *Tristan and Isolde* from the Wagner family box.

His music reflects his dual personality, for it can be profound in one work, then superficial in the next; its strengths and weaknesses both spring from the

Caricature of Liszt with a Hungarian sword, a reference to his Hungarian Rhapsodies which are in fact gypsy in style

fact that he was primarily a player. It not only explores the capabilities of the piano, but is designed to tax the virtuosity and physical stamina of the performer to the full. Schumann saw this when he wrote that the *Transcendental Studies* were for no more than ten or twelve players in the world. Liszt's style shows several influences, of which the most important are his Hungarian heritage, Romantic programme music, and Chopin's expressive keyboard writing. His absolute pianistic command is shown in his many arrangements of orchestral and operatic music, notably the Berlioz *Symphonie fantastique*, the *Reminiscences of Norma* and the *Liebestod* from *Tristan and Isolde*. These go far beyond the *pot-pourri* served up by lesser composers, for they transform their originals into truly pianistic terms. At the other end of Liszt's range is the B minor Sonata (1833), which reveals the genius behind the showman. It is cast in 261 a single extended movement, in which four themes are worked out in an apparently free manner involving elements of fugue, recitative and variation. In his own way he achieves a fine inner unity in this work, which in its adaptation of cyclic development is one of the most original Romantic piano works.

It is in shorter pieces, however, that Liszt excelled, whether in the *Mephisto Waltzes*, the *Paganini Studies* (including the brilliant *La campanella*), the dashing Hungarian Rhapsodies or the most famous of the three delicate *Liebesträume*. After the *Transcendental Studies* he composed two further sets of exploratory tone pictures, the *Années de pèlerinage* and *Harmonies poétiques et religieuses*, which with the two *Legends of St Francis* emphasize his stature as a major composer and refute the charge that he was some kind of virtuoso charlatan. Whereas Paganini remained a fascinating minor composer Liszt can take his place beside the greatest of the Romantics.

Brahms

In harmonic richness and emotional warmth the piano music of Brahms might be regarded as Romantic, but its language, characteristically, is restrained by his Classical leanings. His admiration of Beethoven is reflected in his three sonatas, all early works. They have their rhapsodic moments, but even the most lyrical themes are subjected to traditional, sometimes severe treatment. The Variations and Fugue on a Theme of Handel reflect his admiration for the formal style of Bach and show his mastery of contrapuntal writing; he takes a Classical approach, too, in the two sets of Variations on a Theme by Paganini, which really test the muscles of any virtuoso. The more genial side of his character comes out in the shorter pieces, the ballades, rhapsodies, intermezzos and capriccios, all very approachable works which have a regular place in the piano repertoire. Even here, however, there is always a strong sense of logical structure that might not be expected from their titles. He avoided fanciful titles at all cost, and never indulged in any programmatic ideas.

France

Chopin's poetic style took firmest root in France, though Gallic taste stressed its refinement and underplayed its sentiment. First, however, came the odd man out, César Franck, who imposed a chromatic harmonic idiom, influenced by Liszt and Wagner, on to his formally Classical Prelude, Chorale and Fugue (1884) and Prelude, Aria and Finale (1888). There is more poetry – a poetry governed by logic

Ravel, who composed many fine piano works which he subsequently transcribed for full orchestra, winning larger audiences for them

and moderation – in the nocturnes and barcarolles of Gabriel Fauré (1845–1924). His melodies are highly individual, eloquent in the most graceful manner, which has led to their being described as 'Hellenic'. This most serene of piano music is never emotionalized, but it is always emotionally satisfying to the listener, especially if he admires Chopin. Fauré passed on a great deal of his fastidious style to his most famous pupil, Ravel, but had little influence on the greatest of all French composers for the piano, Debussy.

Debussy's use of Impressionism, already discussed in connection with his orchestral music, distinguishes his piano music from that of any other composer. He disliked the term being attached to his music, but even in the early *Images* (1905) it is difficult not to use it. His use of the whole-tone scale allows a mood of unruffled contemplation and particular tonal colours, so that the effect is similar to that of an Impressionist painting. And how else is one to describe the study of moonlight in the famous *Clair de lune*? Whatever label is attached to his piano style, Debussy certainly succeeded uniquely in evoking the atmosphere of visual scenes. The two sets of préludes include such unforgettable pictures in sound as *The Submerged Cathedral* or *La Puerta del vino* (the famous gate of the Alhambra in Granada). Other preludes create impressions of what can be felt rather than seen, the touch of the wind or of a perfume. These impressions are elusive, but not vague; every note seems to have been weighed and tested before being written down. There are examples of delicious wit as well, such as the mercurial dance of Puck and a portrait of Mr Pickwick. The technical features of the music can be analyzed at almost infinite length, but its seductive poetry can be appreciated at a first hearing.

The case of Maurice Ravel is an unusual one, because he turned so many of his piano pieces into orchestral works, in which form they are better known. He was also attracted to older forms (though he spiced them with astringent harmonies), his first piano work being the *Menuet antique* (1895) and his last the suite *Le Tombeau de Couperin* (1917). His music is often characterized by economic textures, as in the *Sonatine*, whose three movements keep within the Classical tradition in spite of the Romantic feeling of the first and the emotional energy of the last. Impressionism does creep into some of his pieces, however, such as the striking *Jeux d'eau* and the virtuosic *Gaspard de la nuit* with its three pictorial movements. 'Scarbo' in particular is highly atmospheric, its macabre picture of the sinister goblin combining wit, cruelty and also the strong Spanish flavour so characteristic of Ravel.

Spain

The nineteenth-century revival of Spanish music brought to the fore three composers of outstanding piano pieces which have become a popular part of the repertoire. Isaac Albéniz established a national style, influenced by the guitar in harmony and rhythm, and having a strong folk idiom. His early pieces are pleasant but facile, and it was not until he had studied in Paris to improve his craftsmanship – and free his creative imagination in the process – that he composed a masterpiece in his *Iberia* Suite, written between 1906 and 1909. This consists of twelve pieces which evoke particular places and scenes in Spain, each making use of a characteristic regional rhythm. They are mostly in ternary form, with a song-like central section usually in Andalusian style, and they are drenched in Spanish colour, sometimes gentle and sometimes passionate. 'Fête-Dieu à Seville', for instance, vibrates with the pealing of bells in the Corpus Christi procession in Seville, while 'El Albaicín', possibly the most evocative of all these impressions, will make anyone who has penetrated the gypsy quarter of Granada overlooking the Alhambra hold his breath in wonder.

Enrique Granados, like Albéniz a distinguished pianist, showed less interest in Andalusian music, preferring a more restrained style reminiscent of Chopin. His imagination was fired above all by the paintings of Goya, and his finest piano work is significantly entitled *Goyescas*, six pieces characterized by the dignity and pride of a bygone age in Madrid. One of these, 'The Maiden and the Nightingale' has become a special favourite because of its exquisite lyricism. Manuel de Falla, who fell under the influence of Debussy and Ravel during his seven years' residence in Paris, wrote some attractive piano music too. His *Four Spanish Pieces* presents his individual conception of Spain, more savage than that of Albéniz and Granados, whose music emphasizes its gentler, rather sentimental nature.

Postcript

The repertoire of the solo pianist is immense, because virtually every composer has written for the instrument, even Wagner contributing two sonatas despite his obsession with dramatic music. Another unexpected name in this context is Mussorgsky, whose *Pictures from an Exhibition* is a work of immense genius and originality and a most stimulating piece for the listener. It presents a series of vivid musical pictures, culminating in the monumental 'Great Gates of Kiev', with a subtly varied 'Promenade' to link them together. (Ravel's orchestral version of the work, a masterpiece in its own right, has unfortunately overshadowed the original piano composition.) There is infinite variety in the piano repertoire in the late nineteenth and the twentieth centuries, ranging from the salon lyricism of Grieg to the spiky vitality of Bartók and Prokofiev and on to the piano rags of Scott Joplin (significantly included in the Classical section of the gramophone catalogue in spite of their 'popular' origin). It is impossible in a one-volume survey even to mention all the composers, let alone individual works, though Sergei Rachmaninov cannot be omitted, for his twenty-four preludes are remarkably original and perennially popular. The vast body of piano music by more recent composers is of more specialist interest, and cannot be discussed in detail here.

SONG

Since singing is the most natural way of making music, the world of song is virtually limitless. Every society, however primitive, has produced its own folksongs, and every composer in 'art' music has written songs. Surprisingly, however, the repertoire that we generally hear in the recital hall is very small, falling into national groupings of songs which in most cases were composed over a relatively short period of time. From Italy, for instance, where composers of vocal music have always devoted their attention almost exclusively to opera, there are only a few songs from the seventeenth and eighteenth centuries, known as *arie antiche*. The main body of German songs, or *Lieder*, began with Schubert and continued through to Richard Strauss, though a few songs by earlier composers are occasionally performed. French song, or *mélodie*, really began with Fauré in the late nineteenth century, while England, which had songwriters in Elizabethan and Jacobean times, later followed by Purcell, then had to wait for Britten to revive the art in any considerable way. There are also fine songs by composers of other countries which appear when there is a famous singer to take them abroad. Spanish songs have been championed by Conchita Supervia and subsequently Victoria de los Angeles; Swedish songs by Kirsten Flagstad and Elisabeth Söderström; and Russian songs, though to a lesser extent, by Boris Christoff and Irina Arkhipova. In general however, the *Lied* dominates recital programmes.

Italy

The *arie antiche* with which singers often open their programmes are mostly love songs written in operatic style, many of them actual opera arias. They vary from simple 'strophic' songs with two or more verses, to the elaborate *da capo* aria form, and they are always distinguished by the seductively flowing line that the Italian voice has traditionally demanded. The accompaniments we generally hear today were provided during the nineteenth century, and are often sadly at odds with the vocal style.

The nineteenth-century triumvirate of Rossini, Bellini and Donizetti left a considerable legacy of songs which have been eclipsed by their operas. All masters of *bel canto*, their songs are particularly grateful to the voice. Rossini's songs in the collection entitled *Soirées musicales* were written as party pieces during his early years of retirement in Paris, and show his melodic gift as sure as ever, as well as the old glint of mischief in his eye. Bellini's songs are characteristically elegiac and refined, often introspective, with melodies that sometimes bring to mind the nocturnes of Chopin. Donizetti, the most prolific of the three, composed songs in three styles, some Neopolitan in spirit as well as dialect, others operatically elaborate, and the remainder in salon style. A later composer, Francesco Tosti (1846–1916), who settled in London to become singing teacher to the royal family, composed in an unabashed sentimental vein, but with elegance and genuine Italian warmth, which has appealed to singers from Caruso to Luciano Pavarotti. More ambitious songs in the Italian repertoire have been written by Ottorino Respighi (1879–1936) and Ermanno Wolf-Ferrari (1876–1948).

Beethoven

Whereas the Italian composers have always put melody first and foremost, German songwriters have paid more attention to words and to the accompaniment. We do not often hear the songs of Haydn, though he wrote quite a variety and was among the earliest successfully to fuse voice and piano accompaniment. Mozart contributed a number of glorious concert arias, like miniature concertos and with orchestral accompaniment. His songs with piano, on which he placed little value, are so attractive in their delicate lyricism that their neglect is inexplicable. Beethoven produced about a hundred songs as well as a larger number of folksong settings (many of them songs from England, Scotland and Ireland, with violin and cello joining the piano for the accompaniments), revealing a surprising lack of stylistic certainty. Many of the songs are quite insensitive to verbal values, but the cycle of six songs *An die ferne Geliebte* ('To the distant beloved') is almost Schubertian in its care for the words and the subtlety of the accompaniment. The best known of his individual songs are 'Adelaide' and 'Ich liebe dich', whose popularity is due to their melodic appeal.

Schubert

It would be no exaggeration to say that the song rose to become a major art-form through the genius of Schubert, whose inspiration flowed at a remarkable rate and with equally remarkable consistency. Franz (Peter) Schubert, born in Vienna on 31 January 1797, was taught to play the violin and the piano by his schoolmaster father and elder brother respectively. At the age of eleven he became a choirboy in the court chapel, and was next first violinist and occasional conductor of the orchestra at his school. His first compositions date from his schooldays, but he was never able to enter on any advanced musical studies, taking up a teaching post in his father's school in 1814 and composing in his spare time. It was in that year that he wrote his first mature song, 'Gretchen am Spinnrade' to lines by Goethe, and during 1815 he composed a flood of works in all forms, symphonies, operas, sonatas and dances in addition to a hundred and fifty songs. He became friendly about this time with Franz von Schober, a law student and minor poet who provided the verses for the justly renowned 'An die Musik' two years later. Encouraged by Schober and other friends, Schubert gave musical evenings ('Schubertiads') at which he would play and improvise at the piano. He also met the distinguished baritone Johann Vogl, then reaching the end of his operatic career and so impressed by the young composer that he decided to promote his songs in public concerts. The significance of his support is noted in a letter of Schubert's in which he writes: 'When Vogl sings and I accompany him, we seem for the moment to be one, which

strikes the good people here as something quite unheard of.' Vogl also appeared in Vienna in two of Schubert's operas, but without success.

Schubert moved for a time in 1818 to become music teacher to the children of Count Esterházy in Hungary, but he grew homesick very quickly and returned to his ever-widening circle of friends in Vienna. His life from then on followed a regular course, though he developed a mania for changing his lodgings. He enjoyed occasional holidays in the countryside, which always inspired his muse, and he made a tour with Vogl to perform his songs in various Austrian cities, but he never travelled far afield. Fame never came his way, yet he seemed content enough with his lot, composing and performing with no thought of international acclaim. He contracted an incurable veneral disease in 1823, and for the remaining five years of his life periods of sickness and depression undermined his usually happy disposition. In 1827 he visited the dying Beethoven, and was one of the torch-bearers at the latter's funeral a few days later. The following year he contracted typhus and died, aged only thirty-one, on 19 November 1828. The composer of more than six hundred

Schubert at the piano taking part in one of the musical evenings held in the homes of his friends and known as Schubertiads

songs, nine symphonies, over twenty piano sonatas and thirty chamber works, he remains surely the most modest of all the great composers, and the most lovable. His constant struggle against illness and poverty seemed to leave no more mark on his personality than it did on his music.

Schubert used his phenomenal melodic gift in the service of all kinds of Romantic expression, especially in such dramatically declamatory songs as 'Der Atlas' and 'Die junge Nonne' and the wistful melancholy of 'Der Wanderer'. Other songs are purely lyrical, such as 'Die Forelle' ('The trout'), which he re-used in the piano quintet of the same name. Sometimes he adopted the ballad style so popular with Rudolf Zumsteeg (1760–1802) and Carl Loewe (1796–1869). His piano accompaniments also serve a Romantic purpose in many cases, suggesting or underlining a pictorial image in the text to contribute to the mood of the song. The accompaniment to his song of Gretchen at her spinning wheel has a double aim – to convey the whirr of the wheel and also the turmoil of the girl's thoughts. The word 'accompaniment', it should be remembered, is really inadequate when applied to Schubert's songs, for he makes singer and pianist equal in importance. This is why he could create such wonderful songs from even the most commonplace poetry: he did not simply translate words into music, but transformed them into an artistic form with a new depth and significance of its own. Everything he touched with his musical imagination turned to gold, as Brahms realized when he said: 'There is not a song of Schubert's from which one cannot learn something.' Schubert also raised to perfection the song-cycle, which Beethoven had tried, turning to poems by Wilhelm Müller for both *Die schöne Müllerin* ('The maid of the mill', 1823) and *Winterreise* ('A winter's journey', 1827). The former has an idyllic character until the tragic ending, with the sound of the mill-stream pervading the piano part, while the latter expresses unrelieved irony and bitterness throughout the journey of the title.

Schumann, Brahms, Liszt, Wagner

The first true successor of Schubert as a *Lieder* composer, Robert Schumann, was a more thoroughgoing Romantic. Schubert's Romanticism comes through in his harmonic colours and lyrical warmth, whereas Schumann's adds to these a quality of rest-

'The Singer', an Italian painting showing the soloist in the kind of artificial pose still occasionally encountered today

lessness. He increased the already considerable importance that Schubert had given to the accompaniment, naturally enough in that until 1840 he had composed almost exclusively for the piano. Brought up among books, Schumann was also more careful in his choice of texts, and he realized that the later Romantic poets such as Joseph von Eichendorff and Heinrich Heine, because they shared his temperamental outlook, offered the most suitable material for his songs. He composed more than a hundred, including the two cycles *Dichterliebe* ('A poet's love') and *Frauenliebe und Leben* ('A woman's love and life') during the year leading up to his marriage, the most eloquent tribute any man could pay to his future wife. A notable feature of this vocal music is the way in which the piano's preludes and postludes sum up the essence of the song, often expressing thoughts that Schumann felt lay too deep for words. His melodic line may be less spontaneous than Schubert's, but it is always warm and poetic.

The songs of Brahms revert to the style of Schubert, Romantic in texture and harmony, yet with a certain

Mathilde Wesendonck, whose love affair with Wagner bore fruit in his Wesendonck Lieder *which served as sketches for the music of* Tristan and Isolde

267

restraint. Their mood is often melancholy and introspective, and the vocal line is given precedence over the accompaniment. It is not surprising that the philosophical *Vier ernste Gesänge* ('Four serious songs') are among his finest, though he was capable too of expressing passion into a variety of love songs. Liszt, on the other hand, turned his songs into dramatic pieces with bold harmonies and almost orchestral colouring in the piano writing. There is something almost operatic about his setting of Heine's 'Lorelei'. Wagner did not write many songs, but contributed five gems in the *Wesendonck Lieder* which were inspired by his love for Mathilde Wesendonck and which served as sketches for the music of *Tristan and Isolde*.

Wolf

The life of Hugo Wolf, who was born at Windischgraz on 13 March 1860, is one of the saddest in musical history, for his genius was almost destroyed by his perverse personal character. He behaved abominably to almost everyone he met, owing to a state of paranoia which drove him to insanity at the age of thirty-eight. He was admitted to the Vienna Conservatoire in 1875, only to be expelled two years later after a violent quarrel with its director. When he tried to make a living at seventeen by teaching music to the children of the wealthy Viennese he inevitably behaved so rudely that he soon lost his pupils, and for similar reasons he was dismissed from an assistant conductorship after only two months. In 1879 he showed a few of his songs to Brahms, and because the latter treated him in an offhand way he decided that the master he had previously revered was a personal enemy. From 1884 to 1887 he worked as a music critic, producing the most spiteful reviews ever written, with Brahms as his main target. (His attack on the Third Symphony is quoted in the relevant chapter.) Then in 1887 the tide began to turn in his favour and during a period of three years he produced his popular *Italian Serenade* and some hundred and seventy songs including those of the *Spanisches Liederbuch*. This was a burst of creativity he was never able to repeat, though he produced the two 'Italian songbooks', comprising forty-six songs, in 1891 and 1896 respectively. Determined to produce a work on a larger scale, he composed an opera, *Der Corregidor*, on the familiar Spanish comedy *The Three-cornered Hat*, but this was unfavourably received in Mannheim in 1896. He was hoping for a production of the work in Vienna the following year, but when Mahler withdrew his promise after Wolf had brought about a typical quarrel, disappointment and bitterness pre-

cipitated the end. Wolf was taken to a private asylum, and though his sanity returned for a time, he tried to commit suicide in the autumn of 1898, subsequently suffering four years' mental and physical decline until his death in Vienna on 22 February 1903.

Wolf's two hundred and fifty songs are unique, comparable with those of Schubert but totally different in style and purpose. They are concentrated and uncompromising works of art inspired by his love of poetry on the one hand and his admiration of Wagner on the other. By placing the name of the poet above his own in the titles of his song collections, as in the case of the Romantic poet Eduard Mörike, and by seeking equality between words and music, he might aptly be described as the Wagner of song. The line he gives to the singer is declamatory or arioso in style rather than wholly melodic as in Schubert. His music in these miniature masterpieces has the blazing intensity of vision and expression that we find in such poets as John Donne and Andrew Marvell. He carried on to its logical conclusion Schumann's conception of the *Lied* as a fusion of voice and piano, often

Wolf, whose songs have a concentrated, uncompromising style which reflect his love of poetry and his admiration for Wagner

adopting the earlier composer's use of the instrumental prelude and postlude. He sought always to express the psychological heart of the poems he set, and as a lyrical genius he was able to achieve this without lapsing into the dryness of a theoretician, in songs which perfectly reconcile truth with beauty. To analyze Wolf's songs is fascinating yet ultimately a sterile occupation: they exert their magic on the responsive listener as do the Shakespeare sonnets on the responsive reader – instinctively.

Mahler and Strauss

To come to the songs of Mahler and Richard Strauss is to return to a less rarefied atmosphere. Both composers had written for the voice in other contexts, the one in his symphonies and the other in opera, and both had a natural feeling for it that Beethoven, for instance, did not have. The songs of Mahler fall for the most part into large-scale cycles for solo voices with orchestra, notably *Kindertotenlieder* ('Songs on the death of children') and *Lieder eines fahrenden Gesellen* ('Songs of a wayfarer'), though a few are heard in the recital hall with piano accompaniment. Strauss too wrote his finest songs, the *Four Last Songs*, to be performed with orchestra, but he contributed many others to the recitalist, including the highly popular 'Ständchen' ('Serenade') and 'Morgen' ('Tomorrow'). There are also a few songs by Alban Berg with a Romantic flavour reminiscent of Schumann which have found their way into the international repertoire, but later German composers have made little impression abroad.

France

French song has been sadly neglected abroad for a number of reasons that have nothing to do with musical merit. Germany is so rich in songwriters that its singers feel no need to look elsewhere for their repertoire, and English audiences have always been encouraged to favour German rather than French music. For many years France has produced few singers of international stature, and singers of other nationalities find the French language the most difficult of all to master. Then there is the fact that the leading French composers have not been nearly so prolific as their German rivals, though they wrote many more fine songs than one might imagine when glancing through a season's recital programmes. Berlioz is encountered most frequently in the concert hall, for his six masterly songs of *Nuits d'été* ('Summer nights') are almost invariably presented in the later orchestral version. These are immediately appealing, and they may be said to sow the seeds of an independent French style of song-writing. Gounod composed many songs, but of indifferent quality.

It is therefore with Fauré that the *mélodie* really begins. His style of music, delicately refined and civilized, was best suited to songs, of which he composed almost a hundred. He used them to explore a whole world of intimate emotion, handling words with the utmost discrimination and matching them with a supple, expressively beautiful melodic line. Singers have always been attracted to a few of his songs, 'Après un rêve', 'Nell' and 'Claire de lune', making them familiar to audiences everywhere, but there are many more of equal distinction. Equally familiar are a handful of songs by Henri Duparc (1848–1933), who gave up composing at thirty-seven when he began to suffer both nervous and physical disorders. He left only fourteen songs, but 'L'Invitation au voyage' alone is enough to prove him a master, capturing to perfection the spirit of Baudelaire's poem. His craftsmanship can never be faulted, and his music has an intensity rare among French composers. Reynaldo Hahn (1875–1947) had a lesser talent, yet one of his songs, 'Si mes vers avaient des ailes' ('If my verses had wings'), is deservedly popular.

Gabriel Fauré

Debussy, who was always inspired by poetry, and whose music never failed to create poetic atmosphere, was inevitably drawn to song, and it is in his early settings of Verlaine that his originality first becomes apparent. The *Chansons de Bilitis* of 1897, settings of three poems by Pierre Louÿs, evoke the pagan past with the same magical under-statement 269 as the orchestral *L'après-midi d'un faune*, the musical commentary being sweet one moment and sardonic the next, briefly impassioned yet always perfectly controlled. His songs do not have the melodic charm of Fauré or Duparc, so they make a less immediate impact, but on deeper acquaintance their subtleties exert an ever greater fascination. The piano part is of great importance, so that it often takes precedence over the voice, rather as the orchestra does in his opera *Pelléas and Mélisande*.

Ravel, by contrast, lays greater emphasis on vocal melody in his songs, despite being a brilliant writer for the piano, and he made many settings of folk melodies from different countries. Among his most imaginative original songs are the *Chansons madécasses* and the three songs with orchestra, *Shéhérazade*, which weave a spell which is erotic rather than merely seductive.

England

The formation of special groups to perform early music in authentic style and on the period instruments has brought back to life a great deal of English music to which only lip service has previously been paid. It is now possible to hear a variety of solo songs, suitably accompanied (usually by lute) belonging to the period when England was a land flowing with songs and 'ayres'. This has also led to a revival of interest in Purcell, whose songs, it is now realized, need to be sung with great skill and imagination but without the kind of sophistication so often brought to them by recital singers in the first half of the present century.

In addition to his melodic inventiveness, Purcell is distinguished for his unfailing sense in setting English words to music, and it is in this respect that he has proved such a valuable model to Benjamin Britten. Britten was not the first English composer to look to Purcell or to folksong for stylistic roots, but it is he who has successfully incorporated these influences into an individual style without self-consciousness. He has also extended the form of English song, producing his cycle of Rimbaud settings, *Les Illuminations*, for voice with string orchestra and his *Serenade* for tenor with solo horn and strings, as well as the *Seven Sonnets of Michelangelo* for tenor with piano accompaniment. All these original and deeply expressive song cycles were composed for his friend and notable interpreter Peter Pears, but they have proved so popular that other English tenors have been quick to take them up and they seem likely to establish themselves in the English repertoire as permanently as the cycles of Schubert and Schumann in the German. Several other British composers have produced songs of distinction, though Britten remains the most successful and the most likely to endure.

No brief survey can do justice to the wealth of songs produced by generations of leading composers, though those already discussed dominate most programmes. Mention must be made, however, of a few other names. Tchaikovsky and Rachmaninov have both contributed in good measure, their songs having the same attractive lyrical quality as their music in other forms. Mussorgsky reveals more striking originality in his two ambitious cycles — *The Nursery*, songs in which children's speech is set with a total absence of the adult sentiment, and the *Songs and Dances of Death*, which present the horrors of the battle-field with almost unbearable expressive power. By contrast the gentle songs of Grieg have a comforting charm, yet they represent his lyrical gifts at their best. Many Spanish folksongs dating back over several centuries have been arranged by composers of the late nineteenth and twentieth centuries, including Granados and Falla who have also written original songs in the old style. There is also a variety of lighter songs which find their way into recital programmes, often as encores, including succulently melodic Neapolitan songs. A special case is that of Gershwin, a born songwriter in the manner of Schubert, a superb melodist with a spontaneous style, whose denial of a place in the recital repertoire is due in great part to a snobbish attitude taken towards his 'popular' idiom. Time alone can tell whether he will ever be accorded a place beside the more respectable composers of song.

CHAMBER MUSIC

Although the term 'chamber music' has a specific meaning today, it was originally used to denote any kind of music which was not composed for the theatre, the church or the public concert hall. Now we use it for mainly intimate music for two or more instruments, each with a part of equal importance – thus excluding, for instance, the recital at which a pianist merely accompanies a solo violinist going through his Paganini paces. The major categories of chamber music are the duo sonata, usually a piano with violin, cello or wind instrument; the trio, which might comprise three string instruments, or two string instruments with piano; and the string quartet, comprising two violins, viola and cello. Others are the quintet, sextet, septet, octet and nonet, though

*An early trio playing to a small audience who have
more important matters than music on their minds*

these are less numerous. It is ideal music for playing
in the home, though as music-lovers have tended to
become listeners rather than amateur players themselves, it has passed more and more into the public
domain. Since the 1830s the string quartet in particular has become a regular feature of the professional
scene, though its audiences are far smaller than those
who attend symphony concerts or opera. This change
is to be regretted in that chamber music was really
intended for active participation, though on the other
hand the later quartets of Beethoven and the quartets
of Bartok demand such expertise on the part of the
players that only professionals can do them justice.
However, the music's intimacy is preserved, for the
instrumentalists who regularly play as a quartet develop a personal rapport that cannot be achieved in
a huge orchestra whose personnel is constantly
changing.

There is no reason why most people who regularly
attend symphony concerts should fight shy of chamber music as they undoubtedly do, whether in New
York or London. It would appear that the term itself
is unattractive, for when the BBC presented chamber
programmes under the title 'Music in Miniature' they
enticed infinitely wider audiences than any 271

advertised chamber recital would have secured. No doubt the chamber recital lacks the spectacle and glamour of the symphony concert, the weight and variety of sound, the presence of a star conductor and often an internationally celebrated soloist. The chamber recital may be an acquired taste, but once acquired it provides rich dividends, because the music often represents composers at the peak of inspiration.

Much music for duo, quartet and other chamber combinations is rooted in sonata form and follows the pattern of the symphony. In general, the most important chamber composers – Haydn, Beethoven, Schubert and Brahms, have also been the great symphonists, and their development and style in the one form is paralleled in the other. This chapter aims therefore, simply to point out their most notable chamber works and to mention the few sonatas and quartets by composers who are not associated with the symphony.

One of the most famous trios of all time: (left to right) *cellist Pablo Casals, pianist Alfred Cortot and violinist Jacques Thibaud*

The Viennese Classics

Haydn established the string quartet as effectively as he established the symphony as a major musical form, composing more than eighty. He began writing them, in sets of six, quite early in his career, and it took him some time to settle into the form as we recognize it. At first, he composed them in a style that would have been more appropriate for a divertimento or other occasional piece to be played out of doors. It was not until he was thirty-nine, with more than twenty quartets already behind him, that he began to master the form: the two sets of Opus 17 and Opus 20, composed in 1771 and 1772 respectively, mark his emergence into maturity and are the earliest quartets to have a place in the repertoire. Fifteen years later another set of six were published with a dedication to King Frederick William of Prussia, and are consequently known as the 'Prussian' Quartets. Here the level of technique and the force of imagination are at last equal to the symphonies he was composing at the same time. His finest quartets undoubtedly belong to his later years, fourteen in all excluding the last, which was left incomplete. With these works, dating from 1793 to 1799 and bearing the opus numbers 71, 74, 76 and 77, Haydn gave the string quartet a firm basis on which composers have built ever since.

Mozart also took time to find his style in the string quartet, his first fifteen essays in the form fluctuating between a sunny, Italian idiom and a more serious Haydnesque manner. For ten years, as though uncertain in which direction to move, he did not compose any quartets, though he wrote the Flute Quartet in D in his lightest, most charming style, and the Oboe Quartet of more serious character. Then in 1785 he produced six quartets dedicated to Haydn more concentrated and consistent than any he had composed before. They are far from being mere imitations of their dedicatee. Their themes have the singing quality which is Mozart's hallmark. With the four later quartets (three of them dedicated to the King of Prussia), these are his best. Mozart was even more successful with the string quintet (adding a second viola to the quartet), especially with the Quintet in C and another in G minor, both dating from 1787. Even more famous than these, and an undoubted masterpiece, is the Clarinet Quintet composed two years later. Mozart also used the keyboard in chamber music, with his violin sonatas, piano trios, quartets and quintet.

Just as he carried the symphony to such expressive intensity that he almost broke its Classical framework, Beethoven took the string quartet to a point from which Romanticism would inevitably follow. At first, however, he worked along the lines laid down by Haydn, though even the early quartets of Op 18 have many individual features in matters of a thematic or harmonic nature. He scored a great success in 1800 with his serenade-like Septet for strings, clarinet, bassoon and horn. Other chamber works of this first period in his development were three violin sonatas and two cello sonatas, forms which he was later to develop to a new level. Three years after the *Eroica* Symphony came the three quartets, Op 59, dedicated to Count Rasumovsky, all of which have the fire and boldness of the Beethoven who was casting earlier influences aside and gradually becoming his own man. Also from this period comes the celebrated 'Kreutzer' Sonata for violin and piano and the equally popular 'Archduke' Trio. Finally, in his five last quartets, he summed up his musical ideas in an almost metaphysical way, producing music which remained beyond the grasp of most of his admirers at the time. In expressing his final thoughts, Beethoven had recourse to more than the standard four movements in several of these works, and also to a more complex musical language. A great fugue was originally the last movement of the Quartet in B flat major, Op 130, but was later published separately as the *Grosse Fuge*; it is one of the composer's most monumental achievements.

The Romantics

Schubert wrote fifteen string quartets altogether, starting when he was only fourteen, and though the earliest have Haydn and Mozart as their models he was soon raising a voice of his own. From this exploratory period one work stands out in particular, the Quintet for piano and strings known as the 'Trout' because of an additional movement consisting of variations on his song of that name. As might be expected, Schubert's chamber music is filled with songlike melodies, which in his last three quartets are worked out with newly acquired skill. There is a mood of sadness in some of the movements from these works, yet all are made immediately appealing by virtue of their easy lyricism. They are surpassed only by the String Quintet in C major, in which the additional instrument is a second cello, enabling the composer to secure some of his most Romantic sound effects. More popular perhaps, because of its happy, relaxed air, is the Octet in F major, written for string quartet, double bass, clarinet, bassoon and horn, and clearly modelled on Beethoven's Septet.

Mendelssohn contributed a good deal of chamber music which adopts Classical construction tinged with Romantic colour. In addition to six string quartets and two quintets he wrote two piano trios and a sextet for piano and strings, all poised and tunefully pleasing even if they do not significantly extend their forms. He proved more original in the Octet of 1825, an astonishing work for a boy of sixteen, its Scherzo having the shimmering dash that he was to display to such advantage in similar movements of his more mature works. Schumann plunged into chamber music in 1842 by composing three quartets in quick succession and then adding to them the magnificent Piano Quintet (in which Mendelssohn played the

piano part at sight at the first performance). Being primarily a composer for the piano it is natural that he should also excel with a piano quartet and three piano trios. Brahms too, who expressed himself more Romantically than usual in his chamber music, favoured the piano. His Piano Quartet in G minor has always been a favourite, notable for its second movement in the form of an Intermezzo and its lively rondo Finale in Hungarian style. A more powerful and complex work is the Piano Quintet in F minor (1864), in which the tone is more Classical, and an equally striking masterpiece came later with the Clarinet Quintet of 1891, profound and somewhat Beethovenian in its purity of expression. Brahms also composed some of the most impressive of all sonatas for a single instrument with piano: three for violin and two each for cello and clarinet.

The Romantic use of themes which recur in different movements characterizes the chamber music of César Franck, the founder of modern French chamber music. He proved highly successful with his String Quartet in D major and Piano Quintet in F minor, while his virtuosic Violin Sonata in A major, which features several really winning melodies, has become one of the most popular of all works in the form. His achievement is paralleled by the chamber works of Fauré, less full-blooded in its Romanticism and leading towards the Impressionism of Debussy.

Smetana may be most important in the field of

A performance by The Allegri Quartet, a typical chamber group who work regularly together to achieve maximum rapport

opera, but he established a precedent in chamber music by making his two string quartets programmatic and autobiographical, the first ('My life') expressing his love of the dance, the second the 'whirlpool of music in a man who has lost his hearing'. Dvořák was more prolific as a chamber composer, and more distinguished too. He has often been compared to Schubert as a spontaneous melodist, and nowhere is this more apparent than in his chamber music. Also like Schubert, he was to win a popular success with a piano quintet and to reveal a great deal of warm personality in his string quartets. He poured nationalist spirit into these, using dance movements such as the polka, dumka and furiant. His most unusual chamber work is a set of twelve pieces for string quartet with the title *Cypresses*, arranged from his earlier songs. The Czech tradition reached another peak in Janáček, whose two quartets and other chamber works have all the vigour and originality of his later operas and orchestral music.

Tchaikovsky made his mark with his First String Quartet, which incorporates a beguiling folk melody in its slow movement, but despite a wealth of attractive tunes his chamber music does not represent him at his best. He admitted disappointment over the Piano Trio he composed in 1882 in memory of his friend Nicolai Rubinstein, and the work has been accorded considerable critical disapproval. Audiences, however, have continued to enjoy it immensely, especially for the splendidly imaginative variations of its central movement.

The Moderns

As composers increasingly reacted against both Classical and Romantic influences, chamber music has grown ever more diverse in style. Only a few selected works of interest can be mentioned here, beginning with Debussy's String Quartet in G minor. It features both cyclic form, influenced by César Franck, and variation form, with transformations of a single motive appearing in all four movements. The dreamy side of his character is revealed in his three late sonatas, for violin and piano, cello and piano, and flute, viola and harp. No less delicate in style are the chamber pieces of Ravel, though they are more Classical in outlook. His attractive Quartet and Piano Trio have been overtaken in popularity by the Introduction and Allegro for harp, flute, clarinet and strings. Elgar turned late in life to the string quartet and piano quintet, so their music is restrained, even sedate in style, though with many beautiful moments. Sibelius is solely represented as a chamber composer by a string quartet with the title *Voces intimae*, which has kept its place in the repertoire because of its personal idiom and charm. The most substantial quartets of recent times are the fifteen composed by Shostakovich which probably express his personal feelings more directly than any of his other works. The most original and intense, however, are still the six by Bartók, perhaps the only quartets to be compared in imaginative power, complexity and richness of thought with those of Beethoven.

A Christmas card drawn by the composer Paul Hindemith

CHORAL MUSIC

The rise and early development of western music took place within the church, as did the art of painting; for it was religion that brought people together in a shared experience. The celebration of the Mass gave birth to various styles of unaccompanied vocal music in different Catholic countries. All were based on plainsong, the traditional ritual melody of the Christian church which owed something at least to the music of the synagogue. The church attempted through the power of the papacy to impose uniformity of style, so for several centuries music was regulated by edicts and reforms not prompted by aesthetic considerations. But with the rise of European courts the church was no longer the sole patron of the musician, and the songs of the troubadours in Provence and their successors throughout Europe began to influence styles of composition.

The complex history of vocal music is of interest to the scholar but of little concern to most music-lovers of today. They may find that Medieval and Renaissance music can be fascinating and enjoyable as a change from the familiar later repertoire, though not a part of their regular musical diet. Early instrumental music has enjoyed a considerable revival of public interest, but it too lies outside the 'mainstream' and is therefore beyond the scope of a book dealing with music most widely encountered in the concert hall and opera house. There is a large body of choral music, however, which is regularly performed in the concert hall as well as in churches and town halls.

The conservatism of the church could not hold back the development of sacred music indefinitely, and a polyphonic style (one combining several parts or 'voices' in a coherent whole) gradually developed between the ninth and the fifteenth centuries. The great polyphonic period may be said to have begun with John Dunstable, who was active between 1420 and the 1450s. This English school flourished until the death in 1625 of Orlando Gibbons, a famous keyboard player as well as a composer of church music, madrigals and instrumental works. No less important was the Franco-Flemish school of composers, who between about 1450 and 1550 passed a great part of their lives in the service of the Emperor, the King of France, the Pope or the Italian courts. Guillaume Dufay, Johannes Ockeghem, Jacob Obrecht and, most of all, Josquin des Prez dominated European sacred music until the time of the 'Prince of Music', Giovanni Pierluigi da Palestrina (?1525–94). He took his name from the small town near Rome where he was born. Italy had taken the lead in music about this time, having learned from the Flemish composers who had come to work for its dukes and princes, and Palestrina was to bring the Italian polyphonic

Palestrina   *Schütz*

style to its summit. He was very much a son of the church, his music for the Mass having a detachment in keeping with a sacred mystery; purity of spirit and perfection of style are his hallmarks. In contrast to Palestrina, Tomás Luis de Victoria (?1548–1603) – the Spanish master of church music – expressed himself with an exalted mysticism which sometimes led him into a subjective ecstasy. On the whole, however, sacred music remained calm and reflective until the beginning of the Baroque.

The growth of opera and its expressive style of solo singing had repercussions in church music, particularly in Italy. St Mark's Cathedral in Venice was famous for its elaborate music, which often used choirs of voices and instruments antiphonally – that is, answering each other across the domed spaces of the Byzantine building. Such music reached a peak of ceremonial splendour around 1600 in the work of such composers as Andrea and Giovanni Gabrieli. When Claudio Monteverdi became *maestro di cappella* at St Mark's he continued this tradition but also introduced recitatives – solos with simple chordal accompaniment (continuo) in the operatic manner. Both styles are used to great effect in his *Vespers* of 1610, a choral masterpiece which was unknown thirty years ago, but which is now being taken up by choral societies alongside *Messiah* and *Elijah*.

The new style was taken north by Heinrich Schütz (1585–1672), who studied in Venice and then returned to Germany where he spent most of his life as Kappellmeister in Dresden. His reputation rests on his sacred music, which extends from simple psalm settings to the large-scale *Christmas Oratorio* (1664) in which the narrative is presented in rapid recitative while the 'scenes' are handled in arias and choruses with orchestral accompaniment. Another work occasionally given today is his oratorio-type *Seven Last Words*, but his passions, composed towards the end of his life, have proved too austere to compete with those of Bach.

Bach

Johann Sebastian Bach brought the music of the Lutheran church to its peak. He was born at Eisenach on 21 March 1685 into a family that had already produced several generations of musicians. He secured his first appointment as an organist at the age of eighteen at Arnstadt. Two years later he made a pilgrimage on foot to Lübeck to hear Dietrich Buxtehude, the most celebrated organist of the time, whose playing and composition had a lasting influence on him. He held another brief appointment at Mühlhausen, where he married his cousin Maria Barbara; then in 1708 he became court organist at Weimar and chamber musician to the reigning duke, with more freedom to compose. During his nine years at Weimar he wrote many of his great organ works, and by 1717 he seems to have felt he had exhausted this particular creative field and decided to move on elsewhere.

Bach found a more sympathetic patron as Kapellmeister at the court of Prince Leopold in Cöthen. Leopold grew up to treat him as a personal friend and even invited him back to the court after he had left. The Cöthen period saw the composition of instrumental music – the 'Brandenburg' and other concertos as well as chamber works – and it culminated in the *St John Passion*, commissioned for St Thomas's Church in Leipzig, where Bach became Cantor in 1723. This was a somewhat lower position in the professional and social scale than he had held at Cöthen, and his choice perhaps confirms that religion was the mainspring of Bach's music, just as his faith was the sustaining force of his life. He certainly needed his faith at Leipzig, where he worked until his death, because he had a great deal of earthly vexations to contend with. His duties involved the teaching of singing, elementary Latin and the Lutheran catechism, as well as composing such music as was required for the church, including weekly cantatas for the Sunday services. From the beginning he was in constant conflict with the town council which employed him and also with the university authorities who did not approve of the link between the university and St Thomas's School in the first place. Fortunately his domestic life was happy and orderly. His first wife died in 1720, but he had married again the following year. The two marriages produced twenty children, of whom three sons were to become

Bach, who brought the music of the Lutheran Church to its peak

composers of some distinction. Comforted by his family life, he was able to work with unremitting zeal throughout his twenty-seven years at Leipzig, producing an unequalled body of sacred and secular compositions before his death on 28 July 1750. Leipzig showed little gratitude, not even marking his grave in St John's Church. It was not until almost a hundred and fifty years later that a search was made for his body during repairs to the church, and the skeleton scientifically proved to be his was placed in a fresh coffin and put into a vault beneath the altar.

The bulk of Bach's surviving sacred music consists of the nearly two hundred cantatas, which differ from the Italian model in the important part played in them by the Lutheran chorales. Most of the thirty cantatas composed for Mühlhausen and Weimar follow earlier north German models, having a brief instrumental sinfonia and the vocal sections usually arranged in a symmetrical pattern. There are choruses at the beginning, middle and end, leaving two sections for solo recitatives and arias, or sometimes duets. Such is the pattern of *Gottes Zeit ist die allerbeste* ('God's own time is best'), No 106. Bach's response to the text in the early cantatas is subjective, the music emphasizing the poetic imagery with imaginative freedom. The Leipzig cantatas are less free and subjective, and more influenced by the style of

277

opera seria, though by then his mastery was to assure that within the stricter formal limits he set himself he was able to achieve tremendous variety of expression and a seemingly infinite wealth of musical invention. In addition to these sacred works are some two dozen secular cantatas, which Bach titled *dramma per musica*, the closest he ever came to operatic composition. The most popular of these is the *Coffee Cantata*, which presents a comedy situation of a father worried by his daughter's addiction to coffee-drinking, and the catchy, unbuttoned *Peasant Cantata*.

Of his sacred masterpieces the *Magnificat* is perhaps the most melodious and also the most influenced by the Italian style. An extrovert, joyous work, it has rare lightness and clarity, introducing such dramatic effects as the chorus suddenly taking over from the solo soprano's 'Quia respexit'. Another most attractive work is the *Christmas Oratorio*, a series of six cantatas for the Christmas and Epiphany festivals, which presents narratives from Luke and Matthew in recitative, with arias and chorales to reflect on the various episodes. Bach used a more dramatic style for the *St John Passion*: the narration is sung in recitative by the Evangelist (a tenor), accompanied only by continuo; while ariosos and arias are given to other soloists sometimes representing individual characters, including Christ, and the choruses express the reactions of the crowd or the congregation. The *St Matthew Passion* (1729) is even grander in conception, justly considered the most inspired treatment of its subject in music. The work takes the same form as the *St John*, except that Christ's recitatives are given a kind of musical halo by being accompanied by the strings. The peak of Lutheran music, the *St Matthew Passion* reveals Bach's gift for dramatic and pictorial music within a majestic framework. Even the *da capo* aria, the artificial mainstay of Baroque opera, falls naturally into place within this context. The work expresses Bach's fervent devotion to his Saviour through the tenderness, bliss and grief which illuminate it. The importance he attached to it is shown by the large forces it needs: two orchestras, two choruses and a group of boy singers as well as the soloists.

The Mass in B minor, a less personal work than the passions, occupied Bach intermittently for a number of years and was not completed until about 1738. An objective, majestic work, it is too long for use in the Roman Catholic service, though in both form and spirit it harks back to the time before the division in the Christian church. It uses melodies from Gregorian chant, elaborate fugues, arias with all the florid ornamentation of the Italian operatic style, and other contemporary forms. In its ambitious scale and intensity of expression, it transcends the limits of any one denomination to become a declaration of universal faith like Beethoven's *Missa Solemnis* of some eighty years later. Bach probably never heard a complete performance of the Mass, though sections of it were performed at different times. Like the passions, it fell into oblivion on the composer's death, and it was not until Mendelssohn directed the *St Matthew Passion* in 1829 that these supreme works began to be revived and finally appreciated for their true worth.

Handel

Unlike Bach, who was a sober Lutheran serving his God, Handel was a pleasure-loving man of the world serving the largest possible public with music in the more popular Italian style. When opera was the fashion he wrote operas, and when the fashion changed he turned to oratorio to win the new middle-class audiences. This involved no great change on his part, for his oratorios were simply operas with sacred subjects designed to be performed in concert rather than on the stage, the only striking difference being the new emphasis placed on the chorus. The most famous of his oratorios, *Messiah* (1742) is also the least typical, for while its music is dramatic enough in spirit it does not tell a story. It is not as subjective as Bach's passions, for Handel's religious experience seems to have been less intensely personal than his contemporary's. The poet Edward Fitzgerald rightly declared that the Hallelujah Chorus is 'a chorus, not of angels, but of well-fed earthly choristers, ranged tier above tier in a Gothic cathedral, with princes for audience'. This explains perhaps why *Messiah* has won a popularity far wider than that enjoyed by any other sacred work – and in England has become a national institution. The music of Palestrina and Bach belongs to a rarefied world: *Messiah* may have its head in the skies, but its feet are firmly planted on the ground. It provides a feast of melody for everyone to enjoy at first hearing, while familiarity reveals layer after layer of more subtle delights. Among many shorter sacred works the Coronation Anthems, especially *Zadok the Priest*, give similar proof of Handel's mastery of the difficult art of writing for a chorus so that the melodic line moves freely in spite of the full texture.

Top: *A performance of Haydn's* The Creation *in Vienna in 1808 which marked the last appearance of the composer in public*

Bottom: *Beethoven's funeral, an occasion attended by all the musicians, singers, poets and actors of Vienna in full mourning*

279

The Viennese Classics

With the development of the symphony and the corresponding increase of interest in the orchestra, composers began to devote more and more of their energies to works for the concert hall and away from the church. Haydn, for instance, composed fourteen masses, three oratorios and several shorter choral works, but these do not occupy nearly such an important place in his work as the symphonies and string quartets. Like other Austrian composers of his period, he gave a certain flamboyant character to his masses, always wrote for a full orchestra, and introduced elements from both opera and symphony. On his first visit to London in 1791 he attended a performance of *Messiah* in Westminster Abbey and was so moved by the Hallelujah Chorus that he declared Handel to be 'the master of us all'.

Six years later he himself turned to oratorio, then sliding out of fashion, and composed *The Creation*, using a German translation of an English text based on Milton's *Paradise Lost* which is reputed to have been rejected by Handel. It fired Haydn to brilliant, and brilliantly sustained, flights of imaginative writing. The orchestral prelude, 'Representation of Chaos', is a superb example of early programme music, introducing Romantic harmonies before their time, while the opening recitative and hushed chorus leading to the glorious C major outburst on the words 'and there was light' produce an overwhelming dramatic effect. Although the work is religious in its conception, Haydn emphasizes the innocent joy of nature in music that is affectionately pictorial. There is a good deal of naive charm in *The Creation*, but it is the naivety of genius blazing at full force. Its immediate success prompted Haydn to compose *The Seasons* two years later to a German translation of James Thomson's poem. This less exalted work is nevertheless a sincere and compelling expression of Haydn's simple pleasure in nature. Of his devotional works, the most frequently performed is the 'Nelson' Mass of 1798, which gives eloquent music to the soloists and some impressive figures to the chorus. Audiences today are unlikely to complain, as Haydn's contemporaries did, that his masses are too cheerful.

Mozart concerned himself only intermittently with sacred music, but he was always able to compose so easily and quickly that his contribution is considerable. Like Haydn's, his masses combine the operatic and symphonic idioms of the time, though reverting to the old polyphonic manner for certain sections. Their music has all the elegance of his operas and piano concertos, which has led many people to think that they are too worldly to be truly devotional; but to take that view is to misunderstand the spirit of the eighteenth century. It is worth noting that Mozart wrote only two or three masses to commission, others being composed 'in service' or out of friendship, and the late C minor Mass, the finest of all, to fulfil a vow he had made during the course of his engagement to Constanze. For this reason it is more personal than the other masses and strikes a deeper note, even though it was never finished. The Italian side of Mozart appears in the writing for the soloists, especially the soprano arias, the soprano duet and the trio for sopranos with tenor, while the German tradition makes its influence felt in the Sanctus. The composer's other towering achievement, the *Requiem*, is also unfinished. It was commissioned anonymously, Mozart never learning that it was to be passed off by an aristocratic dilettante as a work of his own. This final work, of which the manuscript lay on his death-bed (it was later finished by his pupil, Süssmayr); has strong Baroque elements, the Kyrie and Dies Irae recalling Handel, though the rapturous Recordare belongs to its time.

Although Beethoven composed five cantatas, two masses and an oratorio as well as some miscellaneous pieces for chorus, only the *Missa Solemnis* (1824) is regularly heard today. It is a shame that the oratorio *Christ on the Mount of Olives* (1803) is so neglected, for it includes much impressive and appealing music. It was originally cold-shouldered because it was operatic rather than devotional in flavour, considerations which should no longer concern the musical public. The *Missa Solemnis*, on the other hand, has always been accepted as a natural successor to Bach's B minor Mass, at once profoundly personal and wholly universal. It differs from Bach's masterpiece in its revolutionary form, that of a unified work in five symphonic movements. It is infinitely richer than his earlier Mass in C, and the treatment of the chorus is far more advanced – indeed, it has been said that he employs voices and instruments in the manner of a double orchestra, so completely are they synthesized. The music is more truly dramatic than that of *Fidelio*, for Beethoven seizes every opportunity to give powerful expression to the words, mystical in the Sanctus, awesomely martial towards the end of the Agnus Dei. The miraculous fusion of liturgical, symphonic and dramatic elements places the *Missa Solemnis* on a plane of its own.

The Romantics

The Romantic movement tended to be ill at ease with sacred music. Only Cherubini, in his two *Requiem*

marks of his subsequent music: obsessive rhythms, simple melodies and percussive violence. *Carmina Burana* falls into three sections concerned respectively with the coming of spring, drinking and love. It is aggressively of the modern age, yet makes a direct appeal to the senses. It may sometimes be vulgar, but is certainly never dull.

To set against this preponderance of secular choral works there are four highly successful religicus compositions in different styles. Janáček's *Glagolitic Mass* (1926), the Catholic rite with a text in Old Slav, is complex musically, but so exultant in its visionary joy that it affords a thrilling and moving experience. Stravinsky turned to Latin texts for his *Symphony of Psalms* (1930) for mixed chorus and orchestra. a work that is equally impressive in its musical architecture and its mystical imaginative power. William Walton's *Belshazzar's Feast* (1931) brings a lively sense of colour and excitement to its Biblical subject, rising to moments of almost barbaric splendour without sacrificing tonality. Finally, Britten's *War Requiem* (1962) was composed to mark a special event, the consecration of the new Coventry Cathedral to replace the earlier one destroyed by the wartime bombing of the city. It is unique in its three-tier construction: tenor and baritone soloists, representing dead soldiers, sing settings of poems by Wilfred Owen with chamber orchestra accompaniment; a soprano soloist sings in the Mass itself with full chorus and orchestra; and a boys' chorus, with organ, suggests the mystery of innocence in a stricken world. The work rises above the occasion for which it was composed, even above its very personal anti-war statement, to become one of the few religious works to reach across denominational frontiers, appealing directly by virtue of the intensity of its musical inspiration.

Performance of a Bruckner Mass in the Staats-Theater, Darmstadt

Index

Note: Bold numbers refer to biographical information.

287